THINK

By WILLIAM RODGERS

STEIN AND DAY/*Publishers*/New York

THINK

A Biography of the Watsons and IBM

Copyright © 1969 by William Rodgers

Library of Congress Catalog Card No. 69-19394

All rights reserved

Published simultaneously in Canada by Saunders of Toronto Ltd

Designed by David Miller

Printed in the United States of America

Stein and Day/Publishers/7 East 48 Street, New York, N.Y. 10017

SBN 8128-1226-3

Acknowledgements

Many people helped me in the preparation of this book. Some work now, or worked in the past, for IBM. Only when I was given their permission did I mention their names. But I acknowledge with thanks the help of them all, whether identified or anonymous.

I am necessarily, and most of all, grateful to the late Thomas J. Watson himself. As a man and industrialist, Mr. Watson liked to say what he thought, or thought he ought to think, and he said it in enormous volume over a period of forty-two years. The record he left is part of this book.

I am indebted to the libraries of some of the large universities— Columbia, Harvard, and M.I.T., especially. Orian Fleck of the corporate records division of Harvard's Baker Library was, among many others, most helpful and obliging as was Anthony Grech of the library of the Bar Association of the City of New York.

As for IBM itself, the company made it quite clear that no book of this kind was welcome. Wallace McDowell, IBM vice-president at Endicott, New York, visited me early one morning in the autumn of 1967, after reading a newspaper item that reported my involvement with a book on Watson, and told me that the company felt one biography of Mr. Watson and IBM was enough. He was referring to the book authorized by the company and prepared by Mr. and Mrs. Thomas Belden. Mr. McDowell said he thought it only fair to warn me that, at some point in the research and writing project, I would need the help of the company and that it would not be forthcoming. Thus, other than the routine information I obtained in printed material offered to stockholders—material I received by virtue of owning two shares of IBM stock—I relied on material obtained unofficially from corporation sources, or from sources outside the company.

Watson's old friend, Dr. Benjamin Wood, the Columbia professor who helped develop the IBM educational and training programs, was enormously cooperative. Even though he will doubtless disagree with my interpretation of the material, Dr. Wood felt that no person or company owns history and that my pursuit was legitimate and, possibly, useful.

5

Dr. Wood loved Watson with his whole heart and mind, and whatever conclusions I have drawn about Watson and IBM here that contradict Dr. Wood's own sympathetic views are entirely my own. I have, of course, given Dr. Wood's own account of his years with Watson, undiluted by any interpretations of my own. I respect Dr. Wood very much and am indeed grateful to him.

I am indebted also to Theodore Merrill of *Business Week;* Thomas A. Wise, an editor of *Fortune;* and other writers and editors of business periodicals who provided me with helpful information.

Quite a few former IBM people sat down with me for long taped interviews, Dr. Herbert Grosch and Thomas Mechling among them.

I am grateful for a good deal of peripheral help, gleaned from the works of Daniel McCracken, Jeremy Bernstein's delightful account of the life of Charles Babbage, and of course Mr. and Mrs. Belden's book, *The Lengthening Shadow*. For encouragement, for help in research, and for various forms of personal assistance, I thank Ann Therrien, Colin C. Webster, Ariadne Thompson, Catherine Jennison, George Kendall, Lin Root, Nora Kubie, Carol Williams, Brian Johnson, Steve Hambelik, Tom Cawley, Dr. Charles De Carlo, William Cowan, and my wife Kathleen. I have probably forgotten others.

I thank IBM too. Very few large corporations could stand up to examination and review and fare as well.

William Rodgers
Arch Hill Studio
Briarcliff Manor, N.Y.
June 15, 1969

Contents

Introduction

----◆----

IN ALL THE WORLD one corporation dominates the shape of the future. With installations and operations in 105 countries, it is a corporate network of awesome size, wealth, and influence, whose products, management, and services pervade and largely determine major qualitative and quantitative aspects of human life. Its activities govern much of the world's advanced technology in space, on earth, under the seas, and in thousands of industries, governments, institutions, and individual occupations.

The corporation is International Business Machines—universally known as IBM—the world's largest nonunion company, with a quarter of a million employees, more than half of whom are college graduates, with a current corporate stock value far in excess of all the gold ever hoarded in the underground vaults of Fort Knox in the United States of America.

IBM has brought riches to thousands of individuals canny or lucky enough to have obtained and held some of its 120,000,000 shares. It has made millionaires out of common workmen, multimillionaires out of its long term investors; it has banished economic fear and want from the households of three generations of employees.

In 1967, IBM swept past United States Steel to become the seventh largest industrial corporation in the United States, coming within a few hundred thousand dollars of unseating Mobil Oil and Chrysler in the sixth and fifth position respectively. In 1968 IBM advanced to sixth position in gross sales, and became the third ranking American corporation in terms of earnings, with only General Motors and Standard Oil of New Jersey ahead of it. In view of the fact that General Motors had gross sales of $22.7 billion and Standard Oil $14 billion, it was a formidable demonstration indeed for IBM, with a gross income of 6.8 billion, to rack up larger earnings than Ford Motor Company, with sales of $14 billion, General Electric with $8.3 billion, and Chrysler, with $7.4 billion. In growth and in profit, IBM was without equal in the industrial world. It is more than probable that, in the years ahead, IBM will become the largest corporation on earth. With the commanding power of its patents, its research and development facilities, established markets, and absence of contrary power to deflect its momentum, there can be little doubt about its future.

From its beginning as a consolidation of unrelated, cast-off companies with combined assets of a little over two million dollars, as of 1967 its annual sales volume had increased by a factor of 1,325. A hundred shares of its early stock, with a value at the time of $2,700, could be traded for a fortune in excess of eighteen million dollars and would, in 1968, have produced average additional income from dividends of $18,200 a year for the past fifty-four years.

The company that has become a dynastic empire, in which the qualifications for citizenship were defined by one man and enforced by an ever-changing hierarchy of subordinate executives, was ruled for more than forty years by a patriarchal boss, benevolent and tyrannical by turn, a man of great kindness with an intuitive business genius. Thomas J. Watson was an ex-country-bumpkin, a lachrymosely sentimental leader of granite will, and a compulsive master of detail, who saw himself, his company, and the world of business as a corporate holy trinity to be worshiped by the faithful under his divine right to reward fidelity, exile heretics, and rehabilitate the doubtful.

Without implying similar motive, one must look to such autocrats as Mao Tse-tung, Hitler, Stalin, perhaps to the Papacy for the combination of mysticism, evangelism, nationalism, and faith developed by Thomas Watson and transmitted throughout his corporate domain during his leadership.

He made IBM a kind of international state in which the quest for promotion and reward was institutionalized and in which the sovereign patriarch's index of manners, conduct, and accomplishment was both a standard and an ideal. It was a standard which, in the process of evoking from subordinates and employees a full measure of energy and total involvement in their work, simultaneously molded them into the outlines of the organization man, town criers of dubious Watson dogma who could not distinguish their own nonsense, their critical faculty suppressed if not atrophied, their response to ambition, success, reward, and greed so sharply honed that it became the cutting edge of a dangerously conditioned human reflex.

Introduction

IBM was Watson, and to a diminishing but discernible extent remains so. The ghost of old Watson, which official company biographers ominously called the Lengthening Shadow,[1] remains in the course he set and policies he enforced. His power is embodied, too, in his two sons, Thomas John Watson, Jr., chairman of the board and chief executive officer, and Arthur Kitteridge Watson, for years head of IBM's World Trade Corporation and now vice-chairman of the board. To them, their father transferred not only trusts, shares, and unchallenged administrative power, but a measure of his Methodist fundamentalist morality. They also inherited a full measure of his volatile and often irrational temper which, exercised at the highest level of management for two generations, has made employment at IBM for many a traumatic and sometimes humiliating, if otherwise rewarding, experience.

Thomas J. Watson did not create IBM. It was founded by a brilliant nineteenth-century financier named Charles R. Flint, an educated, high-living pirate of a man who virtually invented the system of combining corporations into trusts. Watson took command of the company in its infancy and nurtured it through adolescence to the giant monolith it seems, in retrospect, it could scarcely help becoming.

Watson was a durable bridge between the manual, agricultural, small-town world of the nineteenth century and the congested, technologically sophisticated, urbanized world of the present. With persuasiveness adapted from the backwoods peddler, refined in time to emulate the suaver city drummer, with techniques developed in Billy Sunday camp meetings and along the Chautauqua lecture circuit, with a straight-laced code of personal conduct that in no way impinged upon an insatiable desire for praise and commendation, and with a personal style that combined courtliness and conservative dress with a deadly, dedicated concentration on his work, Thomas Watson left the imprint of his resolute will on corporate life at IBM, and on a whole new breed of men fashioned in his image.

The phenomenon that is IBM has not declined since Watson's death. Watson had an intuitive vision, although considerably less than full grasp, of what he had set in motion. From a handful of little factories that made meat slicers, grocery store scales, time clocks, and primitive tabulators promoted as "business machines," Watson goaded, educated, and sermonized into existence the explosively expanding enterprise that has produced the tools and technology to compound and multiply mankind's knowledge to levels that enable us to rebuild or ruin our own world—or to escape beyond it to the stars.

[1] *The Life of Thomas J. Watson: The Lengthening Shadow,* by Thomas and Marva Belden, Boston, 1962.

THINK

1.
Genesis

WHEN THOMAS JOHN WATSON died in New York on June 19, 1956, the afternoon newspaper in Rochester, one of many owned by his friend, newspaper tycoon Frank Gannett, published an obituary that contained these paragraphs:

Watson spent four years in Rochester at the turn of the century. He was sent here in 1899 as branch manager of the National Cash Register Co.

Often called "America's No. 1 salesman," he failed to sell a single machine in his first ten days with the National Cash Register Co.

He took time to ponder the reason and began anew, fortified with his favorite slogan, "Think." This time he clicked and the expression has become prominent in the IBM corporation. "Think" signs hung in every room of every office.

Thus are myths and nonsense perpetuated. At the turn of the century, Watson had not, it is safe to say, thought of THINK, a word he turned into a corporation crucifix, the graphic symbol of a business that was an evangelical religion. Nor was he cleansed of ineptitude by revelation and reflection, converted in the manner of St. Paul on the road to Damascus. When he failed to sell cash registers at the beginning of his career with The National Cash Register Co., he was not fortified by any inner resource that led him, in the face of despair, to success. He was bawled out and humiliated by an enraged boss who told him he was probably lazy, not very bright, and foolish to be making a complex project out of a simple matter. In a state of fright, combined with a subordinate's admiration for a commanding figure, Watson observed his boss selling

15

cash registers, and like a gifted plagiarist, a born imitator of effective practices of others, he fathomed the system and excelled over all.

Watson was an apprentice to a tyrant, the legendary John Henry Patterson, founder of the National Cash Register Company, who laced his tyranny with heavy-handed benevolence. In an era when it was commonly believed that character was developed by hard work enforced by fear of failure and punishment, John Henry Patterson was an internationally famous and successful director of men, one of whom was Thomas J. Watson. Patterson developed the dynamics and art form of salesmanship into a partially disciplined vocation, if not quite a bona fide profession: something requiring less demanding study, for example, than pharmacy; offering fewer opportunities for self-delusion and job advancement, but no less respectability, than journalism.

Watson's fame as a corporate educator, as an innovator of training programs that took the personal hazard out of obsolescent skills, was deserved. It was an object lesson to hard-hearted industrialists, unrestrained by nagging doubts about social obligations, who dispossessed and disposed of men and women whose skills had become outmoded through no fault of their own. But Watson himself learned the lesson first at the plants and offices of The National Cash Register Company in Dayton, Ohio—*The Cash*, as it was called—in the years between 1903 and 1914. There, Patterson influenced the life of Watson as master artists of the Renaissance influenced their apprentices. The Patterson influence was as profound and effective in its day on the development of distribution and sales in America as Watson's business machines were to be later on administration and record keeping. It was leavened by such factors as Watson's early environment: his stern and domineering father, his responsibility as head of a household filled with women, and his careful imitation of people, styles, and practices that attracted his intuitive fancy.

The Watsons, some of whom later changed their names in a family squabble over religious affiliations, emigrated to New York State in the 1840's. The families were headed by three brothers, John, David, and Andrew, who claimed membership in the Buchanan clan and whose family, Protestant and Scot, had left the area around Clyde sometime after 1800 to "engage in the linen business," as an officially approved family version of the migration put it, in the vicinity of Castle Berg, Ireland.

"Engaging in the linen business" in Ireland in the years of the potato famine was both unprofitable and difficult. It was a euphemism for long and exhausting days gathering and treating flax and spinning it onto spools turned by foot-operated wheels. The object was to produce fibers, which could be more easily manufactured in England by fast machines that had made the skill of spinning obsolete in preceding generations.

It was poverty that drove Protestants from Scotland to largely Catholic Ireland, and it was the fear of imminent death by starvation that, by and large, caused the emigration of two million inhabitants of Ireland in the six-year period preceding 1850.

Thus in the 1840's—the date is not recorded—the Watsons arrived in America as refugees from a land of famine. David stayed in Brooklyn, New York. His brother John, whose four children included two sons, Thomas and Andrew, made his way inland to the valleys south of the Finger Lakes region and settled on farmland in Hornby Township in Steuben County. The third brother, Andrew, put down roots in Orange Township in nearby Schuyler County. A day's buggy ride away in the tiny hamlet of Richford, the father of another family of Scots, William A. Rockefeller, was in the business of buying and selling lumber, with interim ventures in the field of peddling patent medicines. William had a son—five years younger than the newly arrived Thomas Watson— named John Davison Rockefeller, who went on to become the most famous native of the area.

The records of the local courts show that the migrating John Watson, grandfather of IBM's first president, became a naturalized citizen of the United States on November 5, 1855. His sons, Thomas and Andrew, went to work in their teens for one of the lumber operations which, like some of the oil, mining, and development opportunists of a later day, were indiscriminately stripping the land of natural resources at a rapid and highly profitable rate.

Andrew Watson became a master sawyer, while his brother Thomas, with a wider range of interest and, apparently, a more encompassing outlook on his job, became something of an expert in judging the value of timber stands and in various phases of milling, curing, and selling lumber. He worked and wandered through the timber territory of New York, Pennsylvania, and Ohio, usually following the riverways, for the next fifteen years. Then he returned to Steuben County and opened a lumber business on his own. Andrew joined him, and together they leased timber tracts and began marketing lumber.

A remarkable photograph of Thomas shows him at studied ease, immobilized for a time exposure, his shoulders slightly squared, head erect. Fierce, dark-browed eyes fix the viewer with a level look. Forelocks of black hair hold off from an expansive forehead the curved brim of a rakishly tilted black felt slouch hat. His features are handsome and unsmiling; his mouth, full chin, and lower jowls are enclosed in a black walrus mustache which blends with a well-brushed, but cropped, beard. A low, stand-up, white starched collar, narrow bow tie, and a patch of checkered shirt puffed up under a black vest and coat, each with satin piping, complete the picture of a splendidly attractive but no-nonsense man of the mid-nineteenth century.

In the old country, the Watsons had known a family by the name of White, of Strabane, Ireland; they, too, had emigrated to the woodland and farm country north and west of the Susquehanna River along the southern tier of New York. Thomas became reacquainted with the family and the young lady who was to become his bride. She was Jane Fulton White, whose Scots ancestors, like the Watsons, had migrated to Ireland. She was related to the family of Robert Fulton, the noted inventor, and had sufficient education to be qualified as a school teacher.

Jane Fulton White and Thomas were married and purchased a farm house at East Campbell, a rural region not sufficiently populated to be called a hamlet, between Bath and Corning, New York. The original property is now expanded to a site of 500 acres and contains a replica of the original Watson homestead that was destroyed by fire. In the farmhouse, which remained the headquarters for the Watson lumber business for ten years, Thomas John Watson was born on February 17, 1874.

About this time both the father and the latter's brother Andrew changed their names back to Watson after perhaps fifteen years or so of presenting themselves as Thomas and Andrew Wasson. The downstate New York branch of the family having got themselves intermarried with a Catholic or two, the upstate section of the clan, in a move to obliterate any connection with the papists of either Rome or Brooklyn, had changed the spelling of their name. For father Thomas, however, a conflict arose at the time of his marriage, especially since he had the name Watson tattooed on his arm, and after his namesake was born, he resumed his correctly spelled identity. No significant complications ensued at the time, although some lingering problems affected Watson relatives. In the late 1950's, a man named David Wasson, a cousin of the late chairman of the board of IBM, appeared before the Supreme Court of Steuben County and testified that he was a grandson of the Scotch-Irish immigrant John Watson and that *his* father had adopted the surname of Wasson without bothering to mention it to the courts. The court granted Mr. Wasson permission to return to the appropriately spelled Watson fold and a share of his cousin's estate.

The Thomas Watson family grew until it contained, in addition to young Thomas, four additional children: Effie, Jennie, Emma, and Louella. Thomas was about seven years old when the family dwelling burned to the ground. Another house was built on the site, but the family did not live there long. The father's lumber business was constantly endangered by competition and diminishing stands of timber, and the Watsons moved to a new address at intervals, as the focus of the father's business opportunities changed from town to town. By moving about in this way, he managed to remain modestly, though sometimes marginally, prosperous.

They went to Cooper's Plains, about five miles away from East Campbell, for two years, thence to a house near Addison for seven years, and to Painted Post for five years, where as a youth Tom got his first job. All these Steuben County villages were very small, the largest of them being Painted Post, once in the heart of Indian country, which, seventy-five years after the first Watson's tenure there, had little more than 2,500 inhabitants.

Few people alive in the late 1960's remembered Watson as a boy or as a youth, and fewer still whose memories were reliable. One of his cousins, Martha Leavey, long widowed at the age of ninety-two and a year younger than Thomas Watson, remembered the stern and bearded father whose occasional moods of happiness diminished with the years until he became as dour and remote as a caricature of the laconic Scot.

When he had the lumber business on the homestead, Mrs. Leavey recalled, "he would walk the two or three miles up here of an evening to visit. There would not be much talk, but he was pleasant then. He would have a bowl of warm milk and bread with us, just a little treat, you know, then he'd say good night and walk down the hill in the dark. Tom, his boy, was going to the little red schoolhouse with maybe twenty-five or thirty other young ones. I went there myself when we had forty children, from six years old to seventeen or eighteen, all the young for many miles in that one room. Mr. Watson had the schoolhouse moved, and you can see it down there on the homestead now, with the copy of his old house he had built. I think Mr. Watson did have a happy childhood, though, for his mother and the sisters were usually cheerful with one another. It was a family with strong ties."

Martha Leavey lived all of her ninety-two years within walking distance of the old farmhouse. For many years she lived on funds provided in trust by her cousin, Thomas J. Watson.

Down the dirt road, down the slope of a hill once adorned with fruitful orchards, now in need of pruning and attention, another cousin of Mr. Watson lives in a neat, comfortable trailer. He is Thomas Messer, aged seventy-eight, and named after Thomas J. Watson, he says, by his own father in conscious acknowledgement of his admiration for old Tom Watson's tall, attractive fourteen-year-old son. Mrs. Leavey and Tom Messer were the last two surviving relatives from Thomas J. Watson's youth.

Watson grew tall and strong; he remained lean until he was in his thirties and, indeed, stayed trim, if hefty, most of his long life. Wherever they lived, there was always a horse or two to feed and groom or a rig or wagon to take care of. There was compulsory church and Sunday School attendance on weekends, and more often than not prayer meetings or additional church activities in midweek. The Watsons belonged to the Methodist Church in Painted Post, and Thomas J. Watson had the local church rebuilt in later years. He also gave the money to have the Painted Post firehouse erected.

As a boy, Thomas Watson was afflicted with asthma. He was, if not altogether a loner, something less than gregarious. Undoubtedly any tendency toward uninhibited expression was subdued by old Thomas, who was not known for his personal warmth and sunny disposition. Brusque, stern, domineering, and fiercely attractive, he was physically strong and had survived his share of lumber camp altercations unscarred. Young Thomas did not appear in his teens to have inherited his father's physique. Instead, he was lanky and intense, with a flaming temper that clung to him like a curse nearly all of his life.

He was shy at social gatherings and church affairs; a look of dissatisfaction usually clouded his features. He did not go swimming with the other boys who enlivened the community of some 600 inhabitants, and in fact he never did learn to swim. Nor did he join other boys in the hunting and fishing forays so common to the place and time. He did, however, leave the mark of his identity around the village; he loved to write his name repeatedly on things in a bold and heavy hand—on the village monument, in the stairwell of the local public hall, and on other sites convenient for graffiti.

When Tom finished school in Painted Post, the senior Watson, ambitious for his son despite his inability to establish a warm and open relationship with him, wanted him to study law. He suggested that Tom join the office of a lawyer friend as a "reading" clerk and student, or go to the little city of Ithaca at the southern tip of Lake Cayuga to enroll at Cornell University. No part of this plan appealed to Tom, who was certain, he observed later, "that I was a smarter man than my father; I was positive of that."

Like Mark Twain, young Tom Watson noticed that the intelligence of his father increased considerably in the period between his own adolescence and voting age. But he would not study law. Instead, he told his father that he would apply for a temporary teacher's certificate, teach for three years, and enroll at Albany Teachers' College. A single day of teaching ended that plan.

"I can't go into a schoolroom with a bunch of children at nine o'clock in the morning and stay till four," he declared as he quit.

His next decision was to go into business. Tom feared that his father, whose patience was tied to a short fuse, would send him out to work on the farm. Instead, he made Tom's decision to go into business conditional upon a year in business school. Off Tom went to Elmira, twenty miles away, to enroll in the Miller School of Commerce. He completed the short courses in accounting and business there in May, 1892, and immediately landed a job as a six-dollar-a-week bookkeeper in Clarence Risley's butcher shop in Painted Post. He was eighteen years old. It was a good salary; families were living on as much, although not, of course, living very well. Yet Tom Watson was bored. In a matter of weeks, he complained that "he couldn't sit on a high stool and keep books all my life."

The Watsons had a house on High Street in the village, close to a merchant named Willard Bronson, who operated a hardware store in conjunction with a free-wheeling sales operation. He acquired pianos, Estey organs, sewing machines, and even caskets from manufacturers and took on drummers, or peddlers, to go about the countryside selling them on consignment. Caskets, of course, were a soft-sell item which required some need on the part of the consumer prior to transaction, but in the case of sewing machines, Chickering pianos, and the little organs, any marketing technique that worked was a fair play.

Willard Bronson is still remembered in Painted Post, not unkindly, as a sharp, shrewd entrepreneur on whose face a distinct look of pain appeared from the unpleasant friction that occurred when he had to release his grip on a dollar.

"I just never trusted him," one old lady said, "until he got old enough to be afraid of death."

Bronson was Tom Watson's Sunday School superintendent at the Methodist Church. Even as a bored bookkeeper, Watson had not yet thought of going on the road as a salesman. But a new young man named George Cornwell had come to town to peddle Bronson's wares. Tom Watson met him at a Sunday School picnic and made an important, on-the-spot discovery. He found that despite his shyness and a good deal of inhibition, he got on well with the outgoing George Cornwell. Cornwell immediately stated that he needed a helper on his wagon run through the nearby sales territory, and proposed that Watson make an arrangement with Bronson to fill the post.

That evening, Tom went to Bronson, mentioned the talk with Cornwell, and left with the job. His salary was ten dollars a week and use of the wagon. He had to supply his own horses. The life of Tom Watson, salesman, had begun.

2.
On
the
Way

———◆———

It was a summer day when George Cornwell and Thomas Watson started on what for Tom was a great adventure. Except for his school term in nearby Elmira, he had quite literally never been anywhere. The land area that bounded his world was isolated countryside which, even including Elmira, extended east to west for about thirty miles and north to south for perhaps a little less. If either Thomas or his sisters had traveled any farther than a day's wagon ride in any direction from the site of the family farmhouse, there is no record of it. There must have been a good deal of visiting among the numerous Watson clan, but none of the relatives except the contaminated Brooklyn element with its infusion of unwelcome Catholic spouses resided outside of what became, in the summer of 1892, Watson's sales territory.

"I had a lot of cousins," Watson said in a later explanation of his good sales record as a beginner.

He also had a lot of industry, determination, and stamina. For it was very hard work, for all its adventure and fun. Watson knew nothing of selling, but he was a perceptive imitator and a quick study. Before George Cornwell departed for another job in more promising territory, Watson, often holding the horses while the more experienced and confident Cornwell made the presentations, and now and then a sale, studied everything about the first salesman he had ever encountered beyond the range of his own shaving mirror. He paid attention to minute details and to general impressions, to what worked and to what caused the eyes of a prospective customer to turn away, either in boredom or in rejection of some stylistic mannerism.

About the only skills Watson possessed, other than elementary bookkeeping, were the ability to groom and handle horses and a familiarity

23

with wagons—the natural legacy of a farm boy who in summers had handled a team and a stone boat, working the reins off to the side while a pair of horses cleared the land of boulders or extracted stumps from the earth. In addition, he had the personal advantage of being clothes-conscious, with a flair for sartorial identity in a world of careless, some-what unwashed and ungroomed men. The man, his team of horses, and his clean, yellow "Democrat wagon," as it was called, inevitably looked good. The value of first impressions did not have to be learned; he seemed to know it from the beginning.

Watson drove the organ wagon, with its bed and high seat covered, when necessary, by a canopy, and at least one piano and several smaller organs anchored by rope and chocks to keep the cargo from shifting in the rutted roads. The roads followed ancient Indian paths for the most part, curving and rising with the contour of the land, running parallel with streams to shallow points allowing a fording. The shaky tax base of local government provided money for only a paucity of creek spans and covered bridges. Here and there were sections of plank or corduroy roads—wooden planks or logs to carry the wagons over swamp and marsh areas—but for the most part the roadways were dirt, dusty in the dry season, mud-rutted in the rain, frozen in midwinter.

From Painted Post, the young men went to other villages on market day and did their selling from the wagon tailgates. They bedded down their horses and slept at farms along the way, often with one of Watson's cousins or with a family who knew his relatives. Because of the expense, they avoided the small inns and boarding houses along the canals and railroads.

The miles they traveled often depended on the condition of the four horses which hauled them and on the weather. The horses required care, feeding, and grooming to keep them looking smart and healthy, and the young men themselves sought to look dignified and responsible as good peddlers were expected to look. They were not tinkers or gypsies of dubious repute, like the itinerant salesmen of an earlier time, but solid citizens, emissaries of Bronson the churchman back in Painted Post.

Watson's sales territory probably did not encompass ten thousand people. But when they congregated at early autumn fairs, Watson was there with Bronson's wares, alternating with Cornwell in making spiels from the tailgate, or welcoming people he recognized. Sometimes, the young men would simply stop in a village for a time, rent a ground-floor office, and while one would keep store, the other would try to round up prospective customers. At other times he and Cornwell would heft a piano or an organ into a farmhouse late in the afternoon of a day on the road, and George would play chords and sing, with a delighted family joining in. This, of course, made the household vulnerable to a sale. An organ or a piano, to be sure, was an enormous expenditure for a household, but it was often the primary means of family entertainment. Sewing machines, on the other hand, were prized as a household necessity.

After George Cornwell departed for a better job with more money than could be extracted from Bronson, Watson worked the wagon route alone. It was the most "responsible" job he ever held, Watson said, for he managed every phase of the off-premises sales operation. He settled up with Bronson every week and then started out again. Sometimes he had to take livestock or goods as partial payment for a sewing machine or an organ. This required dependence on skills of barter and trade which courted disaster unless mastered quickly. There were times in the course of Watson's education as a peddler when his mother and sisters had to put a tub of half-rancid butter through the churn again to make it salable, or when he had to take time to break a horse he had unwisely accepted in trade without subjecting the animal to a road test. But he managed to survive the terrible panic of 1893, the worst economic breakdown the country endured in the nineteenth century.[1]

He also grew up. His thin frame filled out. He became extraordinarily handsome. Then and later on when he had more money, he experimented with his image, as young men will, imitating other salesmen he admired and determining in his own mind the kind of a man he wanted to appear to be.

Watson saved some money in his two years on the road for Bronson. He was well pleased with his ten dollars a week advance until he learned from another salesman that commission on his sales would have been as high as seventy dollars a week.

But factors other than money motivated the next drastic change in Watson's course. One was his physical maturity; another was the development of his personality. He had met and, in a manner of speaking —through persuasion and service—conquered people. Limited to the sales territory he could reach by wagon from Painted Post and dealing only in long-life items precluding repeat sales to the same families, his job had little, if any, growth potential. Moreover, he was disillusioned by the knowledge that Bronson had paid him a good deal less than full

---

[1] Grover Cleveland, starting his second term, was forced to summon a special session of Congress to deal with the panic of 1893. It was precipitated, in part, by fear which swept the country when the U.S. gold reserve fell below $100 million. Before the year was over, 491 banks had failed.

value for his labors, and any deprivation of what he thought he deserved evoked pain and latent hostility in Watson. In two years, Bronson had given him no raise nor, for that matter, had he gone out of his way to be pleasant to him. But Bronson was aghast when Watson quit.

Bronson's quick offer of a substantial raise, even an offer to sell him the business with payment to be made from income, backed by a signed note, left Watson unmoved. He did, despite his disdain for old Tom Watson's intellectual capacity, discuss the idea of purchasing the business with his father, who advised him to get out of Painted Post as soon as possible. And so the youth, not yet old enough to vote, co-operated with Bronson until the business could be sold.

With Bronson's business disposed of, young Watson climbed aboard an Erie Railroad coach one morning and rode off to the rough lake port city of Buffalo, second in size in the state only to New York City. The destination was suggested by his father, who had been impressed with the size and vigor of the city on his wanderings to and through it.

Cities like brawling and heartless Buffalo were a world apart from the small villages and towns that were simply flagstops along the tracks of the Erie, the New York Central, and the Delaware, Lackawanna & Western, which led to America's largest inland port city. For Thomas Watson, the search for a foothold in a hostile urban world was depressing and frightening. For many lonely weeks he went to wholesale firms, distributors, any office he could get into, in search of a job. Only in selling could he offer any experience. He was nearly penniless, nearly driven to sending a rescue call to his father for a train ticket back to Painted Post, and probably to oblivion, when he got a commission job selling sewing machines for the Wheeler and Wilcox Company. He had scarcely started, however, again peddling sewing machines in the outlying countryside, when he was fired. It wasn't, apparently, a case of giving Watson a trial and then rejecting him; it was a matter of the company just deciding, after engaging him, that he wasn't needed. He was near the end of a low road. Dispirited, a stranger in a strange town with no place to go for human companionship except to the saloons, he was back in the bruising business of seeking work in offices where he was unwelcome.

In his short, lamentable career with Wheeler and Wilcox, Watson had met a co-worker named C. B. Barron, a flashy fellow sporting the sartorial style of the city slicker. Watson himself, because of his youth, uncertainty, and general lack of resources, had not yet refined the image of himself that was then in the process of development, nor could he afford the wardrobe the image required. He looked up to Barron as the nearest ideal at hand, even though the latter had also been dismissed. Watson's undisguised admiration for his genial and confident friend, who was something of a crook in the guise of a top-hatted drummer, pleased him and doubtless evoked a morsel of the ready-handed willingness to be of service that frequently lurks in the heart of the charlatan like Barron, particularly if he is in search of an associate or victim.

Barron had made a connection with a recruiter for the Buffalo Building and Loan Association who was staffing an on-the-road sales organization to peddle stock shares in the company as a prelude to opening branch offices in outlying towns. It was his plan to canvass the possibilities along a string of towns southwest of Buffalo. He invited Watson to come along and try his hand, on a straight commission basis. Although lacking confidence in his ability to sell anything as incorporeal as a share of stock, Watson lacked an alternative even more. So, with Barron this time, he set out on the road once more.

The first impression of Barron was doubtless the best one, and sometimes the only favorable one, for the longer the time spent in association with him, the more it appeared necessary to resort to a diminishing scale of values in describing him. Unfortunately for Watson, *his* intuition and reflexes in judging people had been awakened and exercised only in or near the community of neighbors, relatives, and people of generally similar outlook. Barron was a new breed altogether to Watson —the kind of man who would deliberately resort to showmanship and insupportable claims, smoke an expensive cigar in the hotel dining room to project the image of the man of the world, and have himself paged by the bell captain to impress the local set. He dressed the role he played, too: silk hat, cutaway, striped trousers, piping on the vest. In due time, Watson adopted some of the man's style and devised his own variation of evoking confidence, but he deplored Barron's disreputable conduct.

Barron and Watson reached Silver Creek, a little village on Lake Erie, halfway between Buffalo and the Pennsylvania border. Unable to induce the local prospects to part with cash, Barron went to their hotel, and Watson stepped into a saloon and introduced himself to a cluster of imbibers. The latter responded with mirth and rejection as the tall, earnest youth opened his prepared sales talk. Their interest remained on the drink in hand and the one to follow. Watson's own recollections were that the pubkeeper himself was drawn to the group as a gesture of friendliness in the face of so much disdain. But when the gesture of good will had been completed, the saloon keeper had some building and loan stock, and Watson had a cash commission of two dollars.

Watson felt a surge of spirit. The magic was back; he was selling again. He strolled down the street to a tailor shop and emerged, after successfully exercising his power of persuasion, with a commission of five dollars. With mounting excitement, carefully held in check, he continued his canvass of merchants and prospects. It was a Wednesday; when the week was over, Watson had made one hundred sixty-nine dollars. It was more money than he had thought it possible for any man to make.

Quickly and noticeably, the Watson wardrobe improved. No longer was it necessary for him to sit in a tailor shop closet, in shirt and drawers, while his only suit was being pressed. The difference between Barron's somewhat excessive, not quite authentic elegance and young Watson's more commonplace but appropriate appearance was soon narrowed. The image and the reality were coming closer together. Possession of money, making sales, taking in commissions—these were the index of accomplishment with which came confidence, at least transient fulfillment, success, and even esteem. Apprehension was tempered, more easily repressed, beneath the cloak of the well-dressed, well-groomed salesman, whose commissions were measures of respect and high regard. The successful salesman, when he was channeling frequent signed orders to the home office, felt loved.

With his own money and some borrowed from his father back in Painted Post, Watson set up a butcher shop in a residential quarter of Buffalo. He chose a butcher shop because the business was familiar. Back home he had kept books for a while for Clarence Risley, and while he disliked the job as a bookkeeper in a butcher shop, he didn't mind owning one. He had read about an entrepreneur in Philadelphia, Thomas B. Hunter, who opened a store with three hundred fifty dollars and built up a large chain of outlets.

He employed a clerk to work in the shop while he pursued prospective stockholders for the building and loan company, for it was his intention to develop the chain of retail outlets as a sideline. In order to reinforce the honesty of the clerk and guard against the diversion of the shop's income to less pertinent uses, Watson bought a secondhand cash register. He was learning elementary business techniques, measuring the risks one had to take, and diversifying his labor and interests toward the exclusive objective of making money, or—as he called it— getting ahead.

Watson's careers both as stock salesman and emerging chain store tycoon collapsed more or less simultaneously. Before he could raise the money to open a second store, he had to sell the first one. Barron had absconded with all the building and loan funds, including commissions, he could get his hands on.

Thus in the early autumn of 1895, six or seven months past his twenty-first birthday, Watson was once more overtaken by misfortune. So far the heroes he had patterned himself after had left him with a short, effective course in door-to-door selling, and a tested flair for fashionable dress—and nothing else. However, he had to recover quickly, for in setting up the butcher shop he had made some financial commitments. Aside from the money borrowed from his father, who at sixty-one and in failing health was barren of both resources and prospects, there were still installment payments owed on that secondhand cash register.

Watson went back to the local Natonal Cash Register Company office, from which he had purchased the machine, and arranged for the new owner of his butcher shop to take over the payments. While there, as he did everywhere he went, he tried to get a job—and encountered for the first time the man in whose likeness he would, in part, mold himself. John J. Range was the manager of the Buffalo office of *The Cash*, a big talkative Irishman who continued and improved upon the tutorial work in sales instruction previously assumed by Barron and George Cornwell.

If repetitive recall of an experience is an index of its impact, the impression made by John Range on young Watson was critical to his development. In hotel dining halls and convention centers around the world, Watson repeated his account of how Range demonstrated by example, by the use of reproof and persuasion, by withholding and granting favor, the techniques of converting a man into a dedicated, demon salesman. Thousands of IBM salesmen, managers, and staff people recall Watson's simplified, ritualized report of his years with Range in Buffalo. There was no doubt that Watson learned how to play the role of the father-figure boss of salesmen by first being a willing target of the techniques himself.

At first Range wasn't interested in taking on Watson, even on a commission basis. Watson, however, showing some of his subsequently overdeveloped tenacity, made repeated trips back to Range's office. The National Cash Register Company was a famous, even slightly infamous, company. It had nearly monopolized manufacture and distribution of the business machine which John Henry Patterson made virtually indispensable to modern business. Besides knowing the stature of the company and Patterson's reputation as an innovator and ball of fire in industry, Watson remembered that a salesman in Painted Post had told of collecting a thirty-dollar commission on the sale of a *single* cash register. In October 1895 he prevailed upon Range to hire him for a probationary period, the duration of which would be dependent on results. Range told him to study the company sales manual—a kind of catechism and prescribed sales dialogue, devised and enforced on NCR salesmen by Patterson himself—and sent him off to work on the west side of Buffalo.

Obedient to the letter and working from Patterson's set of rote instructions, Watson's efforts were unrewarding for the better part of two weeks. He was, in fact, foundering. He did not, as myth would have it, by taking time to ponder the reason and by fortifying himself with his favorite slogan, *Think*, start anew and persevere until he achieved success. He did, however, encounter the ire of John Range, who told him in so many words that he was making excuses, that he seemed devoid of understanding about the nature of his job, that no special endowment of intelligence was necessary to locate people who needed cash registers, and that Watson was going about a fairly simple task in naively inept fashion. He bawled the daylights out of the big, gawky youth on whom the stamp of the farm country was still too clearly visible.

Range knew the technique, which he had refined almost to an art form, of peeling the hide off a man, cutting it to ribbons, then piecing it back together again and leaving him, not resentful over the humiliation—for fathers must be forgiven—but grateful for the advice, counsel, and expressions of parental concern that followed.

Of course, some men would not or could not endure the treatment, either because they did not respond to the patriarchal or father-figure projection or because they were disinclined to be measured in terms of periodical selling output. But such men did not usually become or long remain salesmen in John Henry Patterson's empire. Watson himself said in retrospect that he was waiting for Range's first tirade to die down so that he could quit. But Watson was, in fact, quite capable of extraordinary, even complete, subordination. He also needed to learn more about the ego-shattering trade of selling, and he was intuitive enough to sense that Range was the authority who could extend his vocational training.

Range's intent was purposeful; he was a salesman of long experience, and he knew by training and by observing Watson how far he could go in using harsh talk and the shock of temperament to evoke zeal and determination from his young subordinate. As easily as Range had turned on his rage, he turned it off and warmly, without apology, comforted Watson. He said with sympathy that he knew exactly what

30

Watson's difficulties were; it was people who *didn't want* to buy cash registers. If all the merchants in his territory wanted to buy cash registers, "Why, they would just come in here and buy them, and we wouldn't need any salesmen out walking the streets." The thing to learn was why nobody thus far in Watson's territory wanted one.

In the manner of a man offering encouragement and assistance to a besieged compatriot, Range suggested they get in the buggy and together call on some of Watson's more promising prospects. They started off, taking a big ornate cash register with them, a supreme act of confidence in itself that was fully justified when, with Watson in attendance and observing every tactical nuance, Range sold the machine. On three additional occasions Range accompanied him, and the amazed Watson saw three more sales completed.

Watson absorbed this instructive experience into his whole being. Guided by Patterson's manual, with its explicitness for all occasions, but enormously impressed with the Range style of dealing with a customer —making him feel confident, gently persuading him that a cash register would save money, guard against losses, and help him organize his record keeping, not to mention the psychologically supportive matter of the joyfully ringing bell each time a sale was rung up and money tucked inside—Watson within a year became one of the most successful cash register salesmen in the East, making a hundred dollars a week in commissions. A large part of this went to pay for the support of his parents and sisters, for the family had by then moved to Buffalo.

Watson alternated between meeting and selling the shopkeepers and merchants along the streets of Buffalo, and making two- and three-week buggy trips to the back country of New York State and deep into Pennsylvania. He rode the trains, too, knew the characteristics of different train runs, committed the timetables to memory as did many salesmen on the road, and was a well-known figure in that transient community of wandering, hustling, often harried men who kept the consumer products factories going in the latter days of the not-always-Gay Nineties.

One week he made more than $1,200, his lifetime record on the road, but during the darker days of the depression year of 1897, he would make no sale at all in many weeks. During the bad periods, Range would go with him into the territory—and invariably sales would pick up.

Watson was twenty-five years old, the top salesman in Buffalo, doing better than Range himself, when in the summer of 1899 he was tapped by Patterson to go to Rochester as agent in a branch office. The family bought a house, and all the Watsons moved into it, to be joined in due course by a new member of the family, a National Cash Register Company salesman who married the oldest sister, Effie.

A young furniture manufacturer, Frederick S. Miller, who died in 1951, was one of Watson's first friends in Rochester. Miller, noting that Watson in social situations was stammering and shy, introduced him to business friends and almost always invited him to take a seat at his own table at Chamber of Commerce luncheons. Watson remained grateful for this early welcome to the community, and thirty-one years later, when Miller's son Austin was graduated from Princeton University, the young man was offered a job as an IBM salesman in his home town of Rochester.

An offer of any kind of a job in the depression year of 1930 was looked upon as a stroke of good fortune, and Austin Miller snapped it up. Mr. Miller remains with IBM in Endicott today, a veteran of many of the rewards, passing anxieties, and tribal life of the paternalistic corporation. His failure to achieve his sales quota and win membership in the One Hundred Percent Club during the first nine years of his association with IBM—a failure that would have doomed another man to dismissal or to harassment so unendurable as to make departure the most blessed of alternatives—produced a crisis for Miller, but he was able to survive. An attempt to fire him backfired in part because a negative judgment made of his work was palpably unjust and because dismissal of an old Watson family friend, except for unforgivable reasons—like wearing a yellow shirt or cashing one's pay check in a saloon—was unthinkable.

When Watson first arrived in Rochester, he sold a cash register to the saloon keeper next door to the National Cash office. The man appeared as Watson was hitching his horse to a post to complain about the poor reputation the company had in town because, apparently, the previous sales agent had got drunk and provided terrible service. It is said that when the man finished his unsolicited report, Watson started to talk, and when *he* finished, the saloon next door had a cash register. The same report of Watson's arrival in town disclosed that he disposed of still another cash register en route to investigate a complaint from a dissatisfied customer, when he stopped along the way to fortify his spirits by negotiating another quick sale. With the thirty-five per cent commission he made as sales agent—in contrast to the fifteen per cent previously paid him as a straight commission man—Watson started off in Rochester with at least $125 or so in commissions. However, as manager he had to pay operating expenses of the office. But profits were kept in the family; before there was a subordinate commission salesman on the staff, his sister Jennie occasionally sold a cash register, for which she was rewarded, sometimes with presents.

Rochester was not considered a desirable territory at the end of the century, which was probably the reason why Watson, as one of the most junior of four hundred salesmen at work for the company, got the job. His record in the Buffalo office was, of course, known to John Patterson, who kept himself fully and minutely informed on the performance of every employee connected with cash register sales. Aside from the recommendation that John Range conveyed back to the home office in Dayton, it was most likely that a man named Hugh Chalmers, one of NCR's crack managers and salesmen who was close to Patterson, had a good word to say about Watson when his name came up. Watson had once shared a commission with Chalmers and later got to know him a little better when he went to company conventions in Dayton.

Given his youth, character, and total involvement in his job, the only possible course for Watson in Rochester was upward. Under the system which Patterson devised for measuring and evaluating the performance of about 160 branch offices, Rochester was near the bottom of the list when Watson arrived. Within a few months, under his command, it was sixth from the top, where it remained until well into Watson's second year. Then sales fell off and he did not reach his quota. One reason was temporary near-saturation of the market in many quarters, with an estimated 160,000 cash registers already in use, one for every four hundred persons in the country. More specifically, Rochester was one of the cities where competitors who had not yet succumbed to *The Cash* sales methods were still thriving in business. The Hallwood Company, having hung on through repeated assaults against it, was selling cash registers in spite of the Patterson doctrine that NCR was able to produce quite enough alone. Watson was expected to take over Hallwood's slice of the Rochester market.

The methods by which the two rival sales offices fought for the Rochester market are no secret, but neither of the rivals was an innocent, and neither published accounts of skirmishes or strategy in the contest. It was said of Watson that he was a "rough customer, but a square shooter," yet he conceded feeling ashamed, or at least regretting, certain of his sales techniques. It was necessary to know John Patterson, as Watson was later to know him well—to the point of copying in breadth and some detail his executive style—to appreciate the intensity of the pressure from the Dayton office on the Rochester agent. The directions were to get the business; from Patterson this meant no equivocation and little concern about means or methods. He had no compunction about the rights of the competition and resorted to some brutally crude references to men he intended to put out of business.

"The best way to kill a dog is to cut off its head," he would respond to suggestions that restrained measures might serve in a competitive situation.

Watson may have had a momentary reluctance, even remorse, about the issue, but he got the Rochester business nevertheless. A Hallwood salesman, perhaps off his guard or simply not aware of the range of Watson's zeal for carrying out Patterson's directives, happened to mention that he expected on the following day to call on a promising prospect twenty miles away. When he arrived the next day to see the merchant, he met Watson just departing. By way of greeting, he observed that Watson must have got up pretty early that morning. Watson, who had started off with his horse and rig at dawn and now had the order for the merchant's cash register in his pocket, replied that he'd had a job to do.

For a good many years Watson told the story of his encounter with the Hallwood salesman, whom he considered, or so he said, a friend. He would tell it as he recounted other "salesman" stories, rambling a bit and filling out the dialogue, terminating the account by saying that he enjoyed his triumph over a good breakfast. But as the years passed, and as Watson proclaimed the Golden Rule as the guideline of business and the ethical index of capitalism, the story changed in tone and so did the moral of it. Instead of interpreting it as an exercise in opportunism, as an example of the way in which an alert IBM salesman was expected to get the advantage of a competitor, he cited the incident as an example of regrettable conduct. In time, this bit of nostalgia disappeared entirely from his repertoire of recollections.

Watson had secured enough business to support a fully staffed office after three years in Rochester, with trained men assigned to the city and surrounding territory. Each man was expected to have a working knowledge of the Hallwood machines, as Hallwood men knew The Cash mechanism, for the purpose of preventing them from functioning. What Watson's feelings were on such matters at the time, he never said.

One of The Cash methods was intimidation and threat of ruin, which Patterson's agents were compelled—and trained—to carry out. Watson would stand outside the Hallwood office in Rochester and observe—spotting, it was called—who came and went. He and other NCR salesmen were under explicit orders to report every contact between a Hallwood agent and any prospective purchasers, who were coded on The Cash records as PPs. Men especially trained in persuasion and tactics of intimidation, sometimes in company with regular salesmen and sometimes operating as separate squads, would swoop down on the prospective purchaser of a Hallwood or other competitive cash register and "warn" the customer that the machine was no good, that it infringed NCR patents, that the manufacturer was being sued, and that anyone who bought and used a Hallwood machine would, likewise, be sued. These arguments were reinforced by an offer to give the customer a National register at a fraction of the price of a Hallwood.

In Rochester, Watson did his work so well that he distinguished himself in the eyes of Chalmers and Patterson. He was not then restrained by the delicate scruples or Golden Rule concepts which, in the generation that followed, he sought to impose not only on businessmen but on government leaders, including Hitler and Mussolini. With the assistance of the home office, Watson made National the monopoly company in Rochester, and after that he was destined for more highly significant work.

In Dayton, Patterson was taking Watson's measure in his own way and for his own as yet undisclosed reason. Hugh Chalmers had just been elevated to the position of general manager, second only to Patterson, a move that would often bring Watson's work to Patterson's attention.

Patterson felt he had built the cash register business single-handedly, and any oversight that allowed predators to trespass on his personal preserve had to be remedied. Although The Cash nearly always had between eighty and ninety-five per cent of the business, perhaps half of the sixty or more other companies in the field had disappeared by 1910, principally with the help of The Cash. The remainder died out on their own until National had something approaching a complete monopoly.

Patterson was absolutely certain he had the exclusive right to all of the cash register business in the United States—and in the world as well —notwithstanding the existence of trust laws and strictures against restraint of trade. His ego was, therefore, offended by the growth of the market in secondhand cash registers, a business which had slowly developed over the preceding ten or twelve years and which returned some profit to people in many cities who were too often beyond Patterson's control. People making money in cash registers without Patterson's permission infuriated him, at first by their very presence and finally by the fact that they had developed the secondhand business into a viable, nationwide commercial operation.

With Hugh Chalmers, Patterson devised a heady, aggressive, and palpably criminal plan involving espionage, money, and the assignment of secret agents to clear the field and take possession of the secondhand market across the country.

Watson's four-year record in Rochester, where his unquestioning loyalty to The Cash and his devotion to the neutralization of competition had been put to the test, was seen by Chalmers as appropriate combat experience for a seize-and-destroy assault plan on a national scale.

What Watson would understand more fully before long was the practice of barratry which Patterson and his highly trained band of enterprising pirates had devised. By filing patent infringement and libel actions against smaller competing producers, thus engaging their executive time as well as imposing legal and court costs on them, Patterson after a time found that he could obtain concessions from his competitors simply by agreeing to call off the legal harassment and free them of the costs of defense.

But Watson, not yet privy to the full dynamics and mechanics of predatory industrialism, had no advance warning of the role he was to play when he was summoned to Patterson's office. While he had resolved, with some help from headquarters, the competitive problem in Rochester and left, as he somewhat boastfully declared, "one of the best organized and cleanest territories that had ever been turned over to another man" for his successors, he had seen Patterson only once before—at a sales meeting two years earlier. Now, one morning in October of 1903, Watson stepped into the simply furnished office of a short, compact gamecock of a man who made him an astonishing proposition.

With a million dollars to spend, Watson was to establish an apparently independent concern posing as a competitor to, but in fact fronting for, the National Cash Register Company and thus drive out or take over control of the used cash register business in the United States. At twenty-nine years of age, scarcely known to the NCR sales staff, since he had been isolated in Rochester for four years, he was asked to take on a kind of industrial underground mission.

Watson probably did not yet have a thorough knowledge of the restraint of trade laws, in particular the much ignored thirteen-year-old Sherman Anti-Trust Act, but there was no doubt at all that Patterson, a well educated fellow Scot, knew what he was about. As for Chalmers, he was vindictive, ruthless, enormously smart, and badly abused under Patterson's roughshod leadership, and he knew all there was to know about the combative avarice of Patterson and the willingness of the ambitious, subordinate Watson to do superbly well anything he was directed to do.

Thomas Watson did not, as it was often said, "invent" salesmanship, nor did he introduce very much that was new or original to the field. He gave extension and exposure to the sales system developed by Patterson: a case of the disciple overtaking the master. Industrial paternalism was not new even to Patterson. He knew of the work of George Mortimer Pullman, who founded his own model community where even the public works were owned by the company that had a corner on the bedroom and lounge cars of the Pullman Palace Car Company. In 1889 the community of Pullman was annexed to Chicago following an uprising of the beneficiaries of company paternalism and an acrimonious strike of Pullman car workers.

But Patterson harnessed paternalism to a system of specialized training and self-help projects that offered a religious hope for materialism offset by the fear of damnation. He believed that man responded best to the fear of punishment and the promise of money. Those who could not accept this doctrine with enthusiasm, or sublimate their doubts with conviction, were fired. He fashioned and installed in the cash register business an elemental force that was not previously known. Thus, to the extent that he created and set in motion what was not in prior existence, he was a genius. He was a violent and vengeful eccentric, a man obsessed. From reserves of energy previously unsuspected, he turned to problems of design, advertising, marketing, employee relations, plant construction, financing—every aspect of industrial management and commercial selling.

When Patterson acquired the sagging National Manufacturing Company, producer of Ritty's Incorruptible Cash Register, he first changed the name of the company and then studied the mechanism of the machine it produced, simplified the design of small parts to make possible improvement in the manufacturing process, and in a short time had several patents in his own name. With this accomplished, he turned over production, styling, and engineering to others and launched a selling and sales training program of unparalleled effectiveness. He established the quota system and the guaranteed territory, altering a competitive concept which in the past had pitted one salesman against another in the same circumscribed area, and often resulted in diminishing the size of a territory as a man began to develop business in it. Patterson not only guaranteed to keep competing salesmen from his own and other companies, where possible, out of a man's territory, but credited the salesman with *any* sale made in that area, whether generated by the salesman or by advertising at company expense. This idea ran contrary to previous experience but became commonplace practice as selling and market distribution became increasingly sophisticated.

Patterson told men how to dress and how to act. He made them memorize sales talks and threatened them with dismissal if they deviated from them, or at least if, in deviating, they failed to sell. He summoned the men to group meetings, made them cheer each other, stand up and make public confessions and appraisals of their failures and successes. He transformed the world of selling with generous commissions, with rah-rah conventions, prizes, threats of punishment, and a system of territorial quotas enforced by carrot-and-stick applications. By developing the direct mail technique to a level of unheard-of effectiveness, he had buyers imploring the company in Dayton to direct salesmen in the field to call.

Patterson borrowed money and built on high ground at the family farm a stunning factory with glass walls, vines covering the support columns, and beds of blooming flowers in season. Production employees had never worked in more cheerful, brighter, safer surroundings. There were private lockers, dressing rooms, showers and a swimming pool, lunch rooms and free hot meals, medical care and counseling on family affairs. Patterson was widely known, something of a national public figure, for such benevolence. He loved the publicity but scoffed at the suggestion of benevolence and wouldn't talk about it. When Watson arrived for the mandatory interview, he saw a sign outside the door of Patterson's office, which read: *Be Brief. Omit all compliments about welfare work.*

"It pays," said Patterson of such coddling of employees. "Hungry people, people with bad diets or in poor health, are not good producers."

In return for all of this, employees were expected to be enthusiastic about the same things and ideas that evoked enthusiasm from Patterson; absolute obedience and conformity were required, including attendance at inspirational lectures designed to uplift their souls.

When money began to pour in, as it did after a few years, Patterson built more factories in garden settings, with broad drives leading to them and riding paths leading to outlying trails. Executives were persuaded— compelled is the more precise word—to ride horses for their health and well-being, regardless of their skills or inclinations. Some suffered broken bones and bruises until they learned, and one family breadwinner on Patterson's management staff was thrown from his horse and killed. Horseback rides began at dawn; the men were called "the National Cash Rough Riders" by the populace. But Patterson was in dead earnest about horsemanship, and Watson was not with the company long before he, too, was out on the dawn patrol. When Dayton unveiled a monument to Patterson's memory, it was predictably in the form of a great heroic statue of him on a horse.

This was the man who summoned Watson to Dayton and who, with enormous drive, mastery, and occasional sadism, dominated his life almost without interruption for the next eleven years, and in some indirect ways for the remainder of his life. Men who came under the influence of Patterson, those men who could endure the tension and the totality of dominance, or rationalize the humiliation they had to bear as the price of learning the techniques of combative leaders of industry, could never quite shuck the effects of Patterson's volcanic personality, volcanic in the sense that violent eruptions punctuated prolonged periods of mild-mannered repose. Watson was joining a company of men who, before emerging as industrial leaders of the early twentieth century, subjected themselves to the rewarding tutorial instruction, the irrational temperament, paternal counsel, insults, weird faddism, and occasional cruelties of the strutting little genius who taught America how to turn men into instruments of selling.

3.
The
Sorcerer's
Apprentice

WHEN WATSON SET OUT to eliminate competition in the secondhand cash register business, he was launched upon a task clearly illegal under antitrust laws that were extremely difficult to enforce. If John Henry Patterson and Thomas J. Watson, along with their zealous associates, had been more moderate in their avarice and techniques—if the band of co-conspirators, working together to enforce a monopoly and ruin competitors, had remained unified instead of breaking into hostile camps (largely as a result of Patterson's intemperate personality)—it is doubtful that the depth and breadth of NCR's corporate conduct would ever have become public knowledge. How many corporations—by silencing men opposed to excessive applications of power, by making it comfortable and profitable for executives and officers to function in unity, rather than in dissension—are able to conceal from view matters whose exposure would be in the public interest?

While Hugh Chalmers presided at the top of one pyramid of NCR management, charged with the job of knocking out some thirty manufacturers of cash registers, Watson presided over a staff that grew to fifty-six men who "cleaned" out the country of secondhand competition as he had earlier cleared the whole Rochester territory of intruders.

"Business was business" in the old days, it was said, and the ethical standards professed by a religion-oriented world were not so much relaxed as pragmatically ruled out of a competitive arena in which a winner lived and losers were destroyed.

It was said that Watson's success was a unique and commendable victory, a personal triumph over the accepted practices of his time, because in winning—that is, in eliminating competitors—he treated the losers with consideration, making their failures acceptable financially and personally. Settlements offered by Watson were "generous and negotiations honorable," it was reported. When Watson got his way, he did so by persuading the competitor that the outcome was good for the loser, who was then sometimes hired by Watson to assist in any future projects involving further work against still surviving competitors. It was the sort of consideration and generosity that used to be acknowledged in old Western movies by smiling bad men who felt condescendingly that it was no inconvenience to be nice to a man if you were planning to kill him.

After a month or so of intensive study and planning in Dayton, Watson slipped quietly into New York, his identity and purpose unknown both to NCR people and to their competitors. Acting the role of an independent merchant, Watson struck up an acquaintance with Fred Brainin, who operated a secondhand cash register business on Fourteenth Street, then in more or less uptown Manhattan. Before long, another store appeared on the street, close to Brainin's, under the store-front name of Watson's Cash Register and Second Hand Exchange. Watson reported to Hugh Chalmers exclusively through telephone calls and personal meetings. Unsuspecting members of the NCR clan in New York were led to believe that Watson, having acquired some capital of his own to back up his Buffalo and Rochester experience with The Cash, had departed and had entered the cash register business as an entrepreneur at the retail level.

Brainin and Watson were able to exchange views on the difficulty of trying to do business with a product whose manufacturers frequently cut the price of new machines below the cost of secondhand ones. Since Watson's function was not to show a profit in his store, but only to sell machines below the price Brainin could meet, the anxiety of failure was not common to both men. Thus when Watson, having conditioned Brainin to consider the possibility of a profitless future, hinted that he might be able to raise the money to buy Brainin out, Brainin's only objection was to Watson's suggested price. After some negotiation, plus continued sustained losses as Watson consistently sold machines at less than Brainin paid for them, Brainin agreed to give his business to Watson for about $21,000.

The National Cash Register Company credited the money to one of Watson's old connections in Rochester, whence it was conveyed to Mr. Brainin after the latter signed a contract of sale under which he agreed to stay out of the business in the future. Watson put the new consolidated business into the hands of one of his own men and moved on to repeat the process in Philadelphia. When he had consolidated his secondhand business there with an independent merchant named Silas M. Lacey, whom he bought out, he took on a somewhat more complicated task of cleaning up the Chicago area on behalf of NCR. By this time, with the help of aides, Watson had stores in quite a few cities.

Amos J. Thomas operated a secondhand cash register store on Randolph Street when one of the thriving Watson enterprises opened up across the street. Once established on Chicago's Randolph Street, Watson and his old Buffalo tutor, Jack Range, now part of the covert operation, alternately paid calls on Amos Thomas.

"The first store [dealing in secondhand machines] in Chicago was A. Tuckhorn and Company, and another was C. T. Walmsley's," Mr. Thomas recalled when he was called upon to give his account as a witness for the United States Government's later prosecution of NCR for its knockout tactics. "Tom Watson followed. . . . He led me to believe he was buying up the businesses. He bought up in the East from Mr. Brainin. He tried to get me to put a price on my business. He wanted to control the secondhand business.

"I told him I would not sell. Jack Range and Joe Warren kept dropping in three or four times a day."

Repeated visits by Range, Watson, and Joseph E. Warren, another of NCR's undercover specialists, began to wear Thomas down. One day, in an attempt to discourage the campaign, Thomas put what he thought was a high price of $20,000 on his business. He would, he declared, sell for no less.

Meanwhile, in absolute secrecy, NCR had acquired control of the American Cash Register Company, successor to the defunct Hallwood Company. Watson opened yet another secondhand store in Chicago under the name of the American Second Hand Cash Register Company. Since neither Amos Thomas nor anyone else knew that Watson's group had a hand in the American operation, it was possible for Watson to point to the new American cash register store as further competition for all of them and to suggest that Thomas sell out before things got worse.

Thomas was "invited" to visit the NCR plant at Dayton, where he was courted and dined at the Officers' Club, a hideaway of dining halls, cardrooms, leather lounge chairs, checker and billiard tables for executives and managers of Patterson's industrial empire. He met Hugh Chalmers and Carl G. Heyne, head of the "competition business," as it was called, of NCR. Heyne made the situation absolutely clear to Thomas. If he still declined to sell out at a "reasonable" price, Heyne would "rent" another store in Chicago regardless of the cost, as near to Thomas as he could get, for the express purpose of underselling him until he was out of business. "He then offered me $12,500 for my store," Thomas said. "We split the difference and I took $15,875, plus an on-the-spot cash bonus of five hundred dollars."

Thomas went back to Chicago and begged Watson to "take care of" L. W. Roberts, a devoted employee for whom Thomas had high regard. After the conversation in Dayton, of course, Thomas knew that Watson's operation was clearly a restraint-of-trade organization in the service of NCR's development of a full monopoly in the cash register business. It was only a matter of time until everybody in the trade knew it and NCR publicly acknowledged it. By that time competitors had been pretty well bought up or run off. It was not, however, until those who were hood-winked and those who had been bought off or ruined paraded by the score to the witness stands in federal courts that the audacious system of espionage and deception was fully disclosed.

Not long after NCR launched its assault to capture the secondhand business, Patterson satisfied himself that Watson working directly with Chalmers would perform well in his new assignment and departed for Europe. There, between surprise pounces on cash register sales offices on the continent, he sought in the health spas of Europe relief from failing health and tension arising from excessive and compulsive work. Thus Watson was spared frequent confrontation with Patterson until he had developed a towering reputation in the company and wherever cash registers were sold in the United States. By then he knew most of the secrets of NCR, its methods of selling and, more important, the variations of illegal warfare conducted against all business opposition.

Watson's work was one front of NCR's three-pronged attack, or raid, on everybody else in the cash register business. A second front involved litigation—as many as seventy-five patent infringement suits at one time —against competitive companies and their customers. The third front, under the direction for some years of Carl G. Heyne, was the NCR competition department. The latter was, after a fashion, an early American form of industrial espionage, and once this department set out to wreck a competitor company, there was little use in wasting compassion on its fate. Everybody in the competition department except plant technicians was a present or former salesman, trained by Patterson himself. Later on, after he was elevated to sales manager of the company, Watson took over most of the training work insofar as it related to instruction in selling. Strategic and tactical training in techniques for destroying the foe remained in the hands of Patterson and the special competition department.

The main assault forces of the department were at first called "knockers" or "knockouts." A knocker was a specially trained salesman working, not under the authority and generally not in the pay of a district sales agent, but for the company itself, out of the Dayton executive offices. From one to five such knockers would be sent to a district where Hallwood, or Ideal, Kruse, Lamson, or one or more of the competitive companies were showing signs of life. They would do the sort of sales work Jack Range or Joe Warren had done for Watson in Chicago, except that their function was to prevent the sale of competitive machines to prospective purchasers. Failing in that, they would use threats of lawsuits or resort to sabotage to prevent a machine from working properly, offer to take in the competitor's machine on trade for thirty cents on the dollar, and so on. A favorite form of knocker tactics was to urge the buyer of a competitive machine not to pay for it, with NCR guaranteeing to pay legal defense costs if the manufacturer brought an action to collect. This was a tempting proposal to customers whose scruples were no more developed than those of the NCR knockout men.

Knockers, in conjunction with the needs of district agents, also placed paid advertisements in local newspapers, announcing pending libel or patent infringement suits against local sales offices of Hallwood or some other competitor. Circulars would be distributed containing a reprint of the advertisement, together with defamatory material about non-NCR cash registers and anybody who bought or used them.

In one court action, the judge observed that in view of the fact that NCR seldom seemed interested in pressing patent cases to final decisions, it was quite apparent the motive was simply to use lawsuits to "prolong the monopoly." Patterson himself frankly conceded this point, although not in the same context. In a letter to a Rochester agent that became part of the evidence in one of many court actions, Patterson outlined the benefits to NCR of an infringement action against the Lamson Cash Register Company, which he ultimately bought and closed down:

"If a patent is granted to the Lamson Company, we will bring suit. If we lose, we will take it to the Court of Appeals. It will take five or six years of litigation and probably cost Lamson $100,000 before they would have a legal right to use their special key arrester and key coupler, and we would still have the right to go on using the key arrester and coupler."

A "knockout machine" was a cash register manufactured by NCR to resemble closely a competitive model, even to the point of copying decorative features and design identification, and sold at one-third or one-half of the cost of the offending model. Sometimes this fakery was carried so far as to indicate that the machine was actually manufactured by Hallwood, for example, when NCR had in fact produced the machine. Hallwood would be left then to explain to customers who had bought its $200 register why a merchant down the street could buy an identical, or nearly identical model for $65. Hallwood's explanation that somebody else had made the machine and *called* it a Hallwood was somewhat unconvincing. In most cases, the cheaper fake Hallwood would break down in short order, thereby producing further grief for the company which had not made or sold the register in the first place.

With public disclosure, often through newspaper coverage of litigation instituted either by NCR or its competitors, of the employment of knockers and the use of knockout machines, the very words fell into disfavor. Watson himself began referring to knockout men as "special salesmen," and in company literature the NCR began to call knockout machines "displacement models."

The competition department functioned like an espionage service, which is what it was much of the time. Companies scrambling for the five to ten per cent of the market not controlled by The Cash found frequently to their dismay that their own district agents, plant technicians, or salesmen were receiving two salaries, the second from the National Cash Register Company. There were times, too, when salesmen for one of these companies would not know for a while that it had sold out and that NCR, rather than being their competition, was in fact their employer. There were agents and double agents, and it was not unusual for a man to be confused about whose side, if any, he was on.

Patterson was without pretense or restraint in the matter of dealing with competitors, in either human or machine terms. People in any phase of the cash register business, other than NCR, and the machines they sold were anathema and fair game for ruin. He was fond of showing visitors to the Dayton plant through a place called the Gloom Room, which contained heaps of rusty registers—a graveyard of machines that couldn't stand NCR competition, he said, and that symbolized the presumptive fate of anything mechanical or mortal that opposed Patterson.

On a memorable occasion, Patterson was accompanying a delegation on one of his public relations tours, including a visit to the decayed remains of cash registers unworthy of even a decent burial, when he came upon one of his own new nickel-plated beauties, awaiting shipment to the discerning customer. With his customary argumentative and didactic style, Patterson punched a button to demonstrate the technological ease with which the shiny and composed guardian of money was supposed to function—but, to his dismay, the button stuck. It was a dreadful moment; even the weather, it was said, dared not disagree with Patterson. He depressed a second button, and it, too, failed to register and spring back as required. Patterson strode off and returned with a heavy hammer, with which he pounded the offending and unresponsive cash register into a shapeless mass of writhing springs, fragmented gears, and malformed rubble, quite worthy of interment in the Gloom Room.

That, he said, was what they did with machines that didn't work around there. After a short lecture on quality control at the National Cash Register Company, the tour continued.

Even the simplest account of Patterson's life at NCR must resort to hyperbole. That adult men would tolerate his temperament, whatever residual rewards followed, seems improbable until it is remembered that successful men out in the field for NCR were paid extraordinarily high salaries for the times. In a day when fifteen dollars a week was an adequate wage for a family, men of The Cash who engaged in knockout work were paid fifty dollars a week and expenses, often with a commission on profitless knockout machines they could sell. A certain commando camaraderie—the knowledge that many men were individually and collectively working for the common goal of complete monopoly—militated against any feeling of personal wrongdoing, especially when it was so well rewarded.

For Thomas Watson, life at NCR was better, or at least less turbulent, when he was moving from one city to another knocking out the rival secondhand business than it was when he was summoned back to the Dayton office for more conventional executive functions. When Watson or any other associate was out of Patterson's sight (just as, some years later, when a man could avoid sustained personal contact with the imperious boss of IBM), he was likely to feel safer, out of the line of fire. The closer any man was to Patterson, the more likely he was to get scalded. It happened all the time at NCR—and later at IBM.

Patterson, after a long stay in Europe, returned home and propelled himself back into the temporary calm of NCR with strident battles against the city administration of Dayton, and with demoralizing new rules of conformity and conduct imposed on his executives and plant employees. Watson and Chalmers watched, Chalmers restraining his impulse to interfere, while Patterson allowed a weird little physical culture faddist to stir up a storm that had lasting effects on all about whom it raged.

The intruder was a man five feet tall, a cockney gymnastics trainer and rub-down specialist named Charles Palmer, who billed himself as "the strongest man in the world." Patterson had recruited him as a personal servant after meeting him on a visit to the London gymnasium of Sandow. Patterson had sought from Sandow a physical rehabilitation program to restore his strength after he had gone on a thirty-seven-day fast that left him weakened and in impaired health.

Palmer shared some of Patterson's eccentricities about diet as well as the "eat less, chew more" enthusiasm he had picked up in consultations in Europe with Horace Fletcher, founder of Fletcherism, advocate of *New Thought* and Yoga. Patterson's preoccupations with health and diet had taken him several times to the sanitarium in Battle Creek, Michigan, of "Mr. Cornflakes," who was John Harvey Kellogg, the cereal man, and on another occasion, led him into a survival demonstration in which he proved that for fifty-eight days he could perform a regular schedule of activities on a diet of nothing but potatoes and water.

As something of a Rasputin in Dayton, Palmer exercised a form of hypnotic influence over Patterson. He was made a director of the company and given power over company health and calisthenic programs. In addition to early morning horseback runs through the Ohio countryside, there were now group exercise sessions and health lectures, with compulsory participation and attendance. Palmer claimed to have occult powers, with a special capacity for detecting the true character of people by studying their physiognomy. Certain indications began to appear that, with Palmer's guidance, Patterson was reevaluating the worth of some of his executives, once in a while firing someone who was vibrationally out of line. The camaraderie among the uneasy subjects of Palmer's scrutiny, particularly those whose cranial topography had been tactilely explored by the tiny terror from a London gymnasium, was badly shaken, and a measure of understandable depression settled over the billiard lounge and dining hall of the Officers' Club.

Watson, Chalmers, and others at NCR who were regularly exposed to Patterson's histrionics were well aware of his volatile nature and unstable reactions. They tried to dismiss it as eccentric conduct, but now and then it seemed considerably other than harmless. Once in a while, for instance, Patterson liked to slip into the office of an absent executive and clean out the entire room, throwing away family photos, personal effects, and everything in the desk drawers. His idea was that everybody should "start fresh" now and then.

On one striking occasion, an absent manager returned to the Dayton office to see his own desk and office furniture outside on the lawn doused with kerosene and consumed by flames. He was so shocked—perhaps the effect Patterson desired—that he turned from the blaze and walked off to make a fresh start with another company.

Chalmers and Henry James, reported observing Patterson do some outlandish things. Standing before an easel, red chalk in hand, he would be making some sales point when, crushing the chalk in his hands, he would rub it vigorously over his face and hair and throwing his arms up, looking like a tousled but well-tailored Comanche, shout at the top of his lungs:

"Dramatize, verbalize!"

Joseph E. Warren, one of Watson's aides in the used cash register extermination project, told a court that Patterson yelled, "Kill them . . . crush them!" at sales meetings, meaning kill and crush the competition. "I have seen him knock a table down and smash it," said Warren, "tear off his collar, take a pitcher of water and smash it against the floor."

But Patterson's antics seemed to take on added irrationality with the arrival of Palmer. He had the salesmen marching through trite morality plays in the Hall of Industrial Education—the training school where knockout men were instructed in special work. In one such embarrassing performance, the stage set contained a huge bag suspended high over the players and marked with dazzling dollar signs.

Below it, disabled men on crutches and others seen as blind, impoverished, or crippled struggled vainly to reach the elusive riches. One by one onto the stage came tailored NCR men in dark suits and white collars, composed, courteous, sure of themselves. Each carried a rectangular step labeled in large letters; the legends read, *Use Advertising Matter, Analyze, Dramatize, Cut Out Cigarettes.* With a sufficient number of these props piled up, a heroic figure climbed the pyramid built of labeled virtues and pulled a cord. A cascade of money, purchase orders for cash registers, commission vouchers, and membership cards in the One Hundred Point Club poured over all.

The irony involved in expecting the salesmen to walk over, indeed to step on, the verities they were instructed to honor while clambering upward toward the money bag was lost on Watson. When he built the IBM equivalent of the Hall of Industrial Education, known more simply as the School House, at Endicott, New York, in 1934, he had the risers labeled beneath every step that led upward to the building where Opportunity resided. Chiseled into the concrete are the words, one for each step, *Read, Listen, Discuss, Observe, THINK,* etc.

Watson did his best to stay out of Palmer's way and continued to show up for calisthenics sessions and early morning horseback rides, but Hugh Chalmers was seething over the chaos and morale problems caused by the newest NCR director's interference.

Chalmers, whose contribution to the success of NCR was great and who managed, despite mounting difficulties, to work *with* rather than against Patterson through every crisis, found more than he could endure in Palmer. When the omnipresent Palmer, whose orders had the power of unappealable law, banned the presence of cigarettes, tea, cigars, salt and pepper, butter, and eggs at sales lunches with customers and at conventions, Chalmers, second only to Patterson at NCR, balked and complained.

Patterson instantly fired him, along with a half dozen or so of Chalmers' closest friends and associates. Watson alone, among the top sales staff, was spared, principally because the secondhand business was making money and probably because, despite the fact that he had been recommended and supported by Chalmers, he had remained as invisible as possible in the rising furor over Palmer. With Chalmers gone, Watson gradually moved into his place.

Word of Palmer's grotesque capers reached the Dayton press— indeed, it was the talk of the town and much of the business community elsewhere, for Patterson's paternalism and welfare programs among employees, including the dawn patrol, had attracted widespread attention. Someone at NCR, convinced that Patterson had gone daft, leaked accounts of some of the bizarre incidents to the newspapers. At *The Dayton Daily News*, feeling against Patterson was running pretty high. Its editor, James M. Cox, a young Democratic Party partisan and later governor of Ohio and subsequent candidate for president of the United States, carried on a long and bitter feud with Patterson, trading insults and libel suits. One called NCR "the glue factory," poked fun at Patterson for whining and threatening to pull his company out of the city, and raised pointed questions about his relationship with Palmer.

The press dutifully reported that some of Patterson's ideas—for flood control and city manager, among others—had merit. But *The Daily News* enjoyed itself with ribald accounts of Palmer's interference in the business, ordering executives about, evaluating their competence and potential usefulness by phrenology readings, providing Patterson with ex post facto reasoning for dismissing people he no longer wanted around and for the enforcement of The Cash equivalent of kosher dietary laws.

When some men departed in a rage when Chalmers and his band of fellow victims left the NCR grounds, *The Daily News* said Patterson was ruining the company, endangering the economic base of Dayton, and acting the arrogant fool as well. Patterson, after emerging victorious from a fight with his own board of directors—a board which included the powerful Palmer—retaliated by filing libel suits against the newspaper, closing down the NCR plants and throwing two thousand unemployed workers onto the city's streets.

With the factories shut down, the great complex of silent structures amidst the flowers and gardens was a monumental rebuke to Dayton. Unyielding, probably well aware of his own pleasure in Palmer's offensiveness, Patterson simply announced that he didn't have time to operate the factory in view of the costly lawsuits to which he was compelled to devote himself. For six months he made the city grovel.

Watson's importance increased in relation to other managers because with production halted, the secondhand business had become the sole source of income for the company. He attended public mass meetings promoted in tribute to Patterson, forums in which *The Daily News*, Editor Cox, and others who ridiculed NCR were roundly denounced. Obsequiously, and presumably with spontaneous unanimity, company officials signed a statement for publication intended to neutralize the rollicking press accounts of Palmer's ludicrous exercise of power at NCR. "The simple rules of health and exercise which have so often been referred to and ridiculed," said the statement, "have been beneficial to us and of great value to the company."

But the hardship on the city, and Patterson's obdurate insistence on complete vindication, precluded anything except a lugubrious playing out of self-imposed roles.

The Daily News finally published a grouchy revision of its earlier criticism, which amounted to a softening of position but remained something less than an apology. Is a large business enterprise, on which a community depends, altogether "a private affair," an editorial asked, an affair "which must be held to be sacred, and the newspapers denied the privilege of mention?"

Out-of-work employees, joined by Dayton citizens, gathered at a large mass meeting to hear ringing speeches in praise of John H. Patterson, and in criticism of those who scoffed. One of the speakers who commended him was a loyal executive who had broken his leg when thrown from his horse on the dawn patrol.

This was praise and punishment enough; Patterson relented. Lawsuits were settled without going to trial; NCR obtained some of the railroad siding concessions it had sought, in return for which Patterson withdrew his threat to move the company to another city. Patterson still thought the city government incompetent and corrupt and regarded politicians as unfit to govern; businessmen, he said, should take over, since government was largely a business operation anyway. Having gotten in his last licks and arranged with his management staff to reopen the plant after he was out of the country, Patterson and Palmer departed for Europe in the spring of 1908. The executive offices of the company were transferred from Dayton to New York, the factory reopened, and The Cash recovered from the staggering blow which long idleness had imposed upon it. With Patterson out of range again, Watson picked up the pieces of the sales department and began cautiously to rebuild it.

For many weeks, as the fight between Patterson and Dayton raged, Watson's tenure at NCR had seemed to hang in the balance. Patterson had apparently decided, after Chalmers and his friends were fired, to dispose of Watson, too. One morning Watson had arrived at his office to find it occupied by someone else and his staff dispersed. It was reported that Watson simply went away; he returned each day and, finding his office still closed to him, visited various branch offices and conducted his business from there. When he and Patterson met, cool civilities were observed, but no direct comment on the freeze-out was exchanged. When, finally, Patterson departed for Europe without resolving the matter, Watson was given an advance in status and joined the migrating executive staff in setting up offices in New York City. Why Patterson hesitated to cut the final thread holding Watson to his job was not revealed, but the suspicion lingered that Patterson, having clearly demonstrated to Watson his displeasure with anyone in the Chalmers management pyramid, was simply too preoccupied with other affairs at the time to carry the matter any further. Besides, of course, Watson's operation was showing a profit.

Watson took on as his assistant a former company salesman from Utica, New York: Joseph L. Rogers, an ex-Canadian and a man of considerable experience and ability. Together, and to the extent they dared risk the ire of the absent Patterson, they instituted subtle changes in the selling style of the company. Emphasis on rote learning from the NCR primer, then twenty years old, was diminished, and individuality was mildly encouraged. The teaching system was unchanged but less bathos-ridden. Watson was more earnest and less volatile on the podium than Patterson. His chalk talks, illustrated with pictographs and short phrases on the easel, were simplistic but relevant to sales experience.

Instead of putting Patterson's emphasis on knocking out competition, Watson promoted an early version of "Positive Thinking" and directed his attention to hard, concentrated selling of the NCR product. He did many of the things Patterson had done, but with a change in content. In his chalk talks, setting forth a list of rules for handling a prospective purchaser, he would add a new admonition. Across the bottom of the large sheet of paper on the easel, he wrote in bold letters: "DO RIGHT."

One day, when Patterson was around, Watson was trying to command full attention to some sales message. He wrote across the paper one large word, THINK. He was proceeding with his pep talk when Patterson strolled in to observe. The one-word directive caught his fancy, and he ordered it made into signs and placed in every department. Watson, in turn, liked that idea and, at IBM, made THINK signs compulsory in every room, and at times on every desk, throughout the company. Any tendency to thought that Watson considered negative or that led to doubt or uncertainty was discouraged. For all thinking had to be positive and, like Watson's own criticism, "constructive."

During Patterson's stay in Europe, Watson was, by all reports, more at ease and even somewhat gregarious with the men. This was in contrast to the obvious tension, compressed lips, and pinched face that characterized his visage when Patterson was there. Now he could sit, smoking cigars and talking at length with the men, gaining their confidence and being helpful.

By the time Patterson returned from nearly two years in Europe, having disposed of Palmer somewhere along the way, Watson had established a measurably distinguished record as a sales manager and executive. He doubled the company's volume, and the sale of cash registers rose to one hundred thousand a year by 1910. Part of this success was attributable to technological improvements, to be sure. Charles (Boss) Kettering, who went on to devise the self-starter for cars and become the "genius inventor" at Delco and General Motors, had developed a little electric motor which eliminated the manual operation of the cash register.

Like the fender fins and automatic gadgetry on automobiles in the middle of the twentieth century, the electrically operated cash register had status value and was heralded as a scientific advance of notable achievement. It propelled salesmen into their territories to proclaim the scientific breakthrough as a stunning discovery. It allowed the promotion of the "trade up" concept of sales expansion. The difference was that, instead of pushing buttons and depressing a manually operated handle to register a sale, open the drawer, and sound the gong, one now pushed the buttons and activated a switch, which turned on an electric motor, which registered the sale, opened the drawer, and released the clapper that rang the bell. It was sheer, dazzling, idiotic progress in which a minor manual operation had become tantalizingly complex; the market was grateful for it, and sales boomed.

Patterson, his disgraceful treatment of Watson forgotten by both, promoted the latter to sales manager, discarding the old qualified title under which he had worked. Patterson also broke up the executive offices in New York and dispatched everybody back to Dayton. Now that he was back home, he wanted them around; Watson went back to his drawn, anxious look again. His relaxing and informal talk sessions over cigars with salesmen and agents were curtailed. Patterson immediately took over all the command posts, and feelings of disquiet and apprehension, an atmosphere of unpredictability, of the impending adversity of fate, enveloped all. The city of Dayton, schooled by experience, braced itself.

But Patterson ignored Dayton and, with Watson in tow, made a country-wide tour of NCR installations. It was evident that a larger adversary than Dayton had NCR, Patterson, Watson, Jack Range, et al., in its sights. It was also apparent that Hugh Chalmers and his dismissed platoon were conveying damaging intelligence to that new adversary: the government of the United States.

The signals were clear that the federal government was moving in on Patterson and the National Cash Register Company. One of The Cash's highest ranking salesmen, Harry F. James, resigned in 1909 to take over operations in Michigan for the American Cash Register Company. American was the latest and best financed of a series of companies possessing rights to manufacture the machines made by Hallwood, which went into receivership and died at the hands of NCR's competition department and lawsuits. As an expert on NCR operating techniques, James filed suit to oust NCR from the state on the grounds that it was organized to maintain a monopoly.

Watson was hurriedly dispatched to Detroit to help James's successor, George Lingham, get organized. Testimony at the Michigan trial accused Watson of telling Lingham's sales staff that James was a "dangerous" competitor who had to be stopped. One witness declared that Watson warned NCR men to have nothing whatsoever to do with their old associate Harry James and not even to "speak to him on the street."

American Cash Register Company salesmen told a woeful tale of murderous competition from NCR: sales agents and customers were harangued and harassed; American salesmen were bribed, its cash registers imitated and produced by NCR at prices below cost; in some cases fist fights, smashed show windows, and damage to store interiors followed the trail of the competitors.

By this time too many people had heard Patterson's views about his competition and his techniques for disposing of them for NCR denials to be altogether convincing.

"We don't buy out, we knock out," was Patterson's summation of NCR policy. Actually, he bought out often, and accused some operators of going into the business solely to get bought out, but when purchase offers fell on unresponsive ears, the knockout operations came into play.

Chalmers took Harry James into the Chalmers motor car company when the Michigan case remained pending for several years. Meanwhile depositions were being gathered around the country for the anti-trust case which Patterson was careless not to have foreseen.

Some of Patterson's ideas on restraint of trade were completely contradictory. For instance, in praise of his monopoly, he declared it allowed the company to put the highest quality of materials and workmanship into a product, without fear of being obliged by cost-cutting competitors to cheapen it and inflict added cost on a customer in the long run. Yet with equal fervor he would stand before his subordinates, or address his salesmen in communications, and state: "We have no intention of making improvements in our cash registers unless forced to do so by our competitors."

He was a ready-made case for federal prosecution, and with Hugh Chalmers gleefully prepared to testify against him, the inevitable occurred.

On February 22, 1912, John H. Patterson, Thomas J. Watson, John J. Range, Joseph L. Rogers, Edward A. Deeds—thirty "Cash" men in all—were indicted on three counts of criminal conspiracy in restraint of trade and maintaining a monopoly. They were to be put on trial in Cincinnati.

Earlier anti-trust cases, and in particular the Rockefeller–Standard Oil trial, received close scrutiny and an enormous volume of press publicity. But the public, rather than finding satiation in the restraint of trade and conspiracy cases, increasingly enjoyed them; the trials seemed to serve as mass entertainment. That the very wealthy, the barons of corporate power, could be so conspiratorial, wicked, and avaricious made the average citizen feel morally superior, putting into shadow the petty cheating and modestly larcenous conduct of the more common folk, to whom "combinations of capital" was more likely to mean assembling the resources required for a four-dollar ton of coal or a ten-cent gallon of Mr. Rockefeller's kerosene.

Moreover, the trials gave the prosecutor, who enjoyed the role of folk hero for a time, an opportunity to appear as a Galahad, the defender of public virtue, protector of the upright, God-fearing little businessman whose hearth and home stood endangered by rapacious overlords of opportunity and the iniquitous organizers of the hateful, un-American trusts. The prosecutor at the Patterson-Watson trial declaimed with majestic fury that the reprehensible conduct of the NCR men was without parallel in the civilized business world, and compared it to the "methods of Mexican bandits," who loomed large in the American press in the days before the United States Army went loping off unsuccessfully in pursuit of Pancho Villa. Seldom had the leaders of industry been in such disfavor.

Just short of his thirty-eighth birthday, and after he had been indicted and was awaiting trial, Watson met the woman who was to be his wife. He now had a home that Patterson built for him and a Pierce-Arrow motor car, exactly appropriate for a dignified bachelor of his status, and also a gift from the boss.

With some prodding from his mother, Watson had become increasingly open-minded about marriage as he approached forty. It had been often noted that he was shy in any approach to possible romantic involvement, but the impression lingers that Watson was perhaps less shy than inexperienced. His compassionate assistance to underpaid school teachers in Rochester was not altogether missionary work, nor was it his only association with young ladies. His sisters reported that Watson's favorite horse, Dexter, would trot directly and unguided to the residence of the young man's favorite companion of the moment. New experiences and situations gave Watson pause, but the countryman's uneasiness in urban social life wore off. When Watson was moving over ground on which he had traveled before, reticence might remain if it was appropriate or useful, but shyness did not.

According to one account, he was once engaged to an opera singer from Philadelphia, whom he knew when he lived in that city on his mission to take over the secondhand business, but the relationship failed to flower as a result of career conflicts between the two. Another girl in whom he was seriously interested frightened him off when he overheard her in a vehement quarrel with her mother.

But Jeannette Kittredge was precisely right, and both seemed aware of it simultaneously. She was a trim size ten with a good, lightly rounded figure and soft, appealing eyes. Nine years younger than Watson, she was the daughter of hellfire-and-damnation, teetotaling Presbyterian parents who were church leaders in Dayton. Her father had been president of a railroad car manufacturing company in Dayton, and Patterson knew him rather well.

They met officially at a country club dinner, after seeing one another without the formality of an introduction at several local gatherings.

55

Jeannette Kittredge gave Watson a mark of merit at the party because he alone among the diners at the table—except for herself, of course—had not lifted the wine glass before him. She had been to Wooster College and to Wheaton Seminary in Massachusetts and was living, unmarried and nearly thirty years old, with her parents on Ludlow Street, directly across the way from the house in which John Patterson himself lived when in town. The family's proximity to the president of The Cash, the fact that the Kittredges and Patterson were not only acquainted but from about the same stratum of Dayton society—added to the fact that it was about time both Watson and Jeannette married *somebody,* if they were ever going to—made the budding relationship an appropriate one for all concerned.

Like the house and the Pierce-Arrow, Patterson had chosen for Watson, Jeannette Kittredge was also his choice for Watson's bride. The decision to marry was arrived at with dispatch, and when Watson went to Patterson to tell him that he and Miss Kittredge were secretly engaged, Patterson was genuinely delighted and said he had been hoping all along he would ask her to be his wife.

The secrecy of their engagement was not kept very well; before the end of the year nearly everybody knew it, but the couple had hoped that the impending trial might bring an acquittal for Watson and that they could announce their engagement at a more joyous time.

The trial opened in November and ran for three months. The defendants sought in vain to have it moved to Dayton, but Judge Howard C. Hollister, of the southern federal district court of Ohio, ruled against them and opened the trial in Cincinnati. Several of the most damaging witnesses, notably Henry F. James and Hugh Chalmers, would almost certainly have been under indictment with Patterson had they not been fired or left NCR to work for a competing company.

Chalmers despised Patterson, who, he felt, had demeaned an equal, but Chalmers didn't dislike Watson; he had, in fact, at one time befriended him—in part, to be sure, because he and Patterson needed an ambitious, solid, conventionally moral, clean-living citizen to do some rather dirty work. Thus when Chalmers invoked the power of the United States Government in his vendetta against Patterson, he meant to cut him down. But he did little more than cite the evidence against Watson. He was very nearly to ruin them both.

The testimony was voluminous, with the expected polarization of outlook, but undeniably overwhelming in support of the government's charges, although the government's case was somewhat sullied by the relish with which former colleagues sought to ruin one another. Counsel

put none of the defendants on the stand, mercifully sparing them unwelcome cross examination. Watson had to stand as his name was
mentioned by witnesses and let the jury identify him when his invasion
of the secondhand business was recounted. James recited the name of
one cash register company after another that NCR, by one means or
another—most of them illegal—had driven from business: Globe,
Hallwood, Century, International, Ideal, Cuckoo of Detroit, Latimer,
Peck, Navy, Metropolitan, Osborn, Simplex, Sun, Toledo, Union, Weiler,
and others. Watson subsequently declared out of court that in his years
at NCR he had seen two hundred and fifty cash register companies open
and die. The figure was wildly overestimated, since the number doubtless did not exceed sixty, but even so it was more than the cash register
business needed. By 1912, NCR had no competition of consequence.

James told how he had put one Andrew W. Sinclair out of business
in Detroit, then hired him as a special knockout man for NCR to "undo
the work he had done" with American in Detroit. The job led Mr.
Sinclair to a highly successful career with The Cash and to a seat among
the defendants in the criminal proceedings.

Incriminating letters, some bearing Watson's signature and some
signed with a rubber stamp, instructed salesmen how to set prices on
both bona fide and masquerading knockout machines, and assigned
special salaried men to go to prospective purchasers disguised as
commission salesmen for the purpose of installing price-cutting displacement machines.

The experiences of James R. Waller, who had managed the Los
Angeles office of the Hallwood company, were something special and
were corroborated in part by an editor-writer for *The Los Angeles
Commercial Bulletin* in an article under the headline, "Dirty War Being
Waged Against American Hallwood Cash Register Co., Spotters Spy on
Offices and Follow Salesmen About."

The writer said *The Bulletin* was "unable to believe that a company
of the standing of NCR would tolerate such despicable and un-American
tactics," which it then described. On its own, *The Bulletin* investigated
the complaints of American Hallwood.

Mr. H. Beadle, proprietor of a barbershop at 622 Spring Street in
Los Angeles, said NCR men "have used my barber shop and cigar stand
as a hangout for weeks. They are here to spot against the [American]
cash register company across the street. They make no bones about their
business and what they are here for. . . . I have no interest in the matter
either way. . . . While they are good customers of mine and good fellows
personally, I can't help saying it is dirty work."

A Hallwood man once left the office in a horse-drawn rig. Immediately, there swung in behind him "a man in a heavy runabout," while the investigator from *The Bulletin* followed. The Bulletin man overtook the man in the runabout and asked, "Are you an employee of NCR?" He answered, "You bet I am." "Why," asked the reporter, "are you following that man?" Realizing his blunder, and that he'd been caught in a three-way horse and spy race around town, the NCR man "whipped up his horse and said, 'Oh, they're crazy.'"

Quoting other merchants who watched the day-by-day harassment of Hallwood by the larger-manned NCR operation, *The Bulletin* despaired of the conduct of competitive industry. Of James Waller, it said: "His conduct in this fight, as far as *The Bulletin* has been able to ascertain, has been honorable in every particular."

The Bulletin quizzed Earl B. Wilson, Los Angeles manager for NCR, when the latter appeared at the newspaper office to explain the "horse race" and the harassment. "There has been too much of this following of men—more than I thought," Wilson was quoted as saying. "But my men are eager for business, and they may resort to things that I would not permit. . . . But these men have never been authorized to picket the Waller office. I don't like that word, picket. Hallwood was organized years ago for the sole purpose of forcing National to buy it, and it has been a bitter fight."

The Bulletin pointed out to its readers that the Hallwood company had long since been forced out of business in the war with NCR, and that the present company was another corporation altogether.

Hugh Chalmers arrived on the stand with secret and long suppressed sales contracts containing agreements signed by cash register companies bought out, or knocked out, by NCR. These contracts made startling reading indeed and showed that Patterson had a special and heretofore undisclosed regard for two of the least populated states in the union—Nevada and Montana. In disposing of the Lamson company of Lowell, Massachusetts, Patterson forced the principals to agree to the following clause:

"In case we desire to re-enter and continue the business of the manufacture and sale of cash registers, the states of Nevada and Montana offer, in our judgment, an ample and sufficient field for all of us." Company after company thus found that it was free to sell cash registers, competing freely with one another without fear of knockout tactics from NCR in that vast, underpopulated area.

Chalmers rattled off his own credentials: President of the Chalmers Motor Car Company and owner of sixty per cent of its stock, gross sales of sixteen million a year, employing 4,200 men. He said he was still in the cash register business, as president of a Michigan company employing two hundred men. He said NCR owned 1,400 patents relating to cash registers and more than fourteen thousand patent claims. Patterson's salary was $144,000 a year, he said, and his own had been $84,000.

Yes, he testified, he had bought out many cash register companies for Patterson and paid for them: $8000 for the Metropolitan Cash Register Company, $115,000 to the Toledo Scales and Cash Register Company, $9000 for the Weiler company, $35,000 for the McGraw (Century) company, and so on.

One of the more interesting accounts was his report on Watson's secondhand operations and the details of the contract under which the Ideal company of Bound Brook, New Jersey, was exterminated. Chalmers recalled that Patterson had feared several companies whose cash registers of advanced design and low price constituted a fancied threat to NCR. Ideal was one of them, and Patterson agreed to go as high as $125,000 to get it. Chalmers negotiated an unusually good sales contract providing:

$12,000 to be paid as hereinafter specified; said Ideal Company agrees to sell, and does hereby sell, to said National Company all its right, title and interest in and to all its patents of the United States and foreign countries, all its applications for patents, all rights to inventories and all rights of actions arising out of patents . . . all tools used in the manufacture of cash registers . . . $1000 to be paid in cash, and the balance in ten days. . . . No officer of Ideal Company will engage in the business of manufacturing cash registers or similar devices in the United States (the states of Nevada and Montana excepted) or any foreign country, for the period of twenty-five years.

It is mutually agreed by and between the parties that the terms of this contract are not to be made public but are to be treated as confidential.

Patterson agreed to drop patent suits against Ideal and also guaranteed "that a pending libel suit against [Dr. Pierce, an officer of Ideal] will be at once dismissed without cost."

Watson may have been astonished as some of the grubby details were put into the record, but at no time did he indicate any reaction or emotion other than to say that he and NCR were being wronged. He had been correct at all times, he said.

On February 13, the foreman of the jury, R. E. Morrow, read the verdict to the standing defendants: "We, the jury, herein do find the defendants guilty in the manner and form as charged in each of the three counts."

Patterson, Watson, and his friend Joe Rogers got the maximum sentence, a year in the Miami County jail and fines of $5000 each. The others got similar sentences, although several of the jail terms were nine months instead of a year.

"You men belong to the walk of life which should set the example," Judge Hollister told them in passing sentence. "Yet you have lost the opportunity given you by the methods you pursued. In your desire for gain you forgot everything else."

Patterson was released on $10,000 bail, Watson and others on $5000, "to guarantee their appearance before this court from day to day as the court may require."

In spite of a certain amount of bluster and bravado, some of the defendants were shocked and frightened, and Watson after a while was among them. No one had ever gone to prison on an anti-trust conviction, and while this was heartening to some, it left others with the feeling that *they* might be the first. The judge in the famous Rockefeller case didn't order Standard Oil men to jail, only the dissolution of the company.[1]

It was generally suspected by Watson and his fellow defendants that it was Patterson's excesses and offensive style which had brought down wrath and retribution on their heads—and, of course, all that overwhelming evidence from the lips, letters, and records of the defendants themselves. Patterson's lawyers, while denying the charges through witnesses and exhibits, were not able by reason of judicial rulings from the bench to present their evidence of alleged patent infringement on the part of competitors they drove out of business.

Dayton reacted with horror and anger when the verdict came. The city that had knuckled under to Patterson's demands and irrational whims remembered only too well the months of unemployment, destitution, and breadlines when the NCR plants closed down following the original blowup with Chalmers. The press reports of Patterson's family weeping and clinging to him were saddening indeed.

Watson maintained he was totally innocent. Without asserting that he had not done what he was said to have done, he said only that he had done nothing wrong, that he did not "consider" himself a criminal, that he was not "ashamed" of anything he had done in his seventeen years at The Cash. To friends in Painted Post and elsewhere, he wrote that he was unworried, not at all humiliated, and willing to have the

---

[1] This was something less than punishment; it was, in fact, a favor imposed on the oil companies, which had been excessively centralized. The federal court verdict forced autonomy onto many of the constituent companies, which resulted in vastly improved organization and immediate, although not uniform, advances in technology.

whole world know what he had done—which, in fact, the world now knew anyway.

A whistling-in-the-dark posture may have given Watson a pretension of confidence he did not altogether feel. In spite of the feelings of his former roommate John Hayward, the only one of the convicted men who was a lawyer, that a conviction could be reversed on appeal, Watson brought his own attorney, the well-known and expensive John B. Stanchfield, into the case to serve as his individual defense counsel, a move which irked the others.

Jeannette Kittredge, emotionally prepared to demonstrate a fortitude which previous experience had given her few opportunities to express, was not at all willing to accept Watson's intention to continue putting off formal announcement of an engagement that was more or less common knowledge anyway. No one could predict how much time appeal would take or when hearings would begin. Aside from the facts of age and arithmetic, which would impel a lady to avoid an indefinite and open-end postponement, and aside from the fact that no thirty-year-old spinster could be expected to look forward with unrestrained pleasure to another year or two at home with her parents, there was a sound reason for getting married as quickly as was proper and appropriate. Tom Watson and Jeannette Kittredge together represented more strength and perseverance than was possible for them singly. It was a case of their collective, or fused, character being greater than the sum of its parts. They were that kind of a pair and, while Watson may have suspected it, Jeannette knew it as a certainty. As the wife of a man like Watson, she was unsurpassable.

With a firmness of spirit and in pursuit of her own interests, Jeannette pressed for an immediate wedding, as soon as she could get a trousseau together, and never mind the indictment. The defendants' legal Bill of Particulars had to be prepared in the next four months, and the Court of Appeals verdict would follow—heaven knew when. Whatever else was said of them, the ladies in the temperance movement, not unlike the suffragettes, had will, toughness, and fervor; they responded to disfavor with spunk and pride. Jeannette Kittredge had a large measure of the kind of spirit that restored Watson's confidence in his days of doubt then, and for all of his time to come.

Jeannette Kittredge was a full and true partner in Watson's life, and they made a formidable, durable pair for forty-two years. They were mama and papa to thousands in a patriarchally managed society. They praised and paid court to each other—with the IBM family looking on, approving and applauding—at public affairs of honor, adulation, and dedication. They offered parental security, comfort, direction, counsel, and punishment to their far-flung family; they would be hurt, disappointed, and sternly critical of a member of the family who failed them, or who failed to see the family as the strength and solace of all, but they also showed their delight in profuse praise, in rewards that evoked both mercenary and emotional pleasure, when the family worked, produced, and worshiped together. They were, in fact, the epitome of marital and corporate togetherness.

Dayton, in that dismal prewar year, was beset by heavy and constant spring rains. Jeannette, accompanied by her sister Helen and their mother, went to New York on a shopping expedition. Patterson and an entourage entrained for New York to try to arrange, through high placed financial and political connections there, an appointment with President Woodrow Wilson to seek his helpful intervention in the anti-trust case. He was, mercifully, dissuaded from this plan. He met Watson and John Hayward for lunch instead and left them to return to Dayton, which then lay in the wake of a tornado. It was a disaster of dreadful proportions and a piece of phenomenal good fortune for Patterson, who made himself and his fellow defendants into national heroes.

Swollen by heavy rains, the Miami and Mad Rivers meeting above Dayton were unable to contain the floods unleashed by the tornado. Easter Sunday rains made matters worse; by March 26, its levees swept away, the city was inundated in torrents of water eighteen feet deep. Patterson was on the last train that reached the city before it was nearly wiped out, closed off from the rest of the world. Ninety thousand people were without living quarters or shelter; fires and explosions broke out until more rain subdued them; people clung to life on the eaves of floating homes and tottering buildings. It was the worst disaster of its kind in America since the Johnstown Flood in 1889.

Watson joined the Kittredge ladies, along with John Hayward and a young aide, Robert Houston, at the Waldorf for dinner. Word had reached Houston of the Dayton disaster. National Cash Register, on high ground, with Patterson in charge, was equipped to salvage what was left of the nearly destroyed city. The only telegraph line in the flooded region connected NCR with its office in New York, where Watson manned a rescue operation.

Governor James Cox, the editor and old adversary of Patterson, gave the latter virtual power of martial law. But even in disaster, Patterson reacted first to his opposition. He sent off a telegram to *The New York Times* declaring that he would throw into jail the Honorable Howard C. Hollister of the southern federal district court of Ohio, who had sentenced him, if he caught him lurking around the disaster area. Watson intercepted the telegram and, quite shaken, tore it up. He did not feel that they were in any position to antagonize the court, nor did he feel that such a message should occupy telegraph facilities when word of life-and-death importance was awaited over the line in Patterson's possession.

But Patterson was working and organizing. He quickly redesigned a company assembly line to make rowboats at the rate of one every seven minutes. Plant facilities were opened to all who could make their way to the island. From the stables of the dawn patrol he distributed fresh hay for the homeless to sleep on and directed that it be changed nightly. He rounded up all the woolen stockings that could be located and made his refugees wear them. Stores of bottled water, now no affectation or health fad, but a stroke of fortune in an epidemic-prone situation, were available to all, and each person drank from his own paper cup. Company first aid stations and its hospital were the sole facilities available and were used twenty-four hours a day by doctors ferried to the place. A half dozen babies, some named after their savior Patterson, were born there on one day.

In New York, Watson and the NCR staff organized a relief train laden with drugs, clean water, food, and supplies, and dispatched it to Dayton within hours of learning the terrible news. New switches had to be installed in uprooted railroad tracks and roadbeds shored up, and even so, the first supplies reaching the city were carried the last few miles on the backs of men moving in pack trains along the muddy flats. Before the first train reached the end of the rail line, another was on the way. A third, a hospital train with John Hayward in charge, followed. A telegram from Patterson advised that further medical help was unneeded; The Cash was able to manage.

The press lauded Patterson to the heavens. Watson and his associates in New York were included in the praise; everybody associated with NCR and Patterson was a saint or a hero. A press room was fitted out in the NCR plant, and visiting reporters were guests of the company; the NCR office in downtown Manhattan was the flood's press center in New York. Patterson was photographed conferring with the Army Chief of Staff and cabinet members, planning the preservation of law and health measures while himself under prison sentence. The commander of the Salvation Army, speaking before the multitude of refugees, said God would reward Patterson. Governor Cox had already rewarded him with praise. The flood, it was implied, would wash away both NCR's sins and the anti-trust convictions. Overzealous friends sent a petition on March 30 to the President, urging a pardon for Patterson, and the following day he telegraphed a message to President Wilson saying that he had nothing to do with the petition, was opposed to it, and wanted no pardon anyway, "only justice." He added, "I am guilty of no crime."

Watson went back to Dayton to marry Jeannette Kittredge as planned and in spite of the catastrophe. The wedding took place in the family home that two weeks earlier had been flooded halfway up the first story. Patterson started a campaign to raise money for reconstruction and to bring flood control to the Miami County region.

Watson and his bride left for a honeymoon through the scenic west and on their return, with Jeannette already pregnant, went to live in Patterson's wedding present, a summer house he had built near his own. Watson should have been uneasy about the gift of two houses, the car, and the close relationship they implied, knowing Patterson's proclivities for ridding himself of associates who stayed too close too long.

Shortly thereafter, Joe Rogers, Watson's assistant who was supposed to handle the Hundred Point Club Convention in July, was incapacitated by a nervous breakdown. Watson had to see to all the details of the most sacrosanct of NCR assemblies, this one held at Patterson's estate, Far Hills. Tents had to be set up, banners raised on high; there were flags and bunting and interminable speeches. The anti-trust trial hadn't hurt business; the salesmen in the field were doing well and by and large were cheerful. R. H. Grant, successor to the long deposed and now despised Chalmers, made a speech. Watson followed him, and stammering a bit, but projecting sincerity and an affinity for the problems of a salesman, he evoked applause. Of course, audience response was expected at these affairs. The applause recognized and acknowledged that Watson was one with those applauding.

Then Patterson, with a prerogative that transcended both courtesy and procedure, walked to the podium and all but displaced Watson to make an unprogrammed and unexpected speech of his own. But this was not unusual; he could and did interrupt anyone and any proceedings as often as he chose.

So, in fact, would Watson, and he did so—many times—at IBM meetings, Hundred Percent Club assemblies, and the like. And in the years to come he would do to other speakers what Patterson did to him on that July day outside of Dayton. Patterson simply interrupted Watson to praise R. H. Grant, the preceding speaker, but he did it so pointedly, and with such exaggeration, that he might as well have inscribed the message in handwriting on the wall. Patterson was finished with Watson.

He was sealed off, unloved, unsettled, and uncalled for. His telephone didn't ring, and he was neither summoned to, nor welcome at, executive conferences with Patterson. There were clearly implied accusations that Watson, in handling the New York end of the Dayton flood operation, had been grandstanding, that he had shipped tainted food to the suffering city, that he had grabbed publicity.

After being systematically humiliated, after enduring it for many months, after having done so wonderfully well all that he was directed to do and having been convicted as a criminal for doing it, Thomas Watson was fired.

Watson's emergence from his position as apprentice and subordinate had evoked the destructive egotism that was a measure of the Patterson character. The latter could tolerate in his presence no vision of a replica of himself. In this case it was a false vision, for Watson had been content to remain subordinate, although his apprenticeship had taught him all Patterson had to teach.

Now he would convert his association with Patterson into a fortune and a vast industry, emulating his teacher, even to the point of personal shortcomings, in many ways.

4.
The
Shaping
of
IBM

WITH FIFTY THOUSAND dollars in the bank, a parting consolation from the boss to add to the nest egg he had saved, a shocked and disbelieving Watson waited out the remaining weeks of Jeannette's pregnancy until the second president and chief executive officer of International Business Machines Corporation was born on January 14, 1914. They named him Thomas John Watson, Junior.

Watson felt abandoned. He had seen men fired for whimsical reasons, yet could not seem to relate the knowledge to his own fate. NCR was his home, his life, his world. To be ejected from the company, to leave the house built for him and Jeannette as a wedding present, was completely demoralizing. It was not a question of a job; he could have gone with any number of companies—the Dodge Motor Car Company, which would have been appropriate, since so many NCR men moved into the burgeoning automobile industry; Montgomery Ward, Frigidaire, Remington Arms—but these were salaried jobs, and Watson was a commission man. He wanted his income equated to individual accomplishment. He was accustomed to this form of remuneration. Even when he became the highest paid executive in the United States in the 1930's, some of his income was salary, but a larger share of it was a percentage of the company's earnings, paid to him under a formula he devised for himself.

Patterson had kept Watson on when he fired Chalmers and his aides, but this time Joe Rogers and Robert Houston, his assistants in the sales manager's office, were dispatched, too. They cast about and commiserated with one another. Watson was at such loose ends that when he was offered financing to support any business venture of his own choosing, he had no choice to make. He knew in general what he wanted; there was nothing imaginative about it: executive power and money. But the truth was that temperamentally he was not ready for command. He had executive ability but little experience in being the boss.

Years earlier, Watson had heard a noted American financier and exponent of monopolistic capitalism address the Chamber of Commerce in Rochester. The man was Charles R. Flint, munitions trader, organizer of trusts, key figure in the development of the United States Rubber Company, gun runner, double agent in the incessant revolutions and military coups in Latin American republics, and a charming, witty, educated egotist.

Irvin S. Cobb, noted American humorist and lifelong friend of Flint, said the latter had "found romance in business"; he also found vast amounts of money along the way, and numerous ways to attract capital to his schemes, some of which were highly remunerative, and others of which provided pleasure, travel, and risk, but not necessarily any financial profit. Said Cobb:

"The more dramatic commodities—munitions, ships, explosives, speculative inventions—these are the things he dealt in. . . . He was a pioneer investigator of, and investor in, the automobile and the aeroplane. He had a direct hand in the earlier development of the submarine and dynamite gun. He owned and sailed the fastest yacht in American waters. He built and captained and largely designed the swiftest steam yacht that ever split the salt. . . . He was the first to shape and perfect a giant industrial combination in the United States. He is the only man alive or dead who ever assembled to order and sent to sea a full-sized navy intended for belligerent uses—and did it all in six weeks time: a fleet of war vessels, armed with modern ordnance and modern projectiles and manned by crews of jaunty gentlemen who neither knew nor cared for what cause they were enrolled to fight nor under what flag they would serve."[1]

Watson, through friends, looked Flint up in New York. The latter was a figure of prominence in both the United States and Europe. He also knew John Henry Patterson and the two most famous citizens of Dayton, Ohio—Wilbur and Orville Wright. Flint, after some years of unsuccessful efforts on the part of the Wright brothers to market their invention, offered a half million dollars to Wilbur and Orville for rights outside the U.S.

Wilbur wrote from Berlin that Flint agreed to pay the half million "in cash upon delivery of one machine after a demonstration consisting

[1] From a Foreword by Irvin S. Cobb in Flint's memoirs, *Memories of an Active Life*, published by G. P. Putnam's Sons, New York and London, 1923.

of a flight of fifty kilometers. . . . Their [Flint and his associate, Hart O. Berg] idea seems to be to depend on getting possession of the market by being the first in the field rather than by depending on patents alone, or secrecy alone." Flint's offer was conditional upon a secret demonstration flight, but Wilbur Wright complained they were "watched so closely by the newspapers and some others that a secret flight would be impossible."[2]

Flint and Berg had helped introduce American electric automobiles to the European continent, and had acted for Simon Lake, inventor of the submarine. When he met Watson in New York, Flint was one of the leading capitalists and entrepreneurs in the world. He had been a friend of President McKinley, who thought so highly of a Flint speech defending monopolies and citing J. P. Morgan, Henry Ford, John D. Rockefeller, Charles Schwab, and other titans of industry as "endowed men" that he had a half million copies of the speech printed and distributed nationally. Flint felt that "labor leaders, socialists, and legislators . . . sometimes had opportunities to be of service to their fellow men," but he doubted they could accomplish anything outstanding. "The application of any theories which presuppose conditions in opposition to this fundamental fact inevitably result in chaos such as that in Russia."

Flint's confidence in the endowed or divine right of monopolies notwithstanding, he was a man of distinction, energy, and color, and a superb teacher. All that Watson had learned came to fruition under the tutelage of Flint, who found Watson—for he was a shrewd judge of ambitious men—something quite different from the common breed of combative personalities of the period. Somewhat gleefully predisposed to piracy himself, Flint saw in Watson a mystic who could learn, imitate, improvise, and pour limitless energy into an undertaking, doing whatever was effective or required, and ascribing to it all a measure—a condition—of truth and goodness. Flint and Watson talked long and often, the former evaluating his man carefully and deciding, in time, that he wanted him to manage a small, relatively new trust he had organized from thirteen original companies three years earlier. As Flint himself explained it:

In 1911, I made a departure from my practice of bringing about consolidations of allied interests, that is, by consolidating similar, but not identical products. . . . The Computer-Tabulating-Recording Company is of this class, and although it has not been the largest, it is the most successful.

2 The Wrights' account of their association with Flint is related in the book *Miracle at Kitty Hawk, The Letters of Wilbur and Orville Wright*, edited by Fred C. Kelly; published by Farrar, Strauss and Young, New York, 1951.

At the outset, I pointed out to the Guaranty Trust Company that the proposed allied consolidation, instead of being dependent for earnings on a single industry, would own three separate and distinct lines of business so that in normal times the interest and sinking funds on its bonds could be earned by any one of these independent lines, while in abnormal times the consolidation would have three chances instead of one to meet its obligations and pay dividends.[3]

The formation was, in fact, a holding company known as C-T-R; the products manufactured by the component companies were not, as Flint knew, identical, but they were not as dissimilar as he seemed to think, either. All measured or counted something—time, weight, portions or units. One of them was the Tabulating Machine Company, whose chief asset was a man named Herman Hollerith and his patents, transferred to Flint for stock in the company, and who was to drive Watson nearly out of his senses. Hollerith, a graduate engineer from Columbia University, had developed a system of recording statistics for the United States Census Bureau back in 1890 by punching holes in sheets of paper. By adapting techniques he observed in the player piano and the Jacquard weaving loom, which was regulated by cards in which holes were punched to represent a pattern to be woven on the loom, Hollerith had, in fact, devised the forerunner to the ubiquitous punch card with which IBM changed the world.

Flint and his board of directors, including Hollerith as chief engineer, had gotten the combination of companies off the ground with a bonded indebtedness of $6,500,000—twenty-five times its then current assets—$4 million of which had been borrowed from the Guaranty Trust Company in New York. All of the companies together, located in Toronto, Dayton, Detroit, Washington, New York, Endicott, and Binghamton, had approximately 1,200 employees.

When, finally, Flint and Watson came to terms, and the latter was proposed before the board of directors as the new man to manage the profitless, debt-ridden consolidation of companies, one of the directors is said to have growled: "What are you trying to do—ruin this business? Who is going to run the business while he serves his term in jail?"

The question must have occurred to Watson as well, for the ever-present threat of prison did not subside that winter. And other questions irritated Flint's fellow directors: Why did Watson leave the highly suc-

[3] Flint was writing this in 1922, eight years after he hired Watson to manage the company and two years before it was renamed International Business Machines Corporation. The quoted passage is from his autobiography, *Memories of an Active Life*.

cessful National Cash Register Company? Because, said Watson, Patterson insisted on it. Was all that damned foolishness true about horses, phrenology readings, capricious dismissals, and thirty-two chews per bite? Watson conceded it was all too true, but he pointed to the fact that Patterson's methods sold cash registers.

When it came to talk of salary, Watson was less interested in immediate rewards than in a percentage of the future. A committee of three was named to work out terms: a gentleman's salary of $25,000 a year, more than 1,200 shares of stock, and a profit-sharing arrangement which, in time, worked out to five per cent of profits after taxes and dividend payments. Within twenty years, the arrangement led to a salary of a thousand dollars a day for Watson which, coming in the depth of the depression of the thirties, was sufficient to make him confident in the soundness of American industry, even though there appeared to be a certain amount of general evidence against it.

The directors balked at making Watson president, fearful that his conviction in the anti-trust case would haunt them all. As general manager he went to work at 50 Broad Street in New York in May, and within two months the verdict in the Michigan Supreme Court case was disclosed. NCR was found guilty and fined $10,000. Later in the year, the appeals court heard arguments in the federal case, with Watson and Rogers—no longer with NCR—filing individual briefs. While the Justice Department condemned the defendants as pirates and greedy monopolists, Watson's attorneys argued that it was largely overzealousness on the part of "a few" subordinates, not policy approved throughout the company, that had been to blame for the offenses charged. The inference that "all" officials in the organization approved of these deplorable practices was said to be unjustified. That this excessive zeal emerged from detailed training and executive orders as an extension of old and successful policy was not discussed. The court heard all the appeal arguments, and the case awaited decision.

Watson, harassed by anxiety and bedeviled by questions from the directors, took charge of sales operations while deferring on other matters to Flint, to the volatile inventor Herman Hollerith, and to George W. Fairchild. Fairchild was a large mustachioed man of considerable wealth who, as chairman of the board, evoked from Watson a carefully controlled subservience from which there was no escape until Fairchild's death in 1924. Thus from 1914 until 1924, Watson worked in relative obscurity, if not anonymity. On the national scale his name did not appear in that inventory of both trivial and galactic significance, *The New York Times Index*, until 1923, by which time the president of C-T-R (the name of IBM was not adopted until the following year) was forty-nine years old.

Besides Hollerith and Fairchild, Watson had to deal with such well-known directors as Edward Canby of Dayton, Ohio, who operated the scale manufacturing company and who, as part of the Dayton industrial community, knew the background of NCR and the court trials. Another director was Harlow E. Bundy, pioneer of the International Time Recording business, a compulsively frugal man whose theories on corporate management extended to his Binghamton household; it was reported that for many years Mr. Bundy deducted from his wife's house allowance the market price of vegetables taken from her garden for the dinner table, the deductions being adjusted to account for the cost of bringing the produce to harvest.

When Watson went to Binghamton to inspect the C-T-R holdings there, he called on the most famous citizen of the area, George F. Johnson, head of the Endicott-Johnson shoe factory, and established a comfortable, informal relationship with him. In seeking out Johnson for counsel, Watson was in one respect pursuing the obvious, since Johnson was, for all his reputation as an unconventional character and an up-from-the-tannery shoe tycoon, the dominant power in "The Triple Cities" of Endicott, Johnson City, and Binghamton.

Johnson's concept of capitalism was part conservative and part revolutionary, spiced with Fabian condiments and sauced out with a flavor that might have emerged from the criticism of George Bernard Shaw. Johnson added his own vision of a Jeffersonian transplant of an agricultural society to the world of factories. "My picture of a real factory," Johnson wrote, "was the shop out in the open country, with the homes of the workers around it in a little village. Then the men and their families could have gardens, could get fresh air and sun, and bring up their children decently, away from the crowded city."[4]

What Patterson at NCR achieved in the style of a benevolent tyrant and a temperamental martinet, Johnson accomplished with personal warmth, camaraderie, and physical labor in the most grueling and unpleasant jobs in the factories. He built his own home among the homes of the workers' families, joined them in clambakes and ball games, had his medical needs attended to at the factory clinic. His son, George H. Johnson, went to work as a common laborer, and both were called by

[4] *George F. Johnson and His Industrial Democracy,* by William Inglis, copyright by Endicott Johnson Corp.; printed by Vail-Ballou Press, Inc., Binghamton, N.Y.; first edition, 1935; second edition, 1947.

their first names. When young George was of age, his father offered to send him to college, to which the young man replied, "I'll be wasting time. I want to learn the shoe business." His father congratulated him on his superior judgment.

As paternalists, Watson and George F. Johnson were of a different breed but within the same species. Johnson was sure, open, communal in his style among employees and their families; he could chat and laugh about inconsequential matters in a group lounging about the running boards of his touring car parked at a picnic area. He could wear a tanner's apron, dip his gloved hands into the dye vats, don the supervisor's linen duster, hit the road as a drummer, or occupy the president's swivel chair—and maintain in all these roles a robust, physical dignity, the entity of a whole man, a man who was what he himself chose to be.

To as many as 20,000 employees, many of them immigrants recruited in the Balkan countries of Europe, Johnson wrote endless letters published in the company's newspaper. He invited anyone and everyone to write in return, in disagreement or otherwise. He despised real estate speculators, whom he called "home gamblers," and earned their enmity by selling profitless homes to his workmen for deductions from their weekly pay.

A wary distrust of authority was as characteristic of Johnson as a tendency to defer to it was of Watson. When Johnson donated vast acreage to Endicott as a park for the families of employees, police on patrol discovered that young men and girls used remote and quiet areas as hideaways for experiments in the inducement of affection and, no doubt, conversation. It became rather a sport for policemen to move in stealth on such revelries and march the apprehended pairs in embarrassment back to unsecluded police stations.

When the pleasure of conducting such surprise assaults on young lovers wore off, the police made a report to Johnson and suggested that he forbid the use of his park for such indulgence in rampant sexuality. As expected, Johnson's sensibilities were offended; in fury, he reacted by having notices posted about the grounds barring the police themselves from the park.

This sort of thing was not Watson's style at all, and as C-T-R grew, turned into IBM, and in time dwarfed the shoe company with its diminished total of 8,000 employees, Johnson and Watson lived and worked in their different ways; the employees and their families looked, spoke, behaved, and even dressed differently enough to indicate a mild disdain, and on occasion, a contempt for one another.

Watson had heard many times before he first went to see George F.

Johnson that Endicott-Johnson wanted a corner on the Binghamton labor market and would try to keep other industry from entering or expanding in the community. Known as "The Parlor City," owing to its abundance of individually owned homes containing that popular status symbol of the time—a separate room for the reception and entertainment of callers —Binghamton was said to loath the prospect of "dirty" industry, such as a railroad car shop. All of this was pure myth, of course, one of those mysterious falsehoods with absolutely no basis in fact except that somewhere, at some time, some spokesman, admired perhaps for routine acumen, had deduced a theoretical probability that had become a popular assumption.

One of the first decisions Watson had to make, as the non-president manager of the C-T-R operations, and one that would have to be carefully explained to the touchy board of directors, was the question of possible relocation of the holding company's operations around Binghamton. Watson had misgivings about the local labor capacity and the advantage held by Endicott-Johnson in attracting new arrivals and young people coming of age. How could the loosely organized companies that made up C-T-R, each with its own board of directors, management, sales force, and production staffs, compete for labor with the universally famous "industrial democracy" of Endicott-Johnson?

"Locate your new plants here," said Johnson. "Labor will come to you. You will see." He went on to comfort Watson in other ways that Watson remembered throughout his life. He often said that Johnson had persuaded him to make the Binghamton area a factory home of IBM. Watson also recalled the framed motto which was always near Johnson, on his desk or on a wall, with its biblical injunction that even the least literate of workmen and little children could quote: "And let us not be weary in well doing, for in due season we shall reap, if we faint not."

Johnson, at the time of his early meetings with Watson, was concerned more about the intrusion of the federal government into the shoe manufacturing business than the unlikely possibility of any little upstart company like Watson's drawing off his labor supply or diminishing his status as an enlightened modern employer. The fact was that Endicott-Johnson, in part because Johnson was an innovator in industrial mass production, had a highly competent, stable labor force in a manufacturing field characterized by a high proportion of hard, unpleasant jobs in noxious surroundings.

Watson inspected his company's properties in Binghamton, some of which were little more than sheds, paid visits to other plant locations, and returned to New York to start building a sales organization.

The main offices of C-T-R were across the street from Flint's headquarters on Broad Street in Manhattan's financial district, but the hazards and problems of Watson's job extended outward to a score of cities,
to twelve hundred employees, and most specifically, to about four
hundred demoralized and poorly supervised salesmen. Part of the problem was the nature of the company and the absence of experience and
tradition in operating a conglomerate of plants and people lacking collective purpose or corporate sense of identity. Having emerged from an
organization where the word of the boss had biblical status, Watson was
shocked to hear salesmen boo and hiss the president of one of the subsidiary companies. Yet he did not assault this blasphemy frontally, since
his own position did not yet command the respect he meant it to evoke.

In a series of small meetings with salesmen, he spoke authoritatively
of what he called "the competition proposition"; in fact, that word
proposition was used by Watson to cover a multitude of meanings: one's
job, an assertion, a sales talk, a product, political theories, and so on. It
cropped up three and four times in a single sentence if his intimidated
assistants didn't surreptitiously weed it out.

Unsentimental salesmen, who wondered how the new boss could talk
about competition, virtue in business, "square shooting," and the like,
when he himself had carried out policy for one of the roughest, most
ruthless competitors in American business, were impressed when the
grave, somewhat stuffy Thomas Watson raised the question of the
realities of combat in the field of competitive selling. Watson spoke with
the conviction of a man who had never seen, heard, or spoken evil, but
who acknowledged its theoretical existence.

"You must not do anything that's in restraint of trade," he said at his
first sales convention when it was suggested that as far as Watson himself was concerned, he had possibly been more successful in former days
than his future might allow. He went soberly on to say that salesmen
must not do anything that could even be "construed by anybody as
unfair competition." Then, quite as though his simple rhetoric was really
intended to convey a fundamental thought process developed at C-T-R,
Watson declared that "no man ever won except in the one honest, fair,
and square way in which you men are working."

The men were pleased to hear that their honesty, high mindedness,
and square shooting were so clearly evident to a man of Watson's status.
Quite convinced that Watson was sincere, one salesman said that the
talk sounded almost "sublime." In some of his early inspirational pep
talks, Watson would appear before the men with an easel and write these
words in vertical alignment as in the rungs of a ladder:

> The Manufacturers
> General Manager
> Sales Manager
> Service Manager
> Sales Man
> Factory Man
> Office Manager
> Office Man

Then in imitation of John H. Patterson, but with a style more serious and sober, Watson would address himself persuasively to the men: "We have different ideas and different work, but when you come right down to it, there is just one thing we have to deal with throughout the whole organization—that is MAN."

Moving decisively, briskly, he would draw fore and aft chalk lines through the prefatory words and suffix syllables, leaving visible, not very surprisingly a column made up of nine *MAN*'s. Something considerably more than the actual content of this elementary, if not kindergarten, message seemed to come through to the spectators. The presentation itself was impressive, with the tall, conservatively attired Watson moving solemnly around the easel, chalk in hand, obliterating the excessive verbiage, stripping away all that preceded and followed the three letters of MAN—the ultimate IBM MAN—who emerged as though from confusion, the mist and darkness of creation.

It was evangelism in the sales room, yet it suggested the inner conviction of the unarmed crusader rather than the shoot-to-kill sectarianism of Patterson and NCR. It was the evocation of confidence and faith, a summoning call to an inner, if not a higher, power in place of the curse, the lance, and the sword. What was seen and heard was not individually or significantly measurable; what was felt by those to whom the sermon was addressed was the fire that feeds on newly evoked desires, on the vision of being held in high esteem and of being materially rewarded for work.

Before long the growing admiration of the men was channeled into song, for a crusade is part chorus. And so they sang, to a melody no longer remembered, the words that praised the man—Watson; the company—C-T-R; the virtues of honorable heroes; the spirit of playing the game; and how to make it all worthwhile in terms of pay and profit. They sang the first in a long repertoire that was revised through the years, old songs abandoned and new ones written to praise new products and to permit incantations against threatening spirits, songs that made up the hymnal of the company, sung with the regularity and reverent confidence of a psalm, with the ritualistic fervor of the Greater Doxology:

> Mister Watson is the man we're working for,
> He's the leader of the C-T-R,
> He's the fairest, squarest man we know;
> Sincere and true.
> He has shown us how to play the game
> And how to make the dough.

Under the spell of the camaraderie that replaced earlier insularity and distrust, Watson got on well with the men in sales, and although income (sufficient to allow dividend payments totaling $313,719 the preceding year) brought in a profit of $1,313,062 during Watson's first year, dividends were passed up. The two card manufacturing companies in the combine, one in Washington and the other in Dayton, had enjoyed notable success over the preceding five years, with growth measured at 19 per cent in one year and 24 per cent in another. The plant that made scales had put 275,000 scales on the market not only on the domestic scene but as far off as Europe, South America, and Australia. Meat and cheese slicers were doing well, but other operations were skimpy, and the special applications of time recording devices required costly and detailed servicing. Nevertheless, dividends were resumed after a lapse of one year and continued without interruption, notwithstanding foreign losses when World War I broke out in full.

Watson had been on the job a little less than eleven months when the federal appeals court, in a decision involving a single issue, granted the defendants, Watson among them, a new trial and set aside the earlier conviction. Watson and Jeannette went off to North Carolina on a vacation to celebrate not only the court's decision but the decision of Flint and the board of directors, formalized within forty-eight hours of the news, to elevate Watson to the presidency of C-T-R. The court decision meant that the case would have to be tried again, since a new trial had been granted solely on the grounds that the presiding judge had erred when he declined to permit NCR attorneys to submit evidence alleging that at least some of the companies wiped out or bought out by Patterson had infringed on NCR's patents.

But no second trial developed. Instead, the case was closed by a consent decree, which Watson declined to sign. He said it would have been an admission of guilt. Since he was no longer connected with the convicted company, the government simply let him go. Technically speaking, he could have been tried a second time, but with Patterson, NCR, and other defendants now out of the case, and with Watson's consent to a more enlightened policy at NCR wholly meaningless now that he was out of the cash register business, the case simply died away.

Although he was president of C-T-R, and although sales and income allowed the declaration of a four per cent dividend after a one-year lapse, Watson was saved only by Flint from being held to the actual status of general sales manager. Internecine stress and Watson's own personality kept from full expression his desire—in fact, his need, if he was to discharge his management responsibilities effectively—for command. He had been too long in service, too long subordinate to the overpowering Patterson, to emerge, even with Flint's help and frequent encouragement, from the suppressed and repressed role of master in name but not in fact. He was no Uriah Heep, to be sure, for in the area of sales and product improvement and development he was, by combining his intuitive judgment with the training and motivational formula copied from others, increasingly successful. He was simply not running the business.

The internal strain was compounded by a cabal of officers and directors acting, if not with Flint's knowledge, certainly without his interference, to create by manipulation a price rise in C-T-R stock wholly unjustified by demand or value. Uneasiness, even fear, for the company's future, plus the anxiety and tension produced by Herman Hollerith's and George Fairchild's interference with Watson's work, depressed and upset him, and he was frequently ill. His manner with the touchy Fairchild remained submissive and deferential.

As a holding company, C-T-R was vulnerable to manipulation, an activity that attracted the attention of some directors and officers. Watson, as a man with little stock and no capital in the company, wanted a more solid form of growth and development. Flint upheld him when Watson, over some objections, wanted more emphasis on returning income to the business and less on dividend distribution. Flint's basic interest was in making money, rather than in how it was made. But he appears to have sensed that Watson, regardless of his immediate failure to exert leadership and command the power that was there to exercise, had the correct concept of the company's future. Thus when Watson disdained participation in a stock pool where carefully staged buying and selling activity would give the illusion of demand and consequent rises in price, Flint stuck by him. Again, it was an indication that when Watson had the courage, the will, and the daring to move, the charming old rascal Flint was ready to support him.

But Watson, so long unused to command, could not make the complete and final move. He never did make it, either, until after Fairchild died, but he did keep the stock speculators from doing possibly irreparable harm to the young company. The price he paid was perhaps ten years of needless obscurity in an organization that was to be the growth company of the twentieth century.

5.
Propagation
of
the
Faith

———————◆———————

WATSON MAY HAVE MOVED slowly at the beginning, but he moved surely as well. He made people like him in situations where distrust and hostility had prevailed. Internecine jealousies among the subsidiary companies may have prevented Watson from making consolidations in accounting procedures, inventory controls, and other fundamental practices of good business, but he kept his temper in control, did not fire anyone, and gradually won favor as a persevering leader, impartial in his dealings, and patient even with such men as Herman Hollerith.

Hollerith had sold out to Flint and presumably relinquished management prerogatives when C-T-R was set up, but emotionally the irascible inventor couldn't let go. Another tabulating machine on the market was, in Watson's opinion, a competitive threat to the C-T-R Hollerith machine, for the simple reason that it was technologically better. Watson's experience in building knockout machines and his trained eye for a better design impelled him to set up at once the equivalent of the NCR competition department. In this case, it was a form of product research, designed to improve the Hollerith model in order to compete with a superior Powers Company product. The work was done in a downtown Manhattan loft, and the method used was one learned from Patterson: dissect the competitor's machine and make design changes and improvements as required.

Hollerith was uncooperative with Watson's research, but Watson had on his staff his old NCR colleagues Robert Houston and Joe Rogers, and together they not only improved on the tabulating equipment they inherited, but emerged in a few years with a completely new machine. This infuriated Hollerith, who appeared to have ideas of his own for developing an improved accounting machine, along with data processing

79

accessories, without the accompanying intention of handing them over to C-T-R.

By 1919, Watson and Clair D. Lake, one of the company's most inventive and durable assets for more than thirty years, along with a draftsman and machinists under the supervision of a manager, E. D. Ford, brought the company far out in front of the competition in the profitable tabulating machine business.

Without this early accomplishment, it is altogether likely that the Powers Accounting Company would have got a strong lead in the lucrative and exciting tabulating field. C-T-R, left with its meat slicers, grocery store scales, cheese cutters, and other elemental measuring devices, would undoubtedly, given Watson's indomitable perseverance, have remained in the business machines field, but not as the leader it was to become.

The last serious obstacle to be overcome before the company was to plunge "ever onward," as its hymnal foretold, was a financial one, some of it attributable to nagging debt and some of it to botched and cumbersome bookkeeping, out of place in an organization which made the equipment to prevent the problem. Even when bills went unpaid to the last possible moment, there was seldom enough cash.

But the Guaranty Trust Company, which had financed Flint's operations in the past and to which C-T-R was already deeply in debt, extended more credit. Alexander J. Hemphill, president of the bank, advanced Watson $25,000 with which he established, again duplicating a practice long in force at NCR, a "future demands" department, which was a little product development shop at Endicott, N.Y. It was the first loan, apparently, that Watson obtained without the interference of Flint or Fairchild. It was also a manifestation of Watson's farsighted caution; he wanted not only to win the current sales skirmish whenever possible, but to be prepared for the one that had not yet begun.

Watson's pride in that insignificant loan was personal. Before company gatherings, usually with Mrs. Watson smiling beside him, he said many times that obtaining that first $25,000 loan and persuading Jeannette Kittredge to marry him were "two of the finest sales" he ever made.

Willis H. Booth, vice-president of the Guaranty Trust, joined the company's board of directors and remained an important financial advisor and colleague of Watson's for life—a friendship that withstood one of the harshest and most pithy descriptions of Watson ever uttered by so exalted and trusted a friend.

Speaking over a public-address telephone hookup to the upper level sales and management staff of IBM one time, Booth commented that a good description of Mr. Watson could be summed up in two words. The first, he said, was "benevolent," and, after a theatrical pause, he followed with the second, "despot." No account of this shocking moment was reported in the company's publications, and Mr. Watson's response was left to be imagined.

Watson's style became more assertive as he slowly, over the early years, shucked off the drab plumage of the subordinate in favor of the more princely posture of acknowledged head man. The change was encouraged, more subtly than overtly, by the aging, affable Flint, who all but invited Watson to exert his own management muscle. It was concurrent with the departure of Fairchild, and prompted by the development of new designs that isolated, and indeed subdued, the quarrelsome Hollerith.

Gross income was a little more than four million dollars in Watson's first year with the company. Four years later, profits had nearly doubled (to $2,134,000), and reserves were planned for a major expansion of production facilities. With sales at fifteen million, Watson grandly set a growth objective of one hundred per cent in one year—double the company's sales and production capacity. This walk-on-water confidence was fortified by a fine new tabulating machine plant on the flats of Endicott, erected in the wake of high wartime profits that accrued notwithstanding the loss of European sales in World War I. His earlier predictions of increased yearly growth, not only for the company, but for the American economy, held up for six heady years, but in the seventh—a famine year after the fat—they fell apart in the postwar panic of 1921, a short-term catastrophe that produced a nationwide wave of bankruptcies. In part by misfortune and in part by an uncharacteristic failure of Watson to remain in command of the facts about his own business, he was dealt a nearly mortal blow.

Everybody's wages from Watson to the factory hands were cut ten per cent, while the company house organs editorialized that no hard times were a-comin', only easy times ending. Skilled men were laid off, and the prized "future plans" department was obliterated, with forty-six of its staff of fifty sent away. A major miscalculation had occurred in the scale division, which produced some $3,400,000 worth of business that year against a predicted total of $15,000,000—or half of Watson's heralded company total. Upon analysis, it developed that this arm of the business was in very serious trouble; eventually, in the depth of the depression, it was sold to the Hobart Manufacturing Company, which made it pay very well. For many years, IBM annual reports showed tidy profits from Hobart with no further risk or headaches.

Watson had based his 100 per cent growth predictions on inner mystical confidence arising from a count of smoking factory chimneys, the length of freight trains, scrap iron sales, and similar indexes of industrial health, alleged to be useful for decision-making. Company reforms followed these errors in judgment; credit was sustained throughout the panic, although at the cost of borrowing 80-cent dollars at eight per cent; and Watson, who continued to predict peace, prosperity, the ascendance of virtue, and stability through wars, depression, alleged moral decay, and world chaos, nevertheless kept a closer watch and tighter rein on company affairs. When, subsequently, he thought it might be symbolically inspiring to set a goal, for example, of a 30 per cent growth increase to celebrate his 30th anniversary with the company, he permitted himself to be talked out of it; goals were established not altogether free of such arbitrary considerations, but not altogether dependent on them either. Watson had to wait until 1937 for his $30 million year.

Nevertheless, the company weathered a year that brought failure or sale to many others. Watson's income, because of his profit-sharing formula, was cut forty per cent. But he was soon rewarded with a new five-year contract and an improved formula, providing him compensation on top of a salary of sixty thousand dollars a year. Charles R. Flint's admiration for Watson, and his faith in his own judgment in backing him, increased almost year by year, and he included a full-page photograph of him in his memoirs, published in 1923. Before long, the pendulum of time and circumstance put Watson in a position where *he* was lending money to Flint, or so it was reported, and Flint, not long after that, was quoted in the press as designating Thomas J. Watson, along with J. P. Morgan, John H. Patterson, Henry Ford, Charles H. Schwab, John D. Rockefeller, etc., among the ten great American businessmen in history. And even though Flint's opinion on such matters, authoritative as they were, might have been less than objective, it was far more valid than an earlier listing in Ohio newspapers of former NCR men and their accomplishments: Watson wasn't even mentioned.

The oversight must have hurt him deeply, for reasons of both fact and ego. Watson was quick and eager to acknowledge his debt to the man who had employed him, educated and trained him, used and endangered him, punished him, abandoned him, and, until the day he died in 1922, was generally indifferent to him.

Something psychological, something compelling, seemed to touch Watson about that time. Perhaps it was the assumption of command, the confidence of knowing he now had a fine product line capable of producing profits and growth, and the death of Patterson severed the remaining threads to his old obsequious self. He was at last his own man.

For two or three years he had been saying with a half measure of confidence that the company would go on indefinitely, repeating the expression in the C-T-R press and at meetings until it became a line in the company catechism. Similarly, he had been asserting that the entire world itself was the true territory of this international company and its machines designed to serve business. He rechristened the company International Business Machines, thus obliterating the last trace of the symbols associated with any thing or person other than himself.

Virtually heedless of grousing directors—some had objected to changing the name of the company—he set about creating IBM exactly in his own image. With the death of Fairchild, the position of chairman of the board was eliminated, not to be reincarnated until Watson himself needed it as the pinnacle on which to establish his throne and from which to look down upon his son, his heir, his president. Watson's new position as chief executive officer was secured, not by stock ownership, for that was minimal; not by intrigue or by corporate politics, in which he kept the balance of power; not by his broad and varied experience in business, management, or finance. His strength now was his mystique, his indispensability; his unrelenting dedication to the company added a measure of meaning to his simplest, most nonsensical, platitudes. The metamorphosis was complete. Watson *was* IBM.

As a thoroughly decent person who truly wanted to do good, Watson completed and more or less arrested his own development as full command of the company came to him. From then on his patience diminished considerably. His authority took on stern overtones; deference to superiors within the company was no longer required since there weren't any; deference to outsiders was selective, often reserved for heads of state, men of learning and wealth, and federal authorities. Courtesy was his way of life save when irritated or angry, which was often. And the mystic in the man required the creation of a doctrine, a company litany, a host of angels, a hierarchy, devils to curse, the exorcism of evil spirits, and a heaven at the end. Hell was for those of little faith and unfulfilled sales quotas.

The tempo of indoctrination, of defining the faith and propagating it, quickened. So, in fact, did the tempo of everything and everyone else around IBM. The size of the company had, roughly, tripled under his care, and so had the amount of dividends. The market value of the stock, now worth eighteen million, had increased by five times. Offices of subsidiary companies were consolidated in St. Louis, Chicago, Boston, and Philadelphia, a process of bringing all activities of all the companies together that continued until it was complete. The holding company itself disappeared in 1933.

Otto E. Braitmayer, who was reported by company writers to have "sneered openly" at Watson when Flint first hired him, and who might have been fired for his insolence had not Watson ignored every manifestation of ill will at the time, was elevated to vice-president from his position in a subsidiary company and sent to Europe. There, a new plant opened at Sindelfingen, Germany, and plans were begun for a Paris factory, which opened the following year.

At home, in 1924 the largest and most dramatic sales convention in the history of the company brought an evangelical fervor to a high, sustained pitch. Although IBM was only thirteen years old, the first meeting of the Quarter Century Club for employees with twenty-five years of service was held at Atlantic City. Any time served by any person in one or more of the original companies before Flint formed the industrial combination was counted in order to produce Quarter Century Club members.

In a collective marketing research study, IBM joined with, of all companies, NCR, the competing Burroughs Adding Machine Company, Elliott-Fisher Co., the Remington Typewriter Company, and several other producers of specialty products, to direct the R. L. Polk Company, publisher of city directories and other source material, to analyze sales possibilities. From this undertaking, Watson determined that IBM had in the U.S. at the time more than two million prospective customers. Moreover, he knew pretty much who and where they were. From this information, district office locations, sales territories, and quota systems could be more accurately and more efficiently determined.

To all of this activity was added an important corporate project, a new seventeen-story headquarters office at 310 Fifth Avenue in New York to house the sales offices of all divisions. The building was completed, and schools for executives, salesmen, and—a new feature—manufacturing employees opened there in 1925.

"We want manufacturing men to feel that they are executives in the company," said Watson. "The farther we keep away from the 'boss' proposition—of being the 'boss' of the men under us—the more successful we are going to be." Part of the IBM spirit was that no man was to have thoughts of being a boss. It was the equivalent of sin, something like inducing carnal fantasy in a state of grace, to set oneself thus apart. One could be a leader; leadership was encouraged, but only in a one-to-one relationship, one man offering guidance to another. The leader was instructed not to tell people what to do but to help them to do it. Paraphrasing Coué's nostrum, Watson said: "The man who utilizes every minute of every hour becomes a bigger, better being every minute."

The IBM man was not a visible part of the roaring twenties and the dissolute life that distinguished them, first of all because he was a serious fellow, intent on making something of himself, but also because Mr. Watson would fire him in a minute if word of excessive frivolity, any drinking whatsoever, or unacceptable incidents of boisterous or embarrassing conduct got back to the leader.

Every man in the IBM organization had an equal opportunity to follow in Watson's footsteps as president, he told both his own people and non-company listeners, with pride. He was distressed, even in the summer of 1926, at the common tendency to regard men as impersonal assets rather than living beings of flesh and feelings. And, again, he said it did not much matter what a man's capacity was, the presidency of IBM was open to him on an equal basis.

"Sometimes I think we overemphasize the mechanics of this age," he mused in an article. "Often we lay too much stress on machinery in production. When we start thinking of men as automatons, clicking their respective ways through the process of life with mechanical exactness, that day we lose our own identity and become automatons ourselves. . . . When a man comes into this business, no matter what his capacity, the job of being president is as accessible to him as is the next job above him."

Tom Watson, Jr., was twelve that year, and in case his appearance before a company convention and the applause for his first speech on salesmanship gave him heady ideas about the presidency of IBM, he had his father's sobering words to reflect upon. On the other hand, there was his father's little closing homily to think about, too: *"Never feel satisfied."*

There was not much opportunity to feel satisfied at IBM; too much was going on, too many activities and too much sales competition; they excited one's ambition, spurred one onward, and sometimes scared the daylights out of one. The balance wavered between hope of satisfaction, which was brief at best even when attained, and the well-nourished fear, which Mr. Watson himself aroused at nearly every opportunity, that the widows and orphans were looking directly to the salesmen for their bread and butter, their shelter, and the clothes on their backs.

Although Mr. Watson was earnest and sincere in his grave compliments to the salesmen, whom he regarded as the elite corps of the corporation, he was careful not to overfeed their egos, and as an expression of this caution, his commendation frequently had a cutoff point just short of making a man who had met his quota wallow in the slough of conceit. In this instance, his closing remarks to the men who had made

1926 a record-breaking year, were helpful in building defenses against the cardinal sin of pride.

"This selling proposition isn't surrounded by any great mystery. Any young man of ordinary intelligence who is honest, and willing to work, can 'make good' selling our products. . . . *Constructive criticism is the trail blazer to success.*"

Watson made six separate addresses before the Hundred Percent Club meeting early in 1927. The extraordinary success of the preceding year had Watson so fired up with the spirit of IBM that he had devised a new method for salesmen-proselytes to reach "the men who are not here," i.e., those who had not met their quotas.

Earlier, delegations of plant workmen had visited meetings of Hundred Percent Clubs, and salesmen who had not met their quotas were conducted on tours of the factories, meeting the production workers, chatting around work benches, visiting model shops, and the like. Watson talked to the factory men who had welcomed the salesmen to their shops and who were now in New York as guests of the Hundred Percent Club. Watson invited this captive audience to exert a new twist to the screw that turned on the IBM spirit.

"We want each of you gentlemen from the factories to select two or three salesmen whom you have met on their visits to our plants and act as sponsor for them. Write them and ask them what you can do to help them get into the One Hundred Percent Club. Tell them about your visit to the One Hundred Percent Club meeting. Tell them you missed seeing their faces there. . . .

"It is a shame for any man, if he is in good health, to put in twelve months in a territory in our business and not come through with 100 percent of quota. He is not cheating anyone as much as he is cheating himself and his family. . . . Let us see if we cannot help them to take a little more interest in doing more for the people who are dear to them— their own families, their wives and children."

There is no evidence to suggest whether this was a successful method of inducing the IBM spirit among backsliders. The idea seems to have sprung from Mr. Watson impulsively, unpredictably, as did frequent imaginative suggestions that inspired zeal and energy throughout the corporation. But whether this idea or others produced the desired results, results surely came as the faith was propagated and the IBM spirit moved men.

Watson's thoughts on company matters, patriotism, public issues, morals, the way things were, the way things ought to be, began to appear in company publications. A treasury of his thoughts, and an almost clinical account of the development of IBM, as seen largely through the language and proprietary vision of Watson himself, was disclosed week by week in the company publication called *International Business Machines,* the first word being dropped when the company itself took that name. *Business Machines* was alone in its class as a house periodical. It sometimes appeared in rotogravure, or an issue might contain thousands of dollars worth of halftones of a single convention, and as many as two dozen photographs of Watson presenting or receiving awards, in posed discussions, or—more likely—before bunting-hung rostrums or daises, addressing the awed, or at least attentive, multitude.

Each IBM installation of any size had its own publication. *Business Machines* itself was aimed at the whole IBM family and was also useful in the trade as a public relations channel to show what Watson wanted, or permitted, to be known about IBM. Sometimes special distribution procedures were called for. On one occasion a 56-page special issue in rotogravure, commemorating a year late what was, in fact, Watson's 25th anniversary with the company—but which was incorrectly publicized as the 25th anniversary of his "founding" the company—was mailed to 50,000 names in the telephone books of Johnson City, Endicott, and Binghamton and was widely distributed in New York City, as well as being sent to its regular receivers.

While significant space was devoted to Mr. Watson's speeches or to inspirational messages that pleased him or that he had prepared himself, news ranging from the trivial to the company's annual sales convention, considered any year's major event, was reported with devotion and in detail. When the company's prestige publication, *THINK,* was inaugurated in the Thirties, many of Mr. Watson's loftier messages, as well as literary contributions and philosophical tidbits invited from non-company contributors, graced its pages, and *Business Machines* stuck more strictly to IBM affairs.

Mr. Watson thought so well of these publications and the merit of his prodigious contributions to their content that two volumes of what he and others had to say in *THINK,* speeches he had given before salesmen or public gatherings, and his interviews and magazine articles were published and circulated at company expense. A third volume, entitled *As a Man Thinks, So Is He,* anthologized editorials from *THINK* and reproduced them in an outsized work of elegant printing and binding. Its publication coincided with the celebration of Watson's fortieth anniversary with the company in 1954. The anthology was in honor of both Mr. and Mrs. Watson; the dedication hailed the "rare quality of thinking for which Thomas J. Watson is noted," and the tribute was published over the simple printed phrase, designating the donor: *The IBM family*.

This official record of some of Mr. Watson's thoughts, while at times flawed by self-consciousness and the unmistakable public relations touch, was remarkable for the consistency of its style, easily recognized as Watsonian in its ideology, and for the inventory of issues that concerned him in the years he prepared his revelations for publication.

If some of his thoughts seemed over-simplistic, or burdened with needless weight that might better have been discarded in a merciful trimming of the rhetoric, it should be remembered that the periodical reflections of very few businessmen—in that time of Sinclair Lewis's "Babbitt" and H. L. Mencken's "boob and baloney" disclosures—would have withstood the analysis of succeeding generations with less erosion than Mr. Watson's homiletics.

Most men and women are probably content, and perhaps relieved, if devoid of any special gift of language and the compulsion of confession, not to have old positions and speculations preserved in print; Watson was not one of these. He had inscribed his name on the wood, the walls, and the stones of Painted Post; and by extending the Spirit of IBM, impossible as it was to define, by expropriating the work THINK, propagating the faith, and putting the Watson name on patents, thoroughfares, structures, propositions, projects, and an endless output of didactic essays, he continued to spread the tracery of his signature across American industrial culture.

Besides the company's intra-communications publications and *THINK Magazine,* which by the 1940's was circulated to 70,000 persons and businesses, Watson's speeches were heard and reprinted for numberless thousands, and possibly millions, of people. They were The Word, the very embodiment and interpretation of the IBM Spirit. He must have made in the neighborhood of four thousand speeches in his career, not counting impromptu tirades to small groups of managers or invitations to "say a few words" on other business occasions.

A large measure of the IBM Spirit involved the veneration of money. It was not "altogether the hallmark of success," said Watson, but a man's success in general "is measured by his prosperity." He would then instruct the men to put their savings in "five successful companies with good earnings," and warned them to resist the temptation to sell out and take a profit "as long as the companies increased their earnings. . . . There are men in this business who have been buying IBM stock for the last fourteen years. Some of them have never sold a share and keep on buying more."

Watson was absolutely correct about that. In the Binghamton-

Endicott area, where employees for some years received a portion of their pay in stock, a sub-cult developed of IBM workers who had amassed fortunes. One of the first women hired after Watson became president was a factory worker, Fannie Sexsmith, who borrowed five hundred dollars from a local artist and woodsman, Foster Disinger, and started buying company stock. From a poor but respectable family, she looked upon Watson and George F. Johnson as heroic figures; she had often bolstered Mr. Disinger's sagging spirits when he was escorting her home from church by slightly altering Johnson's biblical injunction: "Be not weary of well doing, for in time ye shall reap if ye faint not."

Fannie Sexsmith neither wearied of well doing, nor did she ever faint until she was very old, by which time she was a philanthropist of some note, financing a share of the restoration of the old houses in the New England Pilgrim country, endowing a church home, and making $25,000 contributions to local institutions. Disinger himself, to whom Watson had shown his collection of John Taylor Arms etchings, and who often trekked to the Adirondacks to paint mountainscapes, made a little money by putting outrageously high prices on his oils of "Indian Lake," "Pines in Winter," and the like, which Watson, quite astonishing him, bought by lot for inclusion in the early traveling exhibits sponsored by the company.

Fred E. Lee, a bachelor who had never made more than about $5,000 a year as a draftsman at the Endicott plant, lived with his sister, Viola, worked every day of his adult life, and acquired a million-dollar fortune by accumulating IBM stock. Upon his death, Viola Lee became one of the town's wealthy women, the fortune having grown to more than two million, despite her disbursements of a half-million dollars to the Fairview Presbyterian Home, $250,000 to the local Y.M.C.A., a large gift to the Masonic Home, and so on. Fred Lee's best friend, Floyd Jackson, who invested $5,000 in IBM in 1925, left a million-dollar estate which scarcely anybody except a lawyer named Herbert H. Ray, who became something of a specialist in handling estates of wealthy IBM workmen, knew he had.

Attorney Ray and his wife experienced a different facet of the Spirit of IBM. He had some clients who endured regret and bitterness over their own failure to assimilate the IBM faith. They were people who had complained when, in their view, Watson had persuaded them to take a portion of their wages in stock against their better judgment. Their objections resulted in the recovery of the stock payments and a restoration of their full wages, thus dooming them to live out their lives as comparatively impoverished object lessons whose loss of faith represented the irrevocable loss of millions of dollars. Watson, who had inaugurated the stock purchase plan for no other reason than that of giving his employees an opportunity to take his advice to become wealthy, was so angered by imputations that he was palming off shares in the company as a substitute for cash that he suspended the program altogether; IBM workmen did not regain the right to buy stock in such a painless manner until after his death.

One of the unhappy complainants, an elderly lady at the time of her death, left among her modest effects an unexercised warrant for some IBM shares that had lapsed and become valueless. In a time-consuming bit of legal service on behalf of the lady's estate, which amounted to nearly nothing, the attorney traced the warrant, with the help of Watson's office, to its origin. Somewhat to his surprise, he received from the corporation a check payable to the estate in the amount of $4,200, for division among two or three poor heirs. Ray had no corroboration for his suspicion that Watson had been personally responsible for the welcome little landfall. The heirs and the lady herself lived in an area of about ten square blocks in Binghamton in which an insurance collector, making his rounds periodically to accept premiums at the households of his clients, regularly called on twelve people known as "IBM millionaires." News accounts of wills probated in the area still frequently report the accumulation of fortunes ranging from two or three hundred thousand dollars up to two or three million. The faith and spirit of IBM which may elude definition by analytical observers takes on, to the beneficiaries of these wills, a revealed meaning of stunning clarity.

Ray knew Mr. and Mrs. Watson rather well and was invited on occasion to attend with his wife, as guests of the Watsons, sales convention dinners and other company affairs held at the IBM Country Club nearby, a sumptuous piece of real estate among the rolling hills, woodlands, and greensward of Broome County. One of three company country clubs, its membership fee to IBM people has always been a dollar a year. At a dedication dinner on one occasion, at which Nelson Eddy "rendered selections from *Indian Love Call*," according to a company publication, Mrs. Ray happened to mention to Mrs. Watson, gracious, smiling, and warmly responsive to her guests, that her daughter, Beverly Ray, suffered from a chronic asthma and sinus condition —a legacy from long Binghamton winters and late springs—and had been directed by the family doctor to transfer from the University of Rochester to the University of Arizona.

When Miss Ray arrived at the arid campus, the IBM branch manager in the Tucson area, whom the Rays had neither met nor heard of, called on her and invited her to a dinner party in her honor, a gesture of welcome to the West. Jeannette had repeated the incidental bit of intelligence to Watson, who, no doubt remembering his miseries with asthma as a youth, had been moved to intercede.

When the sniffling but grateful Miss Ray showed up at the dinner dance, a young bachelor salesman for the company, lonely himself and ready for companionship that had not come easily to him as a proper, thoroughly well-behaved representative of the corporation, was on hand —instructed, it may be surmised, to look after her. Love bloomed in the desert air, and Beverly Ray became Mrs. Robert Coope, thus enlisting two more families in the legion of those who admired Mr. and Mrs. Watson.

Admiration for Watson was vast and genuine in the optimistic years of the late 1920's, both on the basis of this quiet and often impulsive assistance to people who least expected it, and because of his optimism and confidence in the future. IBM's great year in 1926—during which the number of IBM stockholders nearly doubled and its foreign operations extended to fifty-four countries—sent Watson's optimism spiraling beyond its normal heights.

He sent Otto Braitmayer, who had begun as Herman Hollerith's office boy, and who managed IBM's overseas expansion, to China and the Philippines, "where we have some installations of tabulating machines . . . and from there he is going to Australia and New Zealand. Probably by that time, we will hear of something farther on, which will take him somewhere else. Everywhere he stops there will be IBM machines in use. The sun never sets on IBM."

Watson would continue, rapturously: "When I talk to a group of IBM people, I cannot help but talk of IBM. I think it is the most interesting thing for me to speak about, and I don't think there is anything that is more interesting for you to listen to. We are one great big family. . . . If you look upon me as the head of the family, I want you to come to me as often as you feel that I can do anything for you. Feel free to come and open your hearts and make your requests, just the same as one would in going to the head of a family."

Sometimes he would engage in conversation with a workman at a lathe or assembly bench, and the workman as often as not was addressed by name—for Watson, with his elephantine memory, would either know a man's name or learn it before dropping out of a touring entourage to approach a factory worker. If the visited workman was calm, courteous, neat, and confident, knowing his work and exuding pride in it, Watson

91

might turn to one of his male secretaries and say, "Double that man's salary."

Or, he might order a reward of another kind—an extra week of vacation, a day off, and so on. Reports of such incidents may have been exaggerated, but some were factual, too.

There were no specific rules about decorum, grooming, and apparel, but a certain style was expected because Mr. Watson approved of it. At both executive and lowly levels, the distribution of largesse and kindly treatment went to those who won his approval, which was often dependent upon his mood or some recent justification for optimism.

On rare occasions, even something that normally irritated him evoked a contradictory attitude. A shop foreman once saw Watson approach a drill press operator, ask the man's name, then say: "Can you lend me two dollars?"

The embarrassed fellow extracted the money from his pockets and handed it to Watson.

"Now, young man, I would like you to take the rest of the day off and take your wife out to dinner or a motion picture. But first you will probably want to get a haircut. I will pay the bill for it and for the evening, and here is the down payment for it." And he handed the man back the two dollars.

Word of these sorties into the factories spread through the plants and were said to be very good for morale. Later on, when the work force expanded beyond the range of Watson's ability to involve himself so deeply in the affairs of IBM people, a variation of the practice continued. Some new office staff member, or a service man obliged to deliver equipment to customers, might somehow have slipped through the employment screening process and, after reporting to work, begin to appear in a despised colored, or striped, shirt. If his boss had assimilated the Watson style properly, he would not summarily dismiss the offender but rather keep an eye on him for a few days. If the offense was repeated, the supervisor would go to him with a gift of perhaps a half-dozen white shirts, and suggest calmly that he was considered a good man to have in the company and that the shirts were intended only to make his work more satisfactory to all concerned.

It was not necessary to put into writing the rules for grooming, clean white shirts, neckties, and conservative attire. Servicemen with tool kits who came to repair the plugs on a calculating machine, or check the operation of a high-speed card sorter, appeared little different from the IBM-trained salesman who had placed the equipment in rental operation. It was said that Watson himself communicated his insistence on dark suits and white shirts by standing at a podium at one of the early sales conventions and, looking at the forward rows of attentive salesmen, their stiff collars and shirt fronts gleaming in the morning light in contrast to their dark suits, said pointedly to the executives gathered about him, "My, but those men look nice; I am proud to have them represent the company." It was quite enough, and the expression of approval instituted a universal, undeviating policy.

By the same indirect but unambiguous methods that made white shirts and ties standard IBM attire, modes of conduct were established. Church attendance, for instance, was not imposed by order on IBM families, but it might as well have been. Watson, a Methodist and an admirer of the bishops of his denomination, quit one church when the minister's sermon offended him, and joined the Episcopal Church in Short Hills when it seemed appropriate to do so. Later he associated himself with the Brick Presbyterian Church in Manhattan, where services were held for him when he died. It was of no special consequence to him which church a man attended, but attendance itself was not an issue of choice; an IBM household was quite simply expected to be at least modestly religious.

It was almost exclusively a male world at IBM, except for certain factory jobs, clinic nurses, and some typists. Male secretaries were the rule until World War II compelled a change in policy. Prior to the war, employees were overwhelmingly male and Protestant. The message to personnel interviewers evoked no less response by reason of the fact that it was oblique, unwritten, and theoretically unofficial. Watson liked the kind of men who were calm, polite, devoted, and subjugated editions of himself, whose ambition found expression in a total involvement in their jobs, leaders who were enthusiastically content to be followers. They were an industrial ethnic group, nationalists of the company, expected to serve and represent the company above all other considerations.

It was at no time formally noted that Catholics, Jews, women, and Negroes were incapable of response to the indoctrination, incantations, and Watsonian philosophy prescribed in the dictates of IBM. Nor was the company distinguished by its exclusionary policy, which was practiced in much of the country, by both intention and oversight. IBM did not create this aspect of the American character; rather, it exemplified it and subscribed to it. Enlightened departure from the policy came years later under the pressure of World War II, when women entered industry by the millions; in the scientific and technological revolution when educated Jews and scientists broke the barriers in such numbers that an IBM space center at Owego, New York, became known—pejoratively at first—as "Little Israel," and later, to both the new inhabitants and a more tolerant countryside, as "Israel West."

Catholics were not so much overtly excluded from employment as preference was given to Protestants, although job applicants with the ring of Erin in their names—Shaughnessy, O'Sullivan, Ryan, and the like—were turned away in disproportionate numbers, especially women, even though some were non-Catholics originating in the Orange state of Northern Ireland. With the specific question of religion unasked, for discrimination was not conceded, secondary symptoms of identification were enough to produce exclusion.

As for black citizens, any chance of employment at IBM was virtually hopeless, consistent with employment policies prevailing in much of America, except in menial and service tasks. Few Negroes resided in the vicinity of the principal manufacturing operations at Endicott, but the policies that were perhaps more accidental than intentional there also prevailed elsewhere—in Washington, D.C., for example. Not until the civil rights outbreaks of the 1950's did company management become concerned with discrimination against Negro workers; then there gradually developed an accelerated program under which it was mandatory upon division heads to give Negroes some preferential treatment in training and employment.

In these respects, the largest number of IBM workers in the United States, residents of the southern tier area along the New York-Pennsylvania border, differed from the larger and more boisterous class of working people of the Endicott-Johnson "industrial democracy." Thousands of the latter were first and second generation immigrants who had left their Ukrainian, Slovakian, Hungarian, Italian homelands to take steerage passage to Boston and Ellis Island in New York—where, it was said, they uttered their first question in English, hastily memorized before departure: "Which way E.J.?"

Poor, pleasantly respectable, largely Catholic, they established ethnic colonies in the valley, attended the churches of their linguistic origin, sang their native songs, kicked up their heels in vigorous folk dances, and made hundreds of millions of shoes for E.J. They were people in theatrical contrast to the men and the families of IBM. They made wine in their cellars from dandelions and from the grapes diverted from the half-somnolent vineyards which, in the Prohibition era, were saved from extinction by the grape juice industry. They brewed equally illegal yeasty beer to enliven their feast days and festive parades, in which ebullient marchers swung past the factories of abstemious IBM workers, shouting to their sober onlookers the taunt, "While you're thinkin', we're drinkin'." They wed and bred and stayed in the valley towns, in the succeeding generation or two distinguishable to an ever diminishing degree from the conservative, careful, nonunion, mostly Republican, clannish IBM families. They, too, had been brushed by the subduing spirit.

The industrial sub-culture that devolved around the IBM family, something of an ideal style of work and life that even the more militant labor unions both begrudged and forgave, did not offer quick and easy assimilation for everyone. But it paid in the currency of security, respectability, status, promotion and the hope of promotion, social life, and increasing fringe benefits. These, while arbitrarily preferred and sometimes as arbitrarily withdrawn, alleviated a measure of the anxiety and economic hazards that afflicted families dependent upon jobs in seasonal industry, service trades, or manufacturing operations which did not enjoy IBM's growth and profit possibilities, or which lacked the guidance of a perpetual force like Watson.

For some IBM people, it was difficult to determine with confidence where allegiance to the company might let up, perhaps freeing them to exercise individuality which, while not inimical to the corporation, might nevertheless be unacceptable. A form of seat-of-the-pants learning had to be acquired. One seldom erred, in living by the faith and spirit, if he pretested company attitudes before venturing into any uncharted waters. But the assumption that the company might not care about trivial or personal matters could be inappropriate.

Sex, of course, was a matter of moral significance and was impermissible, if not unattainable, except between a husband and wife. And while a married couple was not in theory discouraged from pursuing their conjugal relationship, in practice the choice of a residence in which to do so was not always theirs to make. Where IBM families lived could be their own decision only if prior conditions were met.

Preferably, employees were expected to reside relatively close to their jobs. Marginal allowances were made, depending on the individual manager enforcing the rules. As factories and research installations arose in Westchester County suburbs, Poughkeepsie, and other towns, mileage perimeters around one's place of employment were informally prescribed, and residence within the perimeter suggested. But a foreman or inspector at the Fishkill factory or the typewriter plant at Poughkeepsie was not allowed to live in a substandard section of Newburgh or Beacon, even within the prescribed circle. Not that most IBMers would want to: it was simply understood.

One young Hundred Percent Club man and his wife in Endicott, residing in an acceptable development, acquired a handsome nineteenth-century barn and made plans to convert it into a distinctive house. He had been promoted to an enviable job as aide to an upper management personage and wanted to upgrade his status in Endicott circles. Even though it was the man's wife who initiated the project and who was reported to have the money to see it through on her own resources, the husband was called in by a personnel official and told that in view of the fact that the property was located in a section of town not considered suitable for company people, it would be inadvisable for the couple to live there.

An IBM man to the core, he had to comply and had an unhappy review of the aborted project with his disconsolate wife. He compounded his resentment against the system by going out on a mild and forbidden drunk and denouncing the injustice to a colleague. The latter, putting sympathy for the couple ahead of his obligation to report the heretic, kept his silence; no reprisals ensued, and somebody else got the beautiful, but outlawed, barn.

The point emphasized by the case of the banned barn was a difficult one to comply with; it showed that members of the IBM family could inadvertently overreach themselves and approach damnation before recognizing a doctrinal violation. A man must not strain the spirit of IBM democracy by ostentation, by ambition too overtly exhibited, by ascension in the material scale inconsistent with his position in the corporate zodiac. Sensitivity and delicacy were called for, preferably exercised in a style that forebore acknowledgement of their usage. This was managed best among those to whom the practice, no matter how strained or contrived, seemed natural.

Yet discipline and order in the IBM family were not uniformly rigorous. In small cities and towns company mores could effectively forbid drinking, induce church affiliation, confine the therapy of copulation to the lawfully married and prevent backsliding among monogamists —or at least drive the faithless to the uplands, beyond immediate patriarchal jurisdiction. But the same purity controls were not easy in populous urban areas. City congestion provided an escape into anonymity; deviation from the faith was less visible, and therefore less enforceable.

Watson was not as comfortably permissive as George F. Johnson, nor was he as unrelentingly autocratic as Patterson—which was, in a comparative sense, his saving grace. Watson would go to church, of course, sometimes arriving at the office on Monday mornings with the church service program on which he had scribbled memoranda to himself and his secretaries about business matters that had occurred to him in the course of meditation or the sermon. There was no contradiction or disrespect intended and none involved, since Watson through his business and promotion of the Golden Rule in the universal affairs of mankind was confident of serving God with not much less dedication than he expected from the deity whose protection and help he invoked. He—Watson, that is—frequently deplored, in talks and messages directed both to the IBM family and to the world at large, the human condition in which mankind forgot that this was God's world, not man's world. Coaxing the fullest measure of work from his salesmen and production staffs, he often reminded them that prosperity offered man his maximum chance for happiness in this world, and that the success of the company offered the people in those countries IBM served an opportunity for the prosperity that would bring happiness if their faith in both the company and God was sustained.

Upon returning from his trips and conferences with company employees abroad, he would report confidently that there was a consistency of acceptance of the IBM philosophy everywhere he went. "This might just as well be one of the conventions back home," he assured his organization in Germany. And back in New York, he would report: "Our people over there looked just the same to me. They said the same things, they had just the same qualities."

Mr. Watson, never hypocritical and never cynical, was quite certain of his observations. Yet the restrictive code that worked so well in Endicott and Binghamton, in Fishkill and Denver and San Jose, and in the white suburban communities in which IBM invariably located was a good bit less effective in Paris, metropolitan England, and New York. The legacy of Sodom and Gomorrah could be subdued, if not obliterated, in the boondocks, but seemed to cling to the cities. Watson may have felt, as a matter of pragmatism, justified in permitting himself a measure of self-delusion; or his supreme confidence perhaps altered his vision. In any case, IBM's emphasis on churchgoing, the ban on drinking, and the like, was only nominally, and not very effectively, extended to the great cities, and in the anticlerical cities of wine-loving Europe, the policy was considered an eccentricity imported from fundamentalist, abstemious America. IBM men drank wine for lunch in the company cafeteria in Paris.

The clergymen Watson employed to pray at sales meetings, one of whom, the Reverend John V. Cooper, had the title of IBM chaplain, invoked divine blessings primarily on the domestic scene. Even there, Watson sometimes fretted about it. He questioned whether the Lord's

Prayer should be recited or sung at daily convention sessions on the grounds that "too much" religion could conceivably be injected into a day's program. Once he advised resorting to the prayer only on the opening day, and proposed that at succeeding sessions the chaplain substitute for the prayer one of his "good" sales talks. Watson was not an unrealistic patriarch.

He tended to be contradictory, although any record that this was pointed out to him has disappeared with the lost, or suppressed, archives that made the second generation of Watson management self-conscious. There was a never-ending emphasis on THINK and company loyalty. The word loyalty was not visually exalted to the status of THINK, but it was second only to the capitalized directive in continuing significance. THINK was what all were required to do; loyalty was the inevitable result of thought, if it was correctly undertaken. Watson, arriving at the office late, would say to his associates, "Gentlemen, I was looking at my THINK sign for a long time this morning, and . . ." And he would go on to enumerate and review the outcome of his reflections, all of them explicitly bearing on business matters which, ingested and extracted through the crucible of his thought process, became issues of immediate importance.

Every office had a THINK sign, and every desk was supposed to have one on it, within unobstructed view of its occupant. If this bit of iconography was not readily visible in Watson's presence, he was quick to notice it, and his reaction was as reflexive as it was explosive. In the company's building on Fifth Avenue, the THINK sign in the lobby was apparently carried off by a pilferer, and Watson, arriving with an executive from his advertising department one morning, missed it at once. He administered a short, stinging reprimand to his associate on the spot; the latter hurried up to his office, removed his own sign, and returned to the lobby where, without bothering to summon the custodian, he secured the sign to the wall himself. A little later in the morning, Vice-president Fred Nichol dropped in on the advertising man and, having schooled himself over the years to respond as identically as Watson to identical situations, bawled the poor fellow out for not having his sign around. Still later, Watson summoned all his aides and delivered a stern lecture on the text, "You Men Must Learn To Think."

Possibly because it had been a trying day for the advertising man, he and a confederate went back into the building in the night with a container of red paint. The following morning one wall of the meeting room was adorned in flaming letters six feet high with the word THINK. Gerald Breckenridge, a writer for *The Saturday Evening Post,* said that

Watson did not appear to notice any intended sarcasm, and the over-powering admonition remained on the wall until the next visit of the painters.

The proliferation of THINK signs provoked a genre of jokes and cartoons probably unequaled since the "tin lizzies" mass produced by Henry Ford. Levity in such a matter made only insignificant forays into company installations. Once in a while, someone would put one of the signs on the inside of a toilet door, and pencil a comma and an adverbial "too" after it.

Translations of the word were converted into THINK signs in overseas outposts as well, and scatalogical inferences were in rare instances applied to them. At higher management levels, a privileged personage would sometimes discard the sign itself and reflect instead upon a reproduction of Auguste Rodin's famed sculpture "The Thinker," perhaps unaware that the sculpture of a powerful, muscled nude male was Rodin's concept of a man in despair confronting "The Gates of Hell." In any case, sculpted representations of this sort did not make their appearance until the reign of Watson's son Tom.

A memorable but little known instance of irreverence on the THINK business occurred at the IBM Owego center for space and related computer research. Wernher von Braun, the ex-German rocket authority, once visited the facility with an elite group of both American and European physicists, mathematicians, and scholars. As they proceeded from laboratory to design center, meeting their hosts, they got to the office of an important figure who was on leave from other work and attached to a classified research program then in progress.

Discussions in two or three languages were going on quietly in the large room when an eastern European physicist, looking at the desk sign, began to laugh loudly; others joined in the merriment until the place was in something of an uproar.

The letters of the sign were printed in an imitation of the Teutonic or Gutenberg style, and the word itself was a Russian translation of the English word that constitutes both the verb and the noun relating to defecation. As the amused visitors departed down a corridor, some were heard discussing with more heat than thought the nuances and variants of meaning commonly attributable to the four-letter word when prefixed with either "bull" or "horse."

The scholarly administrator who had brought the sign with him to the research center, being only temporarily attached to the operation, left sometime later to become president of a prestigious Eastern university, and his linguistic *objet d'art* left with him. In its original form, unsullied by alien infection, THINK has retained its preeminent place in the traditions of IBM.

Watson spoke of the virtue of loyalty often, and defined it repeatedly, emphatically so when addressing himself to new company recruits. He felt that employment at IBM was not solely a job, but a life commitment. The company was, similarly, engaged not only in operating and expanding a business, but propagating a faith, setting a standard and an example of industrial morality, and demonstrating in action the premise that prosperity was an open doorway to human happiness. Thus, a man who was loyal to the company, or to its vision of itself, transcended mere allegiance to a commercial enterprise.

Taking to the company's publications, Watson declared unequivocally to IBM employees, presumably including the luckless pariahs who had not even achieved their quotas, "If you are loyal, you are successful." Work was "raised to the plane of art," he said, "when love for the task, loyalty, is fused with effort. Loyalty is the great lubricant of life."

In what could have been misinterpreted, by those who could not carefully pick their way, as a slur on THINK, Watson said, "loyalty saves the wear and tear of making daily decisions as to what is best to do." Thus if loyalty was sufficiently developed and inclusive, the necessity for thinking might diminish. Whatever ambiguity and contradiction characterized this philosophy, thousands of people in Watson's employ were intensely, unremittingly loyal to him and the company. They neither quailed nor equivocated, apparently, even under the image of a glorious death which he conveyed.

"The man who is loyal to his work is not wrung nor perplexed by doubts, he sticks to the ship, and if the ship founders, he goes down like a hero with colors flying at the masthead and the band playing."

Without pausing to reflect on where or what the doomed ship's band might be playing at such a moment, Watson reiterated the theme: "Joining a company is an act that calls for absolute loyalty. . . ."

The absolutes, the verities, and the vague content of the IBM faith were firmly established in those first fifteen years or so. The corporation grew and prospered as the Watson personality and the well-behaved cult over which he held dominion extended across the land, across the oceans and into enclaves of other nations east and west, southward to Latin American cities. Important people began to notice him and court his counsel, which he gave with sincerity and dignity—at times as though, in his early fifties, he himself was in awe of the mystic forces responding to his relentless will.

He was admired, respected, and praised, and a disciplined army of capable sycophants catered to him with the fervor and competitiveness of subjects recognizing a sovereign personage: his nod of approval elevated their status in the corporate kingdom; his princess in marriage brought the dowry of a seat by the throne; his favor, a dukedom in a subsidiary company; his disdain, exile; his anger, oblivion; his enmity, loss of one's head. All that was desirable or detestable among men of his company was his to disburse, to bestow, or to withhold.

To Watson men yielded up their right to be different, to question the system that embraced them, engulfed them, rounded off the outlines of their diversity until they became nearly identical reflections in a corporate mirror. They were semi-citizens; by their own consent, they submerged their individuality in a collective society that, in disbursing the rewards of collective effort, altered the meaning of freedom. The quest for success and security was a goal in itself, made possible by the application of men's resources, energy, and personality to the job, to the Company, to that special world of Watson, THINK, and IBM.

In a modern industrial democracy, where freedom, diversity, and initiative were said to be exalted, where dissent and controversy were constitutionally welcomed in the resolvement of ideology, where that cherished uniqueness of each person was to have been tolerated, Watson had fashioned a separate domain in which enthusiastic and agreeable human beings cheerfully, energetically, unquestioningly, yielded to the discipline, the rigors, and the alluring promise of white collar serfdom.

In building his domain Watson owed much to the intuitive, proprietary assistance of Jeannette Watson, who expeditiously produced their four children in five years, and thereafter served much of the time as matron saint of the company, which they both viewed as an extension of their own household and family.

After Thomas Junior, came Jane, then Helen, and the youngest, Arthur Kittredge Watson, nicknamed Dick. Jane married John Irwin II in 1949, and Helen married Walker G. Bruckner. Both husbands, long in the inner circle of the company, have prospered. Mr. Bruckner has been a director of the company for many years. Mr. Irwin served as a director of the World Trade Corporation; he has also served as deputy and assistant secretary in the Defense Department, and is a well-known New York clubman (Links, Century, Metropolitan, among others) and upper echelon lawyer with partnership service in several leading Manhattan firms.

Arthur (Dick) Watson specialized in the overseas development of the company and has long remained a power, a step or two behind his brother Tom, in the corporation. The third generation, the children of Tom, Jane, Helen, and Arthur, have not yet appeared in corporate court circles.

By the time the second child, Jane, was born, the Watsons had moved from their Eighty-Fifth Street apartment in Manhattan to the correct and appropriately sheltered exurban community of Short Hills, New Jersey, populated largely by "downtown men," commuters to the Wall Street financial district, the shipping, commodity, and trading centers of lower Manhattan. Even the name, Short Hills, had a ring of continuity in it for the Watsons. In Dayton, Patterson's place was called Far Hills. The NCR country club was called Hills and Dales. When Watson shortly thereafter acquired a thousand-acre farm and estate thirty miles away in New Jersey, he named it Hills and Dales, too.

Watson enjoyed the five-acre place at Short Hills at times—when he could release the springs of tension that bound him to the business. He merged his two families—the clan and his own household—for great gatherings: his sisters, who with his mother had provided him with the "supervision" he said he needed in youth; their husbands, all but one brought into the company; and cousins, aunts, uncles, and their families, quite literally by the dozens. Watson was the patriarch, at home and afield.

Alone with his children, according to the company biography, he regaled them, a large and somewhat portly man by that time, by masquerading in his wife's clothes and hats, and making up games. More often, he was curt and unforgiving, expecting too much of them. This irreconcilable contradiction—the rare moments of playfulness and skylarking, with prolonged periods of stern demands—left its mark on the boys. Not until Thomas Watson relinquished most of his management prerogatives to his older son did the symptoms of distress that affected the boys in the presence of their father disappear. The girls, while remaining always *of* the company (unlike the boys, who were both *of* and *in* it), were spared the disturbing feeling of fear of their father, and looked upon him as a seraph, one of the worshipful celestial beings of whom they sang in the fashionable Episcopal Church in Short Hills which Watson had joined. Jane Watson was quoted once in a tribute to him in which she used the endearing words *My Joy* as a substitute for *father:* "I am so thankful that God gave me such a wonderful My Joy and am so glad to know and be sure that you are the very best man and father in the whole wide world."

By the time young Tom was five years old, he was taken to a sales convention, and by the time he was twelve he was on the program, making a short speech on salesmanship, which his father thought was very good. The boy was sent to schools around his Short Hills home and emerged from the Hun School, noted for its strict no-nonsense regimen.

The children accompanied their parents abroad from time to time, sometimes to stay with nurses in England if the entourage was traveling, but staying at hotels on the Continent, too, when not in school. One daughter was presented at the Court of St. James, looking solemn and timid in white lamé. Watson himself, in the thirties, was honored at the first levee held by King George after his coronation. A period-piece photograph of that event shows him in gaitered costume, a row of cherished decorations swinging, all in a row, across his left breast, following soberly behind a strutting guardsman across the historic palace yard. Although identified in one local newspaper as "Thomas J. Watson, former Rochester resident and president of IBM," Watson looked exactly enough like an old Scot, at long last acknowledged by the King, to be quite in character. Having one's daughter presented at Court was, for many affluent and properly connected families, the epitome of social recognition in the post-Depression years in the United States. Watson rose to eminence largely along the industrial, rather than the social, route, and the granting of royal audiences to a father and daughter in the same family constituted that special added touch of distinction that Watson, while taking it for granted with studied humility, deeply loved.

Watson sought such honors, along with any other form or manifestation of recognition, so assiduously—and received a good many without having to bid, however discreetly, for them—that he very possibly stands as the all-time record holder for a non-academic, non-royal personage. Only the U.S. armed services, the International Rotary Clubs and the United Nations are represented in more countries than IBM, and only IBM had a well-oiled, pretested plan for bringing the honors-and-decorations grantors of so many countries into conjunction with its receptive and appreciative leader. Those overseas IBM representatives who grasped fully both the family and the international concept of the IBM style did not have to be directed, first discreetly, then perseveringly if necessary, to pursue possibilities for paying homage to the man who translated THINK into an international symbol.

The focus of virtually all adulation and flattery from the outside world toward the company was on Watson himself. Managers and associates who failed to accept and comprehend this understood neither the nuances of the milieu nor the uncodified, but nevertheless unrelenting, demands of the man. When Watson himself spoke of the company, seeing its future, enumerating its difficulties, it was an exercise in self-analysis. Grammatically, and in print, he spoke of the company in the conventional third person. But IBM was synonymous with first person usage: IBM was "I" to Watson, and in the collective, it was "the family."

Where religious concepts in the world have called for a belief in immortality, doubters have long consoled themselves with the thought of living through their sons and daughters, and beyond them, through their progeny. When Watson spoke of "living forever," it was IBM he was talking about. His vision of immortality was, like the Lord's, in the house he had built; in the materialistic edifice of IBM which, in his narrow but towering faith, was ordained to endure through eternity.

Old Watson's spirit remains lively at IBM, not so much revered overtly as embodied in the edifice. Photographs, statuary, and portraits of Watson abound, the THINK sign as ubiquitous as the crucifix in a convent. Among the great laboratories and research centers, often theatrically lighted in the night like shrines; among the temple factories, with architecture and style a tribute to all that is modern, engineered, aseptic, profitable, respectable; among the soundless computers, amorally yielding through aroused circuits and semi-conductors to the magnetic seduction of a priesthood of physicists and programmers, guessing at and guiding man's destiny—among all these the iconography is a reminder of their creator.

And in all of this there is veneration for the Spirit of IBM, as it is called, which is *there*, everywhere, in the lengthened shadow of Thomas J. Watson, in His Presence, as in the spirit present in the Eucharist, in the Host.

6.
Our
Father
in
Heaven

In THE TWILIGHT OF the twenties, Watson was emerging as a national figure on the industrial scene, and had become one of the highest paid people in America. Calvin Coolidge had retired to Northampton, Massachusetts, having chosen not to run for a second term as President of the United States, content with fame as modest as any that had accrued to a man in that office. He had been thrust into the limelight and the Vice-presidency by publicity and accolades after crushing a Boston police strike; he subsided to become the subject of tolerant amusement for his simple explanations of public issues, such as his observation that unemployment was the result of a good many people being out of work.

Watson responded warmly and with admiration to the way Coolidge "quietly and unobtrusively" conducted his life, and in a eulogy at the time of the death of the "elder statesman," paid him a glowing tribute. Coolidge had, Watson said, "contributed something of stability to the daily scene," the scene itself covering the predepression years when stability was an illusion. "He will go down in history as one of our great presidents," Watson predicted, citing "his ancestral heritage of straight thinking. The ideals for which he stood will live on forever. Young men should take time to study the life, and particularly the habit of thought and judgment of Mr. Coolidge. In them they will find much on which to pattern their own lives, their own thoughts and judgments. The more closely they can approximate them, the more satisfactory their lives will be to themselves and the more valuable to the world in which they live."

Watson, for the record, was a Democrat whose partisanship, a legacy from his own father, was so cautiously guarded as to be practically inaudible. His politically impartial praise, first of Coolidge, and

105

next of his successor Herbert Hoover, were more nearly expressions of tribute to their style and probity than of party denial. The fact was that Watson was apolitical; he identified with authority and the repositories of power regardless of party. He placed his name and influence on the line with respect to his own party label only after the Democratic nominee Franklin Delano Roosevelt was elected; and he went all the way to the opposing Republican Party by unequivocally supporting Dwight D. Eisenhower from the beginning of his foray into politics. On matters of tariff and trade, he was, not surprisingly for a man who manufactured and sold his merchandise all over the world, a liberal. In all other respects he was a nonpolitical conservative in the era between Roosevelts.

His unqualified admiration for Coolidge and Hoover seemed to stifle any prescience he might have possessed to sense the crash and the depression that closed out the decade and that nearly ripped the nation asunder. He was far from alone, of course, as few businessmen of note detected the danger. His antenna for spotting any trend contrary to economic growth in general, as differentiated from the expanding development of IBM in particular, had never been reliable, even after the lessons learned in the post-World-War panic. Looking back, one suspects that, economically—other than his comprehensive knowledge of his own company—he scarcely knew what he was talking about.

Ten months before the stock market debacle of 1929, Watson's confidence was undiminished. He foresaw continued prosperity with the same optimism that led him to expect "normal" economic conditions to be reestablished in a "reasonable" length of time during the first two years of the Depression.

Watson's response to the Great Depression was on two separate levels: in the interests of his own company, he resorted to the most intensified selling effort he had ever undertaken; in his growing role as a spokesman and statesman of industry, he explained its causes with a good deal of elemental and foolish reasoning.

It was the low and sorrowful ebb of a dangerous time, which Watson said had come about "because of lack of education." The Depression had come in spite of his predictions of prosperity, and it was prolonged in spite of his analysis that it would be of short duration. The fact that no "meeting of five men could agree on what caused the present state of things," was, to Watson, "proof of our lack of knowledge . . . lack of education." Of course, lack of confidence was both a cause and a result, and poor selling had been responsible, too, he said, along with too much "mass thinking" instead of constructive individual thinking.

In the press and over the air, Watson took issue with criticism of President Hoover, and defended him against charges that he had not moved quickly or effectively enough to halt the disastrous decline. Neither Mr. Hoover nor American business leadership, said Watson, could be fairly blamed for the wreckage, for the increasing poverty and despair among Americans. There was not, in fact, much wrong that better salesmanship and more straight thinking couldn't repair. "The dance of the millions," he said, was over, and a reliance on the old virtues, harder work, and rugged individualism was called for. He expressed his usual confidence, which paralleled Hoover's promise that prosperity was around the corner, with a car in every garage and a chicken in every pot.

Watson remained assured and hopeful, with his vision of a truly international business in every land. When the great German lighter-than-air ship, the Graf Zeppelin, arrived in America on a flight from Brazil, he saw it as a portent of a new commercial transport system for moving passengers and freight in large volume at high speed. He praised the airship's crew and their commander, Dr. Hugo Eckener, and was especially charmed that his own IBM manager in Brazil, Valentim F. Boucas, whom he had personally hired, had had the foresight to sign on the flight as one of its twenty passengers. It was a demonstration of "the pioneer spirit" on the part of Mr. Boucas and the science of aeronautics.

Watson went off on a business tour of Europe, where his men were spared the "handicap" of melancholy conditions. There was "more gloom in New York than anywhere else," and the IBM sales convention in the ancient city of Florence renewed his enthusiasm. He commended the Italian organization as "pioneers" of the true spirit, too.

"I want to pay tribute this morning to your great leader, Benito Mussolini," he told the pioneers. "I have followed the details of his work very carefully since he assumed leadership. Evidence of his leadership can be seen on all sides. The thought came into my mind that your Mussolini is a pioneer. Under his leadership, Italy, one of the oldest of all countries, is showing signs of becoming a very new country. I feel that the present generation in Italy is going to benefit greatly as a result of the pioneering work of your leader, Mussolini."

And, again, he saw a common equation linking the new Italy and IBM:

"One thing which has greatly impressed me in connection with his leadership is the loyalty displayed by the people. To have the loyalty and cooperation of everyone means progress and ultimate success for a nation or for an individual business. I feel that you in Italy, as we in other countries, should pay tribute to Mussolini for having established this spirit of loyal support and cooperation."

Enthusiasm and evidence of commitment, of loyalty, tricked Watson, who placed excessive emphasis on image and pretension, to the exclusion of ugly reality that might be obscured beneath it. He was, of course, not an evil man himself, and if he sensed the presence of evil as he understood it, he condemned it without compromise. His flattery of the most flamboyant and egotistical dictator in postwar Europe was a common enough failing among leaders whose vision was clouded by vested interest.

When he returned to New York and its gloom, he reported that IBM itself, in spite of the national economic decline, was doing well. As for the Depression, he said it "had nothing to do with our business; we have no right to talk or think pessimism, because the first eight months of this year have been better than the corresponding period of any year in the history of the business."

Yet the pull of the depression was inexorable, so great that in spite of IBM's expanding sales, and in contradiction to general conditions, its stock rode downward with the bears, totaling a fall of 202 points by 1932, the lowest in eleven years.

Watson was, virtually from the moment of Hoover's departure, a devoted supporter of Roosevelt and the New Deal. With the passage of the National Recovery Act and social security legislation, American business was swamped with mandated bookkeeping and data-recording operations. IBM machines were leased to government agencies in increasing volume, and to business and industrial companies who required them to comply with federal demands for information on which welfare, NRA codes, and public works projects were dependent. The government became, in time, Watson's largest customer. When the depression was at its depth, and after NRA codes were established to stabilize prices and thus prevent ruinous decline, a new engineering laboratory and a school were built at Endicott. Wages were increased 17.8 per cent on the average at IBM, and at long last all subsidiary companies were consolidated into a single vast corporate operation. Production was started on a newly designed alphabetic tabulator, and new equipment included a bank proof machine for sorting, listing, and totaling checks. Electromatic Typewriters, Inc., a Rochester concern, was bought out in 1933, primarily to get important patents safely into IBM hands, and the Dayton scale division was sold to Hobart Manufacturing Company in exchange for stock. By 1935, Watson had paid off the mortgage of $187,500 on his building at 310 Fifth Avenue, and a year later IBM moved into its World Headquarters Building, still standing at 590 Madison Avenue, adorned with the printed slogan, "World Peace Through World Trade."

When, under Roosevelt, diplomatic relations with the Bolsheviks were established, Watson helped deflect some of the bitter criticism that engulfed FDR who, it was charged by zealots among others, had set in motion Communist Russia's conspiratorial machinery against the United States. Roosevelt and Watson met many times, both in Washington and at Hyde Park, where Mr. and Mrs. Watson went for tea and talk.

In November of 1933 when Maxim Litvinov, at Roosevelt's invitation, arrived on the liner *United States* for nine days of historic conferences, Watson welcomed the event. William E. Leuchtenburg, a professor of history at Columbia University, has noted that "the President drew strength from businessmen in the newer industries . . . typified by Thomas Watson, whose IBM flourished in the nineteen thirties."[1]

After an exchange of eleven letters and one memorandum between representatives of the U.S. and Soviet governments, signifying the restoration of diplomatic relations, Watson spoke at a farewell dinner for Litvinov at the Waldorf-Astoria Hotel in New York. On hand with the diplomats for the festivities were executives of the House of Morgan, the Chase National Bank, the Pennsylvania Railroad, and other converted titans of finance and industry. Acknowledging the fact that something less than national unanimity greeted the re-entry of Russia into America's sphere of non-Communist influence, Watson urged every American to "refrain from making any criticism of the present form of Government adopted by Russia."

Many leading businessmen winced, and some of the more viscerally reactive editorial writers howled, but as President of the American Chamber of Commerce, Watson was listened to. He was ushered into the councils of the Chamber by Willis Booth, an IBM director and adviser to Charles Flint. Booth was the first president of the U.S. Chamber and later president of the New York Merchants Association, and Watson followed him in both posts. Watson thought the International Chamber of Commerce was "in harmony with the basic laws of the universe." He became president of that, too, in 1937.

Roosevelt appreciated Watson, and obliged him by sending messages to his sales conventions. Acknowledging Watson's readiness to play host to international dignitaries, a ceremonial obligation he fulfilled with pride that could approach pomposity, Roosevelt once said that he took care of such matters in Washington, but in New York, it was Watson's work.

Watson fought so hard in defending Roosevelt's policies, including deficit spending (although he later disagreed with the President's plan to increase the size of the Supreme Court by "packing" it), that Roosevelt

[1] *Franklin D. Roosevelt and the New Deal*, New York, 1963.

was ready by the end of his first term to appoint him Secretary of Commerce or even, it was said, Ambassador to the Court of St. James. These offers were declined, but Watson wrote Roosevelt, sometimes twice a week, urging him to promote harmony and confidence by instituting a good neighbor policy with business. Watson agreed with Roosevelt that business should be well regulated, but he wanted it well treated, too. FDR said he would go halfway, that he would try, but not much came of it. The showmanship and emotional appeal of his "soak the rich" pretensions were irresistible to Roosevelt, who enjoyed himself hugely in the role of an alleged traitor to his class, without causing any real pain to the heavily affluent. The business community was overtly leery of the New Deal, nevertheless, and the literature of the period was burdened with predictions that FDR was destroying the capitalistic system.

When Watson went to Rochester to address employees of the newly acquired Electromatic Typewriter Division (an acquisition which brought the total number of IBM employees to more than 8000), he told them, first, that the company had even more advanced ideas in mind than "the typewriter proposition," then launched into a spirited defense of the much maligned National Recovery Act and President Roosevelt. "We must do something to help them," he said. "We have no right to think or talk of the NRA failing. It is not going to fail."

He ordered company employees to take part in NRA parades, and the IBM press became a thunderous propaganda organ in support of business cooperation with the agency FDR and the Congress had set up to cure the great depression. Issues of *Business Machines* were devoted to it. The issue of September 29, 1933, for example, displayed the NRA symbol, an eagle clutching a bolt of lightning, and proclaimed, "We Do Our Part." The edition also contained a glowing report of a successful sales promotion project called World Wide Banner Month for Vice-president Fred W. Nichol, in which all those salesmen who went over their quotas for the month had their names inscribed on a large banner, to be presented to Mr. Nichol. It had generated a good deal of enthusiasm and was appropriate material for publication beside the other project that needed enthusiasm, the NRA.

A photograph eight columns wide and nine inches deep showed four hundred persons assembled at a Chamber of Commerce testimonial dinner to Watson, as a prelude to a Better Times Parade. Other photos showed an IBM color guard leading the procession, flanked by Marine Corps Reserve men of New York State. Marching between flags was Mr. Arnold Meyers, thirty-eight years with IBM, a salesman assigned to Rochester, who had sold his first computing scale in Chicago in 1895. The

IBM factory band, transported from Endicott, was "loudly in evidence," and the "head of the marchers, resplendent in new uniforms, certainly knew his stuff," said the caption. "The band marched with pep and precision and furnished inspiration with its lengthy repertoire of martial music, and playing its own IBM song, 'Ever Onward.'"

Fred W. Nichol's banner was filled with names, and IBM's sales contest was a success. In Roosevelt's first term, the company hired an abundance of salesmen, put them through training schools that became increasingly explicit in hard-sell techniques, including body blocks and sleight-of-hand for use in tabulating machine demonstrations that might go awry. The sales and training projects were a little more, and a little less, than the somewhat rounded, lofty "education" programs designed for IBM by Dr. Ben Wood, a Columbia University educator who had become a consultant for Watson.

Salesmen were dismissed when, flawed in character or manner, they did not meet the quotas, which were usually established at a point just higher than that imposed on predecessors.

Even so, decimated ranks performed better. The legend of Henri Christophe, who led a rebellion of blacks in Haiti in 1815, came to one writer's mind in looking back on IBM methods of motivating salesmen. Christophe's way of encouraging men to their limits, when they were commanded to drag impossibly heavy boulders to a mountain top to build a fortress, was to shoot every tenth man in a line. The survivors were sufficiently motivated, so the unlikely legend allows, to get the stones up the hill.

Watson's salesmen pushed their sales records upward for Watson and IBM. The company itself was substantially assisted when what looked like something of a mistake on Watson's part turned out to be, in confirmation of his faith, an act of profitable foresight. Against advice, he had ordered the tabulating factory to remain in full production, building up dangerously overloaded inventories for a time. The oversupply went into storage and was thus readily available to meet stringent delivery commitments when the government contracts began to come in.

As the depression eased off in Roosevelt's second term, Watson was training salesmen in lots of fifty at Endicott. Screened for manners and appearance, they arrived in the rolling, green Valley of Opportunity, as the company press called it, or the Valley of Tears, as it was said to be for the unsuccessful. Before The Homestead, the company's plush and spacious hostelry adjoining the IBM Country Club, was built, the men stayed in double bedrooms at the Frederick Hotel, were served three meals a day, and were paid seventy-five dollars a month. As graduate junior salesmen, with an assigned territory and quota, they could expect $150 a month, plus a 20 per cent commission on new business. Some might make $5000 in a year, with senior salesmen going as high as eight to ten thousand. The top few men of the One Hundred Percent Club who consistently stayed there and generated a volume of new business could reach $25,000. Those who did not make the Hundred Percent Club in three years were generally eased out, although IBM brass might help them find other jobs to avoid the onus of former company men going on the dole.

The fledgling salesmen punched time clocks on the way in and out of classrooms, wore white shirts with stiff starched collars and uniformly dark suits. They smoked on the sly—it was not expressly forbidden—and never in Watson's presence. They could be dismissed instantly if seen in a beer tavern, which Watson never had the power to close only because the Endicott-Johnson management and the shoe workers wouldn't go along with him.

The education of salesmen included visits to the factories where they assimilated facts about the accounting machines, with 55,000 parts, 75 miles of wire, and a capability of printing calculations and adding long columns of figures from ten to a hundred times faster than a clerical worker could. There were many different models of machines to be studied, with scores of functions. In fact, New York's irrepressible Mayor Fiorello LaGuardia, addressing a throng of 40,000 at an IBM Day observance at the 1939–40 World's Fair, observed with just the suggestion of a roguish leer:

"Mr. Watson's machines will do everything but kiss your wife—and for all I know, they may even do that."

A photograph of an assembled class of the period shows the earnest young men at six rows of identical tables, seated in identical posture, dressed exactly alike, each bent forward slightly, writing on single sheets of white paper placed in the same precisely measured position, pencils poised as in an old Palmer Method handwriting class. Like the Rockettes at Rockefeller Center, they appeared even to be the same size. The sole relief from sameness in the assembled class was provided by one trainee writing left-handed.

They were taught, in simulated real-life demonstrations, to wire the machines' removable plugboards, which could be quite complicated. Sometimes there were pitfalls. Students were mortified at one graduation ceremony when a runaway calculator produced totals off by several million because the machine was improperly plugged. To prepare for such failures on the job itself, they rehearsed, as part of their training, shielding a machine with their bodies, using diversionary motions, always speaking calmly, talking directly to a customer, fixing him with a glance so that his eyes would not wander. If a run of punch cards fouled up, the salesman would direct the attention of the customer to the plugboard and explain "how easy" it was. With an opportunity to correct the operation of the machine, the customer was invited to lend a hand: "Now, you try it." People were generally fascinated by the machinery. Courses in public speaking gave the men assurance.

The basic rental installation was three machines—a key punch, a card sorter, and a tabulator—with accessory equipment providing innumerable variations of work performed. And while customer engineers (installation men) set up machines that were sold, the salesmen left Endicott with a good deal of knowledge about the equipment and ringing admonitions to learn everything possible about the details of business operations in offices they called on.

Worldly wise men were summoned back from the field for additional training. Made imperfect, perhaps, by the crudities of the world, and in need of relaxation from the disciplines at Endicott, they sometimes fell from grace. One group, returning by train to New York at night aboard a parlor and bar car and believing themselves to be beyond the range of supervision, got to drinking and roistering en route. Some were observed, by unexpected supervision which met the train on its arrival in Jersey City, to be weaving along the platform, and an unrevealed number of them, possibly ten or twelve, were fired. It was an impressive lesson for all who remained.

In school and out—at meetings, conventions, company ceremonies, and banquets—the men sang songs. Watson was vitally interested in the songs and their lyrics and would, after attending a musical show in New York, get permission to incorporate some favored number into the IBM repertoire, with suitable new lyrics. IBM songbooks were printed by the thousands, revised, and reprinted. They virtually disappeared in later years when, under the reign of Thomas Watson, Junior, a management self-conscious about requiring men to sing corny company praise withdrew all that could be found. It was a serious and effective operation; the songbooks even seemed to disappear from libraries, possibly because they were not considered worth preserving.

First of all, there was the company anthem, "Ever Onward," listed in an early songbook from the thirties as "written especially for the International Business Machines Corporation." There were two choruses and one verse:

There's a thrill in store for all,
For we're about to toast
The corporation in every land.
We're here to cheer each pioneer
And also proudly boast
Of that "man of men," our friend and guiding hand.
The name of T. J. Watson means a courage none can stem:
And we feel honored to be here to toast the "I B M."

Chorus

EVER ONWARD—EVER ONWARD!
That's the spirit that has brought us fame!
We're big, but bigger we will be,
We can't fail for all can see
That to serve humanity has been our aim!
Our products now are known in every zone.
Our reputation sparkles like a gem!
We've fought our way through—and new
Fields we're sure to conquer too
For the E V E R   O N W A R D   I B M.

Second Chorus

EVER ONWARD—EVER ONWARD!
We're bound for the top never to fall!
Right here and now we thankfully
Pledge sincerest loyalty
To the corporation that's the best for all!
Our leaders we revere, and while we're here
Let's show the world just what we think of them!
So let us sing, men! SING, MEN!
Once or twice then sing again
For the E V E R   O N W A R D   I B M.

Almost without exception, the songs were music of adoration to Watson himself, or expressions of pride and hope in the company, whose success was an extension of his image. The exceptions were those which served simply to bind men together, such as the IBM SCHOOL SONG:

First Verse
Working with the men in the Lab.,
Backing up the men in the field,
Behind each one in the factory,
To a peer we'll never yield.

Our Father in Heaven

Chorus
In every phase of IBM
Our record stands for all to see
The Alma Mater of the men
Who serve the world's best company.
To everyone who's enter'd here,
A memory will long remain—
We build, we work together
To a world acclaim!

Second Verse
Customer and Field Engineer
Men who build and those who sell,
Inspired by pioneers
We will ever serve you well!

Third Verse
With our sights on bigger records
With the training we receive,
With service as our watchword
Success we will achieve.

Fourth Verse
With Mr. Watson leading,
To greater heights we'll rise
And keep our IBM
Respected in all eyes.

Fifth Verse
Trained to make the finest tools
With the best machines in the world
Our apprentices are exceeding
Every challenge that is hurled!

Fred W. Nichol enjoyed an unduplicated status in the hierarchy as an indefatigable worker who, in 1909 at age seventeen, started as an aide and secretary to Watson at NCR and went along with him at the ousting. He was Watson's alter ego and cheerleader, a beanbag to be tossed about on occasion, an industrious and ever-present shadow. He not only admired Watson but seemed, through some arcane communications link, to have a direct connection to his central nervous system. For years, Watson scarcely noticed Nichol in any complimentary sense, but one day found him approaching indispensability. He guarded against this, never wanting the defection that occurred with Chalmers at NCR to be repeated at IBM. But Nichol grew on him with something like the attachment of a living parasite to its host. He extolled the Watson mystique with such fervor, and the company press interpreted his praise in such dissected detail, that he alone among IBM executives was allowed, after he became vice-president and a member of the board in the mid-thirties, to be separately praised in song. An account of Nichol's understanding of Watson's greatness in 1937 showed that Nichol was, with the help of the editorial writer, a spokesman for the doctrine. The piece was called "Our Bountiful Present—Brilliant Future":

Members of IBM who think constructively as they listen to a speaker or read his thoughts in *Business Machines* received considerable inspiration from the address of F. W. Nichol, IBM vice-president and general manager, at the opening session of the 1936 100 Percent Club convention. "It's a matter of common knowledge to all of us and it is a fact for which we should ever be grateful that our present is so bountiful and our future so brilliant because, since 1914, we have been led by a genius with a great heart," said Mr. Nichol as he spoke, not only to the assembly present but to a world-wide radio audience, including hundreds of potential sales leaders. And he added, "This man who leads us has very definitely created for us great opportunities which are ours."

This sort of exercise in explicitly telling IBM people what they *should* think won for Nichol a position as a Watson interpreter that was never equaled at IBM. It was also what won for him the right to be acclaimed in song. One such accolade was set to the tune of "Marching Through Georgia"; another, also martial in spirit, was in the tempo, or *almost* in the tempo of "Tramp, Tramp, Tramp, the Boys Are Marching":

> I B M is his delight
> Thinks it morning noon and night.
> He is always on the job and ever goes
> In the cause of I B M, etc. . . . .

> *Chorus*

> V.P. Nichol is a leader
> Working for the IBM.
> Years ago he started low,
> Up the ladder he did go.
> What an inspiration to our men!

Sometimes men infused with the IBM spirit, in school especially, would make up a song of their own. Thus Second Vice-president Charles Ogsbury, who was in charge of the training school and well liked for his disarming ability to engage in company humbug discourse without conveying the idea that he took it too seriously, was honored by a song set to the tune of "America the Beautiful." It was not in the songbook, and the words are now lost, but it began:

"Ogs—bureee, the Beautiful."

From far above Cayuga's waters, at Cornell University, came a tune, the words of which were not in print, which started: "Hail to thee, our Mister Watson, pride of the companee-eeee."

With the stiff doses of character building that were injected into the curriculum, the men relieved the dreariness with fifteen-minute morning songfests. When Watson was scheduled to put in an appearance, the sidewalks were cleared of ice and snow, if it was winter, and the place cleaned to perfection. The name of the headmaster of the sales school was, perhaps not unmeaningfully, Love—Charles E. Love, distinguished by his tousled, curly locks which would not lie down and behave in the preferred, neatly coiffed IBM fashion. Love would watch until Watson, a bit stiff-legged then—a sign of age, of course, but a motion that also suggested little exercise—hove into view. Love would issue a warning to get rid of all ash trays and cigarettes, smoking having been curtailed in advance to clear the room of fumes. As Watson stepped gravely into the room, the men would greet him with a chorus of "Pack up your troubles, Mister Watson's here—and smile, smile, smile."

The practice of ditching cigarettes when Watson came around was newly acquired among IBM people and had more or less naturally developed when word spread down the ranks that he had quit smoking. A lifelong smoker of cigars, he had always kept a favorite brand in a humidor on his desk and carried a few in his pocket. It was a habit that began in hotel lobbies and the smoking cars of railroad trains and continued through his years at NCR. He walked into Nichol's office one day and told him he would like to make a "deal" with him. If Nichol would agree not to smoke until noon each day, he wouldn't either.

The loyal Nichol was neatly roped in, and began to show late morning tension as he waited for the hour when he could snip the end off a cigar and light up. Watson seemed to find total abstinence easier to bear, or was more willing to bear it, than the rationing Nichol was stuck with in the uninvited deal. As far as IBM men knew, Watson never smoked again.

The veneration of the multitude was evoked now and then at some special banquet and award-presentation ceremony. In the amphitheater among the hills of the Country Club, song, orchestra, fireworks, oratory, and often a good deal of professional talent would be combined with company organization skills to effect that perfect harmony between the beloved patriarch and his venerators. Then, to read the official IBM account of such a momentous ritual was to sear it into one's memory.

Of banquets there were many, honoring different categories of workers. Some brought together for special honor as a group those individuals who, in the course of a year had received checks, or gold watches, or sets of candlesticks in commemoration of time served. Quarter Century Clubs were the most notable of this type. The company maintained accounts at Tiffany's and Georg Jensen's in Manhattan to supply the prizes.

But the One Hundred Percent Awards dinners were the most significant events. Membership in the club, continuously held out as a mark of status and accomplishment, not only conferred on those knighted the privileges of membership, but imposed on them the obligation to assert the privileges. A member was compelled to attend, and a nonmember couldn't. The privilege obliged a member to join the treks to New York, or Miami, or a Virginia resort, to participate in days, sometimes a week, of dinners, songs of praise, pep sessions, speeches, and award presentations. The last night of the convention was the major event; it was ceremonial, obligatory, social, and the presence of wives was no less required than that of their privileged husbands.

The banquet was carefully planned, and all was in order. Guests entering the ballroom of the Waldorf Astoria, for instance, might notice scalloped swaths of silk draped from balcony boxes reserved for noted personages, one often for Watson's old friends in Painted Post or officers of the Genesee Society, an organization of Rochester migrants who had departed for jobs in New York City.

The spirit of IBM was both auditory and visual, both absorbed and transmitted. Guests moved to tables set with place cards as an orchestra played "Ever Onward." From the wings to the beflowered dais came the notables and officials. First was Watson, followed by little Mrs. Watson and a sustained outbreak of applause. Behind them came Vice-president Fred Nichol ("Up the ladder he did go") and his wife, to applause that was somehow a shade lower on the decibel scale. Still standing, the assembly applauded the appearance of Mr. Ogsbury ("the Beautiful") with what seemed disproportionate vigor, considering his diminished position in the hierarchy, except that most salesmen remembered him from their company school days. As the applause dropped to a steady rhythm, lesser figures entered in single file, down, down the lengthening list. When the men and women on the dais were still, there was quiet, then a hush, the benediction, and the scuffle of chairs shifted into position.

After dessert, two hours of personal tributes followed in the form of three-minute speeches by men who had achieved some goal scheduled for acknowledgement. Plaques, cups, oil paintings would then be presented, some to one or the other of the Watsons. Watson would sometimes choke up at these presentations, his eyes shimmering with tears—even though he had previously inspected the inscription and approved the expenditure for engraving it. IBM people understood that the family father figure was no less responsive and no less sentimental over a gift offered by his children just because he had given them the money to buy it and discreetly supervised its selection as well.

Finally, the moment came for Watson's speech, which would call for staggering endurance reaching into the fifth hour. He spoke of optimism, of steadfastness, loyalty, and his and Mrs. Watson's pride in the IBM family; he acknowledged that he himself could not have achieved it all alone, without the spirit and the cooperation of the assembled; he referred with metallic sorrow—and sometimes with irritation—to men who had failed and were not there. He talked of his assistants, of the old days with Jack Range, of John H. Patterson, of his loneliness on the road, of virtue, decency, and the need to make money for one's family, of the limitless opportunities for all. In closing, he implored them to work more and more, harder and harder, "to enjoy more and more of all of this."

All of that ended with the stiffened assembly rising with some difficulty to hear the blessing, and with some of the wives valiantly struggling to remember the words, all would sing together, "Ever Onward."

Seldom did anything go wrong, but if it did, Watson would deal with it. At one such banquet the attention span of two or three men far in the back of the ballroom wavered, and they got to talking softly among themselves. Watson stopped speaking and coldly, at length, addressed himself to them, almost as though they were alone in the room.

"Now, you men there; I don't know what you're talking about, but you can't be listening. You are employees of this company, being paid to come here and listen and learn what your colleagues, and perhaps even I, have to teach you. I am not concerned whether you respect me or think I can tell you anything or not. I would be more concerned if you insult the speakers I am going to introduce to you. I can't understand how you could allow yourselves to do what you've been doing, even when I'm speaking. To men who follow me, it would be outrageous. I want you to understand that this company is going on forever. Unless you realize this, you do not belong in this company.

"As long as you gabble as you have done here, or if it occurs again, just remember the implications of what I've told you. You do not belong in a company that is a world institution that is going on forever."

Naturally that shut them up. Conceivably, it knocked out their power of speech for some time.

Although the IBM affairs claimed his dominant interest, Watson enjoyed the forum provided by other banquets, too. The Endicott Kiwanis Club tried to establish a local tradition, and succeeded briefly, by holding each year the Annual Thomas J. Watson Appreciation Dinner. The first one at the end of the thirties was a great success and was so reported in the newspapers. The second Appreciation Dinner was less successful in terms of output, but the expressions of praise seemed to increase in stridency. A veteran newspaperman who attended them all said it was not a lack of organization on the part of the community that militated against their continuance. "The praise was just so relentless," he reported, "that I thought the man should protest, or stay away until they toned it down." The Third Annual Thomas J. Watson Appreciation Dinner ended the cycle.

It was, in fact, when the praise was toned up, extended to flights beyond fancy, that these affairs were most successful. One of the best of that period was never forgotten. It was held at the end of the decade to commemorate Watson's 25th anniversary, not of the founding of the company, as eager chroniclers reported, but of his association with it.

These were the late precarious days of peace, when Franklin D. Roosevelt was running for an unprecedented third term as President, when Wendell Willkie, who espoused the dream of "One World or None" and who emerged from the American business community, was extinguishing "a flame that had been lighted for the second coming of Herbert Hoover."

It was a summer day in Endicott in 1940, and 120 separate white tents bloomed among the seven hundred acres around the Homestead and the IBM Country Club to house One Hundred Percent Club men summoned to the celebration. Encircling a huge circus tent, in which the club convention was held, the tents had running water, innerspring mattresses, carpeted floors, and were situated along paved walkways. At the end of one row of tents was a complete laundry and cleaning operation, also housed in a tent, to which the visiting men could dispatch the two white shirts and collars required to get through each long day.

Emotion, fed by the IBM spirit, had never run higher in the company, not solely because of the significance of the passing of a quarter of a century for Mr. Watson, but because recent events and a near tragedy had both warmed and distressed the IBM family.

Watson had decided to put on an IBM Day show at the New York World's Fair that a writer in 1940 described as "a kind of mass strength-through-joy celebration that would drown out the din of warring Europe." There was another small din that Watson wanted drowned out, too. He had received from Adolf Hitler a medal, the Order of Merit of the German Eagle with Star, created for "honoring foreign nationals who have made themselves deserving of the German Reich." Only the German Grand Cross possessed higher status. Watson had the decoration, an eight-pointed gold framed cross with a swastika on each point, pinned on him by Dr. Hjalmar Schacht, German minister of economics, when he went to Berlin in 1937 to accept the presidency, for a two-year term, of the International Chamber of Commerce. It was draped around his neck with a broad red ribbon bordered with black and white, and was accompanied by a six-pointed star pinned over the left breast.

Hitler received Watson privately and told him, "There is to be no war. No country wants war, no country can afford it. Certainly that is true of Germany." Watson said he was inspired with the simplicity and sincerity of Chancellor Hitler's expression and went off to the Chamber of Commerce sessions in the German Opera House, where the Reichstag met when, indeed, it met at all. Some 2500 delegates and visitors were on hand, including a contingent of ninety-five from the United States, led by Watson himself. Representatives from forty-two nations were present.

Watson sent a note of gratitude to Hitler for "truly splendid hospitality . . . you welcomed so many delegates in your own homes, I am convinced that such contacts can do much to strengthen the desire for friendly cooperation which is so necessary for our present needs. . . . We shall all return home carrying a deep and permanent impression of all done for our comfort and satisfaction during our stay in Berlin." He had not gone as far, in these politely circumspect statements, as he had with Mussolini, perhaps because he had been briefed by the United States Ambassador to Germany not to trust Hitler.

But intuition and subjective evaluations were, to Watson, tools of measurement, too, and facts allied to cold judgment could leave him unmoved. He was quite capable of seeing ability in men totally devoid of it, such as in certain suave and courteous Latins who enchanted him with their conservative dress and calculated deferential good manners. Hitler could be believed, not only on the grounds of his sincerity, but because Watson was naïvely confident that German businessmen, by enforcing a climate conducive to world trade, would hold him in check.

Concurrently, the IBM propaganda mechanism was revved up for peace. Framed signs proclaiming the word *Peace* appeared in offices and on desks of IBM people next to their THINK signs. Beneath "Peace" was a quotation of Watson's: "The men and women I have talked with are peace-minded, and personally I have no fear of a world war, if people will sincerely think and talk in terms of world peace . . . I suggest to the members of our corporation, wherever they may be located, that they help develop the same spirit of whole-hearted cooperation among nations that we have developed in our own organization."

Watson had, as an official of the International Chamber of Commerce and a trustee of the Carnegie Endowment for International Peace, organized the Committee for Economic Reconstruction, which was made up of economists of trading nations. With a budget of $50,000, they were at work on a plan for a more equitable distribution of raw materials and the rehabilitation of war-devastated and undeveloped economies. Watson felt that such compacts of business and trade leaders, in association with the Chamber of Commerce, could function where governments could not.

Roosevelt's previously warm regard for Watson changed into something of a chill. The President declined to send him a message to read before the big IBM Day observance at the New York World's Fair, where Fiorello LaGuardia made his remark about the extraordinarily diverse functions of IBM machines. Injured and pleading, Watson persisted, reminding FDR that he had always got similar messages in preceding years and that a failure to receive one now might be interpreted as a rift in their relationship that would handicap Watson in future efforts to be cooperative. Intervention on the part of others followed, and Watson obtained a perfunctory presidential message that settled the matter and put his relationship with Roosevelt on a reserved, formal basis thereafter.

When IBM Day dawned in New York, a dozen chartered trains brought 10,000 employees and their wives from the factory towns, and other trains carried them from offices throughout the land. Full page advertisements in the newspapers proclaimed, "They Are All Coming"— and they were. They were put up for three days in hotels; radio networks —the time paid for by IBM—broadcast the ceremonies at the fair, where Grace Moore and Lawrence Tibbett sang and Watson presided. Whole exhibits were bought out and opened, free of charge, to the IBM visitors. A special IBM World's Fair art exhibit with an array of awards attracted critical coverage, some of it grousing. But it was a great day for IBM and the power of public relations—except for a jarring, and nearly tragic, note.

One of the IBM special trains from Endicott, following a second at Port Jervis, New York, collided with it from the rear and sent fifteen hundred or more people piling atop one another in a barrage of broken windows and dislodged seats. About four hundred suffered lacerations and bruises, some of them being painfully hurt, none fatally. Within a half hour, Watson and his daughter Jane, joined by Fred Nichol, were on their way to the wreck, with Watson's command, "Keep this out of the newspapers," ringing in the ears of executives left behind. Suppression was, of course, impossible, and the next day the press reported Watson's statement that he had visited, in hospitals and elsewhere, every one of the injured.

He was in a towering rage at the IBM Day ceremonies for a while; executives of experience and subordinates interested in the continuity of life stayed so far out of range that some were invisible. Anyone he caught up with, whether he had anything to do with arranging the train trek to New York or not, heard from Watson a variation of John H. Patterson's uncompromising appraisal of a man out of favor: "There are two things wrong with you. Everything you say is wrong, and everything you do is wrong."

IBM Day was concluded with shattering fanfare, and Watson, jubilant by then, set off in another special train called the "Scientific Special" to repeat the performance at Treasure Island in San Francisco. The "Scientific Special" carried a number of engineers and technicians and their wives, as a reward for having completed certain training courses. With sales officials and guests, the band of travelers—all assigned to private rooms—numbered three hundred aboard the longest private railroad train ever dispatched over the western mountains. Watson did everything but operate the locomotives, and on one occasion was tempted to do that.

The trip was a nightmare for railroad dispatchers responsible for clearing tracks and keeping the train in transit. From New York to California, Watson ordered the train stopped to view the scenery, to confer with delegations boarding at depots along the way, and to receive garlands of flowers on the deck of the observation car.

Watson's sense of command seemed to soar generally when traveling, which he did as much as any businessman alive. It often took at least an IBM vice-president to make travel arrangements, for no ordinary traffic or reservations specialist could induce a railroad president to have a special train or car ready on a siding in the little time he frequently allowed. As far as Watson was personally concerned, Orville and Wilbur Wright had wasted their time in Dayton and at Kitty Hawk: he hated airplanes. Watson was a train man. On one trip to Europe, he demanded nineteen single berths on a train departing from Paris for Stockholm.

In the historic landmark building on Place Vendome, which he had bought for IBM's headquarters in France—and which horrified French authorities prevented him from replacing with something more in keeping with the modern company style—the company manager worked in desperation. Baron Christian de Waldner, "Mister IBM of France," had married into the Michelin tire family and was not without connections of his own. Moreover, he evoked deference in official quarters beyond Watson's reach. But to commandeer nineteen berths would require the addition of two railroad cars to the Stockholm train, the approval of the American and British occupation forces, and authorization from the French, German, Dutch, and Swedish government-owned railways.

Watson was not especially perturbed by these facts, although Count de Waldner, as IBM men called him, resorting to the most convincing argument at a royalist's command, explained that even when the King of Sweden, ill in Italy, had to be rushed to his homeland, emergency travel arrangements of the type demanded by Watson were impossible. It had been done for Henry Ford, said Watson, overlooking an intervening generation. M. de Waldner went to work and somehow produced an authorized travel plan approximating Watson's impossible requirements. By then, however, he decided to go instead to Bern, Switzerland, and the good Baron's maneuverings had to be undone.

When "Mister IBM of France" resigned two or three times after Watson's death, it was understandable that Arthur K. Watson, head of the IBM World Trade Corporation, made a quick trip or two to Paris to mollify and retrieve the company's most prestigious European manager.

"Why don't you just let him go?" an associate, relatively new to the corporation, asked Arthur Watson. The latter's solemn retort carried conviction: "But father *chose* him for the job! He had a lot of respect for that Count."

On the run from New York to San Francisco, the "Scientific Special" fell so far behind schedule that the engineer, obliged to outrun the high speed Santa Fe Chief back along the track, opened up the diesel sprays and highballed ahead. In the sumptuous observation car, one of the lady guests sensed the scenery disappearing with increased momentum and said something, which Watson overheard, about "just whizzing along." With traumatic scars from the Port Jervis wreck as yet unhealed, Watson shrieked for the conductor, who tried to calm him by explaining that the rail line's speed limit was still intact and that, what with the Santa Fe gaining on them and their own train being two hours late, any alternative to the present course was unseemly.

Watson made a move toward the emergency cord. "If you don't slow up this train, I'll pull it myself."

"You'll hurt somebody," said the conductor, with an added comment about the relationship between locked wheels and propelling bodies. He said he was boss of the train.

"Well, I'm paying for it," Watson shouted. "I'll have you fired."

The conductor restrained him. At the next stop, a cadre of executives and secretaries moved spiritedly to race the length of the train, each eager to convey some aspect of Watson's order to the engineer. That unruffled member of one of the most independent union brotherhoods in the country said he was not aware Mr. Watson was on the train, particularly since he had never heard of him. But Mr. Watson, it was explained, was president of IBM and ran the company. The engineer said he wasn't president of the railroad, but *he* ran the train.

The "Scientific Special" never did make up the time. It arrived in Los Angeles two hours late, where Watson was acclaimed and presented the Robert Dollar Award for his contribution to world trade. The party went on to Treasure Island where IBM Day drew a crowd even larger than the one in New York. They were entertained by Lawrence Tibbett and Lily Pons, whom Watson all but adored, and the San Francisco Symphony Orchestra. In an international broadcast, Watson made a final plea to Adolf Hitler to please abide by the Golden Rule.

The attention and publicity bestowed on Watson on both coasts, his world-wide radio broadcast in which he addressed himself to Hitler, and the excitement generated by the forthcoming twenty-fifth anniversary celebration put Watson into an appropriately solemn and reminiscent mood for that great event.

On the cropped grounds around the artfully designed tent city at Endicott, a vast bed of red tulips proclaimed THINK to a throng of fifteen thousand people who welcomed Watson back from his triumphs, his travail with trains, and his glory. Mayor Joseph H. Kelly opened the anniversary proceedings. Watson went before the Hundred Percent Club convention to unfurl a copy of his own chart used to illustrate his famous "The Man Factor" speech, first introduced a quarter of a century before, and to repeat the essence of that speech. The most complete and interpretive report of the anniversary event was published in a special issue of *Business Machines*, under the by-line of C.T.D. Spidell:

When Mr. Thos. J. Watson, President of IBM, rose to address the largest gathering of members of the IBM organization in its history, his voice shook with emotion despite his experience as a speaker before many groups throughout the world. He faced a vast sea of faces of men, women and children of IBM. Fifteen thousand people filled the great open air amphitheatre in the valley that nestled beneath the IBM Country Club. They sat upon the grassy slopes, they filled the veranda of the club, they were crowded upon the club roof, the surrounding hills overlooking the amphitheatre were dotted with parked cars of the huge overflow audience.

More than 700 acres of IBM property surrounded him. All about him were the buildings, the structures, the plant and equipment of IBM; the homes of more than 4,000 members of the Endicott organization. Gathered into the great audience were representatives of every division of the business, sales leaders in the cities from coast to coast and north to south, customer service representatives from offices throughout the United States who, with their wives, comprised a contingent of more than 1,200. Engineers, inventors, instructors, plant employees, executives from far off lands and members of other branches of the company. Pioneers of the past, present and future were there. In that audience were veterans who had been in the business a quarter of a century.

A fireworks display climaxed the day's events: "the IBM emblem broke out in signs against the sky that kept thousands spellbound at the close of the outdoor ceremony on the grounds of the Country Club." In one blazing explosion, the word THINK appeared in flares that lighted up the sky. Another pyrotechnic display spelled out in full, *International Business Machines.*

Thomas J. Watson closed the ceremony, when the flames and heat had died down, by saying that he was looking forward "with hope and prayer to our better future. . . . My solution is to revive the Golden Rule and instill it in every heart so that every man will do the right thing in dealing with his fellow men."

Fifteen thousand people at the twenty-fifth anniversary celebration heard the appeal for the revival of the Golden Rule, but Hitler did not. After that long spring and summer of traveling, IBM Days on two coasts, the invocation of the spirit, radio broadcasts calling for PEACE, and an unending barrage of slogans and propaganda, Hitler went on with his war of genocide and conquest.

By the end of the summer, Watson became increasingly uncomfortable about the Nazi decoration among his large collection of honors. No response was evoked from Hitler to his warning that the Nazis were making trade expansion between the two countries unlikely. No evidence developed to support his faith that the German business and world trade community would restrain the madman. Once more, his intuition had failed him; appearances, sincerity, constructive thinking, reliance on simple virtues and hard work, loyalty—all had been applied and exercised, and disillusion was the result. A few months after the anniversary celebration, he sent back the decoration to Hitler by registered mail.

He might have returned it earlier had he not so loved his honors and decorations. He was unembarrassed about seeking them, too. On one occasion, when a government of a little republic arranged to decorate him and was overthrown in a coup, he reminded the successor government of the earlier commitment, and it was fulfilled. More importantly, in the case of Hitler, he believed that demonstrations of goodness, and a sharing of the world's raw materials, would dissuade the Nazis. The dynamics of competition and conquest, which in business he grasped so well, eluded him in the Machiavellian scale of government. When mounting reports of barbarism and murder of Jews and Nazi dissidents reached him two years earlier, he might have returned Hitler's medal, but Secretary of State Cordell Hull, so the company said, had indicated that it might be construed as a precipitate act. Loss of the decoration seemed to make him gun-shy, for after the war he said he had sound and definite reasons for turning down an honor arranged for him by an unidentified "Communist" country.

The years of depression and the rise of Hitler in Europe were good years for Watson and IBM, regardless of a nasty anti-trust action brought by the Department of Justice that curbed the company's style and its claim on virtually all of the punch card market; regardless of the unpleasantness about the Nazi decoration; regardless of the death of the NRA in a Supreme Court ruling; and even regardless of a really wretched embarrassment about the amount of money he personally was making.

By 1939, the company's net income on gross sales of $41 million (at home and abroad) was $12 million. The following year, even with foreign sales heavily off, net income increased by more than two million on a gross of $46.5 million. U.S. and Canadian income taxes alone in 1940 were $3.7 million, and were tripled the following year.

For some years, beginning in 1934, the U.S. House Ways and Means Committee prepared and published the income of individuals paid $15,000 or more a year. In the first report, Watson led the country with $364,432, a fact not disclosed until two years later. A quarter of a million of the total was accounted for by Watson's contract, under which he received a share of the profits, after dividends and taxes, on top of his salary of $100,000. Watson was called to task on the matter at a meeting of stockholders and explained that sixty per cent of his income was lost to taxes.

"When I took charge of this company twenty-two years ago," he said, "it was agreed that if I could develop some new things I would receive a percentage of the money made. This agreement has been renewed several times, and today I draw a salary of $100,000, and get five percent of the net profits after dividends of $6 a share."

Watson's defensiveness about his own high earnings was doubtless influenced by his awareness that other leaders of business and industry had in the course of the depression years suffered, as he had not, from reduced income and even bankruptcy. Business failures were commonplace and devastating, and thousands of people in upper income brackets had been reduced to penury. In their biography, Mr. and Mrs. Belden reported that Watson was twice close to bankruptcy, even though his company's growth was uninterrupted and payment of dividends continued.

The depression was undoubtedly the cause of great anxiety for Watson personally, but at no time did his confidence and optimism become muted. Although IBM's stock fell perilously in the depression years, he owned only a small part of its shares. If he had secret fears that the national economic decline could carry him to ruin, it was never reflected in his manner or his interpretation of events of the period. The uses to which he put his large personal income remained largely his own business, and it was altogether possible that his personal resources were so closely tied to the company that, had it failed to grow each year, failed to show profits and dividends, bankruptcy would have become a possibility. The invisible records on such a matter remain invisible, but when companies were toppling, when banks failed to honor their deposits, when the country was nearly inert with poverty, Watson was its highest paid citizen and his lively and aggressive company seemed to remain, whatever dangers were hidden behind the annual reports and his own indomitable confidence, solvent and healthy.

Some of his old friends and colleagues were doing well, too, ranking favorably with motion picture and entertainment personages of the period. Second to Watson on the much publicized report was the humorist and entertainer Will Rogers, with $324,314; then came F. A. Courtway, president of Lever Brothers, who sometimes competed with Watson for preeminence in entertaining foreign dignitaries, $298,000; the actress, Janet Gaynor, with $252,538; Alfred P. Sloan, of General Motors, with $201,693; Walter P. Chrysler, $197,568; Richard H. Grant, a former colleague at NCR who had succeeded Watson as Patterson's sales manager before departing for General Motors, $114,096; William S. Knudsen and Charles F. Kettering, both auto production men, with $201,000 and $134,500 respectively.

Few things in his life upset Watson more than the question of his highest ranking salary; he was angry and defensive about it. When the minister of his church raised the question in a sermon on excessive remuneration in times of poverty and depression, Watson wrote him a letter expressing his testiness and quit the congregation. He was somewhat mollified when his friend and admirer, Nicholas Murray Butler, president of Columbia University, made a public speech rejecting the idea of any relationship between legitimate gain and morality. When the war came, Watson refused to allow his contract to apply to the production of defense goods, and even cut his percentage on other profits, but the skyrocketing growth of the company kept his income, as it had been for some years before the salary disclosures were made, at or near the top.

When IBM began to do business with the federal government, some of the company's own protective and lucrative practices exercised in conjunction with Remington-Rand, Inc., came under scrutiny. Sales policies of IBM, an arrangement between it and Remington-Rand, and the content of contracts between IBM and customers leasing its machines were areas of prolonged inquiry.

Under the Sherman Act and the Clayton Act, the government instituted its case against IBM within two weeks after Roosevelt took office and closed down the banks. Tabulating machines leased to federal agencies imposed upon them a requirement to buy the necessary punch cards, not on the open market, but from IBM. At the same time, IBM and Remington "combined to restrain commerce," as it was soon charged, "by entering into an agreement (1) not to sell machines, but to lease them on condition that the lessee purchase at fixed prices and use the tabulating cards made by lessor, or pay an additional rental for the machines, and (2) to sell cards only to lessees."

The agreement described in the charges was cancelled by stipulation before trial began, and Remington-Rand agreed to consent to any decree entered against IBM, which, at Watson's insistence, declined to settle the issues by consent procedures and elected to go to trial. IBM filed objections to some of the facts, as stipulated by the government, and the judge upheld its position. But on the main issues, Watson was caught and had to agree to desist "perpetually."

Both IBM and Remington-Rand had for years leased machines to the U.S. Bureau of the Census, but Watson's machines were electrically operated, while Rand's were mechanical. They included devices which performed tabulating, recording, calculating, and statistical work. In IBM machines, punch cards moved to a point in the machine where small electric brushes, through perforations in the cards, registered data.

In Rand's equipment, there were no such brushes; instead, small pins moved through the punched holes to produce the recording response.

The two companies made and owned "substantially all of such tabulating machines used in the United States by numerous business concerns, and by [the government]."

By the end of 1935, IBM had, said the court, 4,303 calculating machines, 4,106 sorting machines, and 8,412 punch machines in use in the United States. The company had under lease 85.7 per cent of all tabulating machines, 86.1 per cent of sorting machines, and 81.6 per cent of all the punches. As for the punch card market, IBM income from this source was $2.6 million in 1926 and rose to a high point of nearly $4 million.

The user of machines acquired only the right to use, not to possess, the equipment, and tie-in clauses in lease contracts obliged the user to buy IBM (and Remington) cards, although any producer could easily enough make them. "It is possible for others," the court decided, "to manufacture and sell satisfactory and usable tabulating cards." The manufacture of paper for the cards was, likewise, not subject to patents or secret processes. Nor did IBM restrict its paper stock suppliers except in the case of punch cards. Thus IBM and Remington had all of the card business at fixed prices.

The government itself paid no attention to the covenant, and the U.S. Printing Office made the punch cards on order and sold them to bureaus and agencies leasing IBM machines. It was, in fact, George H. Carter, then public printer for the United States, who instituted the first proceedings against IBM and Remington-Rand with the Federal Trade Commission, which declined to get into the case and refused to issue a complaint.

IBM alone made and sold about three billion cards a year, almost all of them sold unpunched to leaseholders of equipment. Remington, as an IBM competitor, was in the business under a mutual sufferance agreement. Each agreed not to "solicit business from any such user of the other party in the U.S. or Canada for cards, unless such user is a user of machines of both parties."

Watson's lawyers argued, as he did himself, that the "tying clauses" in the leases involved a "reasonable control of the commerce in cards." Any defect in the cards requiring such control might make maintenance of the machines annoying or difficult. However, the issue in court was whether competition was substantially lessened. The facts seemed to be that, outside of IBM and Remington—where the situation was mutually and satisfactorily stabilized—there wasn't *any*.

"Indeed, the more I think about the defendant's argument, the more I feel that it is merely an argument [of convenience], which in its essence stripped of all legal embroideries, could be addressed more effectively by [IBM salesmen] than by counsel for International to a court," said Judge John M. Woolsey.

There didn't seem to be even any competition between IBM and Remington-Rand, which might have normally evolved except for the fact it was neutralized by agreement. To terminate the arrangement, it was argued, would cause "disloyalties" among the buyers, who could shop around, but the court decided that such disloyalties would be transitory and that equipment users would "soon be safe back in the fold again."

The case dragged on throughout Roosevelt's first term, and the U.S. Supreme Court on April 27, 1936, upheld the government's case. Watson responded with more dignity but with not much more understanding than Patterson had done on more serious charges. What the government saw as restraint of trade and monopoly, Watson clearly thought was progress. He took the position that if the government didn't want to use his machines, they didn't have to rent them.

Although rankled and puzzled by a federally enforced morality that allowed others to profit in a business he felt he had built with risk, development, and superior service, and although IBM went on to challenge monopoly concepts twenty years later—and lost then, too—Watson was neither bent nor bowed. His optimism and confidence seemed eternally justified as the company, irrespective of its troubles, soared onward and upward.

He accepted his honorary degrees, accolades, government decorations; he made the same speeches in the same rooms, hundreds and hundreds of times, to successive assemblies of the same kind of people. Thousands learned the ceremonies and the rituals, and in song and pomp paid him homage, personal and laudatory in nature. It became, even with hyperbole and biblical allusions, impossible to overpraise him. His very thoughts, once uttered or printed, were dicta of deliverance, doctrine of belief. The extensive record of his fallibility was neither questioned nor, it may be surmised, critically mentioned.

It was not ordinary conceit that enabled him to endure the endless and profuse acclaim that might have suffocated one with the rudiments of a critical nature or a response to irony. He was, in the view of a scientist and non-IBM-oriented man who had joined the corporation, a man with the confidence of one who had been anointed by God; in addition he had a good and profitable product that, in becoming more profitable and more widely used, constantly confirmed his own view of himself. Thus it was not conceit, not vanity, not even his monumental self-centeredness that enabled him to abide it all.

To Watson, it was only his due. He did not see it as flattery, servility, sycophancy.

It was worship.

7.
To
the
Speed
of
Light

PERFORMANCE ON THE JOB was the first requirement for acceptance at IBM. It took priority over everything else, but once performance was established it imposed on the performer not only the right, but the obligation, to praise and worship the patriarchal leader, and to represent consciously the corporation to which a life commitment had been made. It meant becoming an expert in one's work, for to Watson an expert who could THINK constructively, who was loyal to the company, and who was neat, well groomed, calm, and courteous, was an educated man. Further interest in ballet, music, hobbies, useful reading, sports, and so on, was encouraged to the point that if thirty or more IBM employees, even in France or Germany, made a joint request for a special course in any field, the company tried to provide it. There was no record of any request for controversial courses on concepts and criticism, techniques of revolution, studies of corruption in politics, and the like; the education program was, by and large, job and, at times, pleasure oriented. The emphasis was on what Watson felt people should know first to do their jobs and to "get ahead," and second to provide them with non-controversial enjoyment among their families and counterparts.

It seldom seemed to dawn on Watson that in his predictions, pronouncements, and assessments of larger affairs of political, economic, or social phenomena, he was deplorably uninformed and often wholly dependent on intuition and his sense of how things ought to be. Even while projecting IBM into an infinite future, his vision had a commonplace simplicity about it, an extension of his certainty that everywhere in the world business would always need tabulators, punch cards, devices to measure, record, and assimilate the data of commerce, government, and industry. The system for taking possession of the lion's share of the

133

market had been learned under Patterson and institutionalized under his own direction at IBM. And when any company could command the market, secondary competition might be tolerated—might even be desirable from an anti-trust point of view—as long as patents were safe, the selling organization functioning with near perfection, and the research and planning department in touch with technological changes and the opportunity to develop new products.

Both gifted and schooled in his business, motivated by an ego that provided enough energy and motivation for a dozen men, and confident that his experience and intuition would guard him against surprise assault, Watson felt little need for academic learning that might have broadened his judgment, or allowed him to view the world with something more encompassing than copybook maxims and bromidic verities.

Watson had the good fortune to have the vision of his own corporation substantially widened by a diffident, scholarly intellectual at Columbia University. It was good fortune for which he was ready, and to which he was immediately responsive. His benefactor in what amounted to a step in Watson's own education was Benjamin D. Wood, a U.S. Army psychologist in World War I and, in 1928, a thirty-four-year-old professor of Collegiate Educational Research at Columbia.

Born in 1894, Wood was a tall, gangling innovator with a towering and disciplined intellect against which sparks of imagination impinged with the force of ignition. The son of an itinerant cattle rancher in Brownsville, Texas, Wood was a largely unschooled but self-taught student who entered the University of Texas with no high school credits, but who had absorbed the contents of a crate of books in Spanish and English which his uprooted family carried with them in a barely successful quest for survival across the near desert of Texas. Besides classical works of Spanish literature, Wood had devoured Rollin's *Ancient History*, Chambers' *Encyclopedia*, the works of Plato, Aristotle, Quintillian, Malthus, and a galaxy of ancient and nineteenth-century scholars. His knowledge of the Malthusian theory was preceded by observation. "I knew all about [it] from practical experience. Every two or three years ranchers had to sell for slaughter part of the herd to leave enough water and grass for the remainder." As water and pasture diminished, so did the quality of life.

Wood also learned that academic credits based on time served in classrooms were an incomplete measure of education. He emerged from the university a Phi Beta Kappa with a B.A. degree in educational psychology and Spanish literature, and a conviction that, in the words of H. G. Wells, "civilization is a race between education and catastrophe."

It was a more profound view by far than Watson's enthusiastic concept of education as vocational training, multiple job capabilities, and job proficiency, yet Wood was led to Watson by reason of their mutual interest in a subject they then defined differently.

Wood went into the Army, where he discovered that his encompassing mind, with its encyclopedic knowledge of history, provided some grasp of future probabilities. After the war he went on to Columbia for his doctorate and his life's work. His dissertation examined the thesis of E. L. Thorndyke that "whatever exists at all, exists in some amount," and applied it to the measure of human intelligence.

He was appointed assistant to Dean Herbert Edwin Hawkes of Columbia College, with the task of advising third-year students entering business, journalism, and law. To do this, he needed some form of prediction of their probable performance in professional schools. Because of previous experience with Thorndyke, who was called "the big chief" at Columbia—and who devised the measurement tests which still bear his name—and because he was appalled by the fact that only two out of every seven boys entering college ever graduated, Wood began to devise testing and scoring methods that turned up some truly astonishing findings. In particular, Wood demonstrated a disparity in the quality of education so extreme that seniors achieving the highest possible test scores in some colleges were still below students who got the lowest scores at, for example, Haverford College. His findings seemed incredible, and Wood was pretty roundly denounced as a fake for "mechanizing" measurement best left to human evaluation.

Dean Hawkes weathered the criticism, however, and supported Wood in his investigations. Grants from the Carnegie Foundation, the Commonwealth Fund, and a half-million dollars from the General Education Board subsidized his efforts, and before long the New York Board of Regents and the educational system in Pennsylvania began to reevaluate their objectives in relation to Wood's revelations.

The monumental task of recording and processing test results became a physical impossibility. Handling 35,000 tests at one time costing five dollars each to process was too costly even with large and generous grants. When Wood had millions of tests to deal with, he was harassed beyond anything even his own tests could measure. He was given floor space in Hamilton Hall, which he furnished with wooden boards and sawhorse tables scrounged from secondhand stores and lumberyards, and staffed with "two acres of girls" reading and classifying test answers. A labor problem arose when the girls, numbed by the tedium of the work, gave vent to their wrath over snagging their stockings and clothes on the improvised furniture. Burlap was tacked to splintered surfaces and the uprising quelled. In desperation intensified by the knowledge that the work was enormously important, Wood culled from directories the names of chief executives of ten corporations in the equipment manufacturing business and sent out a call for design and engineering help. Nine answers were "brush-offs from the secretaries of third vice-presidents." The tenth was a crisp telephone call:

"I'm Thomas Watson. I'm very busy and can spare only an hour. Be at the Century Club promptly at twelve; I have an engagement at one." Wood had scarcely said a word, partly out of shyness but largely out of inopportunity.

Trembling, by his own admission, and quite aware that the style of his clothes and his lingering country-boy manner made him something of an eccentric, Wood was at the Century Club fifteen minutes early. "Nobody could have been greener than I," Dr. Wood has said. "I probably still wore some part of my old Army clothes, for I had little money and even less interest in clothes. I had never been on a date with a girl or to a dance, and my social experience had consisted of going to two football games." He was painfully shy, even in the presence of the young male secretary, who accompanied the great man to the portentous interview. Watson motioned the secretary to stand guard outside the door of the private dining room, with an order to "get me out of here by one o'clock." He glanced at the table setting and the prepared lunch. "I hope you like it," he said. "I wanted to make sure we didn't waste time waiting."

At that time, Watson said, IBM had not enlisted the federal government as a customer beyond periodical work for the United States Census Bureau, an account inherited from the days of Herman Hollerith and his statistical pianos. He was hungry, particularly, for contracts with the military. Wood, deflecting him, reported on an invention of his own, a pencil with two electrode points for marking test answers wrong or right, then summarizing them by bringing an electrode across them. It was still, however, a manual job, and hence of no practical use.

Wood seemed to know that he had to interest Watson in the future usage of the equipment IBM was making, in the future "probabilities," to which Wood himself was increasingly responsive. The means by which military contracts might be obtained did not especially interest him, in view of the pressure that was on him to get several million tests scored and processed. He spoke of correspondence he had had with the American pioneer educator John Dewey, and the founding nine years earlier of the Progressive Education Association.

The machines that IBM designed, manufactured, and, for the most part, rented out to customers at that time measured things in quantitative units. Citing the work of Thorndyke and his philosophy of quantitative measure, Wood counseled Watson to keep in mind that, in psychology as elsewhere, whatever exists at all exists in some quantity. If it is zero, it is nonexistent. But all the existing aspects of earth, science, nature, life, intelligence could be reduced to measure. Money and inventories, the hours a man worked, and the price and profit of goods were not, said Wood as Watson turned on a chilly frown, the only things that could be manipulated quantitatively. Everything from virus to super-galaxy— from microcosm to macrocosm—was a matter of quantity. The only way man could ever learn all of the things he needed to know to keep civilization ahead in the race between education and catastrophe was to recognize the quantitative basis of all phenomena.

The machines of IBM could, Wood went on, extend all measure, whether it was for the doctor, who took a temperature, counted a pulse, took a blood sample, counted cells, or for any other field of endeavor in which the need for knowledge preceded judgment or activity.

"There is no aspect of life to which these IBM machines cannot make a basic and absolutely essential contribution," Wood said.

The young secretary slipped into the room, and Watson waved him out. At two o'clock he appeared again timidly. "Shut that door," Watson barked, without looking at him.

Three and a half hours later, at 5:30 P.M., Watson collected the limp secretary and departed. Two days later, a convoy of three trucks and a crew of men delivered tons of tabulators, sorters, card punchers, counters, and accessory equipment to Columbia University. It was followed by engineers assigned to get it operating and to train Wood's staff in converting it to uses for which it had not been specifically designed. Wood was able to confirm his prediction that with IBM machines, work that had previously cost from five to fifty dollars per unit could be reduced to fifteen or twenty cents.

Watson and his wife visited the place at odd times between prolonged absences. On one of his visits, Wood went to some length in describing the wonders of the machines and the miracles of high-speed work they had performed. The emphasis must have been overstated, for Watson narrowed his eyes and asked, "What's *wrong* with our machines?"

Wood, not yet aware of the fact that Watson could scarcely contain his temper in the presence of criticism, erred with an honest reply. Leaning back in his chair, he said casually that the machines were too slow. "It was as though I had slapped his face," Dr. Wood said. "He bristled, and I said, 'Now, Mr. Watson, don't get angry, please. I don't mean—what I mean is, I am convinced these machines can operate almost infinitely faster than they are going now!' "

"How fast?" Watson asked, coldly.

"Well, I don't know how soon, but ultimately these machines, which are now electro-mechanical, since you're using electricity, are going to operate at the speed of light, ten thousand times the speed with which they function now."

A gleam appeared in Watson's eyes, and a new expression, which Wood later learned to interpret, came over his features. "He was going to call in his engineers and give them hell for not having already speeded up the machines, and he was probably visualizing the scene already. Well, he did; he bawled them out."[1]

With reference to measure, Wood and Watson had taken each other's. Watson relished the opportunity to go before his engineers and storm at them, implying knowingly that they lacked imagination and daring, that the speed limit of IBM machine operations was the speed of light itself. When his engineers, some of whom were all but superstitious about Watson's penetration of their profession, tried to explain that the facts of science and technology scarcely justified his grandiose imaginings, he retorted that he didn't care to acknowledge such facts and suggested that they be changed. Wood, with perhaps more intuition and skill than anyone who worked with Watson except Fred Nichol, his former office boy and alter ego, learned how to circumvent Watson's temperament by focusing interest always on the ultimate capabilities of the IBM machines. The two men became lifelong colleagues and friends, and Watson put Wood on his payroll as a consultant for five thousand dollars a year at the start. It was one of the best bargains of Watson's life. Wood remained there until Watson's death, and afterward continued to serve as an informal consultant on IBM educational projects. He even became a stockholder and accumulated a comfortable nest egg.

After the "speed of light" dialogue, Wood found himself somewhat resented, both by some of the IBM people, who doubtless felt Watson's extraordinary assistance to the Columbia experiments were excessive, and by some of his university colleagues, who felt that Wood, rumpled and unstylish maverick out of Texas, as an IBM favorite was a corporate

[1] Part of Dr. Wood's account of this period comes from his own extensive writing, part from seven hours of interviews with the author, and the remainder from the book, Ben D. Wood, Educational Reformer, by Matthew T. Downey; copyright 1965 by Educational Testing Service, Princeton, N.J. Dr. Wood lives in semi-retirement in a house overlooking the Hudson River near Croton, N.Y., where he writes, works, and generally serves as a gadfly in educational circles.

counterpart of a teacher's pet. Watson never billed Wood's department for the IBM installations, which remained in use at Columbia for twenty years. In fact, Watson used to drop around periodically and offer him more money to help speed up the research work.

Wood then needed a few other things a good deal more than money. He still needed a system for scoring inexpensive answer sheets at something approximating the speed of electricity, and money alone could not produce it. IBM engineers and Wood's staff had experimented with electric scoring, using a scanning device to read answers, or an alternative analogue principle, in which scores were recorded on an ammeter when electric circuits were closed by graphite marks on the answer sheets. The second method held out the better promise, save for the fact that the darkness of the pencil marks varied. There was no way to induce test takers to make impressions of identical opacity. The variations could be measured in a range from 500 to 5000 ohms, or units of resistance.

A Michigan school teacher, Reynold B. Johnson, had developed an analogue scoring device using a high resistance unit of two million ohms, thus increasing the total resistance to a level where pencil mark variations were inconsequential. One of Watson's salesmen heard about the teacher and the scoring machine, and called on him. Wood corresponded with Johnson, and soon discerned that—as was then more often the case in science and research than it is now—one man, working alone without help from Columbia or IBM, had solved the problem to perfection. He notified Watson, who brought the young teacher to New York and hired him. The IBM model 805 test scoring machine was added to the company's product line, and Johnson went up through the IBM hierarchy to become director of the Advanced Systems Development Division of the corporation in California. Johnson's invention incorporated a principle basic to computer technology, which remains important in scientific research despite incredible advances in digital systems. Wood had first heard of the invention in a letter from Professor Alvin C. Eurich at the University of Minnesota, whose assistant was Johnson's brother.

From 1927 to 1932 Wood secured a couple of million dollars in subsidies from the typewriter industry, in which IBM itself later became dominantly involved, to experiment with and demonstrate the value of the typewriter as a learning machine. Wood always made an explicit distinction between a teaching machine, used to convey facts and ideas, and a learning machine, "an instrument to stimulate creativity and independent, self-initiated and success motivated learning, and to expedite absorption and comprehension."

By avoiding enforcement of the touch-typing system among the very young, Wood did indeed prove that child typists wrote ten times as much by machine as they could by hand, with no discernible loss of quality and with the corollary benefit that their speed of learning and absorption increased measurably. Moreover, the typists wrote as much or more by hand as those who wrote by hand exclusively. Experiments with children of preschool age were, Wood reported, even more rewarding.

Wood began to put heavy emphasis on kindergarten learning, declaring without equivocation that the age span of one to six was more critical to a human being's educational development than any later period of life. He even hinted darkly that parents might not be the right people to dictate the methods and quality of child education. The governing council of the university, in response to academic carping, complained to Columbia's president, Nicholas Murray Butler, the terrible-tempered and business-oriented autocrat who held that office longer than any president in Columbia's history before or since, and a lifetime friend of Watson.

Wood was summoned by one of Butler's characteristically curt notes, which he took with a sense of foreboding to Dean Hawkes. "That's funny," Hawkes said, reading it. "I received one just like it."

Butler, solemnly projecting his awesome presence, advised them that the Governing Council had found that their department, the Bureau of Collegiate Educational Research which by the implications of its title was obliged to concern itself with research at the college level, had spent in a four-year period twenty times as much on kindergarten and elementary educational studies as it had on more appropriately related projects. Butler said he had verified the accuracy of the complaint and cited the grants from George Eastman of Kodak for experimenting with classroom motion pictures as learning machines as he later did in the typewriter projects, and so on.

"My answer to the complaint was very brief," Butler told them. "It was an old aphorism," and he quoted it in Latin, as his way of endorsing, beyond appeal, their programs. It meant that educational experimentation among the very young was also appropriate collegiate research. Like Watson, Butler dismissed the complaint with a homily that Wood and Hawkes recognized: "As the twig is bent, so will the tree grow."

In addition to his passionate interest in the Columbia experiments, Watson injected himself with vigor into a multiplicity of roles. He was elected to the New York University Council, was made president of the New York Merchants Association and the New York Economic Club, was honored by the City College School of Business, and became a trustee first of New York University and then of Columbia University—the latter a preference that developed after Dr. Wood received the array of IBM machines and his association with Butler began.

Concurrently with Watson's accelerated involvement in organizations and public affairs, the application of IBM machines at Columbia was extended to other areas: enormous excitement was generated when tabulators were successfully adapted and used to make lunar calculations. This important step in the science of astronomical observations was made by Wallace Eckert, who had taken his master's degree in astronomy at Yale, and dropped in at Wood's test scoring operations while working on his doctorate at Columbia. Aside from Wood's speed-of-light prediction, which was shared by others, Eckert was one of the first to see a connection between what was currently going on and the ultimate development of the computer, which had been developed before it could be built in nineteenth-century England.

Eckert had been fascinated by the work of one Leslie J. Comrie, director of the Nautical Almanac Office of the Greenwich Observatory in England, who with his colleagues described the kinds of machinery and calculators required to prepare navigational data appropriate to modern times. A creative and imaginative scientist, Eckert knew that the men at Greenwich were onto something of great significance. As a result of his enthusiasm and of a vision expanding in his mind, Eckert steered the American Astronomical Society, his department at Columbia (where he became famous for a course called Astronomy III), and IBM into his own orbit of interest.

A small and retiring man, Eckert was so soft-spoken that he was scarcely audible, and it was a wonder to his colleagues how he managed it. But he did, and the outgrowth of his quiet persuasion was the establishment of the Thos. J. Watson Astronomical Computing Bureau, the second IBM operation at Columbia. Watson ordered a modified 601 Multiplier, as it was called, sent to the laboratory bearing his name. It had a sequence mechanism in it and was the only machine of its time that would multiply numbers together. A sequence controlled calculator, it was built for Eckert at Endicott out of standard punch card machine parts, with Clair Lake, Watson's top engineer, in charge. With it, Watson donated several standard sorters and tabulators, which Eckert used for astronomical calculations and which were adapted for use in a contract with General Electric Corporation to compute fire control calculations for the old B-29 aircraft.

The first supervisor of this prehistoric version of the monster-sized

Mark I computer, later built for Professor Howard Aiken at Harvard, was a young associate of Eckert, Lillian Feinstein (after her marriage, Lillian Hausmann). Trained by Eckert, she was the first qualified calculator supervisor in history. Eckert's experiences of this period, and Miss Feinstein's, were recorded in a pioneer book entitled *Punch Card Methods in Scientific Computation.*

Dr. Eckert went on to become the first Ph.D. hired by Watson; another, Dr. Herbert R. J. Grosch, was probably the only man who ever purchased a copy of Eckert's book—the rest were given away by Columbia, the publisher, to interested scientists. Grosch, now with the Center for Computer Sciences and Technology of the National Bureau of Standards, was to win unique distinction himself. Besides being a scientist and joining the early colony of IBM men with doctorates, he was the first and only person with a beard hired by the company in Watson's lifetime. To compound matters, achieving more distinction than a man ordinarily pursues, Grosch went into the intellectual circle of IBM scientists twice: first under the reign of old Tom Watson, and second in response to a directive from his heir, Tom Junior—and was fired both times.

With "a little gadget," which cost about three hundred dollars to design and make, added to one of the tabulators, Dr. Eckert put onto punch cards the voluminous lunar tables compiled over a period of thirty-five years by the universally renowned E. W. Brown, professor of astronomy at Yale University. The tables had been a significant portion of Dr. Brown's lifetime work; they were the foundation on which his own lunar theories rested, and furnished the basis twenty years later for Eckert's wartime achievements at the U.S. Naval Observatory. Although Brown's tables had been published and widely used, it remained for Eckert, after making exhaustive preparations and refinements of his tabulating equipment, to run the tables through the machines and confirm to Brown that his compilations were without a flaw. Brown's stupendous task, like the famed Bowditch navigation tables, was duplicated and surpassed in great magnitude in the computer age, but the old professor died content to know that the newly adapted, miraculously accurate tabulating equipment that could have speeded up his work nevertheless could not have done it with more perfect accuracy than he himself had achieved. Eckert himself surpassed Brown in accomplishments in the science of astronomy, and his recent published work on lunar theories puts Professor Brown's into history.

Other scholars began to be drawn to the laboratories of Eckert and Wood at Columbia. Dr. Harlow Shapley, the Harvard University astronomer, was attracted to the scene and carried word of the capability of the IBM equipment to another Harvard scholar not yet widely known —Dr. Howard Aiken, who was to open other gates to the computer age. Eckert, a pioneer in his field of astronomy, stayed on his course, and was snatched up, in the manner of a secret natural resource, and dispatched with his IBM machines to the Naval Observatory in Washington at the beginning of World War II.

Long before Pearl Harbor and the United States declaration of war, merchant tonnage losses of U.S., British, and Canadian bottoms increased to catastrophic proportions. Tankers, in particular, were torpedoed and left in flames within sight of American coastal citizens. The ports at Halifax and the Gulf Coast were graveyards for vessels. With war declared, the situation grew so ominous (although at the time the real danger was not made public) that German submarines along the Great Circle route of the North Atlantic operated nearly at will.

Working in deepest secrecy, Dr. Eckert and his staff at the Naval Observatory were charged with carrying out an operation that meant, almost literally, the difference between life and death to the Allied cause, since on it depended the use of the sea lanes to Murmansk and the United Kingdom. Before such technological miracles as radar and sonar were extensively in use, priority was given to means more readily at hand to disperse the murderous submarines which had sent to their deaths half of the pre-war U.S. maritime tanker personnel and the ships they manned.

Effective air assault against submarines was inevitably delayed by navigation techniques requiring as much as thirty minutes to determine a ship's or a submarine's position, a preliminary requisite to a radio call for help. Manual calculations, even with available tables and a sextant, were too time-consuming and cumbersome, leaving supply-laden ships exposed to torpedoes and destruction in the interim.

Working from Professor Brown's tables, their accuracy confirmed by the IBM equipment at Columbia, Dr. Eckert, a supervisor at the Observatory named Jack Belzer, and a group of young especially trained women began calculating and producing nautical almanacs for air and sea navigators. Limiting the operation to cover a ten-degree band of the heavens over the North Atlantic—it would have required a million pages of condensed type to provide complete almanacs for the navigable waters over the full north-south range—they produced the printed calculations that constituted the first and oldest scientific computer output in the world. It had been done, experimentally, at the old Pupin computing laboratory at Columbia, where fire control equipment calculations for the B-29 aircraft were later done under subcontracts to the General Electric Corporation.

The almanacs were modified to carry very small slugs of type, printed a line at a time. The type was so tightly condensed that every other digit was printed in the initial operation, then the platen on the machine was shifted one-half a notch to open up alternate spaces for the remaining half of the data on each page. This was done to compress the data and reduce the bulk of the document. Calculations were related to specific dates, and production schedules of the almanacs sometimes left only a few hours during which their delivery was absolutely crucial to navigators in the spotter aircraft, in the assault planes, and on the ships. In Washington, planes stood by to fly them to waiting navigators. Eckert and the staff were never more than a week ahead of delivery. But with the data, navigators on North Atlantic patrol and on ships in transit could determine a fix often in a single minute after sighting a submarine, and radio its position to every craft within range. Corvettes from Canada, destroyers, and anything capable of carrying a gun or a depth bomb could then converge on the spot at maximum speed.

In a matter of weeks, loss of lives and tonnage in the North Atlantic diminished; in time, and with new sensing technology, the sea lanes were brought under Allied control.

It was the sequence of events started by the cooperative Watson, in response to the requests of Ben Wood and Wallace Eckert for IBM machines to pursue their work and scholarship, that led directly to these accomplishments. Watson's Astronomical Computing Bureau at Columbia, established after Eckert had read the articles written by scientists at England's Nautical Almanac Office at Greenwich, was the seminal instrument for giving birth to the new machines to measure the phenomena of the universe.

The newest and most apocalyptic phenomena to which Watson's machines were applied were the nuclear fission and atomic bomb projects; Eckert and Grosch labored on these, not altogether certain of the objectives of their research until word filtered back to them about the Manhattan Project and the awesome accomplishments of Dr. Robert Oppenheimer and his associates, who were dispatching instructions by mail postmarked Los Alamos, New Mexico.

Eckert and Wood remained in close touch with Watson until age, failing health, and his son's ascension elevated him to emeritus status. Following his years at the Naval Observatory, Eckert was preeminent among scientists of the world in his field, and thus precisely suitable as Watson's choice to direct, at $30,000 a year, the Thomas J. Watson

Laboratory, endowed and established at Columbia after the world entered the nuclear age. A good and true scientist, he served in the post for twenty-two years and found his own heaven where mystics always said it was, among the galaxies and the stars.

Wood's relationship with Watson extended beyond business and professional interests into his personal and family life, which made the educator something of a rarity among Watson men. Watson was suspicious of friendship with his colleagues and at times coldly disapproved of emotional attachments taking priority over total involvement in IBM affairs. He made few exceptions; Wood's case rested on his interest in and even affection for the Watson boys, Tom and Dick, whom he sometimes counseled on educational matters, and on their father's uncharacteristic respect for Wood's refusal to be intimidated by him. Wood was uncowed by Watson's temper and even made a study of it through a process of quantitative analysis that was second nature to him. While he deplored and was often saddened by the evidence of cruelty associated with Watson's fury and made no attempts to rationalize its excesses, he understood it as a cross, or a curse, which the man, his family, and his colleagues collectively had to bear.

Wood thought Watson and IBM had put several hundred million dollars, much of it unrecorded, into research and educational activities. Included were funds for blood analysis and an infinite variety of laboratory medical research, astronomy, mathematics, design and development requests, teaching and learning programs.

"The ramifications of what he did and made possible," Wood has said, "are incalculable. No one could name them all. We cannot even calculate the value of his contribution to the work Eckert accomplished with Professor Brown's tables, which were a monument to all those years of lonely effort by one man. Watson's machines, his eagerness to help advance knowledge, making IBM engineers and design facilities available to scientists, whatever the cost, tipped the balance in favor of civilization and against catastrophe. I was ridiculed thirty years ago for trying to do things in education that Mr. Watson made possible by his faith in new ideas. . . . He was one of the handsomest of men; his sons looked like young Greek gods. Mrs. Watson, she was an angel. They came often, again and again, to my laboratory.

"No matter what foibles can be attributed to him, or unfavorable things that can be said about him, nobody in the whole history of mankind has ever contributed one per cent as much as IBM and Thomas Watson.

"He had his faults. I've heard him scold his boys in ways that made me weep. When he got mad, his reason and everything else vanished. But they returned, and he made up for it. People might turn away from him, ashamed, but it didn't last."

Sometimes, Ben Wood almost welcomed Watson's explosive tantrums, because in their wake he became sweet reasonableness itself, and the business of cooperating with him could continue. Dr. Eckert, too, not infrequently observed this side of him: "He saw you as one of his family, and he could be abusive to that family. You had to live around it, then go on about your work."

Dr. Wood and his wife, Eleanor Perry Wood, an educator and administrator in her own right, were asleep when the Watsons knocked at their door one night and got them out of bed in their apartment on Morningside Heights. The Watsons had come from a commencement dinner at the home of Nicholas Murray Butler. They had recently returned from Switzerland and had brought with them a "trinket" for Mrs. Wood, a bit of costume jewelry.

Mrs. Watson saw a record player in the room, and said, "That's the thing I want."

"I'll have one sent to the house tomorrow," Watson replied.

The Woods in dressing gowns, the Watsons in evening dress, listened to a Tschaikowsky concerto, after which Watson was in a reminiscent mood. "You know, Ben," he said, "I'm very proud of having been called a successful business leader. But I am much prouder of what I have done for education than anything else I ever did. I could have been equally successful in manufacturing and selling dishpans, but I get a special sense of accomplishment and deep satisfaction when I think of what you told me about the universal applicability of these machines. When you first told me, I didn't believe half of it, but that was enough. Now that I've seen these machines actually operating on galactic problems that could never before be touched, it is enough." Wood said they were no longer just business machines, that they would touch the very soul of man.

Twenty years later, Ben and Eleanor Wood were going over their household effects, and Wood, hefting in his hand the three-section brooch which the Watsons had given Mrs. Wood as a gift from Switzerland, observed that it felt "different" from other pieces of costume jewelry in her modest collection. The crystals in it seemd to be of some special quality. Mrs. Wood sometime later took it to an appraiser and buyer on Fifth Avenue. He studied it under a magnifying glass and said, matter of factly, "I can't offer you more than $1200."

Observing her shock, he bent over the piece a second time, saying that the diamonds were very small, that he had to get his own markup on it, and insure it in the meantime. "I could get no more than $1250."

With the money Mrs. Wood bought three shares of IBM stock at $400 a share. Over the years, growth and splits and stock dividends increased the original value by a factor of 52 to a total of $65,000.

"It was," said Dr. Wood, "some trinket."

Wood saw in Watson and IBM a unique opportunity to impress a healthy influence on education, and a way to pursue a cherished dream of individualized learning. He helped recruit for Watson and his company some extraordinary men, such as Dwayne Orton, President of Stockton College, to develop IBM's educational program and become editor of *THINK Magazine,* and the talented inventor, possibly a genius, Reynold (Ray) Johnson. Wood himself persuaded Watson that correct theory and methods were as important to IBM as to a university, and they were applied to the training of personnel and customers in the use of machines and computers. Closed circuit television for classroom use in customer engineering education and research in the development of Arabic and Chinese typewriters were among Wood's contributions to IBM. He was from the beginning and after Watson's death an eloquent admirer of the man and the corporation and the second generation management at IBM. He thought the company was the ideal American industrial institution, providing seminal contributions to national life. "The world would be much happier if there were more IBM's and corporations like it," Dr. Wood wrote. He saw in Tom Watson, Junior, the father's finest characteristics extended to a corporation management of "incredible efficiency," making "increasingly versatile strategic contributions to human welfare."

Wood and Watson worked together from the day they met at the Century Club in New York until 1956. At the time their association began, mutual disenchantment characterized in general the relations between American industry and education. The collapse of the Samuel Insull utilities empire in the thirties, the moribund state of a good deal of industry in the Hoover administration and the early New Deal years, and the reputation for ivory tower detachment from reality in the universities made the atmosphere resistant to business-subsidized research and study. Nicholas Murray Butler, the businessman's friend and imperious educator, with Watson's money harnessed to the intellect and inventiveness of men like Eckert, Wood, and others, changed the ways of the past and opened up new avenues that led to astonishing developments, some of which were dubious blessings at best.

University educators, administrators, and research scholars found themselves suddenly in league with the government and ambitious corporations, a triumvirate with initial good intentions that over the decades grew into an enormously complex, devious, and secretive operation. Within a generation, not only at Columbia but in other centers of higher education, trustees and administrators, dependent on corporations for contributions and on military research projects for income, often had a commercial interest in educational institutions that had little to do with education itself. Monolithic and arbitrary rule became dominant, dialogue was stifled, and frustrations ignited into riots and anarchy. The outbreaks and the threat of campus revolution had their origins in the working arrangements between the universities, the corporations, and the military in the 1940's—arrangements which were perpetuated and institutionalized when the needs of war had passed.

8.
The
Patriarch

AN ASTONISHING ASPECT OF life in IBM, even after Watson became a world figure and was traveling by train and ocean liner several months of each year, was the extent to which the aging patriarch retained in his own hands the reins guiding virtually every large and small facet of corporate operations, and in his memory the encyclopedia of facts and impressions that affected any release or restraint in the use of the reins.

After he became president of the International Chamber of Commerce in 1937, he devised a system, made possible by the opportunities offered in that post and by his quest for expanding world trade, for extending his own and his company's name into dozens of foreign business communities. It entailed a good deal of time and travel to countries that honored him but did not lessen the impact of his personality and detailed control over his people and plants at home. He would be given a decoration of some sort, usually for his interest in trade, by Sweden, Belgium, Finland, or Yugoslavia—an honor that would precede, or sometimes follow, closer associations with the Swedish-American or Belgian-American or Yugoslav-American Chamber of Commerce and trade groups. Business, honor, influence, and his confirmed role as a spokesman within each country and trade bloc would naturally and normally follow. The total number of IBM employees in a country might be no more than forty or fifty—as in Czechoslovakia, for instance—but it was remunerative to Watson in terms of recognition, decorations, and stature.

He was tireless in his pursuits, extending his interests into Spain, Brazil, Indo-China, Hungary, Ecuador, Peru, and even for a time into China. Simultaneously, he would take on the presidency of the American Arbitration Association, a post in which he was ultimately succeeded by one of his sons, and become a trustee of the Metropolitan Museum of

Art, the Metropolitan Opera, and accept other assignments commensurate with his name and status. Meanwhile, new plants were going up or expanding, the number of employees increasing month by month and year by year.

World War II propelled the company into really big business, with sales leaping from $63 million in 1941 to nearly $142 million in the last year of the war. While income fell off in some parts of Europe because of destruction and hostilities, two new plants were built on the continent, and foreign sales, not previously significant, doubled while the war was in progress. Net income from foreign sales rose from $239,000 in 1940 to $1,500,000 by 1945. In the latter year, net investments in factories, offices, and rental machines in the United States and Canada was $60.5 million, and in one postwar year, 1946, it increased to $76.5 million. The company was exploding with growth.

Watson was everywhere and, it seemed, involved in scores of official and personal projects. As a trustee of the Carnegie Endowment for International Peace, he once left a meeting early to take off for a government arsenal to learn how to make machine guns. Less than a year after committing the company to produce them, IBM had a new plant in operation. The manuscript of a company history of World War II—never published—showed a wide range of development and production utterly alien to the corporation in prewar years. Nearly forty separate ordnance items were manufactured, including bombsights, guns, and aircraft engine parts, while IBM participated significantly in a wide range of development projects. In addition to the work Dr. Eckert had undertaken in Washington to repel submarine attacks in the North Atlantic, IBM contributed to the secret "AsWorg" operation in 1942–43. A staff of seven men, which grew to seventy-three, analyzed results of attacks on enemy submarines. Prior to the war, aviators had not known how to sight a submarine from the air or how to conduct effective attack against it. Mathematical methods of search were applied to supplement sound-range apparatus in new, original scientific operations research. The devastating toll of shipping—German U-boats had sunk 603 Allied ships from the fall of 1942 to early summer of 1943—was brought under control by these combined methods.

Ballistic computations were made on IBM machines, wind-tunnel findings determined, and weather forecasting improved.

On another scale entirely, Watson bought and equipped a farm in Canada and operated it during much of the war to care for Allied refugees. It was his own personal welfare project.

He took time, too, for personal pleasures and family affairs, going down to Fort McClellan, Alabama, two weeks after "the day of infamy" at Pearl Harbor, Hawaii, to serve as best man at the wedding of his son Tom to the hauntingly beautiful Olive Field Cawley. They had become engaged three weeks earlier, and the wedding preceded Tom's orders to the Pacific as a patrol pilot.

He attended personally to the acquisition of land near the then small Poughkeepsie plant for a new country club to serve employees of the Hudson River area. A bit stoop-shouldered then, always impeccably dressed, wearing a vest and jacket even on the hottest summer days, he was as ubiquitous as the morning dew, showing up at installations by arrangement or surprise, personally attentive to obscure employees, bawling out executives, inspecting the wartime products to which many operations were converted.

One of the first women employed by IBM outside the factories was Elizabeth Pegram, an auburn-haired girl from the South, fresh from college and a job in Washington. When she first met Watson, she found him "inspiring," and although she had heard rumors of maltreatment of others, such experience eluded her altogether. After a time, she found him easy to talk with and developed complete trust in him, acknowledging a daughter-to-father feeling for him. When Watson went to Washington, where she worked in the field of customer service, he chatted with her, asked her opinions, and impressed her "with the serious attentions he gave to my answers, and it was heady stuff to a youngster in the business world."

After six years in Washington, she was transferred to the IBM School in Endicott. When the Japanese struck Pearl Harbor, she wanted to go back to the action in Washington, she told Watson, but she was, in fact, homesick. He understood, and talked quietly with her at length, telling her about his lonely days on the road and how homesick he had been for his sisters and family in the old days. Watson told Fred Nichol that she was qualified to coordinate production of War Bond assemblies, a job which involved liaison with the U.S. Bureau of Printing and Engraving, and Miss Pegram was reassigned to Washington with a $50-a-month increase in salary. In three months, however, at the request of vice-president Charles Kirk, she went back to Endicott to serve in a personnel capacity amid the hundreds of women employed to replace men sent off to war.

Watson kept closely in touch with her work, a fact which puzzled her in view of the enormous demands on his time. She tried to have designed and manufactured an attractive work uniform of slacks and tailored blouses, to replace unsafe and individually chosen clothing around factory machinery. When Watson heard about it, he directed her to stop the research. There were two versions of what Watson said; one of them—"I don't want our women wearing long pants"—appears to have been apocryphal. His actual response was more startling. "I don't want our people wearing uniforms," he said. "I don't want them regimented." She was aghast, for regimentation, whether he acknowledged it or not, was as widespread as it was standard. But she did not object, nor apparently did anyone else.

"I think it was his strength of character that impressed me most," she wrote. "Strong character in abundance has been rare in my experience but, happily for me, was the major personality factor in my father, in Mr. Watson, and now in my husband. How lucky can a female be?"

Watson arrived in Endicott one day, very much upset. Personnel managers were working six days a week, interviewing applicants for wartime work. Long waits for interviews were inevitable.

IBM had for many years, and to some extent after Watson's death, sought to maintain an Open Door policy, under which any person could, with a just complaint or suggestion, enter Watson's office. The policy was both fact and myth; many got in and many did not. Executives were known to cross the country and wait three days in the carpeted office at 590 Madison in Manhattan in a vain attempt to see Watson, who sometimes would be hard at work on an opera fund-raising campaign, seeing inventors, or consulting with any number of visitors. He might see a visitor once for a preliminary meeting on some issue, and never acknowledge, or keep, implied commitments to follow up. Or he might see a floor sweeper about some complaint and, unless successfully pressed by Nichol or a brave secretary, decline to read urgent mail.

One applicant, irritated over two broken appointments for a job interview, had written a complaining letter to Watson, who was indignant at the inefficiency and injustice he felt the letter disclosed. He summoned the chief of personnel, and the admiring Miss Pegram, and administered a humiliating tongue-lashing to the harassed personnel man. The man was silent, embarrassed—and summarily transferred. Watson turned to Miss Pegram, saw that she was suffering from the experience of seeing a man shamed, and followed her into the corridor. He said he had to do what he did, that the company's welfare demanded it, and that he was sorry. She said only that she was sorry, too.

Everybody punched time clocks, including the top managers, and even Watson himself intermittently. IBM made time clocks, of course, and they were abundantly in evidence on company property. One job applicant, sitting out the long wait for a job interview, was given a company brochure to pass away the time. Exempt from the draft for some reason, he read the literature carefully, absorbing the tenet that required employees to be steadfast and trustworthy. Emphasis was placed on the matter of trust, and the language was explicit in asserting that the company put "trust" in every one of its people. When the young man's turn for an interview came, his enthusiasm perhaps diminished in the course of the waiting period, he held the brochure before him with thumb and forefinger, and tapped at it with his other hand.

"How come," he asked, "if you trust everybody so damned much, you got all these time clocks around?"

The interviewer slowly extracted the brochure from the gripping fingers, and answered, "I don't really think you would be happy working here."

The war was mounting in Europe, London was enduring Nazi bombing, and American and British ships—protected to some extent by the sea and air navigation tables developed by Dr. Eckert with IBM equipment at the Naval Observatory—were making their way to United Kingdom ports and to Murmansk in Russia. Miss Pegram and a woman designated to become women's personnel director at Poughkeepsie were summoned to the Hudson River town for a tour of the plant, with Watson and John G. Phillips, company treasurer. All wore their plant identification badges—except Watson, who went everywhere without interference by any of the numerous guards. The plant was engaged in highly classified production work. Watson tracked down the supervisor of guards and reprimanded him for tolerating loose security measures.

Security at the Endicott plant was better, at least in the hands of a twenty-two-year-old bride weighing ninety pounds whose husband had been sent overseas and who, in consequence, had been given a job until his return. Every wife of a serviceman received a week's pay each month during these absences, and they were a super-loyal contingent of employees. The young woman, Lucille Burger, was obliged to make certain that people entering security areas wore the correct clearance identification.

Surrounded by his usual entourage of white-shirted men, Watson approached the doorway to an area where she was on guard, wearing an orange badge acceptable elsewhere in the plant, but not a green badge, which alone permitted entrance at her door.

"I was trembling in my uniform, which was far too big," she recalled. "It hid my shakes but not my voice. 'I'm sorry,' I said to him. I knew who he was all right. 'You cannot enter. Your admittance is not recognized.' That's what we were supposed to say."

The men accompanying Watson were stricken; the moment held unpredictable possibilities. "Don't you know who he is?" someone hissed. Watson raised his hand for silence, while one of the party strode off and returned with the appropriate badge. Al Good, director of security, commended the girl, who understood the nervousness of the men in Watson's party. "I guess it was the sort of thing they couldn't mention to him if they were close to him. With me, it was just a job, and it didn't bother him."

Mrs. Burger's husband, Homer, was missing in action sometime after that. She had been notified of the date of his death. Her hope for an error, for a false report, had nearly ended when, one day, she was called into Charles Kirk's office to find him holding mail from men overseas to friends in the plant. One letter from her husband, with a postmark subsequent to the reported date of his death, was in the pile. "They hugged me, and I cried; oh it was wonderful." It was wartime, and IBM people were inevitably close to one another.

"Neither me or my husband had much of an education," Mrs. Burger continued. "We were backsliding Christians. But we're Saved People now, Evangelical Baptists. I feel everybody in the United States should know about IBM. They were wonderful to me. Homer's father worked there, too, and Homer is a silk-screener, a member of the Second Generation Club. The girls today are a disgrace to IBM and Mr. Watson. They shouldn't be allowed to wear those mini-skirts, and they should go back to the principles of Mr. Watson. Why, the other day, my husband said he saw a girl sitting at a desk, in a short skirt, that you could see. . . . Well, it's disgusting. If I had my way, the men would all wear white shirts all the time. They're nice. Mr. Watson wouldn't allow it, what they do. People aren't close any more. Things have changed a good deal."

When the factory won an E-award, a wartime flag given by the government for meeting production schedules, the event was celebrated with a company party and square dance. James Melton and Rise Stevens, Metropolitan Opera stars, were on hand as guest singers. Mr. and Mrs. Watson appeared as the dance orchestra was playing fast and loud, with considerable swinging of partners and stomping. The music slowed and quieted, and the Watsons joined the throng for a few minutes.

After the war, IBM sent the returning servicemen and their wives on a trip to New York, with all expenses paid, where they visited Mr. Watson and his sons Tom and Dick, who gave them tickets to a Kate Smith Broadcast.

Because of his early days in the nearby area to the west, and the fact that Watson had located his main production facilities in the Triple Cities of Endicott, Johnson City, and Binghamton, a special feeling for him and for his wife always prevailed there. His comings and goings were news, and an assembly of IBM employees of any size was a state affair. A tradition of paying respects to such an exalted personage was long established in the community; it had begun with old George F. Johnson, the shoemaker. When Johnson in his later years returned each spring from a winter in Florida, they closed the schools and factories as though it were a national holiday. Each homecoming was marked by a public reception, with Johnson standing in line shaking hands from afternoon to nightfall. Such ceremonies continued until Johnson died at ninety.

With allowances for the unreconstructed Endicott-Johnson shoe element, Watson expected the community to adapt itself to IBM and its standards. The community did, too, for the most part. Local newspapers treated him as an indigenous prince who had to be an expatriate in New York and Europe from time to time.

The Endicott Daily Bulletin, which later merged with *The Sun-Bulletin,* had a city editor named Paul Crumley who, subjected to the more freewheeling doctrine of Endicott-Johnson, did not become immediately imbued with IBM values. He lacked a certain awe of Mr. Watson, although thought nothing ill of him. He was granted an interview one day when the company was in the process of erecting a building on the site of a former farmer's market, at McKinley Avenue and North Street. The foundation had been exposed for some time, and construction had been delayed. The site was something of an eyesore, and Paul Crumley's civic consciousness prompted him to ask: "When are you going to do something about that hole in the ground?"

Watson sprang to his feet in anger and ordered Crumley out onto the street. Watson liked constructive thinking, which excluded questions hinting at his fallibility.

When news of the confrontation reached James Ottaway, publisher of *The Bulletin,* the latter called the staff together, deplored Crumley's breach of etiquette, and declared it permanent policy that thereafter he, and he alone, would interview Watson. The order was enforced until Watson died eighteen years later. Crumley inherited a drug store in Albany sometime after the incident, and departed with a reputation for having been the only local man who had ever talked to Watson like that.

Not until Watson was dead did a single word of irreverence, and rather affectionate irreverence at that, appear in local print about him or IBM. Steve Hambalek, who is one of the area's veteran newspapermen and writers, on occasion recalled his old job of covering IBM affairs, exclusive of personal contact with Watson. "Unforgettable were the interminable trophy orgies that began with dinner at seven p.m. and ended early in the morning after the speech by the man who made it all possible," he wrote in 1957. "In between were countless minor but not necessarily short speeches by lesser IBM guns and the hours-long award of the ton of trinkets for honors in countless categories of IBM sports."

Hambalek remembered the famous, but transient, Annual Thomas J. Watson Appreciation Dinners sponsored by the Endicott Kiwanis Club. The fact that Watson's birthday on February 17th fell between the Lincoln and Washington holidays provided the dinner chairman with an opportunity to have three huge silhouettes made of America's two greatest presidents and of Mr. Watson, which hung on the wall behind the dais. The one of Watson, quite naturally, was hung high in the center, while the likenesses of Abraham Lincoln and George Washington were placed to the right and to the left and a little lower down. Watson had a very strong hold on the community and its people.

One of the most personable and dynamic of IBM executives, Charles A. Kirk, who became vice president in 1941 and who is remembered by aging company managers for his vitality and his ability as a gifted jazz pianist, suffered intensely when he or men subordinate to him inadvertently transgressed on Watson's feelings.

After President Roosevelt and the Congress levied high wartime withholding taxes, some spokesmen for the American industrial community, and a good many citizens generally, protested the severity of the program. It was called "confiscation" and worse in objecting editorials. Watson was then as pro-Roosevelt as FDR's mother and planned to declare himself as such at a large weekend assembly of IBM families at the company's country club in Endicott. Charley Kirk and his staff was in charge of propagating Watson's faith in the FDR tax program. The dinner itself, the forum for the declaration, was on a Saturday night.

Kirk and his associates worked all day and evening to prepare press releases which, because of early deadlines for the Sunday papers, were sent out before Watson actually spoke. The essence of the speech was that Watson and IBM were "proud to pay the new taxes," a view that ran almost heretically contrary to that of some of his colleagues in the National Association of Manufacturers. With the speech or accounts of it already in print by the time he got to the rostrum, Watson wandered rhetorically about and neglected to emphasize, beyond generalities, his unequivocal position on income confiscation.

The public relations people were appalled at the prospect that he had impulsively changed his mind about the matter, or tempered his position out of proportion to the prepublished statement. Kirk was up all night, stalking around in a bathrobe and imbibing forbidden drinks, waiting for messengers and telephone monitors to feed back the treatment of the speech. Desperately, he tried to stop publication, or to have a qualifying paragraph injected into the accounts. But the syndicate tickers were shut off, and trucks and trains were en route to distribution points with the Sunday papers. To make matters worse for Kirk, Watson remained in Binghamton for the weekend. As the passage of the hours and the assimilation of alcohol sharpened Kirk's premonition of doom, he told those gathered at his home for the wake that Watson was certain to be designated as a Socialist, at least for the press release statement he had not confirmed in public.

But someone in Washington, no doubt up all night on matters of state, had seen the early editions and the wires of Associated Press, United Press, and International News. Apparently before Watson himself saw the papers, he received a long telegram from President Roosevelt, praising him for his courage, his citizenship, and his patriotic attitude. He was humble and grateful for such words from his President, particularly when subsequent editions carried stories under a Washington dateline citing Watson for his gallant stand. The shaken but relieved Charley Kirk went to bed, having completed another day at IBM.

After Tom Junior returned from the war, Kirk was chosen to train the young prince for IBM command. He was always grateful to early Sunday deadlines and to fate for preventing his efforts to kill the press release that won for him, in Watson's heart, a measure of fond remembrance. In the summer of 1947, Kirk was in France to attend a function of the International Chamber of Commerce. As executive vice president of the company, Kirk was then being paid $68,000 a year, after a career of thirty years with IBM. He was found dead in a Paris hotel room, the victim of a heart attack induced in part, it was said, by exhaustion, tension, and years of surreptitious heavy drinking. The death was a blow to old Watson, who spoke of his deep shock and sorrow at the next annual meeting. Young Tom, already a vice-president and, under Kirk's tutelage, a member of the controlling Executive and Finance Committee, after a time moved into the job in which Kirk, on no less a judgment than Watson's own eulogy of him, had lived up to the company's high standards of hard work, confidence, and optimism.

Of the many salesmen in IBM who became something of a legend in their own time, few matched Frank A. Bergman, who grew up on the lower East Side of Manhattan, served in World War I, graduated with an automotive engineering degree from Pratt Institute, and went into the auto repair business. He had been part of the National Guard posse that pursued Pancho Villa along the Mexican border, and he was prominent in American Legion affairs. The depression years destroyed his business in the nineteen-thirties, and he moved into door-to-door selling.

"I sold the blue sky with a gold frame around it," he said of his days peddling International Correspondence School Courses. "You never sold the course. You sold the blue sky. I sold straw hats to Eskimos. I was a salesman."

Classified as 1-A in the early days of World War II, Frank Bergman, nearing forty, faced the choice of going back into the armed service or getting a job in a draft exempt industry. He went to work for IBM in Poughkeepsie as a floor mechanic, inspecting machine guns and munitions. Repeatedly, he sought out Charles Kirk, the piano-playing vice-president, and pleaded with him for a job in sales. "They laughed at me," said Bergman, "and told me I was too old."

One day in 1945, Thomas J. Watson attended a huge clambake and picnic, and Bergman waited three hours, following Watson around the grounds, until he apprehended him alone under an apple tree and asked him for a job in the sales department.

Watson was impressed with Bergman's "gall," a word changed to "gumption" when the story was told in a company publication. He called Kirk over and directed him to put Bergman in sales. Kirk was quiet under the apple tree but furious with Bergman when he called him in two or three days later. There were harsh words from Kirk, laced with profanity directed at Bergman's impudence. Bergman, sure of his ground after hearing Watson give Kirk the order, was unintimidated. He talked back. "You don't scare me, Mr. Kirk. You were told to put me in sales, and that's where I'll go."

With a hundred men, Bergman went to the Endicott school. He was forty-six years old, and the next oldest man in the graduating class was twenty-seven. He was assigned to a territory.

"We had the block model 01 typewriter with no covers or means to carry it," he said. "They took a pencil and drew a line from east to west. I wound up with the Bronx and part of Westchester County. It was nothing to make 35 or 40 canvass calls a day. I'd write down the prospect's name, telephone number, hobbies, and other things in notebooks. Then I made the card records at night."

Bergman sold electric typewriters by the thousands to General Motors, Olin Mathieson, and other corporations moving into Westchester County. He made as much as $28,000 in a year, was in the One Hundred Percent twelve times, and in 1955 sat on the platform with Watson, who had given him his chance to become a salesman.

Bergman responded to the IBM doctrine with whole heart and mind. He said, as Watson had often said, that his most important "sale" had been made forty years before to a girl named Ruth, who became his wife. He was the first IBM man to retire, at sixty-five, from the Electric Typewriter Division. In April 1964, he was honored in a company publication under the headline, "Man In Review." Mr. Bergman wrote:

"Go out and carry the IBM banner, take pride in your profession and play fair. Make the calls, give the service—for it's the little things that count in this business. . . . My motto through the years has been—Faith in God, my country, my fellowman, my company, and my product, and I thank IBM for giving me the opportunity to become a happy and successful salesman."

Bergman once obtained from the General Motors Corporation a preliminary order for three thousand electric typewriters, at a commission of ninety dollars each. It was a total commission of $270,000, nearly the equivalent of ten years of the highest salary he had ever made and probably an all-time record for a commission on a single sale. It did not, however, turn out to be a sale. Bergman was nearing the retirement age of sixty-five. As a member of the Golden Circle—the elite among the elite—a Senior Salesman, he stood by to counsel his successors. A General Motors man called one of the younger men one day and wanted to talk about two typewriters. The young man told the buyer to send the order in the mail, and told Bergman that he couldn't be bothered with "running up to Tarrytown and spending the day for one or two typewriters." Bergman told the young man he was crazy, that service was the key to sales, that General Motors required a special kind of hand-holding attention.

Retirement day for Bergman came, and the order was never formally signed. General Motors bought IBM typewriters in smaller lots, from different sources. But Bergman knew what had happened: "They forgot the blue sky." He had no regrets and no remorse. "Watson," he said, "was my ideal. IBM is the finest company on earth."

Bergman retired to his lawn tractors, his machine shop, a 1956 Thunderbird, and his possessions on a hilltop property overlooking the Hudson at Scarborough, New York. The wand of Watson had touched him at the age of forty-six, and he was forever afterward a happy man.[1]

At times, however, men broke down. The stress and shame of failure was unendurable to some, who chose a tragic exit from the world when their faith in themselves and in the company, which Watson exalted above all else, failed them.

[1] Mr. Bergman died following a heart attack on October 12, 1968.

One day in the early nineteen-forties, thirty-one-year-old Donal O. who lived in the Bronx, took his two young sons, Donal Junior, aged eight, and James, seven, to a neighborhood carnival after helping them with their school homework. Mr. O. worked in the company's systems service department out of galactic headquarters, as the World Trade Building at 590 Madison Avenue was sometimes irreverently called. He was, in effect, a repair or service man for IBM machines. His wife was unaware of the fact that for a week Donal O. had been jobless, dismissed after eleven years. He had concealed the bad news from his family by leaving the house each morning, dressed as usual, to search for a new job, the acquisition of which would cushion the blow to his wife when, ultimately, the truth became known. He could not, however, find a job.

When Mr. O. and the boys did not return that night his wife convinced herself for a time that he had taken the children to her family's house, a delusion dispelled at dawn. Police found the two dead boys in a secluded spot near the Bronx River Parkway and beside them Mr. O., a bullet hole in his head, a gun in his hand.

One of IBM's salesmen had become disenchanted with O. over an issue involving equipment installation and had complained to his "leader," who fired him. A statement from an anonymous IBM spokesman said he had been "let out . . . but it had nothing to do with his character." Some aspect of both Mr. O.'s character and that of the complaining salesman, Robert S., had escaped company leaders, for the following day Mr. S. stopped his car on the Manhattan Bridge, brooding awhile in a heavy rainstorm; then he walked across the thoroughfare, climbed to a railing, and leapt to his death in the channel far below. The thirty-three-year-old veteran, also with eleven years at IBM, left a widow and two young children.

The unidentified IBM spokesman expressed, on behalf of the corporation, "deepest regret" over the dual tragedy and evaluated Mr. S. as one of its "finest men from the standpoint of character and ability."

Because it received a good deal of publicity in the New York and Long Island newspapers, the incident sent a shiver through the family, which nevertheless kept its composure and said no more about it. Subsequent suicides received less attention. A good many IBM men over the years drifted into alcoholism under the contradictory pressure of Doing Right and meeting their quotas, of coming to terms with demotion and dismissal after adjusting to a terminal career in Watson's world, but this murder and suicide of four people in two days was a long-remembered deviation from the normal course of patriarchal life. It was thought by some that the tragedy impelled Watson and his men to exert increased influence in trying to find jobs for those who were detached from the blood ties and security of the corporate state. No such influence was ever necessary in the case of Walter Long.

Walter Long, whose wife worked for years for the Endicott-Johnson company, was a skilled mechanic, operating a small garage. In the depth of the depression when his customers became unable to pay him nearly four thousand dollars in arrears, he gathered up his tools and a set of Johanssen blocks, and stood in line until he landed a job with the IBM model shop. He joined a company bowling team, went often to the country club, got promoted, and was known to Watson by name after the latter visited the shop on a number of occasions.

Watson appeared one day in the forties to observe a demonstration of an experimental model of a bank proof machine then in a midstage of design. Impressed, Watson turned to the plant superintendent, and said, "This is a fine bunch of men you have here; I hope you're paying them well." Using every precaution to obviate trouble in his presence, the demonstration was slowed to cruising speed which, even then, represented a remarkable advance over anything previously attempted by the company. Watson did not fully comprehend the machine, and his interest in it seemed vague. As he walked away, Walter Long heard him say that he liked the old machines—the tabulators, sorters, and punchers —better, and that IBM had been built on those familiar products.

Walter Long spent most of his adult life among IBM people and still does, in a suburb of Binghamton in summers and at a winter home in Florida, where retired IBM people constitute most of the community and where Mr. Long, financially comfortable, his own son now firmly entrenched in the middle echelon of IBM men at Endicott, has served his terms as president of the IBM Retirees Club. The silver candlesticks he received upon retirement and the gold Hamilton watch given to him upon completion of twenty-five years with the company remain swathed in flannel except for special occasions, such as an IBM dinner, when the watch is removed from its place alongside the tarnished silver pieces, their Jensen hallmark attesting to their value and durability. IBM was Walter Long's life very nearly as much as it was Watson's.

Probably the least known personage of the IBM inner power circle over the years was a mysterious gray eminence named George Richter, who rose to the $50,000-a-year level and, by steadily buying stock in the company, became a millionaire several times over. Richter's power was due exclusively to Watson's high, almost superstitious, regard for him, and while the feeling of regard was returned, Richter did a good deal of laughing at the IBM system and pulled it out of joint for his own amusement time and time again. He had come to the company early in the 1920's, and from the beginning seemed to be a fellow who worked largely for the joy of it—some of the joy, of course, being a reflection of the fact that he was getting progressively richer.

Richter, who scheduled factory production, made it a practice to provide instant solutions to crises that were likely to upset Watson, and Watson was repeatedly grateful when imminent production or delivery problems miraculously failed to occur. Happily, Richter was more or less in charge both of releasing the evidence of disaster and of quickly adjusting his factory schedules to provide a remedy. He had a nominal, nondescriptive title; he operated at a lateral level remote from high command posts and was never required to preserve the front or represent the IBM image as other management were.

Richter was one of the few people special to Watson. When Watson would telephone him and explain that, for example, a large tabulator account in Cleveland was in danger because a dozen key punchers and sorters were immediately required and none were available or in production, Richter would institute a rescue operation. He would suggest a staggered delivery to some other company, a shuffling around of priorities, and the like, and come up with a complicated formula suggesting that he had hair-trigger control over a far-flung complex of factories and subcontractors. Richter had, in fact, an incomparable ability for holding fantastic volumes of detail in his memory, calling it forth on command. In addition, he always left margins, knowing Watson and his predisposition to overcommit himself, sometimes as an act of generosity and sometimes just to make his managers stretch the company's capacity. Watson himself was responsible for the myth that George Richter had arcane powers. Richter liked Watson, never let him down, and had a wonderful time making Watson and the later IBM management stand in awe of him.

In the late 1950's, when it was time for Richter to retire, Watson had been dead for two or three years. A young man with the job classification of "operations analyst," Ivan Rezucha, was directed to put Richter down on paper—that is, get all of his talents, gifts, and formulae for production scheduling onto punch cards and into computer language. "They were supposed to program George, make a mathematical model of him," said one of the men who knew him well and who often laughed with him over the excessive seriousness with which his alleged genius was taken. The project to simulate George Richter produced a great deal of pleasure for him and a few cronies to whom he confided his joyous method for making the system work for him.

Herbert F. Milligan, in his sixties vice-president of the Marine Midland Corporation, a powerful upstate New York financial and banking institution, had been paid piecework as a shoemaker for Endicott-Johnson when, as a youth, he migrated from Maine to Binghamton. By going to his bench at dawn and working late, he made sixty-five dollars a week, an astounding income, but he had to quit when he declined an offer of a job as a shoe salesman with higher social status and an income about one-third as much as he was making as a skilled tradesman. He got a job as a messenger with a bank and, in time, became a branch manager of the Marine Midland bank.

Watson telephoned him one day, having known him around town, and said he'd like someone to build a plant with about twenty thousand square feet of floor space. Milligan's bank had taken over a retail produce store through foreclosure, and it was being operated for the bank by a fruit peddler, an immigrant from the Middle East, Alex Hider. Hider had prospered modestly, and the bank's mortgage was paid off. Milligan telephoned Hider and told him to "build that plant for Mr. Watson, and lease it to him; we'll finance you."

Within a year, Watson wanted the space doubled; later as IBM expanded it was increased to 150,000 square feet. Each time Watson would simply express his needs to Milligan in simple terms, Milligan would call Hider, who had developed a substantial contracting business, and new plants would arise on the landscape. When Watson wanted a wholly new facility in another location as yet uninvaded by IBM, he would ring up Milligan on the telephone and tell him: "Buy us a couple of farms." As Milligan himself went up the ladder in the Midland hierarchy, Watson trusted him with very large organization and expansion operations. Sometimes with no more than a telephone call, Milligan offered golden opportunities to waiting investors. Once he telephoned an acquaintance in New York and suggested that he assemble a 150-acre parcel of farm land, which required a down payment of $50,000 in cash to tie up some leases. IBM built its $15 million facility at Owego on the acreage, and the fortunate investor found himself tapped by the golden Watson wand. In time, expansion operations became too unwieldy to be handled in the informal manner to which Milligan had become accustomed. By the time the company asked him and Hider to double the 150,000 square feet at Owego, Tom Watson, Jr., was administering IBM affairs with groups, committees, engineering specialists, division involvement, and the like. IBM paid Hider three million dollars for his holdings, and he retired.

Watson's impact on people, the impressions he left on them with his direct simplicity at times, was as deep and unforgettable to some as it was traumatic to others. He was contradictory and ambivalent, objective and irrational, impulsively generous and a man of demonic rages.

Milligan found Watson an uncomplicated man. "You can't do business like that any more," he said. The hawker of fruit, the piecework shoemaker, and the wagon-road salesman from nearby Painted Post got on very well together. But as Mrs. Burger, the little IBM security guard who despised mini-skirts and longed for a return to the principles of Mr. Watson, observed: "Things have changed a good deal."

9.
A
Generation
of
Computers

WHAT CHANGED THE COMPANY and indeed the whole world—more than it had been changed in their time by Copernicus, Galileo, Newton, Pascal, Liebnitz, Einstein, and a galaxy of immortal men of genius— and sent it spinning into the age of anxiety, space, and technology was the computer: the computer harnessed to the speed of light. And Watson, in the role of a patron beyond the Medici scale, had a great deal to do with it.

The computer, electronic or otherwise, was not invented; it evolved. Like some of the ideas and models which sprang from the genius of Leonardo da Vinci, it had been perceived as a possibility and its functions imagined, but it had to await the discovery and development of new materials, miniaturization, the control of power, new languages, a trained community of specialists, and the application of a great deal of money.

The da Vinci of the computer, if not the inventor, was an oddly humorous Englishman, Charles Babbage, born in Devonshire on December 26, 1792.[1] The son of a well-to-do banker, he taught himself mathematics as a youth, went to Cambridge—where he discovered he was far ahead of his tutors—and departed to establish something called the Analytical Society, the purpose of which was to leave more wisdom in the world than its members found when they entered it. Babbage's friends feared he would kill himself working to perfect a "difference engine" and a subsequent machine called the Analytical Engine, and their concern was justified, for he was a compulsively driven man. At

---

[1] An interesting account of Babbage's life, together with an excellent history of computer development, can be found in *The Analytical Engine* by Jeremy Bernstein, New York, 1963.

twenty, in 1812, he began to think of a way to calculate logarithms by machinery.

Babbage, like many thinkers for thirty or more centuries, was enthralled and sometimes obsessed with mathematics and the challenge of calculations. Fingers and toes, stones and tally sticks served well enough in the early stages of mankind. Probably the first device that extended such efforts was the abacus, or counting frame, which still serves very well in large areas of the world. A skilled abacus operator can perform remarkable feats of calculation. In 1946, a Japanese clerical worker named Matsuraki, in a staged competition with an American army man, Private Wood of the United States Occupation Forces, drew world-wide attention. Private Wood, using an electric desk calculator in a series of complicated arithmetic problems, was beaten every time by Matsuraki, flinging his beads along the abacus wires with dazzling speed.

Babbage prepared actuarial tables for life insurance companies, which some critics of insurance rates feel have never been adequately revised since, and was interested in all kinds of problem solutions. He made keys for example, for locks that had been pick-proof until he inspected them. A consulting engineer, inventor, and gadfly, he once chided the Royal Society, which he said should be rescued from contempt in England and from ridicule elsewhere. When Alfred Lord Tennyson, in a poem "The Vision of Sin," wrote that "every moment dies a man, every moment one is born," Babbage hopped on him with mild malice. Nothing but a static population could be expected if people died at the same rate they were born. Apologizing for the fact that he could not carry the figure to its ultimate decimal point, Babbage suggested that Tennyson try to make his couplet scan by conveying that for every person dying, "$1\frac{1}{16}$" was born. That, he said, ought to make it come out about right.

Babbage didn't fabricate the first mechanical calculator, nor did he make one that could be called successful, but he understood and conveyed the theory and function of its usage. Charles Xavier Thomas in 1820 probably invented the first such device sold commercially. It could perform four elemental arithmetical operations. Later, several more complicated "difference" engines were created, and it was these that Babbage in 1833 brought to an advanced state of development. His machine was intended to perform complete computations *in response to instructions,* a function close to the heart of the modern computer.

The Analytical Engine, which consumed forty years of Babbage's life, was too far ahead of engineering and technical developments of the period. Hardware of sufficiently close tolerance and capable of required speeds of operation could not then be produced. Babbage had an admirer, scarcely less fascinated than the physicist-writer Jeremy Bernstein, in Lady Lovelace—that is, Ada Augusta, Countess Lovelace, daughter of the poet Lord Byron. Her reports of Babbage's efforts, together with his own autobiography, *Passages from the Life of a Philosopher,* published in 1864, provide a complete and coherent account of the Analytical Engine that proved informative and stimulating to scientists seeking to develop the modern computer. It was Lady Lovelace who saw a relationship between the Engine and the Jacquard loom with its capacity to weave flowers and leaves from built-in instructions. She also had a prescience about contemporary apprehensions evoked by computer technology, for she wrote: "The Analytical Engine has no pretensions whatever to originate anything. It can do whatever we know how to order it to perform. It can follow analysis; but it has no power of anticipating any analytical relations or truths. Its province is to assist us in making available what we already are acquainted with."

When Babbage died in 1871, he left, not a functioning machine that met his standards, but a legacy on which the modern company of IBM and many other companies, too, for that matter, are built. For it was not butchers' scales, meat slicers, and bookkeeping machines that made IBM's stock value soar. It was the computer.

The keyboard calculator was developed in the United States around the middle of the nineteenth century and improved upon from time to time by machines and inventors in Germany, Switzerland, and England. Some of these are museum pieces, adorned with brass and fine steel, old masterpieces of the instrument maker's art. They found wide usage in accounting, bookkeeping, and commercial computing. In America, too, printing devices were incorporated into adding machines by techniques vastly improved upon by IBM in its development of the business machine market. In 1887, Leon Bollée succeeded in producing a long-sought achievement: a machine that performed multiplications by a direct method rather than a repetition of additions. Then the irascible Herman Hollerith came along, probably the most remunerative asset inherited by Watson when Charles Flint put together the combination that was to become IBM. It was Hollerith, of course, who developed the punch card method of recording data, by means of responses activating sensory systems.

Among the men who had been keeping themselves informed about mechanical developments of calculators were Wallace Eckert and Ben Wood at Columbia, Harlow Shapley, director of the Harvard College Observatory, and Professor T. H. Brown of the Harvard Business School, an early business adviser of Watson. Another was a dour young man, an associate professor of mathematics at Harvard's Graduate School of Engineering, Howard H. Aiken. As much as any man alive, he shares the credit as midwife for the first generation of computers. Watson himself was something of a patron and godfather who welcomed the birth of the calculating baby, but he must have wished at times that Aiken himself had not been born first. The echoes of their clash of egos resounds through the many accounts of their fateful and productive association.

Both Harlow Shapley, the astronomer, and Dr. James Conant, president of Harvard, had observed at one time or another the application to calculations of Watson's gift equipment at the Columbia University Statistics Bureau and the Thomas J. Watson Astronomical Computing Bureau. Dr. Shapley conveyed the details of the successful use of IBM equipment in scientific research to Aiken, who had begun by 1936 to think about bringing Babbage's dream to reality.

Aiken had some knowledge of the modified 601 multipliers, with sequence mechanisms in them, used at the Astronomical Computing Bureau and knew they could never be adapted to the advanced and high-speed calculations he envisioned. He was more or less quietly shopping around for an industrial patron or a foundation grant to design and build the machine that could. He knew by then, in view of the developments in machine tools, circuits, and new metal alloys, that a prototype could be constructed.

In response to Shapley's enthusiasm, Aiken visited Columbia and saw Wallace Eckert at work. From the first, he was something less than smitten with IBM's method of operating, doubtless because he could see early that Eckert, a kindly and much admired man almost exclusively interested in his own science, had taken some indignities, if not abuse, from Watson. Eckert understood Watson to the extent that as a member of the IBM "family," he could expect to be treated as such at times—that is to say, badly.

"Wallace was tramped on by Watson," a friend and professional associate of Eckert's said. "But the old man did that to nearly everybody. There were two kinds of people around the company—those privileged to contact Mr. Watson and those who were not. Even if you were one of the executives, you were entitled, or obliged, to go and sit outside his office door and wait for him to see you. You didn't call up and make an appointment. You might have to sit staring at the Oriental carpets and the Sloane furniture for a couple of days, when all you wanted was authorization for some small thing or other."

Whether Aiken could not get another patron interested, or whether he decided in his own mind that, personal considerations aside, Watson and IBM had the only resources available to apply to his project, he opened a series of conversations with IBM specialists, with whom he got along well enough to get the work done. These were arranged by Shapley, Professor Brown, and Eckert.

Aiken conferred many times with one of IBM's great men, James W. Bryce. Bryce was a thirty-year man with the company who had more than four hundred "fundamental inventions—something more than one a month" to his credit. They involved counters, multiplying and dividing apparatus, and other machines which became components of the ASCC (Automatic Sequence Controlled Calculator), otherwise known to history as the Mark I. Aiken had the greatest professional respect for Bryce who, in turn, grasped the full implications of the project. Watson financed the experiment with an initial gift of a million dollars that grew, according to Ben Wood, into a gift to Aiken (and, of course, Harvard) of "five million dollars, for which Howard never seemed to have any gratitude." Bryce assigned Clair D. Lake, Frank E. Hamilton, and Benjamin M. Durfee to produce the machine according to Aiken's design. Lake was the chief engineer; Hamilton and Durfee, his associates. Aiken himself spent, in addition to uncounted hours in conversation with the engineers, the better part of two summers at Endicott while the great machine was being designed and put together. While the work was in progress in a section of the Endicott plant, Aiken was summoned to active duty in the Navy as a Lieutenant Commander.

David P. Wheatland was associated with Aiken for several years after working as a research associate with Professor Zachariah Chaffee in the physics laboratory. Chaffee, with the university's Dean Westergaard, heartily encouraged the Aiken project and almost certainly added professional weight. This, combined with Shapley's enthusiasm and President James B. Conant's more than nominal acquiescence, led Watson to a vision of another high honor from Harvard to add to his unprecedented collection. Wheatland who presides today as curator over a remarkable collection of beautiful old scientific instruments reposing in several rooms of a crusty Harvard building, had unqualified admiration for Aiken as a professional man driven to complete Babbage's work but also found him difficult and "predictably temperamental." With a young ensign and graduate student, Robert V. D. Campbell, as the programmer, Wheatland helped operate the Mark I in the Lyman Physics Laboratory. Wheatland was not a mathematician; he didn't need to be one to operate the machine. Campbell was, and as such helped Aiken to write the Mark I code book, which was fundamentally essential to the application of the apparatus to mathematical problems.

From the Navy mines school in Virginia, Lt. Cmdr. Aiken was sent on assignment that left him unperturbed but made his friends fear for his life. As head of some secret operation related to the incursion of German submarines into coastal shipping lanes, Aiken was sent with a small crew in a launch to locate a German torpedo that had finished its run, unexploded, along a beach. When the torpedo was located after a long search, Aiken as the ranking officer in the party felt obliged to disarm it rather than direct the accompanying ordnance men to do so. German language markings assured him it was the hostile piece of armament. One of the young officers, in language uncharacteristic of seamen, said, "For goodness sake, don't touch it."

Aiken communicated with Washington and was told to "disarm the object and let us know what you learn," or words to that effect. The torpedo had been designed to sink in the late stages of its propelled run in the absence of explosive contact; it had settled instead in a plowed furrow of sand. As the first torpedo of its kind to come into American hands, it was considered a find of incalculable value in Washington. Its circuits were nothing like those of the calculators with which Aiken was familiar, but he got a disk turned with pocket tools, wholly unaware of whether he was increasing or diminishing his clear and present danger. With a last turn, the disk, under pressure from an interior spring, shot with a zinging sound across the beach.

Asked why he didn't pull off in the launch and try to explode the device with rifle fire, Aiken replied: "Lieutenant Commanders were a dime a dozen. Torpedoes are one of the most valuable things you can capture." His loss, of course, would have insured a delay, if not the death, of the historic computer development project.

The Mark I was demonstrated at Endicott in January of 1943, after which a long period of debugging, testing, and experimentation prepared it for shipment to Cambridge. It was disassembled and transported to Harvard's physics laboratory and into the waiting hands of Aiken and his assistants, David Wheatland and ensign Robert Campbell, along with a group of young IBM men who were soon drafted en masse into the Navy, while still assigned to the computer project. Their favorite conversation seemed to be a continuing review of whether Watson was entitled to his large salary, which had been well publicized; the consensus was that he was worth every penny of it.

After long talks with Aiken, who assured him IBM would take a commanding lead in the computer business after the war, Wheatland began buying stock in the company. He became rather well-to-do, even though he did not, as was sometimes rumored, "own half the state of Maine," where he had acquired some real estate. With his corporately acquired wealth, he began to assemble old sextants, astronomical instruments, and scientific measuring devices of past centuries, which he expects to repose in time in a museum some patron or foundation may endow. In that museum, he hopes to see also some of the gears and machine parts Babbage designed, which Harvard has on view here and there.

Watson involved himself only peripherally in the development and design of the Mark I, once he had made his decision and provided the initial million dollars. But with his passion for ceremonial events, he expected a good deal out of the dedication.

When completed, the machine was a monster by any subsequent standards. A bitter dispute occurred between Watson and Aiken over whether the computer should be enclosed in a case. Aiken wanted the counters, relays, and mechanisms open to full scientific inspection. Watson, appalled at that image, wanted it enclosed in glass and especially fashioned stainless steel, shaped and curved, as befitted IBM's most costly and prestigious product. Watson won the round, but the victory intensified the bitterness.

The calculator was fifty-one feet long and eight feet high. At the left were two large frames of sixty constants, dial switches for setting up known values for use as required in computation of problems. Reading along the room, left to right, were seventy-two storage counters for storing intermediate results of mathematical processes up to twenty-three digits, and for use also in addition, subtraction, and accumulation. The counters took up about one-third the length of the machine. Next came a wall of multiplying-dividing units, a new system incorporated to multiply and divide through the use of nine multiples of the multiplicand and divisor. This, too, had a capacity of 23-digit numbers. A narrower section, next in line, contained functional counters. These controlled interpolation of functions and computed logarithms, anti-logarithms, trigonometric functions, and printing. Three interpolators followed—tape feeding mechanisms that automatically selected values required in the processes. A sequence control directed the machine's operation in relation to solutions sought. Finally a bank of electromatic typewriters, card feeds, and a summary card punch ended the run. Final solutions appeared in printed form. Cards automatically fed into the machine the data necessary. The card punch automatically recorded pertinent data.

Encasing all of this was no simple task, but a contract was let; stainless steel and glass were fashioned in sections, and the gleaming, elongated, impossibly scientific looking brontosaurus of the computer age was dressed for its christening. It weighed almost two tons; it had 530 miles of wire, 175,000 taper plug connections, and 1,210 ball bearings; it contained 765,299 parts, 2,204 counter positions, 3,304 relays, and 225 circuit breakers. The project had taken six years of work, with time out for the Navy on Aiken's part, and four years or so of IBM engineering and fabricating time.

Watson went to Cambridge the day before the dedication. When he found to his dismay that the dedication ceremony was to be a memorial to Aiken, that virtually all the speeches and references were about Harvard, with press handouts and pictures of Conant, Shapley, Aiken, etc., that there was only passing mention of IBM and scarcely any acknowledgement of Watson, he went into one of his classical tantrums, with some reason perhaps. He had already exhausted the first million dollars and made a commitment to provide another $200,000 in operational expenses. This occasioned a statement by Dr. Herbert Grosch, who had come—the lone bearded scientist—into IBM while the computer project was in progress, to the effect that "discounts in the computer business went up to 120 per cent; they give them the million dollar thing free, then add twenty per cent besides."

Aiken, who had held his own press conference before Watson went to Cambridge, emerged as the brain behind the new robot brain. He appeared to be the person whose knowledge of computer history and whose perseverance had involved IBM as the design and work shop to put his own ideas into operational hardware, housing, and control circuits. Watson not only saw the glory of a new business machine getting away from him, but upon further reflection was incensed by the fact that Aiken was behaving as no good IBM man would ever dare. What kind of public relations would accrue to IBM or Watson if Aiken scarcely mentioned the patron's name? Thus, Watson's choleric reaction boiled up over three discernible causes: first, the money. The initial commitment of $500,000 plus an equal amount or more of company engineering time and wages, which had been a gift, was not intended to add luster to anybody's name but Watson's. Second, the virtual absence of deference or respect for Watson on the part of a man he could neither fire nor effectively reprimand unhinged him. It had not happened in twenty-odd years, and Watson was not a man to retire to a previous position of doubtful status, fortified or otherwise. Third, Aiken's posture in the matter was precisely the one Watson sought for himself and had been careless about. He had simply assumed that he, not Aiken or anyone else, would emerge with the principal, if not the sole, honor. It had always happened that way, automatically and without jockeying for advantage.

"I'm just sick about the whole thing," Watson said, trembling in disbelief and anger. He told Aiken that he regarded IBM in the same light as "you fellows" regard Harvard University. At a conference on the issue, he declared that most of the previous ideas at IBM had come from him personally and indicated that the idea for the ASCC was not measurably different.

It was probably the bitterest clash in which Watson was personally engaged and the least satisfactory. He told Conant that the dedication plans were unfair. "Our inventors" had done the actual inventing, he said, putting a diminishing emphasis on a claim of his own by that time, but making it clear that he himself was being robbed of glory that was his. The implication was that Aiken was acting in retaliation over the furor about encasing the machine and heaven knew what other real or fancied affronts. Unofficially—not much of an official nature was reported—Watson threatened to boycott the dedication ritual, withdraw the promise of $200,000 to put the thing into operation, and maybe cart off the fifty-one foot, two-ton machine and take it down to galactic headquarters at 590 Madison Avenue in New York, where he could have a proper dedication. Reluctant or not, Dr. Conant moved fast and appeared himself at the dedication to make a speech commending Watson and IBM. He said the computer was "not only a splendid gift to have presented [to the] University," but that the institution would look upon it as a challenge and an opportunity for service.

Immediately thereafter, with Watson more or less mollified momentarily, Aiken made his speech, pointedly praising James Bryce, the company in general, and the engineers with whom he had worked. The record of the proceedings showed no further mention of Watson. Even those who believed that Watson's anger was intensified by learning that he could expect no honorary degree from Harvard, regardless of his significant philanthropy, were embarrassed by Aiken's ungenerous attitude. Aiken was perhaps no more ungenerous, had their roles been reversed, than Watson might have been.

Watson, however, rather liked to share credit and did so with warmth and pleasure on his own terms and in his own way. He could not tolerate having it claimed. Standing before an assembly, he would read off a list of company accomplishments, citing contributions made by each of many individuals involved. "I could not have done it all alone," he would say. "We did it together." But the patents, press releases, and acclaim went first to Watson, who then, giving bonuses, promotions, and honors as he chose, became the giver of some of what he had received.

Watson's fury was vengeful, and he despised Aiken more or less unremittingly for the next twenty years. He had been accustomed to "initiate" projects by directing his engineers to "build me a machine that will . . .," then going on to enumerate certain tasks to be performed. Upon completion, if patents were to be claimed, they would, as likely as not, bear Watson's name, along with that of James Bryce, perhaps, or some other specialist involved in the design. Aiken possessed at least some of Watson's opportunism in this respect, which was conveniently reinterpreted by Watson not as opportunism but as pure gall.

Dr. Ben Wood, who knew Eckert, Watson, and Aiken as well as or better than they knew each other, saw the Watson-Aiken feud as a clear case of colliding egos in which neither man was blameless and neither exclusively at fault. At the same time, Wood thought Aiken excessively touchy, almost "paranoid," loath to give Watson the praise and credit he yearned for and surely deserved.

One scientist, whose credentials in computer technology are known widely both in Europe and America, has said: "I think Aiken was a real selfish, difficult person. He had no respect for Watson or IBM. But it wasn't just his attitude toward industry. He had no respect for universities either. He was just that kind of a guy."

Aiken has said he was well aware of the debt of cooperation one scientific investigation may levy on another. He believed that time and history have a way of providing each individual with a full measure of credit precisely in accordance with his merit, independent of (or in spite of) any protests he may make in his own behalf. All he would say about Watson was that he was one of the really great entrepreneurs of modern times.

In any judgment of Aiken, it is clear that "a full measure of credit precisely in accordance with his merit" was earned. Even if all he had done was to get a big corporation like IBM to take on the project—and he had done much more than that—his was a significant contribution to the completion of the Analytical Engine which Charles Babbage, drawing on the intellect of the ages, tried for forty years to build. Psychologically, the building of Mark I was a tremendous accomplishment. As a computer, the machine was of little value; it wasn't an electronic computer at all, despite the fact that it was mistakenly publicized as such. But it broke through barriers of resistance, a lumbering giant of primitivism and obsolescence, and cut the trail for the electronic machines of the computer age that soon followed.

Other scientists and mathematicians in other places were concurrently or shortly thereafter laboring to produce "mechanical brains" or "robot thinkers," as they were called. At the Moore School of the University of Pennsylvania, two men and their associates were at work on a machine which, while embodying enormous advances in automatic computing, was less famed than the Mark I if only because it was not operational until two months after the Japanese surrender and therefore did not get credit for helping to win World War II. The co-inventors of ENIAC (Electronic Numerical Integrator and Calculator), which was actually the world's first electronic computer, were Dr. J. Prosper Eckert (no kin of Wallace Eckert at Columbia), an electrical engineer, and Dr. John Mauchly, a physicist. It would have been easily possible for them to build ENIAC twelve to fifteen years earlier, as it would also have been possible to build Mark I—all of the components and the theory required were in existence—except for the fact that nobody put up the money or had the incentive to do so. The patron of ENIAC was the United States government, more specifically the Army.

Instead of the clicking relays that made the Mark I in operation sound, according to writer Jeremy Bernstein, "like a roomful of ladies knitting," Eckert and Mauchly used vacuum tubes; their current was composed of a miniscule mass of moving electrons, subject to an altered state—by stopping or starting their movements—in a microsecond. Because among other differences it incorporated relays operated at one ten-thousandth the time of ordinary vacuum tubes, ENIAC made both the Mark I and its second version, the Mark II, obsolete by the time they were in operation.

The Moore School and the Aberdeen Proving Ground in Maryland were engaged in a joint effort in 1943 to produce artillery firing tables; they used an analogue machine supplemented by a hundred or more girls doing manual calculations. It was a highly unsatisfactory business.[2]

Dr. Mauchly had written a comprehensive report about a year earlier, the equivalent of a set of instructions on how to build a computer far better than the IBM machine. The report was inexplicably lost, apparently before a copy of it was made. The disaster was mitigated, although the intervening time was irrevocably lost, when Eckert and Mauchly prepared another one from memory and a secretary's notebook. A young Army lieutenant, Herman H. Goldstine, who had gone to Philadelphia to try to recruit more girls for his unwieldy artillery tables project, came across the report; as a former assistant professor of mathematics at the

[2] This 1942 analogue computer, or Bush computer, was designed in its original form in the nineteen-twenties by Dr. Vannevar Bush and his associates at the Massachusetts Institute of Technology. It was an electric-powered, mechanical operation of limited accuracy, much improved upon in the model completed in 1942.

University of Michigan, he was able to detect at once that it held the answer to the firing tables program and perhaps the means to shorten the war. The Army put up the money, and ENIAC upon its completion in 1946 was far advanced over any other computing device in the world. Goldstine later became director of mathematical research at IBM's Thomas J. Watson Research Center at Yorktown Heights, N.Y.

Concurrently, John von Neumann, a Budapest-born mathematician and physicist who with Albert Einstein was one of the first permanent members of the Institute for Advanced Study at Princeton University, was a consultant on the deeply secretive atom bomb project at Los Alamos. Few minds the equal of von Neumann's have turned up in the twentieth century or any other. His thought processes were so encompassing and rapid, so orderly and logical, they seemed to leap the span from question to solution with something approaching the time it took to alter the state of electrons in a vacuum tube. He was a legend long before he was appointed to the U.S. Atomic Energy Commission in 1955 or collaborated with his economist friend Oskar Morgenstern to produce the book called *Theory of Games and Economic Behavior*. He joined the Moore-Aberdeen group, having known Goldstine earlier, and went back to Princeton with Goldstine after the war, while Eckert and Mauchly went into the commercial computer business together.

At Princeton, von Neumann supervised the development and production of a machine embodying concepts of his own and of Jan Rajchman of the Radio Corporation of America laboratory. Both made significant contributions to the development of the "core memory" in computers, as did Jay Forrester at M.I.T., who labored independently on his own projects. The question of who deserved the patent for this technological adaptation, indispensable to modern computers, has never been decided to the satisfaction of those involved, and disputes about the issue continued for years in monographs and historical accounts.

Along with the first UNIVAC, which Eckert and Mauchly built for James Rand, von Neumann's own computer went to the Smithsonian Institution in Washington. For a while, one version of his computer was called the JOHNNIAC, which von Neumann disapproved of. Another, produced by von Neumann for Los Alamos, was somewhat meaningfully called MANIAC.[3]

Contrary to popular belief, electronic computers were not in use—they were not even, except for ENIAC, in the planning stage—during

---

[3] Until commercial companies began to identify their computers by numbers—like IBM's System/360, Honeywell's 200, etc.—they were commonly called by a name composed of first letters of the words that more or less described them. UNIVAC,

the development of the atomic bomb. It is an assumption applied to a myth in the making. But the electric-powered mechanical forerunners of the electronic age were crucial to the Manhattan Project and the Los Alamos development, especially in the area of shock wave determinations, neutron collision, and the like. Even the IBM Naval Observatory equipment and Dr. Vannevar Bush's Differential Analyzer saved so many thousands of years' worth of man-hours that the atomic age could be hurried into being. IBM's SSEC computer, which followed the Mark I, could achieve a ten-year output of paper-and-pencil work in a single hour. The computer was profitable and operated for years. Installed at IBM headquarters in Manhattan, it ran twenty-four hours a day at a cost of $300 an hour, and according to a report written in 1949, was always booked solid six months ahead. Government agencies—especially the armed forces—universities, economists, sociologists, and industrialists trooped to the machine in a scheduled stream.

The most important invention of the whole computer age came later. It was the stored program concept, which meant that the "program" or "instructions" could be stored in the machine in exactly the same form as the data. If properly designed to do so, the program could then alter itself. Or, as it turned out, the program could go "wild" if not properly planned.[4]

With the dedication of the Mark I on August 7, 1944, irrespective of its technical obsolescence, and with the superior ENIAC and SSEC on the way, the computer age had dawned. Watson was entering the last of the seven ages of life, and his company was entering a new one. But the machine that Babbage foresaw did inauspicious work. It was Aiken, with a good deal less experience and knowledge of computer usage than others, who shared largely in deciding what to do with the new tool of history. IBM's senior expert in the field was John C. McPherson, probably the first man in the company with an expertise in the application of computer technology. He had once been a junior salesman, out of Princeton University, and rose to an IBM vice-presidency, bound

---

which became a household word in the United States for its use in television election returns, was the Universal Automatic Computer. EDSAC, built at the University of Cambridge and the first-of-its-kind stored program machine, was Electronic Delay Storage Automatic Calculator. ENIAC was the Electronic Numerical Integrator and Calculator. IBM's ASCC, called the Mark I, at Harvard, was an electromechanical exception to the naming game.

[4] The invention of the stored program is sometimes credited to von Neumann, who was surely among those deserving the honor. Many felt, however, that Mauchly, Eckert, Hermann Goldstine, Jan Rajchman, Jay Forrester, and unidentified graduate students accomplished the development in joint and separate efforts. There were also British claims to the invention. In any case, IBM had little to do with it.

to the company's world and placed on a well-paid shelf at the IBM Systems Research Institute at United Nations Plaza in New York. Mc-Pherson, Dr. Grosch, and Dr. Eckert were the first of the company with broad and creative ideas on computer application. But it was Aiken, not they, who was the administrator of early projects.

Immediately following its dedication he rented the Mark I to the Navy, without moving it from the Harvard laboratory. Ensign Campbell and a lady named Grace Hopper, well known as an early technician, were put in charge of programming. She is, after a long period out of uniform, now back in the U.S. Navy as an officer. Grace Hopper and Aiken put the computer to work calculating Bessel functions, later published in a dozen or more thick volumes by the Harvard Computing Laboratory.

To some scientists, the fantastic word size specifications and the twenty-three decimal digit capacity bordered on the absurd, particularly in view of the nature of the computation projects to which the machine was assigned. Admittedly, this was a hindsight judgment of those who thought it would have been quite as possible, since so much money, talent, and engineering time was devoted to the development of the computer anyway, to have assembled an apparatus more nearly the equivalent of the Eckert and Mauchly ENIAC.

The Bessel tabulations were not used much, beyond demonstrating that the ASCC could function accurately and to extended digit range. The volumes were placed in university math and research libraries and in the Smithsonian Institution, but their value was duplicated in other tabulations. They brought in money, even though other computers (human) said they wouldn't have bothered with them. Aiken used the funds to establish a computer construction laboratory that built a competitive machine, the Mark II. It was finally sold to the Dahlgren Proving Ground on the lower Potomac, where it was devoted to ballistic calculations for the Navy—useful, but comparatively primitive, work. Income derived from Dahlgren, together with large IBM contributions, was applied to the construction of Mark III, which Aiken wanted to sell to the U.S. Air Force. By this time, a professional computing society had been established, excitement was building up, and a new industry of unfathomable dimensions was under way, three years almost to the day after the first Harvard dedication.

To build the SSEC, on Watson's instructions the Endicott plant worked twenty-four hours a day, seven days a week, and accomplished the astonishing feat within a year. It was the last of many notable projects for such old seniors as Frank Hamilton, C. D. Lake, and their crew, with a new generation of M.I.T. graduates moving onto the scene. Watson ordered the French Bootery, which Herbert Grosch thought was a showroom for fashionable foot fetishists anyway, removed from IBM property on the 57th Street side, after buying up its lease. The new computer was assembled and put into operation in the vacated space. Three days before the formal and ceremonial unveiling, Watson arrived on an inspection tour. All the programs and literature had been printed, and press releases and photographs prepared. Watson himself was ready to accept, as he often did with tear-filled eyes, the usual plaque with its baroque prose about men of vision penetrating the depths of nature, revealing the phenomena of the universe.

Six cylindrical pillars, about two and a half feet in diameter, polished black marble concealing upright steel girders, prevented an unobstructed view of the installation.

"Those pillars spoil the appearance of this room," Watson said to the men encircling him. "Will you have them removed, please, before the dedication." There was silence, and involuntary nods of acquiescence from men who, knowing the pillars held the building up, suspecting that no less authority than the creator of the world in seven days could meet the schedule, habitually were prepared to follow orders. When Watson departed in dignity, there was an outburst of laughter, in which those charged with responsibility for the high-speed defiance of the law of gravity did not participate. Instead, they held a conference.

Seventy-two hours or so later, guests at the dedication were handed the public relations literature. Glossy photographs of the exhibition hall and a large double-page spread in color—an artist's rendering of the scene—showed the spacious expanse, dominated by the wall-to-wall computer, quite free of the presence of marble pillars, against which guests lounged or around which they strolled during the proceedings. The retoucher's brush, and IBM's capacity for having produced a corrected set of literature and photos, gave the appearance that what still held the building up had been taken away. Mr. Watson thought the brochure was lovely and that the whole place looked much better. If he noted the discrepancy from the rostrum on Dedication Day, he didn't mention it. The pillars are still there.

The monument Watson built for himself, aside from IBM itself, was the Watson Laboratory at Columbia. It was developed under a plan he worked out with the admired and admiring Nicholas Murray Butler, who concluded his long reign at the university in 1944. The Watson art library at the Metropolitan Museum in New York and the company's research center at Yorktown Heights, both of which bear his name, were posthumous memorials. The research center, perhaps IBM's most elegant piece of real estate, is situated on some of the loveliest of Westchester County's countryside. It was once an estate of orchards, trails, and nineteenth-century buildings. Regarded among scientists as quite on a par with such great centers of its kind as the Bell Laboratory, it was built under the administration of Watson's son, Tom Junior. An imposing bronze bust of Watson, designed and executed by sculptor Jacques Lipschitz, greets visitors entering the curved stone and bronze structure.

One story, conceivably apocryphal, or perhaps oversimplified with the passing of time, suggested that Tom was hoodwinked by an enterprising lower-echelon entrepreneur in a matter concerning the apple orchards. He admired the beauty and fragrance of the blossoming trees and their row-upon-row order in the growing season, but was less enchanted with the layers of rotting apples that sent a sour aroma across the landscape in the harvest season. There was the further annoyance and danger of marauding poachers trespassing on the place to slaughter deer attracted to the grounds for a meal of fallen apples. Someone, so the story went, persuaded him that appropriate spraying would permit full blossoming and foliage but stop an apple at its core. The image of springtime loveliness, however, did not deter the reality of fecundity or the subsequent slippery blanket of fruition decayed.

The Watson monument at Columbia first took shape with the purchase of a fraternity house, owned by a moribund chapter, at 612 West 116th Street. This was soon abandoned when the growing Laboratory was moved to another resident house on 115th Street. The house was gutted to the wall, and steel beams installed under aged polished wood floors. The marble fireplaces, over which hung the inevitable large photographs showing Watson in the company of a THINK sign, were restored. It was wartime, and every building material from nails to fixtures was rationed, so the undertaking was not completed with the dispatch Watson preferred.

Herbert Grosch, who was engaged in draft-exempt work for the Farrand Optical Company in the Bronx, read an article in the March, 1945, issue of *Science Magazine,* reporting that Watson was creating a new laboratory resource at Columbia, headed by Wallace Eckert. It was to be independent of earlier research and experimental operations, and Grosch, who admired Eckert not solely because he had weathered some years of association with Watson without visible scars, but because he was a top ranking scientist, wrote him to suggest an experiment in designing optical lenses with automatic digital machinery. Eckert called him and invited him to join the staff, but his draft board declined to release Grosch for any change in jobs.

However, Eckert had accepted a task from Los Alamos, which before that had been to him only a post office box at which Hans A. Bethe, chief of the theoretical physics division, received his mail. Once the Watson Laboratory had established this connection, it was not surprising that an authority in the Manhattan Project, with a well-placed telephone call, had Dr. Grosch mysteriously detached from Farrand to Morningside Heights. He became, beard and all, one of the unlikeliest IBM employees of that or any other time in Watson's life, without a personnel interview, a medical examination, a copy of the songbook, or a brochure containing the essay on trust and the IBM spirit. He also became an admiring and observant Watson watcher: he judged Watson to be an extraordinary man and, simultaneously, a challenge to any analytical, disciplined mind.

In addition to their scientific pursuits at the Laboratory, nearly all staff members had some function or other in completing and operating the facility. Grosch was supposed to put together a research library on the second floor.

A skier, mountain climber, auto racer, and tireless conversationalist, Grosch was an uncommon and unsettling personage in IBM circles, although much welcomed by Eckert, who was Watson's first subordinate Ph.D., and by fellow scientists. He became somwhat secretly, and understandably, known as Fearless Grosch. He found a confusing system of priorities prevailing at the Watson Laboratory, some prescribed by wartime restrictions and some enforced by arbitrary interpretations of the IBM spirit. For example, he was unable to get books for the library.

The Watson kit arrived, and was incorporated into the decor— photographs, THINK signs, and the like. There was some shifting around of Watson portraits, because he himself would sometimes prefer to see on view one of several permissible types, then tire of it and require a change. Eckert had to go down to galactic headquarters at 590 Madison and wait outside Watson's door to get authorization for equipment which the government much of the time disallowed. Circumspect intervention by an anonymous and more exalted authority in one of the bomb projects was called for to bend the priority system.

A budget of $30,000 provided the library with beautiful shelving, W. & J. Sloane furnishings, and matching celestial globes, all of which conformed to the Watson style of decor, but there were still no books.

A requisition was required for each volume, book by book. Fearless Grosch made some pointed objective comment, which, owing to mildly blasphemous inferences which accompanied it, disturbed the chaste ears of Mary Noble Smith, Watson's director of art, auction scout, curator, etc. She served as an advance divining rod to locate temperamentally troublesome areas around which Watson sometimes could be circuited. But between them, flexibility was eased into the rigid system of priorities, and books could then be ordered by lot and catalogue classification. Cartons began to arrive from Barnes & Noble, McGraw-Hill, and other purveyors of source material.

Mary Noble Smith, who knew nearly as much about what Watson liked in art and decorating as Fred Nichol knew about what he liked to hear at company conventions, called upon Watson's vast collection, stored—when not on exhibit or in use—at Manhattan's Hahn Brothers art warehouse. The inventory included a wide range of paintings, ceramic pieces, tapestries, Oriental rugs, objets d'art, and period furniture pieces, along with the plaques and awards that had proliferated over the years. At that time, Watson owned an impressive—by volume, at least—ceramics collection, which he had acquired, nearly all at a single purchase, on a visit to an upstate New York exhibit. The main assortment represented the work of American artists, and while some of it was very good, some of it was less so. Watson had seen it and said, "Fine, I'll take it."

The exhibit director, accustomed to selling a piece or two at a time, asked what he preferred.

"The pieces are for sale, aren't they?"

"Yes, sir, most of them."

"Fine, we'll take them."

Mary Noble Smith had the collection carted off to Hahn, and selected ceramic pieces were channeled uptown to the Laboratory, along with what she determined were appropriate paintings for the walls and an Oriental carpet of the correct size for each room.

Watson's interest in art was sincere and unapologetic, ever since he had bought an oil of a Maine coastal landscape at the age of twenty-four. His interest was business-oriented, too, and much publicized. Franklin D. Roosevelt had once appointed him chairman of National Art Week, and Watson had sought to stimulate artists to exercise more eclecticism in their subject material and styles because, he said, too many artists weren't producing what businessmen wanted and were not, therefore, alert to opportunity.

Mrs. Smith selected a collection of portraits of "Men of Science" for the Library, and Grosch approved in principal. He demurred, however, when romanticized oils of Henry Ford and other well known industrialists arrived. One of Charles Lindbergh might do, since the hero-flyer of the Atlantic crossing two decades earlier had indeed become a recognized scientific investigator. "But what's the matter with them?" Mrs. Smith asked. "What scientists do you *like?*" Grosch accepted portraits of the Wright Brothers as applicable to the genre, and together they located one of Josiah Willard Gibbs, the Yale University authority on thermodynamics, and another that did not appear too repelling an insult to the memory of Benjamin Franklin.

"Newton, Einstein, or Gauss, the inventor of binary arithmetic—people like that—would be right."

Some weeks later, a huge oil portrait of Newton, "with rather a full rigging style about it," arrived and was put on exhibit. Mrs. Smith had commissioned someone to produce it, and Grosch felt he was progressing.

Watson interested himself in the place from time to time in the course of construction, generally leaving in his wake design changes made, on intuition or impulse, on the spot. A decision had been made relating to the placement of urinals and lavatories in locations on different floors, commensurate with the sex distribution of the work inhabitants. What with one change and another, a visiting vice-president determined that a statistical imbalance had inadvertently resulted. In his helpful way, upon discovering a possibly needless inconvenience, he rearranged the location of some of the toilet equipment with respect to urinal vis-a-vis lidded bowl. Such second guessing of Watson was hazardous business. Wallace Eckert, who cultivated the technique of detachment from such nonscientific matters as a sensible approach to harmony and survival, said it never happened—at least not that way—but others less prone to forget the incident attributed his view to a loss of memory prompted by delicacy. The urinals and bowls were redistributed according to Watson's original computations, which through the years allowed a good many men and women, whose functions in separate departments were otherwise unrelated, to meet each other in passage and cultivate friendships in the stairwell. The vice-president who bore the blame for the unacceptable review of arithmetic disappeared into the management of the Diebold Safe Company.

With such important matters ultimately resolved, the day approached when Watson was to make his ceremonial, or dedicatory—as opposed to unheralded—visitation. The harbinger of the event was Mary Noble Smith, who appeared to prepare the establishment in the manner of a Potemkin Village in the path of the Czarina's carriage. She opened an account at a nearby florist's shop and had, for the few remaining days, fresh flowers delivered daily in a rehearsal calculated to remove bugs from the operation. On visitation day itself, the last delivery arrived by midmorning; after that, the account was closed.

An internal communication system kept the Laboratory staff informed. A telephone message reported Watson and party departing aboard a limousine from corporate headquarters, headed north. A second message—Grosch thought monitors must have manned phone booths along the route—confirmed that Seventy-second Street had been crossed more or less on schedule. The last outpost reporting was at Ninety-Second Street, by which time all stations were attended, all systems operational, the back stairs evacuated, polished woodwork aglow, cut flowers at the ready, paintings shown beneath spotted illumination, the low creative hum of researchers at work softly charging the air, matching celestial globes reposing in the frames of each carefully balanced world. Bracketed fore and aft by vice-presidents, with John McPherson as forward scout, the command party entered the foyer.

Occupants at desks rose, smiled, and sat again as Watson passed in dignity. There was no elevator in the building. Peter Luhn, an inventor of gracious manner, took over as escort and guide, casually careful not to body-block McPherson on the rounds. Gathered in what had been the living room, the party assembled in a crescent behind him, Watson looked long and thoughtfully at the solemn visage of Watson meeting his gaze above the large fireplace. On a cream-colored wall, a French oil in warm colors reflected the light and harmony of an earlier century. Erect and handsome, his imposing presence evoking respect and silence, the aging man, slower in his motion now and more deliberate and studied than usual, allowed the surroundings to absorb him. Then he spoke.

"This is *very* handsome."

A quickening of happy smiles and soft assent, all heads nodding affirmatively in unison, brought motion to the tableau. Crisply then, and frowning, a hint of showmanship in his tone, Watson spoke again:

"But it's *all* wrong."

With beat sustained, tempo steady, their imitative frown collective, heads nodded negatively. "This place is devoted to science. We should have pictures of galaxies, exploding atoms, giant telescopes, things that suggest progress and vision."

Mary Noble Smith was silent in her agony; all, in fact, were silent for some moments.

"No, Mr. Watson," said a voice from somewhere behind the party, which divided, like the sea receiving the wanderers, to give Mr. Watson an unobstructed view into the bearded face of Herbert Grosch. Not even a mustache existed in all of IBM, but Watson did not flinch. He listened. "The people who come here are accustomed to that sort of thing. They are—they will be—impressed with this fine art collection of IBM."

The voice of disagreement hung in the stillness; no cue rescued the vice-presidents. Looking directly at the furred face, Watson pointedly changed the subject, and a repressed sigh changed into the opening words of group chatter. Mary Noble Smith returned the next day to say she had decided, on the basis of Watson's comment, to replace the paintings with works in keeping with his vision. Eckert stayed out of it, and Grosch protested that Watson had seemed to accept his reasoning. "Want me to call him up now and ask him?" Grosch asked. "No, no," she wailed. Things remained as they were.

Contemporary literature and magazine articles of the years after World War II when the mechanical brain computers made their impact on public fancy and fear evoked a good deal of speculation on whether or not the new machines could simulate or take over human thought processes, or, as Watson would say, THINK. The question remains a lively issue and is not altogether resolved, in part because of the imprecision of semantics and in part because a substantial output of nonsense passes for serious dialogue. Nevertheless, Watson, Aiken, Vannevar Bush, and John von Neumann, often with sorely tried patience, sought to reassure the fearful that the computers could not replace mortal scientists, mechanize mathematics altogether, institutionalize logic, or demoralize humanity beyond its normal capacity to do so by itself. Howard Aiken somewhat angrily reminded the public that a computer could no more "think than a stone." It was similar to Lady Lovelace's assurance that Babbage's computer could only do "whatever we know how to order it to perform." In contemporary parlance, a computer could not tell you the time of day without a program. The "brain" of a computer was only that of the programmer and his punch cards, the holes in paper tape, and the artful control of power surging through circuits.

The argument has long enlivened seminars of biologists, with the "vitalists" claiming that the human organism is possessed of an essential vital force which cannot be duplicated by mechanical means. "Mechanists" on the contrary, see it as a highly complex, often mysterious, machine. Not all mechanists are atheists or godless communists either, as worried fundamentalists sometimes like to imagine. With the creation of life by laboratory techniques under investigation in the wake of phenomenal biochemical discoveries, the question awaits scientific resolution. And the computer may well have, or at least influence, the last word on the subject.

One man among many who put aspects of the vitalist-mechanist issue under examination was Norbert Wiener, who made the newly named field of cybernetics comprehensible and seemed to lend support to some of the anxiety evolving from advanced computer technology. Wiener developed solid hypotheses by studying the human mind and the capacity of computers to emulate it. Not everything he said or wrote evoked a joyful response, and the implications of his studies had to be taken seriously. They are being carefully evaluated now by some of the new breed of scientists at IBM, in the universities, and elsewhere.

Dr. Wiener had gone to M.I.T. after World War I, and there he and his associates examined the disciplines of both physiologists and mathematicians. One of his companions was Dr. Arturo Rosenbleuth, then of the Harvard Medical School, and when Wiener published his book on cybernetics in 1948, with the Instituto Nacional de Cardiologia, of Mexico. Another was a former student of Wiener's, Dr. Manuel Sandoval Vallarta, a Mexican and professor of physics at M.I.T.

The group assembled by Wiener was, in part, a realization of his "dream . . . of an institution of independent scientists, working together . . . not as subordinates of some great executive officer, but joined by the desire, indeed the spiritual necessity, to understand the region as a whole and to lend one another the strength of that understanding."[6]

Wiener felt that mathematicians need not possess the skill to conduct physiological experiments, but must have the knowledge and cultivated intuition to understand them. Physiologists did not have to prove a mathematical theorem, but had to be able to grasp its significance and to tell mathematicians what to search for. The colony of scientists at M.I.T. had long before agreed on these matters. With the outbreak of World War II, Wiener's functions were determined by his close association with computing machines developed by Vannevar Bush and his work with Dr. Yuk Wing Lee on the design of electric networks.

The scanning process, as employed in television, offered to Wiener a way to increase the data that computers dealt with beyond anything possible in ordinary differential equations. He saw early the necessity of

[6] *Cybernetics—Or Control and Communication in the Animal and the Machine,* Norbert Wiener, Boston, 1948.

performing "individual processes with so high a degree of accuracy that the enormous repetition of elementary processes should not bring about a cumulative error so great as to swamp all accuracy."

He and an associate, Julian H. Bigelow, described the "feedback" flow of the human brain and saw it applicable to computers. They were handicapped by the lack of unity in the literature on the problems and by the absence of common terminology. They coined "one artificial neo-Greek expression to fill the gap . . . we have decided to call the entire field of control and communications theory, whether in the machine or in the animal, by the name of *cybernetics.*"

A joint paper by Rosenbleuth, Bigelow, and Wiener in 1942 was devoted to the problems of inhibitions in the central nervous system. A relationship was examined between the influence of mathematical logic and the organization of the cortex of the brain, which had been under study by a Wiener associate, Dr. Warren McCulloch, among others, at the University of Illinois Medical School. By extension, "a reasoning machine," a far more encompassing term than computer, could be foreseen.

"If I were to choose the patron saint of cybernetics out of the history of science, I would have to choose Leibnitz," Wiener wrote. "The philosophy of Leibnitz centers about two closely related concepts: that of a universal symbolism and that of a calculus of reasoning. . . . Now, just as the calculus of arithmetic lends itself to a mechanization of progressing through the abacus and the desk computing machine to the ultra-rapid computing machines of the present day [the late 1940's], so the calculus ratiocinator of Leibnitz contains the germs of the *machina* ratiocintrix, or the reasoning machine."

Wiener reviewed the studies of his colleagues with Dr. Aiken at Harvard, Dr. von Neumann at the Institute for Advanced Study, and Dr. Goldstine, of the ENIAC project, and gained confidence in a thesis in the late stages of formation.

"It has long been clear to me that the modern ultra-rapid computing machine was in principal an ideal central nervous system to an apparatus for automatic control; that is its input and output need not be in the form of numbers or diagrams but might very well be, respectively, the readings of artificial sense organs such as photoelectric cells or thermometers and the performance of motors or solenoids. With the aid of strain gauges or similar agencies to read the performance of these motor organs and to report, to 'feed back,' to the central control system as an artificial kinesthetic sense, we are already in a position to construct artificial machines of almost any degree of elaborateness or performance."

It had occurred to Wiener long before Nagasaki that "we were here in the presence of another social potentiality of unheard-of importance for good and evil. . . . For one thing, it makes the metaphorical dominance of the machine, as imagined by Samuel Butler, a most immediate and nonmetaphorical problem. It gives the human race a new and most effective collection of mechanical slaves to perform its labor . . . and it does not involve the direct demoralizing effects of human cruelty." At the same time, Wiener was haunted by doubts.

". . . any labor that accepts the conditions of competition with slave labor accepts the conditions of slave labor and *is* essentially slave labor. . . . It may very well be a good thing for humanity to have the machine remove from it the need of menial and disagreeable tasks; or it may not. I do not know. It cannot be good for these new potentialities to be assessed in terms of the market, of the money they save; and it is precisely the terms of the open market, the 'fifth freedom,' that have become the shibboleth of the sector of American opinion represented by the National Association of Manufacturers and the *Saturday Evening Post*. I say *American* opinion, for as an American, I know it best. But the hucksters recognize no national boundaries."

Just as there was no rate of pay at which a pick-and-shovel laborer could live which was low enough to compete with a steam shovel, said Wiener, the industrial revolution was "similarly bound to devalue the human brain, at least in its simple and more routine decisions." He acknowledged that the skilled carpenter, mechanic, and dressmaker "has in some degree survived the industrial revolution," and thought the skilled scientist and administrator would survive "the reasoning machine." But the future was bleak for "the average human being of mediocre attainments." He would have nothing to sell that was worth anyone's money to buy.

The characteristics of the cells of the brain, the neurons—and their equivalent in the stored memory of a computer—are dual: off and on, firing or in repose, working or latent. They pass up response, or they respond. If the computer takes the place of mediocre brains, it makes obsolete in some form many, perhaps most, of the human brains on earth, and science thus puts the outlaw's curse on a portion of the helpless human race. In view of the nature of man which, while changeable, alters slowly, Wiener had rather a gloomy outlook.

"The answer," he said, "is to have a society based on human values other than buying or selling. To arrive at this society, we need a good deal of planning and a good deal of struggle—which, if the best comes to the best, may be on the plane of ideas. . . ."

Motivated by sociological concerns, Wiener tried to pass on his information and understanding to "those who have an active interest in the conditions and the future of labor—that is, the labor unions." He managed to confer, in sympathetic hearings, with one or two persons high up in the Congress of Industrial Organizations (CIO). But, as the labor leaders themselves agreed, in both the U.S. and England, unions and the labor movement are "in the hands of highly limited personnel, thoroughly well trained in the specialized problems of shop steward-ship . . . and totally unprepared to enter into the larger political, technical, sociological, and economic questions which concern the very existence of labor. The labor union official usually comes from the exacting life of a workman into the exacting life of an administrator, without any opportunity for broader training; and for those who have this training, a union career is not generally inviting. Nor, quite naturally, are the unions receptive to such people."

Those who contributed to the new science of cybernetics, as did Watson's patronage and his own engineers, along with scientists of Wiener's status, "stand on a moral position which is, to say the least, not very comfortable," he said.

"We can only hand it over into the world that exists about us, and this is the world of Belsen and Hiroshima. We do not even have the choice of suppressing these new technical developments. They belong to the age, and the most any of us can do by suppression is to put the development of the subject into the hands of the most irresponsible and the most venal of engineers."

The best that could be hoped for was that a large public would come to understand the trend, "and to confine our personal efforts to those fields, such as psychology and physiology, most remote from war and exploitation."

Scientists of the late nineteen-forties were not entirely without hope that computer technology, and the obsolescence of ordinary brain power, might somehow motivate the industrial society of which IBM was so significant a component toward good and humane ends that would "outweigh the incidental contribution we are making to the concentration of power."

But IBM, as a corporation of expansion and growth, could do little about fundamentally altering society's values. Watson was an exemplary international personage to whom corporate growth was good and to whom enormous growth was enormously good. Happiness and money went together. Computers were tools; they couldn't think. If they were to be used to develop a concentration of power, there was still no way—and no motive, as Dr. Wiener clearly said—to suppress them. It would only make things worse.

Unfortunately, as Wiener said in concluding his writing in 1947, power is "always concentrated, by its very conditions of existence, in the hands of the most unscrupulous." As for his own hope for the future, it was sadly "very slight."

10.
The Lengthening Shadow

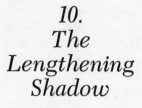

THE PEDDLER WHOSE LIFE began a little more than a decade after the American Civil War, who had inscribed his name on walls around the little village of Painted Post, who had talked with kings and ministers and had been warmed by their compliments and honors, was on, the threshold of old age. Before the end of the nineteen-fifties, he had accumulated nearly thirty national decorations from as many countries, with one or two more to go. The abbreviated recital of his accomplishments and associations was the largest entry in *Who's Who,* and notable among the listings was a long string of honorary degrees from universities in tribute to an intuitive, persevering, uneducated benefactor who had, in most cases, befriended or supported them with his money and technological resources.

He put his son, Thomas J. Watson, Junior, into the company as president in 1950 and stepped up to the restored position of Chairman of the Board, which he had himself abolished upon assumption of total command and the rechristening of his corporation. Tom Junior, however, was still only the boss's son until, slowly and at times imperceptibly, time and circumstance and corporate necessity, in combination with the younger Watson's will, as erratic and as indomitable as the old man's, produced the inevitable transfer of power.

In the dialogue about the implications of computers and the promise or the threat they encompassed in their assault against menial work and the mind of mankind, old Watson saw only glimpses of the promise, of the business of—as Norbert Wiener had said—their value in terms of money saved, of markets created. Watson was a venerable industrialist whose vision of the future obscured the proliferation of uses to which computer technology might be applied.

The technology would help advance some fields of science immeasurably and create the need for the application of new counterpart technology to deal with them. But only in the more generalized ways could Watson see their significance, and largely, but not exclusively, in the field of business and in the area of education which, to him, was the breeding ground for the handmaidens and managers of business. As the patron, rather than the scientist, he could no more be expected to assimilate or project the implications of the technology in whose development he had played a significant part than Duryea, Daimler, or Henry Ford could in the case of combustion-powered vehicles which, in making men highly mobile, would undermine the quality of life in cities and make them all but uninhabitable, while attendant conditions enforced habitation within them.

Concentration of power and the amassing of industrial and financial resources seemed appropriate to Watson so long as moderate regulation, the taxation of which he approved, and a decent regard for people—at least for the people involved—was exercised and applied. With a double-edged gift for reducing the most profound questions to monumental simplicity, he instinctively avoided indulgence in the complexities of human doubt, in reflection on ironic contradiction, and for all his honesty professed concern for international affairs, in sociological and political phenomena beyond his own experience.

To him, said *Fortune Magazine,* "a complex and terrifying world becomes transparent and simple. Let him expound the necessity of giving religion a preference over everything else," as he could readily do the day before canceling the Lord's Prayer in favor of a rousing sales talk, "and you could not help falling to your knees." Art, in which his interest was as deeply genuine as it was narrow, offered the artist an opportunity "to profitably continue to plumb the inspirational potentialities of business and industry."[1] Art, like the company's publications, the great sales conventions, his most significant philanthropy, and his internationalism, were variants of business. Not that he was hypocritical, or altogether a one-dimensional man; it was as far as his vision carried. The fact that a good deal of validity and authority were attributed to his simple values and analysis was scarcely his fault. His manner and life style, his dignified evocation of emotion and conviction of the efficacy of elemental virtues, combined with his phenomenal success in conventional terms, put people off balance so that they tended to see the world as he saw it. To this extent, he could quite inadvertently corrupt. It is an irony that would have escaped him, or have been peremptorily dismissed if noted.

[1] *Fortune,* January, 1940.

Thomas Watson during a marathon sales lecture at National Cash Register in 1913.

International Time Recording Company in Endicott was typical of the ten small companies Charles R. Flint assembled into the Computing-Tabulating-Recording Company (CTR) in 1913.

Left: Charles Babbage's "Analytical Engine," designed in 1820, was a digital decimal computer which controlled itself internally by punched cards and automatically printed out answers, much like modern computers. This small prototype model was constructed, but the limitations of early nineteenth-century materials and manufacturing techniques made it impossible to construct the large steam-driven machine itself. *Below:* Dr. Vannevar Bush with a section of his Differential Analyzer. A mechanical analog computer like this one was slow by today's standards, working only about 100 times faster than a human operator using a desk calculator. Dr. Bush developed his computer during the 1930's at MIT.

Above: Lieutenant-Colonel Thomas J. Watson, Jr. and IBM Vice-President Charles Kirk during World War II.

Top right: This card is an example of Thomas Watson's leadership. It was given to all salesmen. He thought of it at a Hundred Percent Club banquet and jotted it down on the great scratch pad that stood on an easel beside him. *Right:* The IBM Marching Band.

Conception.
Consistency.
Co-Operation.
Courage.
Confidence.

THE FIVE C's

..... *"that we must possess if we want to do our full share."*

Meeting of the Hundred Percent Club at the IBM Homestead Grounds in 1950

Watson plays host to General Eisenhower in Endicott prior to the Presidential election of 1952.

The leadership at IBM; clockwise from left foreground: Thomas J. Watson, Jr., Chairman of the Board; T. Vincent Learson, President; Arthur K. Watson, President of the World Trade Corporation (the international division of IBM); and Albert L. Williams, Chairman of the Executive Committee.—Wide World Photos

ft: Watson crosses the finish line in his cutter Palawan ring an Annapolis-to-Newport yacht race.

A rare touch of humor at IBM. At the Watson Laboratory this abacus is carefully housed, presumably in the event of a computer malfunction.

Because music induced emotion and inspiration, he saw that with all the arts it had a value related to life. But, where emotion and art are to many an often profound experience that nourishes the spirit and expands the realm of what man acknowledges as his soul, to Watson, emotion and spiritual nourishment were expected—since they accomplished such in his own case—to make men work better, THINK better in their jobs, make money, be steadfast and loyal, represent the company in all things, and reap the happiness deriving therefrom. What else in the name of God and man was life all about?

He commissioned a symphony for IBM, copies of which remain in the possession of old IBM men and in scattered music libraries, which could make him cry. Yet he was tone deaf. The IBM symphony, written by Vittorio Giannini, was programmatic in structure. Its first movement was not substantially different, in its intent, from the art of Stalinist Russia; if it didn't explicitly make one love a collective's tractor or deify the adventure in Spain, it did melodically recite the struggles of mankind and cry out instrumentally that IBM was excitement, confirming that there was the place to be, in privilege and hope.

The second movement theme threaded the company anthem, the endlessly familiar "Ever Onward," into the quest for peace and world trade, opening the gates to the final movement and its potpourri of hymns and anthems from various countries whose destinies were thus tied to the business of Watson's IBM, which was in fact the true world.

Who was there to say, other than cerebral critics with forums so small that they were nearly unnoticed, or managers among inconsequential competitors, that the simple philosophy and the extravagant, often whimsical, expenditures did not have any special application to IBM's business? Watson seldom, if ever, had to worry about a competitor's cutting prices or paying higher salaries to attract his people away from the company of opportunity. In the absence of downward trends in IBM, questions about the validity of Watson's methods and style were heresy and could be proved as such. The face of Providence, as the *Fortune* writer wrote, shone ever on IBM and Watson's smiling men, who moved clean-shaven, with barbered heads, stiff white collars gleaming above dark suits on which no dandruff dared to fall, cuffs extended into little white ruffs about the wrists, going competently about their appointed rounds. There was no snake in Eden.

"We love you, and we know you have [IBM's] welfare at heart," Watson would say, sometimes adding the ominous reminder, "or you wouldn't be here."

Watson was no glad-hander and was seldom ebullient. When they sang, "Your glory tide will never stem" to him, or when Fred Nichol fed into ears that demanded but seemed often not to hear praise few men would tolerate, he lived up to it and above it with a demeanor that could transfix the multitude to whom worship was a condition of existence. When he spoke, his face shone with a heavenly light, his suppliant voice, earnestly resonant with sincerity, unfaltering—after he had conquered a mild stammer—even when he lapsed into his countryman's cadence and poor grammar, imposed the finality of resolved truth on phrases which seemed to have passed inspection in dress rehearsal. The content often could not pass analytical inspection, but it scarcely mattered. Style and conviction, authority and bearing transcended meaning.

When he was seventy years old, he exercised his persuasive power on a graduating class at the academy of the Federal Bureau of Investigation in Washington to call for an international police force, modeled on J. Edgar Hoover's G-men, to track down "potential" war criminals. It was necessary, he said, "to detect the evils as they arise," and to "back up the Bureau of Investigation with armed forces and political policies that will prevent any nation or group of nations from bringing about another war."

At times he appeared to be transiently troubled about the kind of world, or the kind of America, that might develop after World War II. In a speech reprinted in a publication of the Carnegie Endowment for International Peace, of which he was a trustee, Watson said he favored one type of propaganda while deploring another. "We are living in very unusual times," he observed. "There is a great deal of propaganda. One type comes from the minds and hearts of intelligent, honest people who are telling us of conditions at home and abroad, which we ought to know about and which stimulates and directs our thoughts along constructive lines. I believe and like to indulge in this type of propaganda.

"There is another kind of propaganda, however, which has a detrimental effect on American institutions and American traditions.

"I feel it is the duty of every right-thinking American citizen in his own individual community to do everything he can do to expose and stamp out this type of propaganda. If it comes from undesirable aliens, there are national laws that provide a remedy.

"If it comes from undesirable American citizens, and if our present laws do not go far enough to cover such cases, legislation should be enacted to take care of that—because our form of government is so fine and precious to all of us that we must assume direct responsibility for its protection."

It was not his advancing age, at least apparently not, that conditioned his failure to hear the significance of his own words. He could be equally inattentive to words, quite aside from Nichol's accolades, directed more or less squarely at him. As an honored guest of the Newcomen Society of England at the Hotel Pierre in New York on May 7, 1948, a speaker listed the impressive array of Watson's directorships, honorary degrees, foreign decorations, and philanthropic causes, then added that Watson could generally be found "at the bottom of practically every worthwhile movement toward international understanding." It was, of course, no more than a slip of the tongue, an unintentional ambiguous observation, perhaps not worthy of note, which caused a ripple of response among the guests, but to Watson it was unheard. Style and presumed intent left him oblivious to content, and sometimes oblivious to facts troubling to many Americans.

In a little statement on "The Faith of America," he was able to see Christianity "as the greatest power for good that the world has ever known," and to see America's "belief in God, religion, and our fellow man" as the reason why the United States had never "denied the privilege of citizenship" to anyone; he added "equal rights and opportunity have been withheld from no one."

Watson was not oblivious to the plight of non-white minorities in the United States, but—and he had much company in his position on the issue—he could believe what seemed appropriate. As the writers of the IBM company biography said, "he could ignore what he did not want to acknowledge." In more explicit terms, a highly educated man who knew and worked for him for some years reported that the racial issue and its attendant turmoil were "repulsive" to him.

Humor, which might have leavened his rhetoric, or brightened it, was almost alien to Watson, as might be expected of one who could speak with absolving conviction of matters that searching minds could not reduce to absolutes. He could seldom handle it, yet he sometimes tried. The response of laughter was, of course, automatic, notwithstanding the feebleness of his well-intentioned effort.

He liked to tell a story about an incident aboard a Pullman car in his years on the road. To white audiences, who saw in Stepin Fetchit and Bojangles Robinson the stereotype of the complaisant black man, his delineation of a kindly old Pullman car porter in white jacket, scratching his woolly gray hair, was not unrealistic. Such a porter, bowing and servile, saying "Yessuh" and "Nawssuh" often, was so impressed with Mr. Watson's appearance and bearing that he timidly approached him and said, in the white man's dialect made familiar by Mr. Bones and Mr. Jones in traveling minstrel shows:

"Mistah Watson, suh, is you a judge of the court?"

"No, Rufus, I am not."

As Watson recounted the story, the porter shuffled off, scratching his kinky white head, with appropriately humble thanks for the encounter. He returned after a time to ask, "Mistah Watson, is you a undertaker?"

"No, Rufus, I am not an undertaker."

On his third approach and inquiry, the porter deduced: "Mistah Watsun, suh, then you all must be a perfesser in a you-nee-versity. That's what you is."

"No, Rufus," said Watson, "I'm a bishop in the Methodist Church."

The features of Rufus became wreathed in sunny smiles as, his first impression confirmed, he responded in triumph:

"Ah jes *knowed* you was a face card in your perfession."

He had another and more genuine response that could be warmly funny when used effectively. After an overblown dinner introduction by Fred Nichol or some local branch manager, Mr. Watson would walk slowly to the rostrum, taking plenty of time, and say something like this:

"I appreciate all those fine things Mr. Nichol just told you about me, but it raises a question about whether he should be so flowery on this occasion. It reminds me of a time down in the State of Maine one time when I was standing by a bridge that went across a little crick on a country road. A farmer was herding three or four cows and a very young calf across the bridge, and the calf just stopped to look down at the water. Maybe it wanted a drink, I don't know, but a big shiny car came up to the bridge and the man driving it was impatient. When the calf stood there, the man sounded the horn very loud and for a long time. The calf was frightened and jumped around some, then jumped into the crick. The farmer went up to the man in the car and said, 'Now see here, sir, you got no call to be in such a hurry.' The man in the car was ashamed of himself and apologized to the farmer. The animal did not seem to be hurt and the farmer calmed himself and said, 'I thank you and I appreciate your apology, and we'll say no more about it.' The farmer started to go away but stopped and went back to the automobile. Then he said to the man, 'Just the same, don't you kind of think that was an awful loud toot for one little calf?' That is all I have to say about Mr. Nichol's introduction."

The awe and reverence associated with the company name produced odd effects on some IBM people, particularly in the presence of outlanders. A motion picture producer who shot hundreds of hours of film of Watson and sales conventions was frequently aware of the self-conscious editing of conversation in his presence. The producer had once cut several days of shooting into a film production of speeches, instruction, and award presentations which consumed six hours of viewing time. Watson had prints of the film, all six hours of it, sent around the country, with orders to everyone to see it. The feedback from the field on the idea lacked the usual enthusiasm.

Riding in a limousine to an airport on one occasion with two IBM executives, one of them a vice-president, the film producer tried to indicate a lack of curiosity about the shop talk in which his companions were engaged. They were discussing arrangements for a sales convention and speculating on the suitability of some parts of the program. Tom Junior at that time had been elevated to the presidency, with authority over the scheduled convention that was, naturally, subject to old Watson's veto. The problem of preparing arrangements pleasing to both the father and the son troubled the two men, who went through the entire dialogue without mentioning either Watson by name. When the lesser executive finished outlining one plan, the vice-president said:

"Yes, that's all very well. But *Someone* might not like it, and we'd better think about an alternative."

The alternative was reviewed for a time, after which the other executive said:

"I have a feeling that *Someone's Son* isn't going to like that idea, either. Now what'll we do?"

The words Someone or Somebody were not uncommonly used in speaking of the Watsons when a third person, within hearing, was thought to be capable of imprudently or inaccurately reporting an IBM man's veneration for a Watson.

Life in the private homes of erring upper echelon executives could be disruptive and unpredictable, particularly among those men and their families who, regardless of their title, status, and large salaries, were often called upon to perform duties that were said to be more appropriately the work of "trained seals." Watson liked to make it clear that his own sufferance was not taken lightly, and that an exalted manager was as much in range of his observation as a lowly trainee. A folk tale known to people in the enclave community of Ardsley-on-Hudson, one of those suburban bedroom villages in which it was considered appropriate for IBM families to live, illustrates the extent to which Watson's presence could alter the most carefully laid plans.

Wallace W. McDowell, an engineer who subsequently was sent to Binghamton with the title of "IBM vice-president in residence," was enjoying himself among friends at a party at his Ardsley home one evening when he was called to the telephone: Watson, who was nearby and wanted to talk with him, would be dropping around shortly. McDowell and his understanding guests were said to have swung quickly into action, running the rum to remote rooms, disposing of the evidence of hyperconviviality, and generally tidying things up, so that when Someone arrived, he looked upon a pleasant household scene of cheerful neighbors engrossed in permissible play and conversation. Even for Mr. McDowell, as dutiful and responsible a subordinate as Watson could ever hope to recruit, the experience was an unusual one, made bearable and free of post-party anxiety by the fact that the Leader had had the good grace and courtesy to make the telephone call before exercising his impulse to visit.

Peter Luhn, the inventor who had escorted the Watson command party on the day Watson inspected the new laboratory at Columbia University, was nearly caught in a disastrous dilemma. Luhn had built two relay calculators for the Watson Laboratory and had displayed them for the first time as part of that memorable tour. Upon studying their performance, Watson was immediately responsive and enthusiastic. "Now, Mr. Luhn," he said, "you ought to do more of this. You ought to build a much larger place for them, down in the basement of the laboratory." The equipment was an early version of a remote access computer utility. Luhn was hastily making notes with Watson pausing now and then to permit him to catch up. When Watson left, Luhn was asked whether he seriously considered dropping other duties which he was expected to perform and devoting himself to the remote access project. "You didn't hear him say anything about money, or staff, did you?" replied Luhn. He filed his notes away and tried not to worry.

Ironically, Watson could have had the ENIAC which Rand ultimately got, had he not been so cocksure that nobody had gained on IBM technologically. ENIAC, the first totally electronic computer, had 18,000 vacuum tubes. There were stories of the lights dimming in West Philadelphia when it was switched on at the Moore School of Electrical Engineering at the University of Pennsylvania. The original design contained no stored program, but this was incorporated by engineers when the machine operated at the Aberdeen Proving Grounds. Dr. John von Neumann, consultant on the design and building of ENIAC, wrote the draft report for the general purpose stored-program computer.

Later, the builders of ENIAC went to the Watson Laboratory to discuss with men there the possibility of joining resources and talent to put their new UNIVAC on the market. Eckert and Mauchly wanted a contract with IBM and the Watson laboratory and to be taken into the company or empowered to produce the computer under some financial arrangement to be agreed upon. Eckert and Mauchly, with a professional reputation among their peers as great as Aiken's in scientific respects, were nearly broke. While they possessed the UNIVAC, they were without resources after their financial backer, a multimillionaire investor, was killed in an airliner crash. Watson Laboratory scientists, impressed by the men and the UNIVAC, were enthusiastic about Eckert's and Mauchly's proposals and recommended negotiations. But word came uptown from galactic headquarters to brush them off. There was, in the words of Watson's decision relayed to the Laboratory, "no reasonable interaction possible between Eckert-Mauchly and IBM."

Remington-Rand put out feelers to the dejected but persevering pair, and the two men went to Florida where, both ashore and afloat on a yacht, they were wined and dined by Jim Rand, who in time produced the revolutionary UNIVAC. The machine and its accomplishments, and especially the publicity it received over television, shook Watson badly and caused tremors throughout the IBM organization. The whole episode, said one of the IBM men involved, "frightened the pee out of the old man, who was convinced he had lost his grip."

Peter Luhn was never confronted by Watson for falling down on the task of establishing the remote access utility, probably because Remington-Rand, which had every capability of doing exactly what Luhn had only orders but no resources to accomplish, likewise overlooked the same development. Watson was not given cause to remember what Luhn could not forget.

In the view of some, Rand was seeking to build his own version of the Watson image, but he continually recoiled from committing the capital essential to the task, the development, and the sales and distribution system. Over and over again, Remington-Rand had the opportunity in UNIVAC to take the lead in the world's newest and most promising industry. Dr. Grosch felt that Rand had repeatedly "snatched defeat from the jaws of victory."

General Electric, which invested more than $500 million in later efforts, got little further than Rand. Radio Corporation of America— even after pirating John Burns, an inside man and efficiency engineer privy to every secret of IBM organization—fell, if not flat, at least to its knees in a subsequent but too belated similar attempt.

Thus the Watson myth was preserved in the wake of an error of judgment of considerable magnitude. There was, however, enough truth left, even with the myth dispelled, to propel IBM onward and upward in a field all but thrust upon it. Competition either did not develop or fell away, and after the depression of the thirties, even after the anti-trust settlements involving the punch card monopoly, there was never any competition that justified the name. Salesmen at conventions were told by IBM officials, including the current president T. Vincent Learson, that IBM time and time again was endangered by competitors—but that was part of the mystique. Salesmen *had* to feel, in accordance with the spirit, that there was an enemy, a devil on their trail, a threat to impel them to exert more and more effort to meet their quotas, win the rewards, make the money, and achieve happiness.

11.
Trust
and
Anti-Trust

———◆———

THE FINAL, TUMULTUOUS EVENTS of Watson's life, aside from yet one more angry and preordained defeat for his company in another anti-trust action, kept him closer than ever to the thrones of the mighty; and in one instance he was instrumental in bringing America's most noted soldier to a seat of status and prestige, from which the unlikely candidate rose to step into the presidency of the United States.

With the creation of the United Nations in June of 1945, Watson felt that his years as a proponent of world trade, as a spokesman for the Carnegie Endowment for International Peace, and as the leading voice in the world for the International Chamber of Commerce had merged into one ultimate opportunity. Support and promote the United Nations, the hope of the world, and all the work of a lifetime might be realized. For, concurrently, IBM would be at the center of the stage, too.

No one was more devoted to, and more hopeful about, the United Nations, nor expressed it with more sincerity, than Thomas J. Watson. Nor did anyone in public life, with the possible later exceptions of such non-industrialists as evangelist Billy Graham and the famed "positive thinker," Norman Vincent Peale, see the functions and goals of the new world institution as clearly and as simply as he did. The IBM publication *THINK* devoted space in nearly every issue to Mr. Watson's uncomplicated hopes and idealism. In fact, the broad program of public relations throughout IBM gave a good deal of emphasis and priority to educating the American populace to support the UN, not only with constructive thinking, but with their prayers and their participation in supporting organizations.

Foreign press representatives at the United Nations, noting Watson's militant support of the deliberative body, thought he might be interested in helping them establish a UN press center for accredited correspondents. He was interested but was advised against involvement by an old friend, Frank E. Gannett, owner of a chain of newspapers and radio stations. Gannett had become touchy about recent scalding criticism of the corporation-owned press in America, criticism for which he was a prime target. Gannett had denounced a critical study group headed by Dr. Robert M. Hutchins, then president of the University of Chicago. Watson, after consideration, declined to sponsor the UN press center; he was just not confortable about it. However, he continued to make occasional speeches about advertising, the educational value of which he found "second only to the public schools."

With Watson's attachment to the United Nations so abundantly evident, some of his closer associates hoped he might interest himself in certain gravely important but controversial matters, such as the rapidly increasing world population, with its prospects of future disaster. Dr. Ben Wood was one of those who thought IBM machines could be put to use in a simulation process that might dramatize the horrors, which many scientists knew only too well, inherent in prolonged life and unchecked fertility. The subject, however, did not appeal to Watson, any more than it did to Eisenhower, who seemed to equate anything involving the Malthusian theory with personal bedroom privacy and, therefore, beyond the range of government interest. Eisenhower later reversed himself on the issue and declared that birth control was, indeed, a matter of world concern.

In the summer of 1946, Watson took time off from his promotion of the affairs of the United Nations to allow himself to be honored at the largest public assembly of his lifetime. It was a testimonial incorrectly billed as a celebration of the thirty-second anniversary of the founding of the company (it was actually the thirty-fifth anniversary of the founding, and the thirty-second anniversary of Watson's association with it).

Company publicity said forty thousand people assembled on the grounds of the IBM country club at Endicott for the great event, and press associations reported the figure faithfully. Special trains and buses carried IBM employees and their families to Endicott from the New England and Middle Atlantic States, and smaller delegations arrived from all over the world to attend the command performance. For Watson it was a day of looking back. His eyes glistening with tears, Mrs. Watson nearly sobbing beside him, Watson responded to the ovations from the multitude:

"I appreciate this great honor . . . but I cannot accept it in my name only. I share this honor with every IBM man and woman wherever they may be located. I share it with Mrs. Watson, who has stood behind me and traveled with me all over the United States and other parts of the world, contributing her personality and unusual talent to the development of IBM. I share it with my children, my sisters, with my mother and father, whose memory I revere so deeply. They gave me a happy childhood and a pattern of home life, civic responsibility, and human relations that I have tried to follow. I share it with my teachers, Miss Jessie Turner. . . ." Miss Turner had been his teacher at Addison Academy fifty-one years before.

While Watson's devotion to the United Nations and its prospects for improving the climate of world trade continued unflagging, he was concurrently taking action on and putting organization power behind his constructive thinking. He had become enormously impressed with General Eisenhower during the period in the mid-forties when both the Republican and Democratic parties were courting him as a possible candidate: the Republicans to help oust Harry Truman from the White House, and the Democrats as insurance to save the party in power if Truman, who was certainly going to be defeated, had to go.

Eisenhower himself reported that, as early as 1943, after Mussolini was disposed of, political feelers were reaching him in Europe, with party leaders trying to convince him that he was proper political material.[1] To an aide, Virgil Pinkley, who conveyed some of the arguments in support of Ike's venture into politics, Eisenhower said: "Virgil, you've been standing out in the sun too long."

Before the New Hampshire primaries in 1948, Eisenhower issued an unequivocal announcement removing himself from consideration as a presidential possibility. His decision was "definite and positive." He felt that the "necessary and wise subordination of military and civil power will be best sustained . . . when lifelong professional soldiers . . . abstain from seeking high political office."

Eisenhower was in the United States and was hoping to retire, but was assigned Chief of Staff of the U.S. Army and took over the responsibilities of General George C. Marshall, only to find that "soon, politics began to complicate my life. . . ." In February of 1948, General Omar Bradley took on the Chief of Staff job. Even before that, when Eisenhower was talking of retiring, he and Watson had met for chats, and while Eisenhower and Watson at that time made no public statements about the recruitment of the General for the presidency of Columbia, it was apparent from Watson's subsequent comment that the matter was reviewed. By the

[1] *The White House Years—1953–1956: Mandate for Change,* Dwight D. Eisenhower, Garden City, N.Y., 1963.

time General Bradley relieved him as Chief of Staff, Eisenhower had begun to talk and sound a little like Watson, with a difference in cadence and tempo; his warm and sunny demeanor, added to the adulation in which he was held for his wartime successes, made him the ranking hero of the Western World.

Watson and Eisenhower warmed to each other from the beginning. Each had enormous respect for the other, frequently stated in terms of commendation and pride. Rhetorically, they were variants within the same brotherhood. As a practical matter, Watson, as head of the Columbia trustees, who were looking for a successor to the enfeebled Nicholas Murray Butler, was in a position to give Eisenhower the kind of employment that would hold him in reserve until needed. This helped a relationship already characterized by warm and mutual admiration, one which grew with the knowledge that they held common beliefs and a more or less identical philosophy that seemed to be easily understood if not easily defined.

Eisenhower could take a relatively simple query and accompany it on a forced march down uncharted roadways of prose, over the directionless terrain of circumspection, with pauses at parenthetical way stations and at refueling stops near little punctuation shops, where dashes and semicolons had to be handcrafted to shore up the load gathered by the subject enroute to some semantically obscure conclusion.

General Eisenhower's rhetoric might meet on the way back a Watson ideological thesis, refreshed and stripped naked as a homily, so peeled of form and spare of definition and bearing its content so lightly that it seemed to have become weightless on its easy jog from nowhere to nowhere. Thus bound by a mutually shared faith in common understanding, their predisposition to an intellectually uncomplicated philosophy, and a no-nonsense respect for each other's ability to command, they became the best of friends.

Watson's influence at Columbia was dominant, acquired in part by the default of other trustees and in part by the fact that, with Nicholas Murray Butler's presidential role unfilled, power gravitated to Watson. Butler and his wife had been promised occupancy of the President's house indefinitely, and Watson visited there and conferred at times with him and Mrs. Butler about a possible successor.

In 1945, following Butler's retirement, Dr. Frank D. Fackenthal, provost at Columbia, was named acting president, while Watson took the leadership in the search for new candidates for the job. It was reported that Butler disapproved of every one of fifty candidates considered. Toward the end of 1946, one trustee suggested that perhaps a candidate under consideration ought to have "insight into and influence upon the course of education," a view held by most senior faculty members, some of whom resented Watson's manipulation of the presidential selection process. For it was Watson indeed, and no one else, who managed it all. He had no personal objections to a professional educator, he said, but felt, on the basis of his IBM experience, that any good man could be educated on the job. His preference for Eisenhower was exclusive, however, and was supported by many members of the New York financial, management, real estate, and political establishment with whom he was in daily contact. They were men who felt correctly, instinctively, and by experience that General Eisenhower need only submit to nomination to become president of the United States. The presidency of Columbia, as an interim occupation for Eisenhower, was ideal in terms of conferring lofty civilian status.

Watson never denied his role in Eisenhower's selection, which he promoted with the dignified zeal and unwavering confidence that were inherent in his persuasive style. Later when, except for political purposes, the choice of Eisenhower as president of the university seemed to be something less than inspired, Watson readily conceded that he had been responsible for it. Eisenhower himself had not sought the honor and responded with modesty to the plan. One of the many candidates said to be under consideration, at least in press speculation, was Dr. Milton Eisenhower, the General's brother and president of Kansas State College. Thus when Watson first mentioned the matter to him, the General thought he meant Milton.

Dissension over the way things were being handled in rejecting candidates while holding the door open to Eisenhower brewed into something of a faculty storm. Butler, with an occasional advisory assist from Watson, had run Columbia for so long in something of the same style that Watson ran IBM that old ideas about checks and balances of power had died of atrophy. No one had examined the statutes or voting powers, and some of the more concerned members of the faculty deplored the spectacle of a great university searching for a president and operating with statutes that had become anachronistic in the 1920's. It was reminiscent of the reign of Louis XIV, someone remarked, in that no one anticipated Butler's demise until after he had disappeared.

Watson moved about in Columbia administrative and policy circles with the assurance of a corporation president available for counsel at a branch office. He had extracted, with the willing help of Butler, concessions favorable to IBM in the operation of the physics, mathematics, and science laboratories. Of course, he had made repeated and generous grants in amounts no one could, or would, tally. The fact that such policies and free-wheeling administration gave IBM an opportunity to draw top-ranking students into the company produced isolated grumbling but no deterrence. The grants were tax deductible; the recruiting and research results, productive. It was one of those ideal arrangements under which Butler and Watson could express their admiration for each other.

Butler was absolutely sincere in his high regard for Watson and once told Ben Wood that everything he had ever told Watson seemed to be "already understood and immanent." Watson seemed to know intuitively what scholars, philosophers, and mathematicians knew by discipline; he could grasp the essence of their knowledge, Butler thought, upon exposure to it.

The tradition of quiescence among the faculty at Columbia had been unaltered for so many years that no real mechanism for protesting Watson's clearly obvious preference for General Eisenhower could be developed easily. Thus the few senior educators who felt a more appropriate president for the institution could be recruited never quite got their protest organized, but they did get it voiced in inside circles. One disdainful complainant disapproved of the Watson-Eisenhower axis on the grounds that policy statements in the course of the proposed presidency would consist of regurgitated or rewritten myths. More to the point, however, was the feeling, first, that Eisenhower was unsuitable in specific, and perhaps even general, terms; and second, that it was improper for a Watson clique which had an alliance with Eisenhower's Republican political backers outside the university to exercise power within Columbia just to put him in a safe if exposed prestige job for interim preservation until he could be sent, polished up with several years of civilian gloss, into the political arena.

Faculty members who did not consider the non-academic Eisenhower quite bright enough for the job, or thought him inappropriately experienced, were subjected to Watson's most persuasive and sincere treatment. He told them Eisenhower would make an admirable president of the university, that he was—and Eisenhower's public statements at the time supported the view—more civilian-concerned than military, and that as a great university Columbia could benefit by Eisenhower's ability to reach out to the forum of the entire world on the institution's behalf. Some apparently underwent a change of mind under the impact of Watson's prestige and persuasion. Others required more objective fare, and Watson provided that, too.

If the faculty would consent to Eisenhower's appointment, his successor would be designated as directed by statutes to be updated; these revised statutes would provide for faculty participation in the selection, together with other improved procedures overdue at Columbia. It was better than half a loaf, although delivery from the bakery was deferred, and the well-mannered but momentarily serious rebellion was settled in that compromise. Watson then went to West Point where Eisenhower was visiting to talk with him, and his selection was made public. Scattered cries of astonishment and wonder received little attention as Eisenhower's popularity drowned them out. If Eisenhower didn't know "beans," as someone said, about Columbia, it didn't matter; he had his old friend Watson to help him. Favorable concessions to IBM, continuing after his term as president began, probably would have occurred under Butler, or a Butler-chosen successor, anyway.

Rumblings of rebellion were largely confined to the faculty level; students, like children of tradition, were then seen but not heard. Watson could subdue the faculty feeling of alienation from the privileged community of a university with a promise not to be so highhanded in the future, but the future he envisioned still saw the institution dominated by Watson's own kind of people—corporation leaders and men accomplished in real estate, financial, and communications operations.

The selection of Eisenhower's successor at Columbia was by no means as arbitrarily engineered as his own had been, but the rift between the administration, the campus, and the Morningside Heights community, which was in evidence as Watson pressed his own and IBM's interests on a complaisant board of trustees, grew wider with subsequent encroachment of the university into a congested community. It took twenty years for the pressures capped by Nicholas Murray Butler and contained by the sort of power and influence exercised by Watson to produce the inevitable explosion—the spring 1968 riots and turmoil that closed down the institution for nearly two months and forced, later in the year, the resignation of Dr. Grayson L. Kirk, the man chosen to replace the departed Eisenhower.

Outbreaks of discontent over the choice of Eisenhower for president of Columbia diminished to complete quiet after the General accepted the post. Nevertheless, Watson had rather a difficult problem on his hands, and the precise means by which he resolved it have never been altogether clear.

The trustees, which as often as not meant Watson, had an agreement with the Butlers permitting them to continue occupying the presidential residency at 60 Morningside Heights. Yet it was neither seemly nor seriously considered that the Butlers and the Eisenhowers might somehow divide the spacious quarters between them.

Butler knew nothing of Eisenhower's selection until it was a *fait ac-*

compli, according to official news sources at the time, although exactly how Butler could have turned down fifty candidates in a row, after finding them for one reason or other unsuitable, and remained as pleased as Watson implied he was after Eisenhower was chosen, was one of those small mysteries in human adaptation which add interest to life. Watson apparently handled the details with finesse. It was disclosed that Butler and his wife had decided not to hold the trustees to their agreement, and they moved from the presidential residence to a Park Avenue apartment. America's newest and most widely known university president moved in.

The official position in Watson circles was that he was altogether unaware of any public speculation that Eisenhower was being purposefully given a chance to remain politically viable throughout a presidential incubation period. However, one day in New Canaan, Connecticut, in the fall of 1947, Watson was glancing through the classified advertisements in a local newspaper, trying to find some kind of a summer home for the Eisenhowers near his own place. His eyes roved from the work at hand to the reports of columnists who, out of the whole cloth as it were, were weaving a fantasy to the effect that Watson and men like William Benton, an ex-advertising man turned statesman; William S. Paley, the Columbia broadcasting tycoon; Paul Hoffman, a leading Republican counselor, and others might be planning to put Eisenhower into the race.

Watson issued a denial, in which he said he was in sympathy with Eisenhower's concept of nonmilitary intervention in politics. Thus, he said, he was not backing him for the presidency. Eisenhower himself repeated his views on the same matter.

An old Roosevelt man, Watson still moved circuitously in Democratic Party circles. Harry Truman's daughter Margaret sometimes went with the Watsons to the opera; in fact she was a bridesmaid at Jane Watson's wedding. The younger son, Arthur (Dick), sometimes dated Margaret Truman, it was reported in Manhattan gossip columns. All of this was, of course, before Eisenhower's Columbia job began, and was directed to the conditions of 1947 and 1948. After that, what had been truthfully denied with respect to one election became true in another.

The columnists and the public had caught onto the right idea, but in view of the well-organized attempt to get General Eisenhower successfully converted into a civilian, they were one election early. Eisenhower himself was surely as sincere as any man could be in saying that he did not want to seek public office at that time. He attributed the uproar in his behalf to "forces" that tried to make him a political threat, some of them being hack press figures trying to become identified with him in the wave of popularity that engulfed the General in public and sorely tested his temperament in private.

Shortly after he moved to Columbia, he began to receive an enormous volume of mail, instigated by the strident voice of the Hearst press gossip columnist Walter Winchell, among others, who asked listeners to send pleas to Eisenhower to seek the presidential nomination. So much mail inundated the university's small post office that Eisenhower suggested it be stored in his own office to await processing. The flood of mail left no room for him, so he simply went off on a vacation; the Columbia Bureau of Applied Social Research, availing itself of an opportunity to study mass psychological reaction, analyzed the letters until the supply was reduced sufficiently to make room for his return.

President Truman sent Watson to The Netherlands as his personal representative at the Fiftieth Jubilee of Queen Wilhelmina, and General Eisenhower, while Truman was being nominated at the party convention, spent the day at an IBM Hundred Percent Club convention at Endicott as honored guest and speaker. Watson booked Eisenhower to make speeches before his favored forums around the New York banquet circuit for many months until the new president of Columbia declined further invitations. On election day, their interest in presidential politics settled for the time being, Watson and Eisenhower went out to lunch together.

They more or less jointly administered the affairs of Columbia; Eisenhower called Watson his "partner" in that period, which extended from the spring of 1948 to the end of 1950.

Eisenhower's own report of his partnership with Watson expressed concern with a "trend in thinking," especially among the young, that seemed to him, as it did to Watson, something less than constructive. He protested against a tendency to "think that we, regardless of our earning capacity, should all eat caviar and drink champagne throughout our lives." For such ideas, he was roasted in a campus newspaper. Eisenhower was disturbed, too, by the whole "drift" toward paternalism in government; he wrote to Watson about it from Denver in August, 1949, to suggest that a biography of the IBM chief's life would constitute a tribute to the free enterprise system. Apparently the irony of the suggestion was lost on both Eisenhower and his friend. He had almost explicitly proposed that the life story of the most widely known practitioner of paternalism in industrial America would be a compelling argument against it in government. Watson did not respond to the idea. His son Tom Junior authorized the biography after Watson's death, and it was published in 1962.

The week before Christmas in 1950, Eisenhower was summoned from a Pullman car, en route to a college speaking engagement in Ohio, to be asked by President Truman to become military commander of the North Atlantic Treaty Organization. Three weeks later he was making a hurried tour of NATO capitals, his tenure at Columbia finished. Watson had to answer some questions about the issue of selecting yet another university president. From Paris, Eisenhower said he wanted out. Conceding that he had been the one who "sold" Eisenhower to the university, Watson urged caution on the part of the trustees. He wanted everyone to be very careful not to let the press get the idea that Eisenhower had been an unsatisfactory choice.

After Eisenhower left Columbia and was living in Marnes-la-Coquette near Paris, where he was still undergoing ardent political courtship as military commander of NATO, he was visited by Paul Hoffman, who directed the Marshall Aid plan for the Truman administration and who became the first president of the Ford Foundation. Other visitors included William Benton, Senator Henry Cabot Lodge, and enough dignitaries to run up a log of seventy-eight scheduled appointments, all of whom trekked to Paris to press Eisenhower to accept the Republican nomination for President of the United States. Watson was not among them this time. Eisenhower wrote a letter declaring himself out of political life for keeps but said he tore it up when he got to worrying about certain Senators who seemed willing to play politics in matters vital to the Free World.

Watson always said he remained generally out of Eisenhower's political affairs after he left Columbia, possibly because he had been an ardent Roosevelt man and, just possibly, because there were confirmed reports that the Department of Justice was going to enter another anti-trust action against IBM. J. Howard McGrath, former Democratic National Chairman, who had arranged for Watson's assignment to the Queen Wilhelmina jubilee in The Netherlands, had become U.S. Attorney General and, recalling his contributions to the party in the past, Watson felt he would do well to have an understanding friend in the Justice Department. Even if he had wanted to reverse himself, as Eisenhower did, on the matter of a military man running for the presidency, prudence dictated retreat.

Nevertheless, Eisenhower remained a devotee of Watson, both for personal reasons and because he was an incurable admirer of successful, hard-headed businessmen; he put a succession of them into his cabinet in the eight years he was president. It was reported that Watson, William Paley, Eisenhower, and John D. Rockefeller, Jr., had conferred at length on Eisenhower's campaign at Paley's home. At the first press conference after the campaign was under way, someone asked Eisenhower what "deal" he had made with the group. The question was aggressively phrased and was not answered.

Although Watson backed off from the Eisenhower bandwagon because of impending anti-trust action, Eisenhower sent Watson a note of thanks for pre-election assistance. After the election, a friend of Watson's wrote to congratulate him on shunning publicity for helping to bring about the Eisenhower victory, a letter of commendation that must have raised Watson's eyebrows, since the last thing he would have wanted at this point was publicity of that sort. The friend further praised Watson for "always" avoiding publicity in his public benefactions, and declared that if the full story were ever told, Watson's part in the Eisenhower victory would be acclaimed as one of the most important services ever performed by a private citizen.

Watson remained uncharacteristically out of the limelight, making no comment on matters normally dear to him, in *THINK Magazine* or anywhere else. Neither his good frined entering the White House nor the departing Attorney General J. Howard McGrath was in a position to help him in his new ordeal. Watson, getting a little frail, just short of eighty years old, once again had to fight the government in another hateful anti-trust action.

Watson's independent career as an entrepreneur-executive approached its end, after a confused but not too internecine struggle for power, with his son in full command and the government again dictating a revised set of operational values which, not being his own, old Watson resented and despised.

The anti-trust action, under review since 1950, was instituted a few days before Christmas in 1952, after young Tom had been named president. Federal agents, presumably seeking ways to assist American espionage and intelligence services, had begun examining IBM records after World War II. Watson was suspicious but had to go along with it. To every business decision he could attribute a measure of moral and ethical importance, sometimes stretching the relationship between cause and effect, but no more so than fellow industrialists equally disposed to improve their public relations image. But what Watson thought was good, the government adduced to be restraint. Growth and expansion of IBM was a matter of merit, Watson said; how could meritorious performance be bad? Because, merit to the contrary, IBM had become so big that it had become a monolith beyond the range of competitive influence, said the government. But IBM built good machines. So it did, thereby reducing the effectiveness of competition. IBM grew during the war, trying to help the government, which admitted that 95 per cent of its punch card machines were IBM's. That was beside the point; patents, research, and a superior sales organization had tightened the IBM monopoly. Intent was not the issue so much as the demonstrable fact.

To Watson, the government's restraint of trade case had no more validity and was no more closely related to the public interest than the cases of 1914, or the punch card monopolies and rental contracts of the nineteen-thirties. What he saw as a simple extension of the guaranteed territory to overseas operations, administered by the IBM World Trade Corporation nominally directed by Arthur K. Watson, was seen by federal investigators as a restriction of the free market. He could neither believe nor accept the fact that the company monopoly was no less real because it had developed through what he *knew* was good business practice.

It was true that chaos and confusion were characteristics of anti-trust law enforcement—it is still true—with one of the earlier IBM cases proving the point. Control of eighty per cent of the tabulating machine market had not been, per se, illegal. In practice, a company dominating, say, eighty percent of a market could expand to acquire eighty-five per cent of it without facing anti-trust action, while two companies, each with ten per cent, could be denied merger on the grounds of restraint of competition. The reason many large corporations are calm, if not disdainful, about anti-trust complaints is, quite simply, that they often cannot determine what is legal and what is not until a federal action is instituted in order to make a determination.

But it was not an idea that Watson could tolerate. The consent decree imposed by the United States District Court was so galling to him that he rejected it, in contradiction to the logic of judicial and federal power and in opposition to IBM management men whose knowledge of the requirements of modern regulation exceeded Watson's piously antiquated and emotional block against it. He was afraid of being "tinged" in the public eye. His vanity, whence he derived his energy and perseverance, was under assault. He would not yield. The company deserved the protection of the government from competitors, not a consent decree providing licensing, release of patent restrictions, and the like. The technicalities of the case didn't interest him; it was the justice of it, the apparent violence to personal principle, that offended him. He contracted for advertisements in daily newspapers to praise the free enterprise system. The ads were less foolish than irrelevant. But they were a measure of Watson's determination to sign no consent decree that would indicate, to himself if to few others, admission of illegal action. He had committed no crime forty years ago and none now. Watson could only *Do Right*.

He argued that IBM was only part of the office machines and appliances industry. But IBM machines had become an industry in themselves, machines whose functions could be performed by nothing else in existence. He would protect his patents against any decree ordering them into the hands, for a fee, of others. He seemed unaware that the technological revolution, which his own patronage had started, would diminish their value, making many of them worthless. He was ready to hang for a principle that was not involved. He could not and would not change, for all of his counsel over the years that change itself was a condition of growth and development.

The case dragged on, and Watson tried to adjust to the realities of modern times, but he was unable to do so. The exercise of power was so diffused and contradictory that the line of command was short circuited. The situation became unendurable, management partially paralyzed, critical decisions delayed in an environment of procrastination. The confrontation between the generations, between the past and the present, the present and the future, had to be resolved.

And it was. Tom Junior committed IBM to the consent decree—countermanding patriarchal power to become, in his own right, the Man of IBM.

Watson thereafter contented himself with writing letters to President Eisenhower, calling on dignitaries, and accepting honors. He and Mrs. Watson "cried with joy" when Eisenhower dispatched his son John to the household with a personal message when Watson was ill in 1955. He said it was a measure of Eisenhower's greatness to think of the "little things that mean so much to your friends." The President said he, in turn, admired Watson for making his business work "on the human as well as the profit side." He became a bit testy, however, in the face of Watson's unremitting optimism about world affairs, especially when the latter saw the Geneva Conference outcome in the usual rose-colored terms. Eisenhower expressed some horror in response to Watson's birthday hope that Eisenhower might live to be ninety-five. "I'll entertain the thought, if you insist," he said. Watson had dispatched the wish after calling on the aged and famed painter of primitives, Grandma Moses.

He was presented with the Horatio Alger award, a public relations ritual that had similarly honored former President Hoover, whom Watson admired so much. Hoover, recognizing an irony that Watson missed, had pointed out that heroes of Alger's fiction were often creatures of luck, who could save the boss's daughter from a runaway horse and get a corporate job and bed the salvaged heroine as a reward. The suburbs of America were populated with well-groomed, serious men and their families who lived in a world of Watson's, not Alger's, fiction; they got there by effort, education, meeting their quotas, going to church, getting promotions, moving Onward and Upward a step at a time—sober, thinking, reading men, making their plan, and planning their work. It was certainly not by luck.

Watson had an interview with Winston Churchill, traded letters with Eisenhower, and called on the even more aged Bernard Baruch, who talked of the changing times and the imminence of death. He continued to dispose of his fortune, which had amounted at one time to an estimated hundred million dollars but had been reduced through gifts to people on his staff, to family and friends, to relatives he had never seen, to aged cousins living on the restored family homestead out beyond Painted Post. He had been criticized for rebuilding the homestead by people who said it was on too grand a scale, that it wasn't, in its tidiness and museum curator's style, anything like the old, primitive farm it had been. But the image of its restoration made Watson happy, and if it wasn't a correct image—well, it was the way it might have been. He got his fortune down to something like three and a half million dollars, all in good time, and in his own way.

The management organized an elaborate, world-wide ceremony to celebrate his fortieth anniversary with the company. It was suitably observed in every country and locale where IBM employees worked, with dinners and memorials. An anthology of his editorials from *THINK* was published in commemoration of the event, signed simply by "The IBM family" and dedicated, with affection and with commendation for the fine philosophy and rare thinking of the Leader, to Mr. and Mrs. Watson.

In 1955, a motion picture crew went to the Watson town house on Seventy-Fifth Street to make a film for another anniversary celebration the following year. A junction box blew out, as the cameras whirred, burning a hole in a sixty-foot flowered carpet in the great room. The technician was horrified, but Watson, who talked with them about his visits to queens and monarchs whose autographed portraits adorned the tables, told them not to worry. "I'll tell Mrs. Watson," he said. The cameraman was mildly reprimanded by the producer for carelessness, but defended himself. "It's an Aubusson," he said. "They'll have a crew over here from France in the morning to reweave it."

Mrs. Watson came to the room as two cameras rolled, a procedure made necessary because Watson, once he began to talk, standing erect as though addressing IBM people assembled all over the world, was not to be stopped. When a reel of film in one camera came near its end, the other camera was started, and the first one reloaded. Mr. Watson did not like to be interrupted by technical problems. It disturbed the flow of his thought and often irritated him as well.

He was thin, his voice quivered, his long stiff legs were unsteady, but his presence filled the room more than the tangle of lines, the hot lights, the recording equipment, and the crew.

Mrs. Watson was fearful that the filming and the long speech would weaken him. Watson was standing there, his eyes looking to the back wall of the world, telling the family of IBM people to be steadfast, to be loyal, to THINK, to take advantage of their opportunities, telling them everywhere that it was God's world, not man's, that they could all be happy if they did their work well and became prosperous, and re-membered every day of their lives that they represented a great institution that would go on forever.

"Do you need all these people here?" Mrs. Watson interrupted. The producer, Sherman Beck, a well-known commercial motion picture man in New York, assured her courteously that they were all essential to the production. "Can anyone here fix my washer?" she asked.

Beck was astonished to learn that the regal lady had been down in the laundry. There was not, for the moment, a servant in the house. He dispatched an electrician to the basement, who returned to report: "Hell, it's an old Maytag from the nineteen-thirties. They ought to throw it out."

"Well, can't you do something to it? She might hurt herself."

Irreverently, the crewman retorted: "The plunger isn't working and the damned thing's throwing water. The worst that can happen to her is that she'll drown."

"Well, jump the fuse or something; try to help her."

The electrician repaired the appliance, and Mrs. Watson completed her task. Watson, who had silently suffered the interruption from Jeannette, resumed. The film was spliced and edited for presentation at the next Hundred Percent Club convention, a presentation that had to substitute for the presence of Thomas J. Watson, for, by then, he was dead.

He had gone to Florida in February to take part in an engineering conference, and in March he dropped in on a gathering of the Hundred Percent Club in Washington. He was quite weak then, dwindling away. In May he relinquished officially to his sons, Arthur at World Trade, and Tom throughout the corporation, executive powers, but would not give up the title Chairman of the Board, although it was thereafter only ceremonial.

In mid-June he suffered a heart attack and was taken to Roosevelt

Hospital from his home at Four East Seventy-Fifth Street in Manhattan. On the night of June 18, the family went to the suite: Tom and Arthur, Jane and Helen—Mrs. John M. Irwin II and Mrs. Walter G. Buckner— and little Jeannette Watson, of course. Fifteen grandchildren, in their family households and elsewhere, awaited the final word.

It came on the nineteenth of June, 1956. Twelve hundred people went to the funeral services on Thursday afternoon at the Brick Presbyterian Church, and the family followed the body to a slope over the Hudson River in the estate country of old John D. Rockefeller—another rich and deceptively simple man who had come from the farm country beyond the Watson homestead. The earth of the Sleepy Hollow Cemetery received the body of Thomas John Watson, who had lived for eighty-two years, four months, and two days.

12.
Heirs
Apparent

———◆———

IN 1955, THE LAST FULL YEAR of Watson's life at IBM, the company's income was $696,294,000, or almost six times the gross business total of the first postwar year of 1946. Nearly 30,000 stockholders owned a little over four million shares, ninety-five per cent of which had been created by dividends and stock splits. Yet starting from a base that had multiplied by 170 times since he had joined Charles Flint's "combination" in 1914, Watson's industrial legacy to his sons, with half a century behind it, was just beginning to grow.

At the beginning of 1968, and before a one hundred per cent stock split authorized on April 29, there were 360,000 owners of 60,000,000 shares to celebrate IBM's first five-billion-dollar year. Gross sales in 1967 were $5,345,290,993, boosted by a gaudy twenty-eight per cent quarterly increase in one three-month period of that year. After the split was announced, the stock rose beyond $700 a share on the New York Exchange, to give it a market value of a collossal forty-two billion dollars.

Such phenomenal, explosive growth in sales and market value from so towering a base may remain commonplace, off and on, for some time to come. A slowdown in long range growth is unlikely. In fact, the Holt Investment Advisory, a commerical counseling firm in New York, advertising for new clients at the end of 1967, estimated that if IBM's growth rate is sustained, annual sales ten years hence will exceed the combined 1967 capital expenditures of all corporations in the United States. If the estimate is valid, IBM will in time become the largest industrial corporation on earth. A lot will depend on the outcome of lawsuits and anti-trust actions piling up against the company.

It is a tribute, a frightening one, to the times, to one company's commanding position in the age of technology, to its ability to recruit talent, to its world-wide sales and service organization, to a national policy which sees value in such growth, and to Thomas J. Watson, Junior.

Young Tom's life began in the year his father, deeply hurt by the ungrateful John Henry Patterson, brooding over his abusive dismissal from NCR and the impending threat of imprisonment, went to work for Flint. His own lifetime has spanned that of the company itself. The company is, he has said, always in his unconscious. As the son of ambitious parents, impossible demands for perfection and performance have left on him the marks of contradiction and repressed rage. There was little of the casual affability, the calm tolerance of youth, on the part of his father to soften and sweeten his young life. Discipline was erratic, often irrational. Their father lectured the boys harshly and sternly, sometimes in tirades, and as often as not punished them by an attitude of disappointment and disdain, withholding rewards as he might from a salesman failing to meet a quota.

In Short Hills, New Jersey, they grew up among the children of the ultra-respectable, largely Republican commuters of the Wall Street community, went to the Episcopal Church, in which their Methodist father was confirmed, went to Sunday School picnics on the family farm, rode their pony in the large, grassy yard, played with their sisters in small houses cut to a child's scale, and later took to the tennis courts and the country club swimming pool. Tom became a Boy Scout and on one memorable occasion endured a bitter lesson in rectitude at the command of his father. Watson financed a summer trip abroad for Tom and his young friends, but the boy had to remain at home in a demonstration of fair play when he failed to meet his Eagle Scout Badge requirements in time.

Before each of the boys was old enough to go to school, they were taken on plant inspections, then on business trips to Europe and to Hundred Percent Club conventions. Tom was put into private schools around the New Jersey area and, a mediocre student, squeaked through to enter the freshman class at Brown University. Dr. Ben Wood at Columbia became, as an advisor to their father, the boys' counselor as well, and it was he who, with a compassionate but objective understanding of Tom's relationship with his father, discreetly engineered him away from the Watson province of Columbia.

Like old Watson, young Tom had little interest in books or libraries, in philosophy or the classics. He lacked the old man's uncaring self-confidence, always nearly impossible to develop in the father's presence, and suffered from uncertainty and his less than illustrious academic record. Inferences that Tom was not very bright, or at best not good college material, drew scoffing denials from the family friend, Ben Wood. Although he looked upon Watson as one of the greatest benefactors of all mankind, Wood had watched the boys "shrivel up and wish they were somewhere else" under the lash of the father's temper.

The two main factors affecting Tom's school years were, first, a lack of confidence in himself, for the overwhelming personality of Watson inhibited any growth of confidence; and second, according to Wood, the college curriculum itself. "Tom could easily have gotten A-plus if he'd wanted to," he said. "He saw that most of the courses were irrelevant to him. At least two-thirds of them were trash. I worked on them when I was in school just because it was less trouble to do it than to get C's and D's. He did well enough in economics, and in whatever he was interested in."

Tom emerged from Brown in 1937 while Arthur was still preparing for his entrance at Yale University. His graduation induced his father to write him a peculiar letter, as though documenting a record, that reinterpreted family history. In it, Watson said he was looking forward to the counsel and help Tom could offer in planning future company programs "along various lines." While he, Watson, had many friends, he felt he had no one, really, to replace his own father; now, however, Tom himself had become someone to whom he could look with confidence. Watson described the relationship between himself and his woodsmanfarmer parent as the equivalent of the one he hoped would characterize the father and son partnership in IBM.

Young Watson found it difficult to produce a mediocre record, whatever the explanation, after that. At the IBM trainee school, he quickly became class president, probably the only such person to do so in contradiction to his reputation as a young fellow who drank. He had not only become something of an imbiber at Brown, continuing the practice at sales training school, but he was honestly and openly rebellious enough to do it defiantly. Moreover, old Watson knew all about it, deciding apparently to foresake application of the previously inviolate interdiction and his rigidly enforced code of "fair play," as he had exercised it in the case of the Boy Scout tour, in the interests of developing new leadership in the company. Dick later was the primary beneficiary of the temporarily adjusted code of conduct.

Tom enlarged his field of social action to become something of a playboy in Manhattan. He was assigned to a sales territory in the financial district in which, it was reported, he ran up a "brilliant" record in the wake of predecessors of lesser skill and determination. He entered the hallowed ranks of the Hundred Percent Club in his very first year, an uncommon distinction which he embellished the following year by reaching his full year's quota on his first day at work after New Year's Day. Company annals, which could as readily disclose as withhold illuminating data on comparative performances, produced no success story in corporate life equal to young Tom Watson's until some years later when Robert W. (Bobby) Sarnoff, son of General David Sarnoff, the chief executive of the Radio Corporation of America, demonstrated the extent to which the first born sons of great tycoons can rise above the vicissitudes of heritage to provide second generation leadership.

Young Tom Watson, however, was not deluded by developments, and he usually conceded that his extraordinary advance through corporate ranks might have been attributable to forces beyond his own control. Upon reflection, he was not ready to believe that the chance to become president of the company was open to everyone, regardless of his father's confidence in the opportunities offered by the free enterprise system. Tom became one of the first top-ranking men at IBM to slip through the loopholes of the IBM myth while, concurrently, respecting it as a generalization. His brother Dick developed a similar degree of understanding, for which he was rewarded by a compassionate board of directors with executive positions and remuneration a little farther off—and a little lower down on the pay scale—in the lengthening shadow. In good time, both young men became the leaders their father always said any relatively intelligent, hard working man could become with the application of hard work, constructive thought, education on the job, loyalty to the company, and an appropriate respect for the IBM spirit. Sibling rivalry, quite understandably, characterized the relationship between the handsome and hard working brothers, with Tom, five years older and fortified by his father's preference, maintaining a clear edge in leadership through the years.

Tom's unprecedented sales career was interrupted by developments in international affairs; three years out of college, he was summoned to service in the New York National Guard. As a civilian pilot with a log of nearly a thousand hours, he went to an Alabama air base as a pilot, starting out as a private. Dick dropped out of the senior class at Yale to enlist in the army.

In three years of service, Tom advanced to the rank of major, which his father and mother—as old Watson, possibly not altogether in jest, expressed it—thought should have been major-general; thence to lieutenant colonel, a promotion which the father, in his "excitement," announced as lieutenant-general before catching himself and editing the phrase correctly. Watson was proud of Tom's record and rank, but as always, his pride was personal, proprietary, and self-centered before it settled into a parental glow attributable to the very real accomplishments of wartime pilots.

Tom developed a good deal in those war years. Tall and athletic, slender, with manly mobility, composed features, and well-shaped head, he was astonishingly handsome—so very handsome, and so graceful for a large and rangy man, that Ben Wood's description of him as a Greek god was, from a scholar of ancient literature and history, a compliment free of hyperbole. When he and Olive Field Cawley were married, the young lady, with her radiance and haunting eyes which seemed to look out on the world in search of some essential elusive beauty, and the young officer were a pair of beautiful people in happy bondage to one another: a storybook couple.

In virtually every type of aircraft except close-combat fighter planes, Tom logged more than fifteen hundred hours of flight during the war, the equivalent of nearly thirty-eight working weeks of forty hours each in the air. His principal duty was chauffeur for braid and brass, transporting them about regions of operations. He was a good, durable, and careful pilot, was assigned to the lend-lease cadre in Moscow, and much of the time piloted American Air Inspector General Julius W. Jones to and from air bases.

When the German armies, thirty miles away, had Moscow under siege, and when Americans, having temporarily overcome their revulsion against the godless Communists, were praying en masse in their churches for heavenly intervention on behalf of their unlikely ally, Tom followed the course of momentous events from his hotel room on the Gorky Street side of the National Hotel. It was a time of apocalypse, when the Russians, sometimes fighting with knives and clubs in their very kitchens and stables, slashed or brained an invading Nazi in the final seconds of their own lives; a time when Tom, no less than others, saw the revelation of greatness in ordinary people, cornered and facing extermination, fighting and sacrificing for their home and land. He ranged over the mountains and plains from Turkey to Murmansk, and in doing so, achieved a pride in himself and a memory of the times that took him a long way out of the patriarchal shadow.

As a pilot he developed discipline; he subdued, if not mastered, fear and occasional danger of death, flew in both real and symbolic flight toward a son's form of freedom. He didn't make it all the way, not with his father standing athwart his world, but came to approve of himself with a sufficiency that is essential to man's maturity. He piloted the big aircraft for so long and so well that he knew a lifetime career as a pilot was open to him, free of his father, free of IBM, if he wanted it—which, then, he did.

Young Watson's closest brush with death or disaster probably came from the trigger fingers of Russian airmen guarding the besieged city of Moscow, men he admired, as one endangered professional man will admire another. Piloting the general, his aides, and an American press correspondent to the Soviet capital from Archangel, Tom brought his plane into the precise flight pattern explicitly prescribed for aircraft approaching the city, maneuvering in the diagram preliminary to a landing, the crew manning their stations apprehensively in the final moments above the corridor's gun batteries. It had been an anxiety-filled run, and safety for that day, after a successful elusion of hostile aircraft en route, was a few thousand feet below them.

Eddy Gilmore, Associated Press correspondent, thought he was the first to see the look on Tom's paled face and the violent and unnatural jerking of one of his legs. He had got his foot, or perhaps the strap of a boot, caught in one of the rudder pedals; he was unable to free it to make the exacting maneuver required at that point in order to keep the antiaircraft guns and escorting fighters from opening fire. The plane was out of the pattern, stable but vulnerable, a highly suspicious intruder in the Moscow skies.

"He was all over the place," Gilmore said. "He goddam near got us shot down."

Russian fighters closed in "like snapping wolves, making passes and getting ready to blow us out of the air." With a final lunge, Tom got his foot free, swept past the hovering guns back into the pattern, and went in with the "bees at his tail" to a safe landing.

"Tom was a great guy," Gilmore said. "A very disciplined pilot. He was a Russian buff; we all were then. His experience in Russia was the greatest of his life. Moscow was a special place for him."

Young Watson's playboy days came to an end when he met Olive Cawley, and in the course of the war his drinking diminished until he stopped altogether, resuming it for pleasure and relaxation, casually and lightly, when he arrived in the upper echelons of IBM.

Drinking was at times a serious problem for Dick Watson. He is a man of considerably more tension, he is more studious, he has an even more volatile temperament than his father or older brother. This occasional combination of alcohol and temperament caused fears for his safety and well-being. Leaner than Tom, somewhat natty, he was more elegant in style, his clothes more crisply tailored, and he had a flair for color. He became a major in the ordnance corps, served in the Philippines, and was reported in company literature to have pressed for equipping mobile truck units with data processing machines that made them increasingly effective in combat. He returned to Yale after the war, made a specialty of languages, studied Russian, and learned to get along nicely in German, French, and Spanish. At the age of twenty-nine he married Ann Carroll Hemingway, taking off with her on a slightly delayed shipboard honeymoon for Europe, accompanied by his parents en route to a postwar business trip across the European continent. Dick sometimes served as interpreter for his father in conferences abroad, but it was not a relaxing experience for anyone involved. No one, especially one of his sons, relaxed very much or for very long in the presence of the patriarch.

Both boys had acquired war bonds and IBM stock as the war went on, an economic step upward arranged by their father, who had been given to sending them birthday checks for twenty-five dollars to supplement their modest allowances. He was also given to dispatching handkerchiefs, ties, fruit, and flowers to other relatives whose anniversaries and birth dates were kept in a businesslike file frequently and carefully brought up to date by Jeannette Watson, who cued her husband at those times when thoughful remembrances were in order.

- After Tom and Arthur were married, the nature and quality of the gifts changed. Carpets and paintings, sculpture, furniture, silver and chinaware adorned their homes, and gilt-edged securities reposed in their safe-deposit boxes, as continuing testimony of the way Watson measured love and generosity. With the birth of each of his fifteen grandchildren, grandfather Watson parted with a gift of money, usually a hundred thousand dollars at a time.

When Tom's duty tour in Russia ended, he returned to Washington, D.C., where, one day early in 1945, an Air Force general remarked that Tom was probably preparing to go back into civilian life and take over IBM. It was one of those moments when Tom's unconscious induced the response that he'd simply never thought about such an idea. Elsewhere in the family hierarchy, though, the thought had long since taken specific form.

As a lieutenant-colonel with his senior pilot's wings and the Air Medal, Tom was discharged from military life, went with Olive on a holiday to Mexico, and at the age of thirty-one, after assuring his father that he was seventy-five per cent better equipped to follow in Watson's footsteps than he had been eight years earlier at the age of twenty-three, went to work for IBM under the skilled tutelage of the company's executive vice-president, Charles A. Kirk.

223

In the Philippines, Dick wanted to forget about going back to Yale and remain half a world away from home as manager of the IBM office in Manila. His father turned down the idea on the grounds that Dick was insufficiently experienced and that such an appointment might be misinterpreted. Dick went back to school.

At forty-three, Charles Kirk was vital, indefatiguable, and already a legend in the corporation as the man who had managed manufacturing operations during the war. In retrospect, he was remembered as something of a superman, with indestructible circuitry taking the place of mortal flesh; when he had almost literally killed himself by remorseless work, old Watson wept with guilt and sorrow, and ordered his hard-driving associates to learn from the lesson of Kirk by slowing down a little. The directive was difficult to comply with, since it involved the contradiction of *appearing* to slow down while proceeding with expansion and quota goals demanded by the seventy-three-year-old Watson himself.

Between the time Tom sat down beside him at Kirk's large desk and the day they found Kirk dead in Paris in the summer of 1947, the young man was considered to be nearly, but not quite, ready for his job. John G. Phillips, personal secretary to Watson, filled in for a time. Phillips had started work as a clerk for the company thirty years before in 1918; he was reputed to be an extraordinarily loyal man, and very modest—so modest, in fact, that he went to old Tom Watson and insisted that Tom Junior should get Kirk's job rather than he, since it was the obvious last step to the presidency.

Watson waved him off, and within two years pushed him upward to the president's office, put Tom in as executive vice-president, and promoted himself to chairman of the board.

The maneuvering was more or less ritualistic, involving little more than title changes on office doors and a redistribution of artifacts and furniture, since Watson himself had all the real power. One of young Tom's least believable published statements appeared in *Time*, after Watson called him into his seventeenth floor office at 590 Madison Avenue and told him he was the new president. "I was completely disarmed," Tom said. In view of the prearranged shuffling around of offices and titles, however, Tom's other quoted comment seemed more appropriate: "It was the most moving experience of my life."

The loyal and modest Phillips moved sideways to become, more or less next to old Watson, vice-chairman of the board. He was perfectly willing to do so, for he loved Watson, the family, and all of IBM. In subsequent conflicts which found young Tom and old Tom in opposition,

Phillips seldom faltered in taking his position with the latter. Young Tom found quite hopeless any attempt to convince Phillips that his father wasn't infallible. Yet he liked Phillips, too, as an old tutor and friend, part of the deep inner circle, who had taught him how to handle a gun, allowing him to tote an empty weapon until, as a growing boy, he acquired enough respect for a deadly gun to load it.

While old Watson maintained total command, young Tom chafed and gave way to his temper. He cringed when his father, in sales assemblies, heaped upon him the kind of praise he liked to hear himself. The young man wrote the old man notes suggesting, politely, that he cut it out. He preferred to be called Tom, not Mister Watson. He may not have known of the Someone-Somebody business, but wouldn't have cared in any case. He went sailing on his own yacht, the Palawan, and was a demonic skier, with his own sumptuous lodge at Stowe, Vermont, where he built a village of town houses and owns half a mountain. The discipline and action of the bomber pilot's life, which he liked, was expressed in active pursuits. He kept his six-foot-three frame at around 190 pounds and tried, not too successfully, to control his terrible, sometimes insulting, temper. Certain crudities of conversation diminished to infrequency, his speaking voice improved when he was out of range of his father, as did Dick's. One close observer of the two men said that Tom often trembled in the presence of his father, and that Arthur trembled in the presence of either or both, but these superficial symptoms disappeared in time, too.

Tom learned not to say impulsively, sometimes in the presence of both subordinates and associates, "Shut your mouth," or "If that's your best argument, keep it to yourself," and the like. When Tom made one of his first major speeches at the dedication of a new plant in Greencastle, Indiana, wholly on his own and far away from the old man, it was a notable improvement in tone and style over any previous public appearance. After his father's death, he acquired real presence, casual though commanding; he used wit handily and even resorted to permissible showmanship, shaking his head of thick, prematurely gray hair vigorously and accenting his remarks with a hand slapping the podium. Where he had once stalked from a room or a meeting in irritation or childish petulance, he learned to do so for emphasis, with studied indignation—"not just leaving the room, but like Richard Burton, making a dramatic exit," according to a veteran IBM man who enjoyed watching Tom develop.

His father noted some of these changes in his son and interpreted his impatience correctly as a compelling taste for corporate power. Nevertheless, infuriated at pressures on him to yield to the hated anti-trust consent decree, Watson held on. "I don't want to be cast in bronze until I'm gone," he grumbled—and he wasn't. Tom, alternately placating him and recoiling, knowing the consent decree had to be accepted or the company would be cut to pieces, could not change his nature. After one fray, Tom went off to the airport, only to find that his father had shown up to make peace. Angrily, he burst out, "Can't I ever get away from you?"

Watson grew more and more formal and eccentric, keeping executives, the same executives he had ordered to slow down, assembled in his office for instructions and a harangue long past the evening dinner hour, dictating for five hours at a time to fatigued secretaries, plodding off to luncheons, dinners, and IBM meetings. He would go into a rage if someone crinkled a paper in his presence, or ramble on in some discourse, all in tenderness and sweet reasonableness, until his listeners nodded to his monotone. He worked at an old desk he had bought in 1914, kept the shades and the red draperies of his office drawn, and just kept going, defying the government, making mountains out of inconsequential molehills, and reducing matters of grave importance to molehills he could step on. He fought and clung and argued, and Tom, circumventing him, fearing and loving him, absorbed some of the power, bit by bit, before it was formally relinquished. He was that kind of a man.

Dick, at thirty-five, became president of the World Trade Corporation, the IBM overseas operation. He was often unhappy, irritable, nervous, taking affront where none was intended, but he, too, possessed the Watson perseverance and fortitude and, in a harder role than Tom's in the hierarchy, provided his share of a different kind of leadership, albeit at the sufferance of old Watson.

Somewhere along the line in the nineteen-fifties, Tom had read—or his speechwriters had—Kierkegaard and Ibsen. He got to talking at times about individuality, courage, decentralization of power, men free of fear to speak and think. IBM needed "wild ducks," men willing to use their daring and imagination, not so damned many tame ones moving in formation, he said. It was heady stuff indeed in the old stabilized family, which, by the mid-fifties, totaled fifty thousand persons. Tom started to kick the homilies around, and thought that more of the ducks, tame and wild, should carry more weight. He lost his taste for, and perhaps never really liked, all the rah-rah and hoopla; it made him self-conscious and appeared to him unworthy of a mature, solid corporation. It was juvenile, all that business of fireworks, great tent meetings, and carnival days on the homestead grounds at Endicott. The big barbecue at the Poughkeepsie plant on the Hudson in 1954, where a mob of nearly three thousand ate 25,000 cherrystone clams, two-and-a-half tons of steak, and 3,400 baked potatoes, was the last of its kind. Tom stopped them, and he wasn't yet the boss.

He saw that IBM was stuck in the past, committed to practices and nonsense unsuited to the emerging technological age. One day in 1955, earlier in the morning than old Watson usually appeared, he arrived unexpectedly in Tom's office. A fearful argument ensued about the antitrust decree, the old man trembling in rage, Tom trying to explain to the unhearing father that the world, the company, wasn't the same any more. He left his father there and went out onto Madison Avenue. Shaken, knowing his course, willful yet saddened, Tom walked awhile, and thought. Then he hailed a taxicab and got in. The driver asked where he wanted to go.

"The Federal Courthouse," he said.

He signed the decree as president of IBM. Justice Department officials were in conference with him when a messenger found him and slipped him a note. The hand of Thomas J. Watson, the hand that had written a name across much of the world, had penned six words, each of which could have been, and indeed had been at some time or other, the subject of a *THINK* editorial. Lined up vertically, one beneath the other, like an old Patterson pep talk, the words were:

> 100%
> Confidence
> Appreciation
> Admiration
> Love
> Dad

Old Watson could not change, but he could yield. Tom was in command.

13.
The
International

By THE END OF THE nineteen-forties when Watson's errors of judgment in the Univac case and the company's problems with anti-trust and technological advances showed no sign of slowing the phenomenal growth of IBM, it became clearer with each passing quarter that the whole world *was* a market, as Watson had said.

Watson had picked up some curbstone knowledge of world trade from John H. Patterson, who sold cash registers in England, on the European continent, and in parts of Asia under contractual arrangements with sales agencies. Charles Flint at C-T-R., who sometimes saw the world itself as a plum to be picked and skinned, instructed and encouraged Watson to get the company's tabulators, scales, and measuring equipment in use in the major cities of the world. He wanted to nail down the advantage that would accrue, so that when the inevitable competitors arrived, they would find it necessary to conduct their assault against a well-entrenched foe.

International Time Recording Company, then owned by IBM, established an overseas office with ten employees in July, 1914, at 77 Avenue de la République in Paris. The operation was more or less immobilized by the war; nothing very fruitful developed until 1920, when a new company, capitalized at two hundred thousand francs, was formed to sell punch card equipment in France. The Société International des Machines Commerciales, with exclusively French management after 1929, was to become I.B.M. France in 1948. A planning office for the continent was established in Vincennes, France, in 1934. By plowing back royalties and profits in addition to supplying capital for expansion, IBM built a solid, thriving business that reached out into North Africa, Madagascar, Indochina, and other pockets of the French Empire. Then came World War II and German occupation, and all was devastated again.

But IBM turned over to the French company much of the equipment it had on lease to the Allied armed services, and the French workers, back from war and prison camps, dressed it up and energetically promoted it as an aid to recovery and a rehabilitated economy. In 1940, 410 employees ran the IBM operation in France. By 1949 there were 2,186 and by 1960, 6,200. Thirty-two sales and service offices served the empire, and French-manufactured IBM equipment went into sixty-four countries.

It was Baron Christian de Waldner, picked by Thomas J. Watson in 1934 to become "Mr. IBM of France," who put a Gallic stamp on the American company. An art collector, bibliophile, and sportsman, he built the organization that ultimately took the computer business from an "authentic" French company, Machines Bull, whose bones were finally picked by the General Electric Corporation. But first IBM nearly wrecked Machines Bull with large doses of competitive capital and sales promotions uncommon in French industry. By 1960, de Waldner's 6,200 employees were turning out more business for IBM in France than the nationally owned Machines Bull was doing around the world.

By the time the United States entered World War II, net annual income from business outside the country for IBM was $630,221. The following year, 1942, in spite of the loss of sales in enemy territory, the net income leaped to $1,578,539. It never faltered after that. By 1950 it was up to $5,698,119. In the first year of the decade of the sixties it was $64.5 million on a gross income of nearly $500 million. In 1967, gross income from foreign sales exceeded $1.6 billion and produced net earnings of $209.3 million.

One of the few corporations in the world growing faster than IBM, financial writers observed, was its collective of foreign operations under the World Trade Corporation. Domestically it had long been the classic growth company of the century, with an uninterrupted record of doubling its size every four years after World War II. Overseas operations after the war were detached from divisional status to establish the wholly owned World Trade Corporation, independently administered in relation to domestic business but not in relation to Watson himself. IBM operated from then on in each country through a national company which, though wholly owned by World Trade, was managed and staffed by citizens; they soon learned that while their national characteristics were not to be totally altered or suppressed, they were expected to be adaptable to the American custom of training and sales. Watson's confidence in the American way of doing business was intense and automatic, but a good deal of flexibility was allowed to harmonize company objectives with each national style of advertising, selling, marketing, and customer relations.

The rah-rah style was not popular in sophisticated, worldly continental cities. As Robert Sheehan, writing in *Fortune* in November of 1960, put it: "IBM abroad was to remain American in its bones though the face might be foreign." By that time, more than 33,000 overseas employees worked in eighty-seven countries, in thirty-six of which nationally incorporated companies had been organized. At World Headquarters in New York only 370 employees looked after the international business.

World Trade had its own adaptation of the Common Market and, like the great oil companies dealing directly with governments and potentates, set up its own state department to deal with boundary and customs matters, import restrictions, tariffs, currency fluctuations, and other questions alien to domestic business. The economy, the land, and the human spirit had been shattered by the war, and low-wage companies were without basic goods and tools when the World Trade Corporation begar building manufacturing plants to produce sophisticated business machines that were really not wanted at that time.

Gross revenue per employee abroad was less than half the domestic rate, in part because the markets overseas were widely scattered and because lower labor costs made mechanization of production less compelling. But such conditions were transitory; the phenomenal recovery of Europe and the revitalizing effect of the Marshall Plan found IBM ready, first with the most, prepared to deliver business machines, many of them manufactured on the spot, to demanding customers. Across Europe, the Americanization of country after country became visible in the presence of drug stores, hamburger stands, higher wages, credit systems, mass marketing, and the idol worship of efficiency. With labor shortages developing, profitable businesses found it necessary to mechanize record keeping, information handling, and the like—which was exactly IBM's business. In the nineteen-fifties, World Trade averaged a growth of 21.7 per cent a year, closely apace with the parent corporation's own growth rate of 22.2 per cent. After that, World Trade outpaced the domestic corporation by substantial margins.

In 1968 IBM had one or more manufacturing plants and laboratories, often in addition to administration and sales operations, in thirteen countries outside the United States: Argentina, Brazil, Canada, Colombia, France, West Germany, India, Italy, Japan, Mexico, the Netherlands, Sweden, and the United Kingdom. In the United States, twenty-five manufacturing and research facilities were spotted in or near principal cities. All of these operations divided the work of ten far-flung divisions and occupied twenty-seven million square feet of floor space, of which six million was leased. World Trade itself had independent facilities in Austria, Belgium, Denmark, Finland, Norway, Portugal, Spain, and Switzerland.

One example was cited by Robert Sheehan to illustrate what was happening in western Europe. In 1950 when World Trade was starting on its own, a man named Joseph Neckermann started a little clothing business in Frankfurt with seven employees. Ten years later Neckermann had expanded into a kind of conglomerate dealing in a variety of un-related goods and materials, disbursed in part through a vast mail order operation. In addition, he was operating ninety-two retail stores for a gross business of $150 million a year. Mr. Neckermann ordered one of IBM's 7070 computer installations to handle his billing, shipping, sales analyses, accounting, and payrolls. The 7070 was one of the company's large and expensive installations, for which Mr. Neckermann paid the national company, I.B.M. Deutschland, $40,000 a month. The company had been managed for years by Hans Borsdorf, a Watson recruit brought into IBM in 1931, who served Watson with ebullient, uncritical servility. Borsdorf had enthusiasm uncomplicated by doubt, plus the IBM-oriented sales training to know something about the possibilities of Neckermann's business.

Vigorously chomping on his cigars and quoting passages from Nor-man Vincent Peale's *The Power of Positive Thinking*—his favorite work of literature, copies of which he handed to prospects and visitors—Borsdorf inspired and provoked his sales staff with no less determination than a Westchester branch manager bucking an updated 100 Percent Club quota. The reputation of Thomas J. Watson was the German com-pany's most profitable asset, said Borsdorf.

Variations of the Frankfurt example became commonplace, and by 1960 World Trade had nineteen foreign manufacturing plants producing ninety per cent of its revenues.

I.B.M. Deutschland and I.B.M. France are the showcase operations in Europe. World Trade overwhelmingly dominates the market in every country in which the corporation operates except England and Japan, and even there it is national trade practices which have given indigenous manufacturers the edge. In England, for example, the government in 1968 distributed $125 million mainly to two British manufacturers of computers, ICT (International Computers & Tabulators) and English Electric Elliott, while the Computer Advisory Unit screened government agency procurements to make sure that an outside computer was specified only when a domestic installation could not meet the requirements.

United States computer manufacturers install ninety per cent of the computers in Europe, a situation which appalls helpless Europeans when they think about it. By and large, IBM gets up to eighty per cent of the total business, although it dropped to about fifty per cent for a short time in France, with England's ICT, Univac, and General Electric (once it took over Machines Bull) sharing second place and splitting the remainder pretty evenly. There are about eight thousand computer installations in Europe, not including punch card equipment which had an initial value of $3 billion. In 1966 United States companies in the computer business were responsible for six per cent of all new plant equipment expenditures on the continent, and by 1970 it will be up to ten per cent. Thus IBM, through its World Trade Corporation, and those competitors who trail so far behind the giant, "will almost fully control an industry which will condition the economic life of every country today," according to M. Andre Chargueraud, president of Diebold Europe, S.A. Chargueraud told a research seminar in New York:

"It is natural that European government leaders are not too happy about this, for this so-called technological gap removes their control of their economic future."[1]

While the national computer manufacturers of Europe and England will receive $500 million in government financing over the next five years, with other supports promised, it will not change the outlook or the division of business achieved. This financial assistance adds up to an average of $15 million a year per company. Each manufacturer and each company in Europe has gone its own way when, according to M. Chargueraud, "it would have been better to build a computer system on a European, rather than a national, basis." Almost no likelihood exists that the technological gap which has struck Europe will be bridged. What Canadians have worried about for years, and what General Charles de Gaulle in France helplessly tried to prevent in the case of a French computer manufacturer, and what they are writing books about in England, is "the American takeover," led by IBM.[2]

Machines Bull was the pride of France and the confirmation to General de Gaulle of French technological superiority. Since the 1930's it had been run by the Callies family, six of whose members sat on its board of directors. The name itself derived from a Norwegian, Frederick

[1] Quoted from the June, 1968, issue of *Administrative Management*, reporting on the paper prepared by M. Chargueraud for the Diebold Research Program in New York.

[2] *The American Take-Over of Britain* is the title of a book written by two British journalists, James McMillan and Bernard Harris (Hart Publishing Co., New York, 1968). The writers report that more than half a million British workers are employed by U.S. companies, and that in seven or eight years, American companies will be producing more than twenty per cent of all British goods.

Bull, who had assigned it some punch card and tabulator patents. Like IBM in the United States, Machines Bull had been the admired growth company of France. Its stock had risen from a fifty-franc par to 804 on the Paris Bourse in 1961. Three years later it had fallen to 167, and in those three years, IBM knocked Machines Bull off its narrow capital base and took possession of the country's computer market. It was a battle of technology and capital in which Machines Bull died. It is now called Bull-General Electric, and GE owns sixty-six per cent of it, General de Gaulle's imperial objections to foreign incursion having had insufficient force to alter the facts of finance and competition. Economic resources and technological superiority, especially when applied in combination, are like love and war to the extent that they acknowledge resistance as largely transitory. IBM, in overcoming Machines Bull, put General Electric into the computer business in Europe by making the French company vulnerable to proposals from a foreign suitor. The once desirable Machines Bull, unsuccessful in achieving what it desired, accepted first what it could get and finally what it had to tolerate.

When the first signs of internal stress appeared, notwithstanding speculative delight over the increasing value of Bull shares, scouts for General Electric, an American giant which had been mauled in domestic encounters with IBM and was determined to show it had benefited by the lesson, paid careful court to the attractive French treasure. As is often the case in such prearranged affairs, money and industrial security were among the more welcome characteristics of the intruder. The courtship proceeded with lowered voices, very good manners, and an air of ceremonial bowing and consultation among the corporate families, the deferential style being industry's acknowledgement of de Gaulle nationalism and of political necessity. General Electric negotiators had been thoroughly briefed on the miffed feelings of de Gaulle, who equated the country's production and corporate growth with the character of France. The problem for General Electric became mainly one of buying its way into the European computer market without having to enter again into open combat with IBM, while at the same time appearing to be injecting into Machines Bull the kind of money de Gaulle could interpret as a tribute to French prowess. General Electric had had such painful experinece with IBM over the years, having paid five or six hundred million dollars in unrewarding capital investment for its education, that its negotiators deferred to de Gaulle's patriarchal pride with something of the same defensive caution old IBM executives had exercised with Watson. If he had sensed anything wrong, the whole arranged affair would have had to start again from the beginning.

The wounds had not yet healed from the humiliating acquisition by

Chrysler of control of the Simca motor car company in 1962. When word
of the pursuit of Bull by GE reached General de Gaulle, he rejected the
match with Olympian disdain, offended at the prospect of a title-hunting
corporate seducer making heady promises to relieve the tensions of a
French computer beauty just coming of age. Although no merger or
marriage had been seriously considered, at least not yet, by Machines
Bull, negotiations even hinting at a betrothal were terminated.

But de Gaulle could not stop the course of true love tied to true need.
While he could prevent negotiations in court or in the drawing room, he
could not police the corridors; in out of the way places, the wary quest
on GE's part for a computer market and on Bull's for a generous protector went cautiously forward. IBM's comparatively mediocre computer
line in the late 1950's had caused the confident Machines Bull to invest
heavily in the advanced but costly Gamma series. Manufacture in 1960
of the highly regarded machines, the first to appear with germanium
diodes, shook up IBM considerably.

Meanwhile, another American giant soundly birched by IBM from
time to time showed up in France. Radio Corporation of America and
Machines Bull came to an understanding under which the latter received
patent rights and U.S. training for its engineers; in return, RCA machines
were allowed in France. IBM all but shrugged in its imitated Gallic
style, pointing out that *it* was selling a true, fully French-made computer
in competition with an intrusive RCA import manufactured in a foreign
land. Bull declared that its behavior with RCA was amicable and correct
and that nothing had been subtracted from its own desirability. However, in preserving its virtue on paternal orders from the righteous de
Gaulle, Bull lost something else not quite so irreplaceable: money. Even
with sales up twenty-one per cent in 1962, profits fell steeply: Bull had
to give as much as thirty-five per cent discount to compete with IBM
machines, and it sounded like the bad old days at NCR. With much of
its equipment on lease, Bull could not wait out the period of return on
rentals. A new company, half French and half American, was formed to
take mortgages on leased equipment and get working money back into
the Bull bank accounts.

"It was not a normal deal," said a Bull man in reviewing the matter.
"Passion was involved, reason was not. . . ."

In the two-year period during which Bull tried to make its superior
Gamma computer the sought-after princess, if not the queen, of the
European market, software, programming, and service problems compounded by capital shortcomings made it necessary to become less discriminating, regardless of de Gaulle and national pride. Having grown

from annual sales of $1,500,000 to nearly a hundred million in thirteen years, a record not achieved by IBM itself, the fall of Bull was all the more humiliating because it was visible to much of the world. A loss of $25 million in 1963 came at a time of record high sales, when the Gamma computer was indeed making inroads on the market, when Bull had service centers all over Europe and Latin America and was selling equipment for Remington Rand's Univac in the United States. Bull simply couldn't keep it up, and in the faltering interim, IBM drove forward with such force that the French company reeled.

Two thousand stockholders, irate and howling, assembled in April of 1964 in the elegant Paris Théâtre des Champs Elysées to hear their president Joseph Callies confess that the company couldn't meet a four million dollar bond payment. Control passed into the hands of the Banque de Paris et des Pays Bas, and a few weeks later Callies was succeeded by the bank's nominee, Roger Schulz. The government promised sixty-three million dollars in capital and contracts, and it was disclosed that an agreement had been reached which accommodated de Gaulle's requirement for the preservation of national honor and General Electric's insistence upon capital control commensurate with about $50 million. The big power in jet aircraft engines and the developing nuclear industries of the United States had bought its way into the European computer market. Callies was not deluded, de Gaulle's touchiness to the contrary.

Reduced to trapping size by IBM, Machines Bull would now be taken over by General Electric, said Joseph Callies; full control was "inevitable" in view of the fact that the annual sales of Olivetti (with which Bull had had a financial and producing agreement), Britain's ICT, Germany's Telefunken, and Bull did not, combined, equal the cash flow of IBM.

A French banker was quoted by editor Stanley H. Brown in *Fortune*, August 1965, as saying France was "faced with a desire to get out of economic diapers," but that the country lacked the financial ability to do so. GE wound up with two-thirds of the company, about what Callies had predicted.[3] IBM recovered the bit of market it had lost for a time when Bull was going well, and things settled down again in Europe to

---

[3] With Simca taken over by Chrysler, and Machines Bull by GE, another blow in the "concentrate or die" dictum struck the French auto industry late in 1968 when Italy's giant Fiat Automobile Corporation, largest European producer and fourth largest in the world, acquired a fifteen per cent interest in the Citroën Motor Company. Fiat had sought a controlling interest but settled for a minority position which would be a great deal larger than fifteen per cent through participation in a holding company which owns Citroën shares.

the old operational balance of power in which IBM took the bulk of the computer market, with all other producers sharing between twenty and twenty-five per cent.

General Electric paid pretty heavily for sixty-six per cent of Machines Bull while accomplishing not much more than a base on which to mount an attempt to accomplish what Bull couldn't. But GE found itself still standing there in IBM's shadow. J. Stanford Smith, vice-president of GE's Information Systems Group, reported to stockholders in October of 1968 that computer operations were costing the company a good deal of money and were having an "adverse impact on current earnings." In that special language that characterizes annual reports, he explained that 1968, like 1967, had brought "reduced operating losses." It takes "massive investments to establish a position in a market of this dimension," he said. However, Bull-General Electric was expected by GE President Fred Borch to become profitable "very shortly." Meanwhile, gross sales in GE would exceed $8 billion in 1968, and over the next decade everything—computer operations, jet engines, and nuclear power plants—would bring in profits at GE. In fact, Mr. Borch foresaw a $20 billion company well before the nineteen-seventies were over. He thought the draining of profits to pay huge development costs would taper off.

General Electric advanced with its renewed challenge to IBM in a merger with Italy's Olivetti. After "l'affaire Bull," it became apparent that the two American companies, IBM and GE, will dominate the struggle for the European and world markets in the nineteen-seventies, a market that will most certainly grow to gigantic and profitable size. It is conceded as possible that GE may gain a lap or two in the uneven race, but the positions of the contenders will remain about the same, with IBM beyond serious challenge. The London Economist determined that, after the GE-Bull matter and the Olivetti merger, IBM increased its share of the French market to seventy-four per cent, retained seventy-three per cent of the German market, and hung onto at least half of the business in Great Britain, notwithstanding heavy British subsidies. In Canada, in the rest of Europe, and in South America, IBM had nearly all of the business, and even in Japan it had forty per cent of the market. Altogether, IBM has kept about eighty per cent of the total world market.

To make things worse for the Europeans, the United States balked at exporting the really large computer installations, needed for defense planning and large aircraft production, for which insufficient manufacturing resources existed in Europe. Thus the embattled defenders made alliances with each other to prevent, if possible, foreign economic occupation. Two British companies, ICT and English Electric, arrived at an "understanding" with what remained of the French computer industry.

They united with the French holding company, Compagnie pour l'Informatique et les Techniques Electroniques de Controle (in which GE exercised considerable power) and agreed to cooperate in building very large scientific computers for experimental and university work. With a projected world market for no more than thirty installations, the plan, however desirable, did not promise continuous profit. It is doubtful that such a plan would have found favor in the first place had not the United States declined to export a few dozen of the enormous Control Data or similar installations; smaller nations need these if they are not to be relegated to curbstone levels in the development of future technology.

General Electric's investments in Machines Bull started with a $43 million outlay, which grew to $65 million in a year or two and exceeded $100 million by 1967. As such expenditures induced second thoughts or timidity, GE began acting like the proverbial absentee landlord and canceled Bull's Gamma 55 and Gamma 115 computers, to the considerable fury of people who had been working on them for years and amid uproar from the French press and labor unions protesting employment cutbacks. The move had repercussions in Italy where, fearing the spread of retrenchment at Olivetti operations, scientists and technicians began looking around for other jobs. The trade periodical, *Business Abroad*, grumbled in early 1967:

"General Electric tried to take the computer operations of three companies with different philosophies and different product lines and blend them into a whole." The anonymous spokesman voiced a thought that must have occurred, possibly with despair, to decision makers at GE who watched hundreds of millions disappear in the sustained attempt to crowd into a market over which IBM seemed to preside with its own sledgehammer and its own mint: "GE probably would have been better off coming in here on its own."

But on its own, GE probably would have got no further. IBM had mastered the arts and sciences of foreign trade, expansion, absentee ownership, and management by citizens of each country in which it operated. Although the purchase cost GE heavily and caused rumblings of protest among stockholders and dissident managers, the company became well entrenched in the European computer market as a continuing challenger to segments of the IBM market, and the association with Olivetti and Machines Bull gave GE nationalistic acceptance and respectability of a high order. IBM will unquestionably retain its thorough dominance of the commercial computer market, but GE has gathered strength to compete in the nineteen-seventies in market areas from which, until it bought its way in, it had been excluded.

As in the United States and every industrialized country, the demand

237

for computers is generated in four main segments of economic activity: service industries like banking, insurance, and finance; electrical, aircraft, space technology, and missile producers; heavy manufacturing like oil, automobiles, chemicals, and steel; and the largest purchaser of them all— sometimes the only purchaser in small nations—governments and their various agencies. The service industries require equipment to handle incalculable volumes of data processing. Heavy industry emphasizes process control machines to anticipate, regulate, and operate factory complexes. The largest computer installations go into aircraft and missile fields to perform technical calculations at a rate of nearly three million additions a second and simulations of infinite variety. IBM is absent from none of these fields, but its world-wide production for the most part emphasizes the universally sought-after "business" machines, which in spite of the uninspiringly conventional name include a vast range of highly sophisticated and perennially profitable computers and supporting equipment.

A splendid example of the kind of business machine that IBM sold in volume throughout Europe in the nineteen-sixties was a compact accounting system designated as the 3000 Series. It was a case of a promising demand being satisfied by a beautiful product, explicitly put together to meet continental needs and kept off the market in the United States. Contrary to usual IBM practices under which domestic operations take care of design and development, the 3000 sprang from the World Trade Corporation. It was the sort of thing Thomas J. Watson, when he was nearly eighty, "wished" he had had back in the early nineteen-fifties.

The laboratories of Herr Borsdorf's I.B.M. Deutschland designed the 3000 originally, but sales and technical people from a dozen different countries studied it in a collective collaboration that made it wonderfully applicable to a large number of unrelated operations. It was a real all-purpose product based on punch card usage, non-electronic, relatively inexpensive, capable of performing basic accounting functions; and it wasn't very heavy or very big. It was intended to captivate the small business man, the little company, and it was a bargain. It could be bought outright for $16,550 and installed in a space occupied by two or three small desks, or it could be rented for $340 a month. Volkswagen, no small business operation, took thirty of them for automobile agencies around the continent at a cost of nearly half a million dollars. In six or seven months, sales of more than $13 million were reported. As fast as they could be produced they were installed, and in a couple of years there were thousands in operation all over Europe. They were exported, too, to Latin America, Africa, and the Far East. But because the 3000 apparently could not be produced at a competitive price in America, it was never marketed in the United States or Canada. Cost-conscious buyers there had to settle for more sophisticated electronic equipment that was more efficient, operated at higher speed, and cost a great deal more than $340 a month.

French engineers at the old Paris laboratory which has since moved to the Riviera near Nice were credited with developing the logic system for the famous and widely sold electronic 1401, the development and design of which were completed at the IBM installations in Endicott, New York. Until the System 360 generation of computers began appearing across the United States and Canada, the venerable 1401 saw service (and, in fact, remains in use) in institutions and companies which could contract for rental fees ranging from $2,600 to $8,000 a month. This was several levels away from the more awesome and more costly 7070, which cost the enterprising Herr Neckermann in Frankfurt, Germany, $40,000 a month and cost his American counterparts a good deal more, depending on the type of installation, the software, and the programming involved.

Within four or five years after the end of World War II, IBM operations in Europe were running smoothly and more promisingly than they had been before the war. It was true that the markets of Eastern Europe were closed off, but with the inauguration of the Marshall Plan, business expanded almost month by month. The nerve center of the IBM operation was a graceful old historic building on Place Vendome in Paris. From there, and from World Trade Headquarters at 590 Madison Avenue in New York City, Thomas J. Watson until his death, and his two sons, Tom and Arthur, watched overseas business in the corporation quadruple in size in the period between 1950, when World Trade was detached from divisional status and organized as a separate corporation, and 1960.

In 1958, the Paris quarters had become so congested, with travelers from America and the continent arriving and departing in an endless stream, that a new plant was built twenty miles up the Seine near the little town of Corbeil Essones. There, the largesse of paternalism manifested itself in some magnitude for the first time among the touchy, individualistic French.

Only pleasure and approbation greeted the construction of a sports stadium and tennis courts, and by that time no one in the company, domestic or foreign, made any effort to impose the kind of rules of deportment that had characterized IBM life in America. It was two years after the death of the venerated old patriarch, and the French character that was allowed to guide advertising and marketing policies was also permitted expression in the company dining rooms, in which wine was served with meals. From other parts of France and from French-speaking lands abroad, trainees appeared to take the courses and participate in sales indoctrination studies very much like those at Endicott, Pough-keepsie, and Sands Point, New York. There were, however, no *chansons* for the honor and glory of IBM or its new leaders. But four hundred men a year, including those from French North Africa, came to learn and departed to man the branch and district offices in the country and abroad. The costs were borne from rising profits. No remittances had been made by the French operation to the parent company for the nineteen-year period between 1935 and 1954, when royalty payments to IBM were resumed. By 1960, IBM assets in France amounted to $92 million.

One aspect of American methods which met solid resistance was the sales quota, which was simply alien to the French temperament. On the other hand, militant French trade unionists were no more successful in France than they were at Endicott, New York, in persuading workers to unite in solidarity against exploitation by capitalists. One aging French trade unionist was quoted in *Fortune* in 1960 as grumbling that an IBM employee was "a company man for life," and described the whole opera-tion as "socialistic paternalism."

There was some trouble when IBM sought to provide pensions for the workers, but again it was more a matter of what was temperamen-tally acceptable than any inbuilt resistance against fringe benefits. French workers insisted that they be allowed to contribute some of their own money to the pension plan. In the United States, IBM had made all the contributions—although in former years, under the late Thomas J. Watson, dismissed or departing employees could be denied pensions to which *only* the company had contributed. IBM yielded to the French system which disbursed retirement income from a pension pool—a plan under which an employee's pension was not dependent on just one com-pany but on a consortorium which assured pensioners that payments would be related to the rise and decline of buying power levels. IBM management compromised on matters of this kind, but there were two areas in which compromise was not allowed—one involving personnel, and one involving corporate power, in which a compromise was made once, but only until the company could buy its way out of the situation in which it had allowed itself to become involved.

IBM personnel policy abroad was in direct opposition to traditional practices in many countries. Its distortion of language in conferring exalted titles on service employees contradicted in European and Latin American countries a reverence for the words *engineer* and *doctor*. In South American republics especially, these were annexed to the names of company men and managers with something of the honor and fraternal acceptance transferred to Kentucky colonels in the United States. In Europe, use of the descriptive title *engineer* was reserved not for IBM men assigned to install and repair tabulating equipment—as in the case of a customer service engineer—but for graduates in engineering. Terminology had to be adjusted, but resistance to titles masked an older tradition that militated against young men.

In his long tenure as chief executive of the World Trade Corporation, Arthur Watson upset the tradition in countries where young executives were more or less detained in holding pens until upper echelon management figures were retired or died off. For many years IBM had promoted younger men to positions of responsibility, a factor which sharpened a man's ambition and made it possible as often as not to reach upper income levels in advance of middle age. In Japan, Germany, France, and to a somewhat lesser degree in England, where veneration for age and experience at times took the form of hostile expression to the ambitions of the young, Arthur Watson directed area managers to move able young men upward in the hierarchy. The policy had a salutary effect on overseas operations over the years, for when young men saw that their contemporaries advanced in jobs normally reserved for their elders in other companies, it created a foreign equivalent of the old IBM spirit. In this respect, Arthur Watson and IBM instituted economic as well as sociological changes in what had been an employment generation gap.

In the matter of languages, too, Arthur Watson recognized the crippling effects of a man's inability to achieve routine mastery of conversation and correspondence in a host country. He had himself, with no extraordinary aptitude for linguistics, become fluent and competent in French, which enabled him to remain both emotionally and officially associated with the strong growth of IBM in France over the years. In addition, he became sufficiently adept in German and Spanish to get along with ease, and even learned enough Russian to avoid reliance on an interpreter in routine situations. Watson knew early and young what every knowledgeable and sophisticated businessman in Europe knew prior to World War I: that one could scarcely engage in business across boundary lines without developing linguistic skills. When IBM insisted that foreign managers and, later on, even middle echelon engineers and technicians master English, the policy met no resistance from Europeans;

they just naturally expected to have to learn the language, and learn it well, anyway. Virtually all personnel marked for upper level jobs get a year or two of living and observing in the United States, where they are expected to raise the quality of their school-learned English to a high level of fluency.

Foreign leaders of IBM like Louis Castaldi, Italian-born European manager for many years, could travel from the Balkans to England, switching languages at each customs stop. When he became head of the IBM overseas area stretching through twenty-three countries from Iceland to Israel and was responsible for recruiting and training men, his emphasis on language ability on the part of prospects was unrelenting. On these points IBM has not compromised abroad, and it shows in the acceptance, growth, and style of the international corporation.

Mr. Castaldi's area was one of seven into which, exclusive of the market in the United States, IBM had divided the planet. Each area is separately developed and managed. In the decade of the nineteensixties, World Trade expansion has been taking place in these areas at a faster rate—sometimes four to five times faster—than their gross national product rates, and in fact the growth rate of World Trade was injecting adrenalin into the economy of some areas by stimulating gross national product development.

In most cases, IBM managers overseas—especially outside the industrialized and technologically advanced countries like England, France, Germany, Italy, Switzerland, Japan, Scandinavia, etc.—just naturally gravitate to the upper levels of national governments. It is generally unnecessary to curry favor with governments; the situation works the other way around. When emerging nations look to censustaking tasks, to the vast range of quantitative measurement required to make national plans or ward off disasters, they find IBM prepared from experience in other lands, ready with the equipment, the programming, and the service to get countries started on their way. World Trade men thus were on hand when the census had to be taken in Ghana, Kenya, Tanganyika, Uganda, Nigeria, Zanzibar, India, and elsewhere on the globe. Where governments have looked to IBM for such help, which in turn gave the corporation an advantage in subsequent contacts and negotiations, World Trade men moved easily into such activities as establishing national manufacturing plants, training job recruits, dealing with tariff and currency problems, and so on. It all just came naturally.

With a single exception, IBM always kept complete ownership of its overseas production facilities, a policy it was not easy to insist upon, since many governments and most Americans accommodated themselves to a policy under which U.S. corporations were at least in part nationally owned abroad. On one occasion, IBM did compromise on this principle, but not for keeps.

Until 1949, the British Tabulating Company, the predecessor to the United Kingdom's highly regarded International Computers and Tabulators (ICT), had an exclusive license to make and sell IBM products throughout the Commonwealth, except for the lucrative Canadian market, second in size outside the United States only to the European market. It was an old arrangement dating from the days of Charles Flint, but it did not altogether fit in with Thomas J. Watson's concept of an integrated world-wide company free of ownership entanglements in foreign lands. The licensing arrangement in England was a throwback to the days when overseas sales agencies were the purveyors, as in the case of Patterson and his National Cash Registers, of U.S. equipment abroad. When things settled down after World War II and Marshall Plan aid programs, Watson made overtures to renegotiate the old British Tabulating Company contract.

With a steady supply of new models and products at no research cost to itself, the British firm had a good and lucrative thing going, and was well aware of it. It held fast until Watson, in an exercise of intuition that sometimes made his adversaries superstitious, gave more than it asked. He offered BTC a non-exclusive license, free of charge, on products then in the IBM line and on patents still pending. In return, rather than giving BTC exclusive sales throughout the Commonwealth, IBM was to be allowed to compete around the world. The managers of British Tabulating agreed, secure in the knowledge that its own experience in the markets of the Empire would provide more than enough advantage over the American-managed operation. Thus, IBM began competing with itself by selling against its own sales agency, not only in England, but in Australia, New Zealand, India, Pakistan, South Africa, and wherever else the sun of Empire had not yet set.

When the World Trade corporation began operating as a separate entity under the name of I.B.M. United Kingdom, Ltd., Watson—who was still very much the sole arbiter of IBM policy—allowed British subjects to own some of the shares in their mother country's own company. Meanwhile, IBM pursued its quest in the Commonwealth, and within the next eleven or twelve years built up $50 million a year in sales, a growth rate that exceeded that of the parent company as a whole.

After ten years during which Britons collected dividends on the jointly owned IBM operation in the United Kingdom, World Trade borrowed $28 million from its parent corporation and bought out the thirty-eight per cent interest that remained in British hands. The price, according to a *Fortune* estimate, was thirty-five times the stock earnings.

Never again did a foreign national own a piece of an IBM company in his own country. When an unpleasant squabble developed in Japan, Arthur Watson and his advisors stood their ground against Japanese pressure to put partial ownership of IBM in that country into the hands of its own citizens or investment institutions. In India, too, where partial ownership was a matter of national policy following the departure of the British, the unwavering IBM position was upheld. Most countries were so pleased to have an IBM installation inside their frontiers that negotiations were inevitably settled on IBM's terms.

Yet the company's own position on the issue reflected good experience and at least the self-serving logic of expediency, regardless of possible longer range considerations. Archaic export limitations still compelled IBM to manufacture parts and components in one country and ship them out unassembled, often across an intervening country, to be stored pending arrival of other parts from yet another country. The manufacture and shipment of a completed product from one country to an adjacent one was often economically prohibitive, if permitted at all.

Of course, that was only part of it. In defending its argument for sole ownership, IBM was able to point to a remarkable record of reinvesting profits in the development and extension of its national companies, the growth of technology, economic expansion, increased job opportunities, and the like. Sometimes the company all but took a country by the scruff of the neck and compelled it to join with others in doing what they might well have collectively accomplished in the first place.

When IBM began making electric typewriters in Europe, for example, it manufactured parts in nine different countries and shipped them around the continent; shipments sometimes passed each other in freight trains going in opposite directions. Yet in each of the nine countries, assembly plants had to be set up to put the completed typewriters together. All of this foolishness was required by antiquated rules which, in seeking to protect domestic manufacturing interests, prevented developments conducive to cost savings and efficiency. This dog-in-the-manger style of protection had frustrated sensible and intelligent business leaders for years; it was a throwback to the era in which the gauge of railroad tracks changed at national borders to provide employment and extract fees for checking and handling goods in transit.

By snipping away at red tape, persuading European bureaucrats to liberalize interpretation of restrictive procedures when they could not be discreetly ignored, IBM and a growing number of western European businessmen got trade practices eased. American persuasion, reinforced with postwar aid funds, naturally lubricated developments. In time, electric typewriter parts could be manufactured in two plants, and with the advent of the Common Market, production was concentrated in one. The concentration of complete manufacture of products or categories of products in individual countries has become commonplace on a world-wide scale.

Each of the seven World Trade areas is managed by men who are free and encouraged—even directed—to make all day-to-day decisions with a minimum of interference from world headquarters. Companies and countries in the World Trade group do not, however, undertake research and development on their own; that is the prerogative of the parent domestic operation. It is true that the Series 3000 accounting system, which was a gold mine for the World Trade Corporation, was created abroad, but it was not technologically advanced equipment; it involved no electronic components and was a relatively simple, if highly useful, product. Equipment and products of the technological age, together with basic research and planning, are controlled by IBM in the United States.

The appearance of a permissive attitude toward competition prevails, but every tremor of the market is recorded and evaluated at world headquarters, now in suburban Armonk, New York. By heavy applications of research and capital, or by expanding sales and service efforts, IBM could drive virtually any company, including governments bent on interfering, up against or close to the wall. It remains, approaching the decade of the nineteen-seventies, content with a volume of business that allows little more than the appearance of serious competition, without thus far permitting it to become meaningful in fact. Its policies and corporate competitive responses insist on retaining sixty to ninety-five per cent of the world business. Whatever its internal policies may have done in the past to mold and shape the white-collar American, IBM has devised, tested, improved, and refined the system of international corporate success to its nearest expression of perfection on earth. And it has done so, as Arthur Watson once said, "as if we had an absolute guarantee that there will be peace forever."

14.
Ever
Onward

———◆———

THE SECOND GENERATION OF management at IBM dates from the middle of the 1950's when the company was in potential danger. It was a time when, as young Tom correctly concluded, the old evangelism was no substitute for coming to grips competitively and intelligently with the scientific revolution that Watson's patronage and self-serving generosity had helped inaugurate. Tom's first move was to get the one-man organization rehabilitated and functioning as a corporation with a dozen separately managed divisions. He brought cohesion to the sprawling bureaucracy, potentially vulnerable to competing men of brilliance and scientific understanding, who saw it as a lumbering giant unable to progress in a world that had evolved beyond its capacity for adaptation. Resorting to conventional management techniques and processes, Tom and his aides steered IBM into an organized bureaucracy capable of absorbing the shocks of growth.

Concurrently and intentionally he began to destroy the evidence of patriarchal worship and evangelism, meanwhile recruiting brains and talent to help him personally. The old songbooks, with their hymns and marches of adulation, were rounded up and disposed of. It was a thorough job, the purpose of which was to deemphasize, without altogether obliterating, old Victorian attitudes toward clothes, conduct, and religious dedication to the IBM spirit, and to substitute for individual missionary zeal a dedication to the disciplines of technology.

He sought continuing counsel from a telephone utility executive, a former friend of his father, and looked around for a proved expert on management to guide him. He assembled an important conference in Williamsburg, Virginia. Here for the first time a more or less complete organization chart was drawn and executives assigned to fill more than a hundred key corporate positions, with duties and lines of command specified, at least on paper. Taking in talent from outside the corporation was treacherous work, and Tom tried to move cagily. Nevertheless, he blundered—dangerously, but not fatally.

About the time of the Williamsburg reorganization conference, he had played golf with John L. Burns, an investment and management authority with the aggressiveness of Genghis Khan. He had made a reputation in the management consulting firm of Booz Allen & Hamilton, a company which had often been successful in diagnosing and streamlining faltering corporations. Tom said he liked the "cut" of the man, his ideas, and his authoritative style. Thus impressed, he went to Booz Allen to discuss plans for making the reorganized corporation function while undergoing inevitable expansion. One of Booz Allen's clients was the Radio Corporation of America, which, Tom assumed, was in conflict with some of IBM's own goals. His assumption was confirmed in part in the course of his discussions, and Tom went to General David Sarnoff of RCA, candidly exposing his problems and disclosing his hope of bringing Burns into IBM if the conflict of interest on Booz Allen's part could be resolved.

Sarnoff assured Tom that RCA's primary interest in the field of computers was related to military logistics, then developing under the so-called BIZMAC project. He had, said Sarnoff, no intention of trying to wedge RCA into the computer market across the board, and thus no conflict of interest need be considered.

Tom thereupon put Burns in charge of a high priority study team, with access to complete knowledge of IBM's secrets, weaknesses, and bureaucratic management problems. He was privy to its plans, its technology assets, and its organization, which he helped devise. IBM was one of Booz Allen's eight hundred clients.

Within two years, Board Chairman David Sarnoff hired Burns as president in a move that shocked Tom Watson, Junior, and shook IBM to its deepest circuits.

"He lied to me," Tom said, and his moral sense was outraged. Tom had—and continues to have—a moral and ethical sense that ranges, not always cohesively, from the trivial to the significant in corporate affairs. His outrage was transmitted to the IBM sales staff, who, while repeatedly admonished to abjure "dirty selling" and the use of excessive power in competition—in line with the consent decree—made something of an exception in the case of RCA. Salesmen were informed they had "damned well better not lose an account to RCA." For several years, Sarnoff and Burns had an extremely hard time in the competitive ring with IBM, and the word was out that Tom wanted the lions turned loose against Sarnoff's plans to enter the computer business. He had been treated unfairly, he was clear to point out, and the exercise of morality was inapplicable in the case of a corporation which he felt had clearly cheated him.

RCA took a hundred million dollar loss in one year, and its computers continued to lose year after year, even following the dismissal of Burns, who set up his own investment firm for a time, then went on to become president of Cities Service. He became, unjustly or otherwise, known as the serpent in the IBM garden of loyalty. Robert S. Weinberg, who was on the corporate planning staff at IBM before he became vice-president of corporate planning at Anheuser-Busch, Inc., told the business periodical *Forbes Magazine* in the fall of 1967 that he would never himself take in Booz Allen experts to counsel him on corporate planning: "They have a fantastic record of their partners becoming your competitors."

To cope with the problems besetting a company that was falling behind in scientific planning and research, Tom hired Dr. Emanuel E. Piore, one of the elite in his field. Formerly chief scientist of U.S. naval research, Dr. Piore was the answer to Tom's anxiety over IBM's failure to keep abreast of the advance of science in its field. He ascended to the post of Director of Research, over the rather well-known Dr. Cuthbert Hurd, who directed what was known as the company's applied science division and who had come to IBM from the atomic energy project at Oak Ridge several years earlier. It was Cuthbert Hurd who, in proprietary sympathy was other old IBM hands loyally bound to Tom's father, clashed with the peripatetic Herbert Grosch and sent him, first, back into the academic world at M.I.T., thence into the computer operational levels of the General Electric Corporation.

Probably only IBM's great size and the inertial force set in motion by old Tom Watson gave the corporation time to get in step with scientific developments. As a company, it was naturally not in any critical danger; but it was manufacturing achievement, coupled to an unparalleled sales and service organization and capital reserve, that set IBM on top of the world. Dr. Piore later became a director of Science Research Associates, which IBM bought and which serves the educational market. The acquisition was the first of its kind by an electronics company. After the acquisition of educational firms and publishing houses became commonplace among diversifying corporations, the Department of Justice made IBM nervous, asking hundreds of questions about the purchase that became so widely imitated. Negotiations involving further buying of similar companies at IBM stopped.

Another famous personage, who had come to the company in 1935, emerged into prominence during the early years of young Tom Watson's reign in the huge, muscled frame of T. Vincent Learson, who rose through sales channels to become vice-president and, as an old phrase from the advertising community defined it, a Group Executive, in 1956. Learson somehow suppressed or subdued an overpowering personality for years, remaining only quietly visible in the middle echelons of vulnerability, until both he and the top management plateau of IBM were conditioned, through vicissitudes and Olympian preparations, for each other. He was not easily hidden in obscurity, being among the biggest of the hundreds of big men in a corporation whose leadership over the years looked with favor on outsized specimens, especially if they could learn and exercise with ease the art of deferential calculation. Learson was ruggedly handsome, craggy of face, lordly of bearing, as smart and controlled as a cobra and—until Tom was ready to assign him to a task of exacting performance—quite as prepared to coil on command into the covered basket of reserve talent to await the cadence and the beat of the new Watson drum.

Except for Tom and Dick Watson, the inheritors—and he has circumvented them at times—Learson became the most dominant, domineering, and self-confidently commanding figure in the whole corporation. He stands six feet and a half, a large boned and sinewy competitive man, relentless and untiring, uncharacteristically unconventional for an IBM executive. He seems to thrive on and derive continuously new sources of energy from life along the razor's edge. He has a faculty for dulling the blade without leaving his own blood and is credited with a capacity for evoking, through fright and explicit directives marinated in threats of doom, incredible performances from IBM men. While Tom rules IBM as chairman of the board, Learson is president.

As the single greatest eminence in the corporation to have come up though old Watson's favorite path of sales, Learson is at the top of his special breed in American business. His skills encompass every conceivable attribute of the compleat corporate executive, save those in the subjective area of sentimentality, the appearance of kindness, or an inherent willingness to give a man in error a second chance. It is not that he couldn't, if he cared, acquire the polish of gentleness, but rather that he regards it as a superfluous characteristic in a man who carries all the weight and power he can use. He is the nearest thing to a contemporary legend in the making in the company, and he has scared grown men in a way and to depths that no Watson ever quite managed. Writers and editors, searching their memories under questioning, have not been able to recall a single kindness attributable to Learson, nor have they been able to bring to mind an error, his own or someone else's, for which responsibility was charged or conceded to him.

The name of Learson, even when softly mentioned around headquarters at Armonk, produces among those assembled the equivalent of an ominous, offstage minor chord of premonition. Only men outside the IBM corral discuss him with any absence of reserve, and they marvel at him with some of the admiration they hold for nuclear power, or the unexplained phenomena of the universe. Learson did not come to the top as a friend of or because of Watson. A scientist who had called him, without rancor, "a beast of a man," saw him as mastering the toughest, hardest job any IBM man ever had, in possession of incredible self-control when he was for years required to withhold any evidence or even the suspicion of a toughness that would have got him fired. But once he unveiled his gun batteries, he was rough not only to those beneath him—others had been that—but actually rougher to those beside him and above him, not excluding the Watsons themselves. Known among IBM salesmen as "the hatchet man," he has fired more men than many moderately sized companies employ. In his march over the limp bodies of the softies, he has left distraught some otherwise hardy souls caught in the debilitating radiation of what they called TV fallout. For T. V. Learson, in the judgment of many men, is without parallel in the computer industry, a towering physical figure with a mind, finely honed to the technological age, to match.

Learson's favorite phrase, used in reference to any manager whose career hangs in the balance with project schedules, is, "I'll cut his balls off." Lacking the scientific expertise common in recent years to IBM commanders, Learson's mind and searchlight eyes focus on subordinates and associates like a laser beam that transmits back to him all the millions of bits of data the questioned man possesses, leaving him momentarily stripped of knowledge or will, his memory core deprived of both a program and a capacity for storage.

After the last stock split, Learson had more than eighteen thousand shares of stock, worth in excess of $6.5 million, an income of $232,000 a year, and dividends of $90,000 a year.[1] He also had the durability of the

[1] Quite a few shareholders own far more stock than Mr. Learson. Walker G. Buckner, husband of one of the Watson sisters, owned (personally and in family trusts) after the split 360,000 shares; Louis H. LaMotte, retired Executive Vice-president, 61,700; Tom Watson, Junior, 366,000; Albert L. Williams, former president, 25,000; Arthur K. Watson, 193,000. The largest stockholder, who became a director in 1925, is Sherman M. Fairchild, a tycoon in cameras, instruments, and helicopter companies bearing his name. He owns 509,134 shares. At an estimated $5.30 a share,

Arctic ice cap and the vision to see that the computer business is as vast as the mind itself—scarcely on the first step toward its ultimate possibilities—and a good deal more profitable, potentially, than dependence on minds in danger of atrophy or displacement by IBM equipment.

Yet there is another profile presented by Learson to his friends and family, and in his personal and public service life outside of IBM. He is frequently sought to lead public fund drives of various kinds, applying his energy and organizational skills with courteous and effective zeal. A devoted alumnus of Harvard University, he serves as an Overseer of that institution, having been elected by the alumni. A close friend and admirer of Learson has written: "He is a gentleman with a very fine reputation among his friends and associates, and he is not only a kindly, generous person, but is a very public spirited citizen who works hard for diverse good causes."

After six years or so of work in the slowly growing scientific community of IBM, Herbert Grosch began to tire of his ten-thousand-dollar a-year post and the Watson Laboratory at Columbia, and instituted a program of intrigue—carelessly formulated, as it turned out—to advance himself, beard and all, into the domain of management. Grosch had been somewhat content, enjoying the action in IBM science circles and advancing both in reputation and in professional organizations, until the company started to take in scientists from M.I.T. and the like at substantially higher salaries. He began to feel like a colonel passed up on the promotion lists but was unsuccessful in inducing management to take him out of the Laboratory. "The beard bothered them," he said, but in all likelihood, even Grosch without a beard was not easily ingested. He simply was not conventional corporation material.

He raised $50,000 and opened negotiations with the American Research and Development Corporation to start his own company in the form of an eastern counterpart of the successful Telecomputing Company operation on the West Coast. But excess profits derived from the Korean War made the idea of a new business venture decreasingly attractive, so Grosch—still with IBM—went to an insurance company, Mutual of New York, with a report that its competitors, Prudential and Metropolitan, were far advanced in computer operations; he offered to help as a consultant in catching up. He neglected to check in the Standard & Poor directory, where he would have found that Tom Watson, Junior, could

---

his income from IBM dividends in 1968 would be $2,698,410. His shares, selling at $375, were worth $191,000,000.

be expected to be sitting with the directors around the board room table when a company associate put the Grosch proposal before a regular meeting. This oversight in research astonished both Watson and Grosch, who was summoned the following morning to hear Tom ask: "What's this I hear you're doing with Mutual of New York?"

Grosch recovered in time to explain that he could not seem to get the IBM management interested in his possibilities, and that he was thinking of starting his own business.

"I understand you had an idea of starting a company computing shop for us down in Washington."

Grosch said he had tried, but that Dr. Hurd and others had balked at what he felt was a sensible idea.

"I'll give you twenty-four hours," said Tom, "to let me know whether you want to go down to Washington, or leave the company." Grosch didn't require all that time for decision-making, but let it pass for the sake of concealing his eagerness, then told Tom he'd take the job.

In Washington, Grosch started a scientific computing operation with Don Gamel and watched, fascinated, as Louis H. LaMotte coaxed government contracts out of Washington authorities by methods that, while apparently legal and certainly effective, reminded him of the niceties of old Balkan diplomacy. LaMotte, who became chairman of IBM's Executive Committee, had been allowed by the old patriarch, Watson, to run the Washington operation like a private kingdom. He was one of the few with real influence over the old man, whom he impressed. LaMotte doubtless stirred latent memories of the old dawn patrol in Dayton by going on horseback rides with the U.S. Quartermaster General, the source of important contracts. He did not, however, care much to have an outlander scientist like Grosch poaching on the IBM embassy reservation. Thus, he was a natural ally of Dr. Cuthbert Hurd, who had misgivings about having his own authority diluted in an out-of-town arena of science.

As fast as Grosch could get computer scientists trained for his Washington bureau, Hurd would requisition them for his applied science team back in New York. When Hurd called for one top-ranking man who had got into the swing of things to go to New York to strengthen the scientific community at headquarters, Grosch balked at starting all over again to train another key man. "He's not going to go up there," said Grosch, "until he's finished with the task assigned to him."

LaMotte said the scientist would go if he and Hurd wanted him out of Washington. "He's not going," said Grosch. But he went—and so did Grosch.

Grosch had been with the company six and a half years. In lieu of notice and of his lost pension benefits, he got a month's pay and departed for M.I.T., reflecting soberly on the cost of trying to impose a rationale on old Watson's domain. "There was little rationality then," he said. "Everything depended on what Mr. Watson wanted, and whether what he wanted could be divined." John McPherson had told him that heroes in the company were men who "guessed right" on Watson at least three times. "You've got to bat a thousand at IBM."

Grosch did design research at M.I.T. for a project that later became SAGE, the continental air defense system, and advised Jay Forrester, later the father of the core memory in computers, to put an IBM pre-701 computer into the M.I.T. center. He went to work for General Electric after six months and spent four years in Cincinnati running the biggest computer in that part of the country. He was one of perhaps fifty men in the United States capable of directing that operation. The job was part of the background that led to a decision on the part of GE to go into the computer business, and the company sent Grosch out to Phoenix, Arizona. Whether word of this move spread was not clear, but one day an IBM salesman, Robert Maxwell, called on him to say that he'd been instructed to find out whether Grosch might be interested in going back to IBM. Already committed to the GE program, he reported that he would return if and when General Electric's venture into the computer business became unpromising. GE put more than half a billion dollars into the project, which unhappy stockholders complained about, flubbing the operation time after time and, like James Rand earlier, helping IBM handily. Of course Rand and GE remained in the computer business, but they continued—especially Rand—to be relatively unimportant in terms of total markets, although significant in specific ways.

Grosch, who had been a charter member of ACM (The Association of Computing Machinery) and president of the American Rocket Society, active in the Optical Society and other professional associations, knew everyone in all these related fields. Knowing GE was faltering, he went to Wernher von Braun at Huntsville, Alabama, for whom GE was doing computing, and persuaded him to take over his staff of sixty people who would be stranded in the debacle. The computing contract, which produced one and a half million a year when Grosch got it, grew to eight million dollars a year. "By a supreme effort," he said, GE managed to lose it in 1965, when Computer Sciences took it over for five and a half million a year. GE had taken thirty million out of the contract, with a five per cent allowable profit, on no investment and no capital commitment. At the time GE lost the contract, the company had five hundred employees in Huntsville computing for the von Braun team, devoted largely to the Saturn space project.

Grosch went back to Tom Watson, Junior, to talk about the job the young salesman had mentioned to him earlier. It developed that that job had been related to one of IBM's more memorable failures, the luckless STRETCH computer. Priced at $13,500,000, the STRETCH was designed to dwarf everything in size and power, and its very projection caused the stock of Control Data Corporation, which had set its sights on the market for massive computers in the scientific field, to sink badly. The market for this type of computer lies in aircraft manufacture, atomic energy installations, and the utility concept of data usage.

The man who wanted Grosch was Charles De Carlo, a maverick and something of an IBM "wild duck," and a remarkably accomplished man. He was a mathematician, a virile artist and intellectual with a baritone voice and opera training; his wife was a superb cellist. He had a love for IBM, music, martinis, and the simple pleasures accessible in an environment of wealth. Sometimes he could get too much of music, martinis, and IBM, for which Grosch was a curative antidote.

De Carlo had achieved an extraordinary distinction not normally sought by IBM men when he both expressed and tested his character by appearing on corporation property now and then in a blue shirt. He achieved a good deal more distinction when it was announced that early in 1969 he would become president of Sarah Lawrence College in Bronxville, New York. When he appeared before the student body to make his introductory address, he charmed the girls and won from them a spontaneous ovation. He told them he was not going to look upon the students as punch cards and clearly left the impression that he was not going to spindle, mutilate, or bend anybody.

In fulfillment of Tom Watson's belief that if IBM had promised Grosch a job it was obligated morally to give him one, De Carlo had to take him on as his executive assistant.

"Have you changed?" Tom asked Grosch when he appeared in his office.

"Yes, yes. Don't worry about me any more," Grosch assured him, not altogether correctly. After a time he became manager of the company's space program. Forty to fifty people altogether were involved, some of them salesmen, in Washington. Within a few months—it was then early in 1959—he was invited to participate in one of the first conferences of its kind in the U.S., a meeting summoned at the California Institute of Technology to examine "The Realities of Space Exploration." Charles Benton, head of IBM's military products division, authorized him to attend. What followed was an indication of how thorough disorder and chaos can become at times on the IBM preserve.

Questions reviewed at the historic conference dealt with the morality of stupendous expenditures for space explorations at a time when race turmoil and demonstrations were spreading across the country, when the decay of the cities—clearly evident for thirty years—was becoming noticed, and when Senator John F. Kennedy, who was thought to be presidential material, seemed to be saying that American urban society was in danger of splintering apart. Some of the scientists at the conference—the Nobel laureate, Harold Urey, for example—had been moved by the things Kennedy was talking about.

But as an IBM man out on public view, Grosch got into trouble and was fired again, still without losing his objective admiration for IBM, Tom Watson, and even for T. V. Learson.

On the last day of the conference, Louis Ridenour, vice-president of Lockheed Aircraft, who had a distinguished career as a physicist and professor at the University of Illinois and as a senior scientist at M.I.T., made a provocative speech. Ridenour was the editor of a famous five-foot shelf of books on radar published after World War II, had been chief scientist of the U.S. Air Force and founder of his own company, called International Telemeter, which was financed by Paramount. He left the company to go to Lockheed.

Ridenour's credentials made his remarks significant, especially when he said that the space program was a typical excrescence of the American affluent society. He said the space agency would fire off "these things" into space, and if they came back, the effort would be called successful, so that more could be built; if they did not come back, they would be called a failure and more would have to be built anyway, just to keep up with the Russians. It was far better, he concluded, to invest in cures for a sick society with "our billions" than to go overboard from space ships.

The tone of the speech was satirical, although critical, and Ridenour's manner of lightheartedness softened its content. Grosch rose to comment that he thought Dr. Ridenour's paper sounded "like the swan song of a dying culture." He had thought it was a closed conference of professionals, summoned for discussion, and was unaware that a Los Angeles *Times* reporter, hungry for a Saturday story, had been given a quotable lead, which a hundred and fifty newspapers picked up the next day.

Harold Urey stood up and said, "Herb, I think you're a bit pessimistic," and cited the tomb of Tamerlane and the fate of Samarkand, in a learned comment. Grosch replied that in the Tamerlane era it took a considerable part of a lifetime to exterminate any small portion of the human race, but that now, "It can be done in the time it takes for a thousand breaths." Further remarks followed, until the assembly, which stayed late for the dialogue, rushed to the parking lots and cab stands. The newspapers said the conference had deteriorated in confusion, with scientists yelling at each other.

Back in New York the next day, a four-striper from the U.S. Navy telephoned Grosch and told him he had received a telegram from T. Vincent Learson "apologizing" for what Grosch had said, or at least for what the newspapers reported he had said. The telegram pointedly said Grosch had not represented IBM, that he had spoken without authority.

When a reporter called Charles Benton out of bed to tell him that Grosch had made news in California, he did not comment at once, but asked the newspaperman: "What's *he* doing out there, anyway?" He recovered and talked awhile; the result was another day of news items identifying Grosch as a "renegade" and "a repudiated IBM scientist."

Benton went to Manhattan to meet with Learson, Wallace Eckert, and others, and plan a counteraction to put back together IBM's reputation, which had not been associated until then with a disintegrating culture. With the soft-spoken Wallace Eckert trying to explain that the Benton and Learson conclusion was incorrect, the two men sent telegrams to newspapers throughout the country disavowing the Grosch statement and more or less killing him off in advance of culture's fate. During the meeting that preceded the dispatch of telegrams Grosch sat by his telephone, hoping that somebody at IBM might want to talk with him.

Lee Alvin DuBridge, president of the California Institute of Technology, who organized the conference—and who was chosen by President Richard Nixon to be his scientific advisor—had taped the proceedings, and sent a copy of the tapes to Tom Watson, Junior, along with a calming letter asserting that Grosch had commented only on the satirical views expressed in Ridenour's paper, not on his views about the space program, or much of anything else.

Benton saw Grosch in his office and offered him a new job at the same salary—$25,000 a year—managing the publication program for the maligned STRETCH computer, which was still on the market, although more terminally stricken at that point than the American dream. The "publication program" consisted of one booklet scheduled for release in six months. Grosch thought this position was a trifle overpaid, considering it was restricted to producing a booklet that could scarcely be more than an operational obituary notice. He said it was against his principles to take it. It was assumed that principle meant money, so he was offered a few demeaning jobs thought to be more commensurate with such ethics.

It was uncommon for a man in IBM to turn down a lifetime job at $25,000 a year.

"Guys like you shouldn't go to meetings like that," Learson told him.

"I was sent," said Grosch.

"Who sent you?"

"Charley Benton."

"Well, I'll check with him about that," Learson promised.

"Why don't you fire Charley Benton instead of me, if he wasn't supposed to send me out there?"

Grosch thought, just for a split second, that Learson hesitated but knew quickly that it was an illusion. Learson and Benton had sent telegrams enunciating company policy based on an inaccurate, if not irrelevant, newspaper account. He could no longer hesitate.

"Why did you send those telegrams?" Grosch asked.

"That's not the point," said Learson. "What we have to do is find a job for you where you can function accurately and vividly in the IBM corporation but not see the public."

Grosch said he thought he was "doing fine" with the public, and suggested that Learson himself "ought to be hiding." Learson told him to go away.

IBM's famous "open door" policy remained a matter of pride with Tom, as it was with his father. Grosch invoked it and was rebuked. He sent Tom Watson a letter, telling him that someone—Learson, it was implied—was preventing him from getting to Watson. Tom wrote back to say, "Herb, you must be mistaken." He said "nobody" could keep Grosch from seeing him if he had really wanted to. Now that Tom knew he wanted to see him, Grosch wrote him several more letters, which either did not reach him or which he declined to answer. Learson administered daily lectures to Grosch while the job offers and dialogue continued. One day, Grosch said to him, "Vin, there are hundreds of guys following you around in the halls trying to do everything they can to be like you and to be liked by you, watching your every mood and your way of acting. Isn't there room in the company for one man who wouldn't be like you on a bet?"

"Okay," said Learson. "Go away."

The next day the fruitless dialogue would resume. People quit speaking to Grosch in the corridors. Former friends walked past him, unable to see the most visible pariah in the corporation. Within two weeks, Louis Ridenour, who had been subjected to great pressure for his exercise in oratory, fell dead of a heart attack in a Washington hotel room. Grosch was distressed at the news and, already discouraged at the hopeless impasse in which he found himself, sadly left IBM, nursing the dubious distinction of having been hired and fired in the regimes of both the old and the young Tom Watson, each of whom he admired.

The STRETCH program failed at a cost of more than twenty million dollars, still leaving IBM with a near monopoly in most of the market, but opening the door for Control Data Corporation and its unduplicated "6600" computer, an eight-million-dollar installation in this highly sophisticated field. William C. Norris, president of Control Data, and the corporation's top technical man, Seymour Cray, who is regarded as one of the finest computer scientists in the world, did not think that the IBM STRETCH program failed so much as that it had been staged to curtail Control Data's entrance into the scientific computer market. Norris was coldly bitter in asserting that IBM, in announcing the STRETCH project, intended not so much to produce the great and costly machine as to provoke Control Data's ruin. STRETCH was, to Norris, little more than an old-fashioned "knockout" machine designed to prevent Control Data from attracting customers.

But the STRETCH program, whether calculated to stop Control Data or not, was abandoned by IBM after a few of the installations were delivered, and Control Data recovered in time from its suffering. Although Charles de Carlo's responsibilities were largely in nontechnical areas, with emphasis on marketing, and although the collapse of the project was said to be caused by design and specification failures, he was selected, among others, by the IBM hierarchy to take some of the blame for damaging the corporation's reputation for unqualified success. He took the burden of blame with good grace and saw his name posted on the bulletin board as the recipient of a lateral promotion to lesser status. De Carlo understood his corporation and suffered only slightly under the lash of such machinations.

The recruitment of scientists by the thousands changed the body and face of IBM after 1957 when the company crossed over into the magic circle of billion dollar corporations. Tom began to engage in activities that had been familiar to his father. He was chairman of the United States Chamber of Commerce from 1955 to 1957, a position his younger brother filled ten years later, moving into the presidency of the International Chamber of Commerce in 1967—exactly thirty years after his father had been installed in the same job in Berlin and got that embarrassing decoration from Adolf Hitler. Both men became important public figures, each filling roles associated with prestige, power, and accomplishment.

IBM entered an exhibit in the Brussels World's Fair in Belgium in 1958, and Europeans seemed greatly impressed with the company that had become known and famous throughout much of the continent and the world. American exhibits in general were acclaimed at Brussels, and the United States State Department under Eisenhower was pressing for developments calculated to end the U.S.–Soviet chill that had continued after the Korean hostilities. Negotiations opened between the two big powers to do something that would expose to their peoples the advantages of each way of life and perhaps exploit them a little for purposes of public relations and propaganda. An American team went to Moscow late in 1958 and returned with an agreement under which the Soviet Government would put on a great exhibition in the United States, in return for which the United States could put on a show in Moscow.

Tom Watson, the old Russian buff from the days of World War II, saw the proposed plan as an extraordinary opportunity in internationalism. Both Tom and Dick were as alert as their father had been to exploit the universal character of the corporation by any appropriate means. Tom had been complimented widely in the press for his contribution to an Eisenhower project inaugurated to define the country's goals in domestic and world affairs, an ambitious program in charge of Dr. Henry Wriston, president of Brown University, of which Tom was by then considered an illustrious graduate. Without consciously imitating the style and persevering forcefulness of the old man, Tom had become in a relatively short time a world-wide figure in his own way. He seemed to be genuinely liked, too, with only appropriate—not worshipful —deference paid to him.

The Russians opened their exhibit at the Colosseum in New York, lifting the iron curtain on a carefully arranged presentation of national lore, industrial achievement, and communal living. There was a special emphasis on their space program. The Americans prepared to return the compliment in international good will with an exhibition scheduled to run six weeks in the summer of 1959 in Gorky Park, but moved to Sokolniki Park at the last minute. It was an event that reintroduced Tom to Russia and sent Dick there, too. First, however, they were obliged to employ another of those extraordinary non-IBM types to represent the company.

Thomas Mechling had been in the State Department, after a varied career that included nearly becoming a United States Senator from the State of Nevada. After World War II he searched around in his home state of Montana for a way of life that held some promise of enjoyment combined with useful work, not necessarily in corporations and not necessarily remunerative beyond the basic needs of himself and his family. He married a second-generation Italian beauty willing to accompany her husband on treks into the wilderness and on study tours through the western mountains and plains. In 1952 they studied the election and residency laws, equipped a trailer as a portable home and drove to Nevada with their children, established an address that qualified them as voters, and filed the documents that made Mechling a candidate for U.S. Senator.

He lost the election, but still determined to serve in government, he went to Washington and got himself an appointment with duties that twice took him to Moscow. In 1958, he was with the State Department team that went to Russia to arrange for the exchange of exhibitions.

Because of his experience in dealing with Kremlin officials and Russian trade agencies, he was recruited by IBM to handle the company's computer exhibit at the Moscow fair. The State Department helped put together four thousand questions, with multilingual answers provided by instantaneous print-out on the IBM computer, to give Soviet citizens a non-Communist view of the United States. Mechling had liked the earlier IBM exhibit at Brussels, where a computer had answered in ten languages questions about the United States; long lines of visitors had waited sometimes for two or three hours to obtain the canned responses to queries of their choice. The machine had been programmed to provide a nonpolitical answer to visitors asking the most significant event of their respective native countries. The Soviet president, Voroshilov, was pleased to be advised by the computer that the most historically important event in Russia was, of course, the revolution of 1917.

Under the terms of the U.S.-Soviet agreement, no censorship or harassment of each other's exhibit was permissible. Dick Watson had studied Russian and tried to improve his fluency with a crash refresher course before he went to Moscow with the IBM party; in fact, he had people on his staff reporting for 7:30 A.M. language classes. Dick found that "no censorship" in Russia didn't mean the same thing as it did at home. But the exhibit was an unqualified success, from the American viewpoint, regardless of the fact that a corps of aggressive and vocal young men stood around the computer, scoffing at fellow citizens waiting in line to ask, not about the lynching of Negroes and other savage aspects of U.S. culture, but how much cigarettes, hosiery, butter, and milk cost, or whether they could be obtained at all. Mechling was delighted to observe that the organized jeering deterred almost no one from shuffling along the lines leading to the exhibit; indeed he became apprehensive at the indignation displayed by guests who shouted down the demonstrators, bawled them out with curses, and demanded that they shut up and show some Soviet courtesy.

Tom Watson arrived in Moscow after imposing on Mechling an extraordinary, and what seemed a hopeless, request. He wanted to be quartered in the same old room on the Gorky Street side of the National Hotel in which he had lived during the siege of Moscow in World War II. The hotel, overlooking Red Square, was all but off limits to Americans at the time, although unofficially so. An American, inevitably taken in tow by the official tourist agency, had nothing to say about where he could stay. Nevertheless, Mechling made some inquiries to support his promise to make the effort, and the matter rested there.

When Tom and his wife Olive and their daughter arrived, they were taken to their rooms, from which Tom telephoned Mechling with unrestrained delight.

"You did it, you did it!" he shouted into the phone. "Come on up and have a drink."

Through the luck of the draw, and perhaps because of Watson's status in international industrial affairs, he'd been given a suite, Number 201, that did not meet, but far surpassed, the impossible request. It was the enshrined Lenin Suite, in which the exiled revolutionary leader had lived when he returned in 1917.

"I know," said Tom, "you couldn't get me my old room because they're painting the rooms along Gorky Street"—which although Mechling was unaware of it, was true.

When Dick Watson arrived, he, too, was impressed with the feat, which Mechling said he had nothing to do with: "It just happened," he said. Dick Watson, however, thought he would like to have Mechling working for him in the World Trade Corporation.

The IBM crew of thirteen, including several Russian-speaking girls, was made up of technicians and engineers trying to keep the computer, installed on a sagging wooden floor, in operation, while a Marine guard tried to keep curious onlookers—some of them too officially curious—away from it. The Marine slept beside the machine when the exhibit was closed.

Meanwhile, censorship was tightened. Newspaper accounts were unfavorable, and Soviet officialdom was red-faced at the excessive attention showered on the IBM operation and the exhibit in general. Because Mechling was not permitted to send photographs of the crowded exhibit back to the United States, he smuggled film out with a Sabena Airlines pilot. He had made the arrangement in Brussels weeks earlier, having surmised that Soviet authorities were not going to like evidence of U.S.

popularity among their citizens. Newspaper correspondents had to sub-
scribe to normal restrictions. Harrison Salisbury, Max Frankel, Henry
Shapiro, Preston Grover of Associated Press, and Robert Kornfield of
United Press International sent their reports through channels, but
wrote more extensively when they were out of Red range.

Tom Watson was highly gratified by the success of the affair and had
never seemed more at ease to observing IBM people on the scene.
Moscow was indeed a special place to him, and he had a wonderful
time, even to the point of enjoying the anger of visitors shrieking at agit-
prop types. "What are they shouting?" he asked on one occasion. "They're
saying, 'Godammit, shut up. Let the Americans have their say,'" someone translated for him. Watson thought it was an encouraging sign.

Watson organized a dinner party for the IBM crew in the private
room of a restaurant. Fine French wines supplemented the menu, and
nearly everybody became, for an IBM affair, uncharacteristically tipsy,
Watson among them. "You are all doing a great job for America," he
said in a warm and pleasant speech. Olive had gone to the Bolshoi ballet,
so Mechling and Watson went off for more quiet drinking, the latter
reminiscing about the old days in Moscow. He told of running up a tab
of about eighty dollars at the Aragve Restaurant just to get a good
Georgian meal, when the Nazis were pushing on to Moscow.

"What I really always wanted to do," said Watson, "was fly, be a
transport pilot. When I got back from the war, that's what I wanted to
be. I flew 'em well during the war, and I could fly 'em well for a living
in peacetime. But I inherited this company from my father."

The chairman of the Board of IBM said, sadly, that he was "in the
wrong business." Running IBM with an iron hand did not appeal to him.
Memory, and the wine, had brought forth an old vision of himself, as it
does to most men—a vision that haunted him, but that died away with
a night's sleep.

Izvestia and *Pravda* denounced the exhibit as a "lie," but Khrushchev
came by anyway and, standing aside while an aide asked the computer
some questions, looked unhappy. He and President Eisenhower had
agreed to pay respective visits to each other's country, but political
pressures in the Kremlin against the idea seemed to sober him.

The Watson friendship in the White House was maintained through
the thousand days of the John F. Kennedy administration, the two
families being sufficiently well acquainted to call on each other in station
wagon visits accompanied by children. A friend of both the President
and his brother, Attorney General Robert F. Kennedy, joined the
Watson-IBM hierarchy when Burke Marshall, who had presided over

civil rights enforcement in the Department of Justice, left government service to become counsel for IBM.

He continued to serve as a family counselor to the Kennedys after the President was assassinated and appeared in 1968 as a family spokesman after an agreement was reached with government agencies on the disposition and ultimate accessibility of X-rays and autopsy findings relating to the murder. After Robert Kennedy was assassinated, one of IBM's big jet planes was turned over to the grieving Kennedys to transport them back and forth across the country, thus freeing them from dependence on commercial or military aircraft. Burke Marshall was with one or more members of the family for days.

A high level lawyer, Mr. Marshall remained an equally valuable consultant to IBM on anti-trust issues under review in the Department of Justice, and from time to time serves as spokesman defending the company against complaints of small competitors that IBM is trying to swallow them up.

As the Lyndon Johnson administration drew to a close following the election of Richard Nixon, it was disclosed that IBM would have even more impressive legal help in anti-trust suits being prepared against the company. Nicholas Katzenbach, who had served both as U.S. Attorney General and as Undersecretary of State, became a company lawyer with the title of vice-president.

Foreign operations were growing fast, with IBM sales of computers, typewriters, and services approaching the two billion dollar figure in the year 1960. The company decided to break ground on a magnificent new building on Ernst Reuter Plaza in Berlin. This delighted the State Department, which saw in the move an opportunity to promote the expansion as an American symbol of its determination to remain dominant in the Free World, a euphemism for non-Communist nations. The ground-breaking ceremony was to get well organized newsreel coverage, with Mayor Willy Brandt wielding the ceremonial shovel and U.S. agencies cooperating in a promotion and propaganda program to depict American industry and free enterprise as superior to state management.

A corporate management meeting at 590 Madison Avenue reviewed tentative plans for the event, which Dean McKay, an inner echelon policy man, and Chet Constable, director of communications at IBM, thought was a golden opportunity in international public relations.

Before the project could be taken to Dick Watson for review and approval, he summoned Mechling, Constable, and several others to his office, where he assaulted them in an unmerciful tirade. No one could reconstruct precisely what he said, but none forgot the way he said it. It was a tantrum of old-fashioned Thos. J. Watson proportions. Although Mechling tried to explan that plans for the Berlin event were still in the exploratory stage, awaiting further development before it was felt Dick Watson's time was to be imposed upon, there were charges of Madison Avenue flackery taking over World Trade policy; there was profanity and incoherent rage.

It was apparently not unusual for Dick to behave this way. Jack Brent, the number two man at World Trade, had been observed standing silent in Dick Watson's office on one occasion, enduring profanity and shrill denunciation, with a couple of male secretaries and junior executives waiting, mute and rigid, until the ordeal was over. "The guy just goes off his rocker," one of those present said. There were other reports of hurled objects and uncontrolled rage. Yet within a day or so, meeting one of the men he had castigated, Dick would throw an arm around him and conduct himself as a warmhearted friend. It was old man Watson all over again, with the exception that Dick's technique and style did not always restore a man's lost dignity.

Mechling left to go to the Xerox Corporation in Rochester, after easing himself out of World Trade and working for the IBM corporate staff for a time. Others left, too, some because they felt like substitutes on the old Notre Dame football teams. "There were always eight people in line for an opening," as Mechling put it. "But I loved that company, just the same. When they did anything, they did it first class. It is a quality company, and don't forget that. Tom, Dick, everybody in it, sees to that."

Some who left gave other reasons. One was the fear that in unexpected dramatic and insulting situations an impulse might get out of hand, and a victim under assault might physically strike back. "It could ruin your whole career," one departing executive murmured.

The other side of Dick Watson was as sociable and pleasant as his tirades were shocking. He might show up in Acapulco with his wife for a sophisticated fiesta. He would sing songs in Spanish, sipping a drink with quiet courtesy, calling on the guitarist to play "Swing Low, Sweet Chariot" or deferring to Mrs. Watson, who preferred to hear "Frère Jacques." Dick and his wife would sing together and talk about going to their island off the coast of Maine, where they had several hundred acres and a summer home. Dick would be wearing dazzling trousers, one leg half yellow and half green, the other half blue and half red.

But he was, for all his worldly cultivation and social grace, a difficult man for all to work with and an impossible man for some. In other ways, so was Tom, but to most people around him, remuneration and promise exceeded the vicissitudes.

Infighting and internecine manipulation for power, as common in corporate life as it is in government, increases in intensity in proportion to the scale of management command. At IBM under Tom Watson, Junior, casualties in the lower and middle echelons were reduced to the point of relative safety for all. But with the elevation of Learson and the establishment of territorial boundaries within which Learson and Tom Watson co-existed by tacit agreement, casualty figures at higher levels became severe. They were considered part of the legitimate human cost of running a world-wide business, which was absorbing new employees at an astonishing rate—at times as many as 25,000 a year, including 6,000 at management level. This influx of new people was sometimes referred to as IBM's "immigration problem." The company acquired a reputation among professional evaluators of having mastered the techniques of using both the carrot and the stick, applying the latter in a way probably essential to an enterprise of enormous size.

In the lower and middle range, the company took care of its people with forgiving and paternal care. Disturbed employees were sent to psychiatrists, to Alcoholics Anonymous, to school, to counselors, to hospitals and clinics. They were protected and preserved under the philosophy that "people" were IBM's finest asset. The use of punishment as policy began in the upper ranges and became painfully visible at about the $25,000 annual salary level.

At that height, the terrain becomes rough; climbers are above the timber line of corporate foliage and subject to pitiless exposure. It becomes difficult for management to determine whether, and how, a high-salaried man is carrying his own weight, let alone bearing the additional burdens that mean growth and profit. Brass knuckles replace the prod, blood flows instead of persuasion, mistakes mean destruction or demotion, plus—for many—a good deal of humiliation. Social and domestic pressures intensify the pain, particularly in the colonies and communities where the fate of IBM men becomes more or less common knowledge. The status of wives varies like the status of women wed to men of military rank, according to their husbands' titles and power. The index of progress is advance, money, prerogative, the subtle and overt acknowledgement of position in the exercise of social responses. In the modernized IBM, materialism was not, of course, everything, nor was status the sole measure of worth; but if they were withdrawn, if a man was laterally disposed of or demoted, suffering could be intense indeed.

In general, IBM policy dictated that a man wasn't wanted in power circles if he made a mistake. Where some companies might tolerate him, give him an advance in title, and carefully diminish his authority, at IBM he had to take his clobbering in full view. Blame for a mistake meant demotion, sometimes a reduced salary, and oblivion from former associates. His name went up on the bulletin board under promotions and transfers. An executive in charge of manufacturing at half a dozen plants might find himself *promoted* to a management job involving one plant. Those who knew how to read such notices knew he had come into contact with the brass knuckles.

Some men, like Charles de Carlo for example, learned simply not to care, to take whatever came—one could comfortably live on even a reduced IBM salary—in the knowledge that no system could guarantee justice or fairness. It was a Machiavellian world, and they had chosen it.

The system, Tom Watson said, breaks eighty per cent of the top men in varying degrees. The remainder, after demotion or lateral disposal, often come back. One of these was John W. Gibson, a vice-president who was said to have guessed wrong about computer circuitry and got the company in trouble with production problems. He was demoted, went to the Fishkill plant, stayed steady and cool, worked his way back up, and became president of the entire components division of the corporation—a vast realm, indeed.

Clarence Frizzell, an engineer of some fame who became a highly valued man as president of the Systems Manufacturing Division, also stayed with the company after a downhill slide, or what looked like one: having been in charge of a dozen or more plants, he became a plant manager in Colorado. Of course, with stock options, he was not badly hurt materially and possibly preferred his new, less exalted, but hardly shameful life. Sometimes Watson just liked to shift people around, realizing that the top jobs were killers, capable of inducing physical and mental breakdowns. The division presidencies, especially, for all their rewards, are endless, exhausting jobs, of which Watson seems to relieve men with a genuine sense of charity.

The IBM practice was one of generally protecting the lowly, but hounding to ultimate performance, and knocking off, the mighty. There were times, however, when the concept was trivially used.

From their corner office windows at Armonk headquarters, Watson and Learson would watch the employees hastening from the suburbs of Westchester and Connecticut to the vast parking lot, surrounded by grassy knolls and orchards. Enough people were arriving late, which meant after 8:30 A.M., to irritate one or both of the reigning pair. Men who could not complete a telephone call to offices in Manhattan much before 10 A.M. and who were exempt from punching time clocks, were careless of the starting hour, especially since they would often be in their offices or traveling late into the evenings. It was decided that everybody, including vice presidents, would go back to punching time clocks.

The intention was to single out chronic late comers. The computerized scoring system recorded lateness on a percentage basis, so that a man who arrived on time for four days but was more than a few minutes late, say, on Friday was said to be twenty per cent late for the week. Black marks of varying degrees of opacity, and seriousness, went into the records.

A high level specialist, whose office was at Armonk but who was traveling much of the time, was nearly discharged when the time clock records were analyzed. He was in Los Angeles for the first half of the week and flew back to New York on the night plane, arriving at 6 A.M. He went to his office at 11 o'clock that day and was clocked late.

One thirty-thousand-dollar a year man returned from an assignment across the continent to be told that he would have to obtain a written note explaining why he was late. He demurred and was bawled out by his manager, who then tried to reason with him.

"Don't you understand? I have to write an excuse for you. If you're late a certain number of times, on the record, you can be fired. You have a good reason for being late, and I have to say so in a note."

The latecomer suggested that he could get a note from his mother, saying, "Please excuse Georgie for being late today."

"It's not funny."

The excuse was prepared and delivered, and the offending professional man was exempted from penalty. An associate went to the manager to complain. "This business is silly," he said.

"I know it's silly, but there's nothing to be done about it. The order came from Tom's office."

The system lasted ninety days; the sluggards were presumably identified, and upper level staff people went back to riding the night planes and showing up, on occasions when they got to bed at daylight, a few hours late.

The company over the years relaxed its policies against women and minority groups, and male secretaries all but disappeared from most divisions and departments. In the past, a woman had been dismissed if she married, except in cases where her employment was continued by sufferance or pending pregnancy, and the rule of dismissal could be applied at any time. As a matter of policy and practice, women did not rise at IBM. Even when the number of employees approached a quarter of a million, no woman entered the ranks of highest management. A single exception to the rule occurred in the latter years of old Watson's long reign when a beautiful woman named Ruth Leach, of Atlanta, served as a vice-president. An expert in the IBM customer service field, she was a member of the first women's training class at Endicott, and was known as Peachy Leachy. Actually, another member of that renowned class of extraordinarily attractive women had been picked by Watson for the honor of becoming IBM's first female vice-president, but she disqualified herself by marrying an Albany banker, and Miss Leach was designated instead. After a few years she, too, left to get married, and males again filled all the top management roles. Miss Leach was said to be so outrageously beautiful that her presence among the men set up an interplay of competitive dynamics not conducive to the type of concentrated positive thinking encouraged by IBM doctrine. Upon the departure of the distracting Miss Leach, complimentary gossips said it was not possible to *replace* her; it was possible only to supplant her. But thus far, no successor has been named.

Secretaries and thousands of female customer service specialists and technicians moved into the corporation in the nineteen-sixties. The ladies at times remain unimpressed with the antics and harsh infighting for position characteristic of corporate politics. A visitor to the headquarters at Armonk met several young IBM ladies for lunch one day and by way of making conversation asked: "What do your bosses do?"

One of them said, "They play office."

As for ethnic and racial issues, Tom Watson, Junior, has made himself unmistakably clear. He directed managers to hire Negroes and minority groups to every extent possible, providing pre-job training and enforcing preferential considerations. Watson has said that no other identifiable category of people in the corporation has caused it the problems that this policy has produced, especially in the suburban installations. He told a magazine editor that IBM would persist, regardless of problems of white resistance, to train, employ, and promote Negroes. "All industry had better do it," he said.

The old Watson Open Door policy, under which presumably any complaining worker could march into the chief executive's office to talk over his problems, was always more imaginary than real, but it remained real enough, and just enough, after Tom took over to keep IBM mythology going. The door might be shut to a scientist like Herbert Grosch, but it opened in an untidy little case involving marital infidelity among the lowly. At the Poughkeepsie plant, a vast installation that by 1965 employed 18,000 people, a custodian and a plant worker got to sharing the sexual favors of the worker's wife. The worker complained to his foreman, seeking redress. The foreman seemed to think the matter too trivial or too private for official intervention and stalled for time in the hope that circumstance and mutual adjustment would resolve the matter. The impatient cuckold somehow got word of the extramarital dalliance to Armonk, where Tom was reported to have required the dismissal of the third person in the menage on the grounds that his conduct was sinful. Among those with knowledge of the incident, the impression was sustained that in IBM each sparrow's fall, and each hair on every head, was under scrutiny.

Tom's commitment to morality took other turns, too. John Dvorocsik, a manager of Purchase Quality Control, complained to the Poughkeepsie plant vice-president, William Mair, that deficient machine parts from one source were causing expense and production delays. As a quality control man, it was his obligation to see that incoming components met specified standards. "Why don't we cut this company off?" Mr. Dvorocsik suggested. "We can get the stuff elsewhere."

The boss promised to take the matter under review, and a department head reported back in a few days. "You've got to put up with it," he said. "The president of this little machine parts company spends most of his life in an iron lung. The orders are—not to terminate the contract."

Dvorocsik once discharged a man for excessive absenteeism, or "goofing off," with the result that the dismissed workman reached Tom's office on a complaint of unjust treatment. Tom sent two vice-presidents to Poughkeepsie where, after nearly a full day of questioning of the principals, the complainant was caught in several falsehoods and his dismissal adjudged to be appropriate.

Tom Watson's reputation as a man vastly different from his father grew as he continued to articulate his thesis that IBM needed more "wild ducks," more nonconformists who dared boldly to let their imaginations range afield. In one article about him in a business publication, he was quoted as deploring the fact that if he were to show up at the IBM office in a pink shirt, everybody else would probably appear in a pink shirt the next day. To some of his colleagues, Tom appeared to be deploring a condition of conformity intellectually, while bound to it by ties and shirts that colored his own will. The idea of Tom Watson appearing in a pink shirt was the equivalent of TV Learson showing up sporting a "Make Love, Not War" button.

There were times when Tom sounded absolutely sincere about the wild duck business, and he could express real contempt for the conformity that was a characteristic of the IBM family. "As you stand up and are counted," he once said, "you will first run into the group who equate newness with wrongness. . . . Second, you're sure to meet cynics, people who believe anyone who sticks his neck out is a fool. . . . Follow the path of the unsafe, independent thinker. . . . Speak your mind and fear less the label of crackpot than the stigma of conformity." It was new and heady stuff at IBM.

A professor named Chris Argyris, chairman of Yale University's Department of Administrative Sciences, cited some of Tom's views, without identifying him, in his writing. Professor Argyris had submitted to a thousand executives, one of them Watson, a report he had prepared based on a book called *Soviet Attitudes Toward Authority*, written for the RAND Corporation by the scholar and anthropologist, Margaret Mead, and published in 1951 by McGraw-Hill. The Argyris study was called "A Valid Description of American Management Theory," but in fact was a precise description of the Soviet theory of industrial organization. The majority of the thousand American executives who read the Argyris study declared that it sounded right to them. The results of the study seemed to substantiate what some economists, including Galbraith of Harvard, knew to be true: that industrial organizations anywhere, whether communistic or democratic, are variants of each other.[2]

[2] An equivalent of IBM training and management indoctrination was going on in Russia, too. The *Literaturnaya Gazeta* of Moscow published in January, 1968, an amusing and informative article under the title "How An Executive Ought to Behave." The advice of economics writer B. Tereshchenko was, in effect, "behave like an American executive." Although the article denounced "sham and hypocrisy" in the United States, it could have been lifted from an IBM house organ. Here are some excerpts:

First of all, the executive must be a manager and not a slave driver. The slave driver drives; the manager leads. The driver always relies on his power; the executive relies on the assistance and cooperation of his subordinates. The executive sets an example and shows up every day on time. The driver finds scapegoats on whom he blames all his mistakes whereas the executive corrects those mistakes himself. The driver knows how things should be done, but the executive demonstrates how they should be done. . . . Here are a few psychological hints for you: keep erect and don't hang your head when you are in the presence of subordinates, or in the plant. Walk straight, keep your head up and you will gain self-confidence in no time. When you meet people, make your handshake firm. A man who is always jittery and quick to lose his temper can never be a good executive. "How do I keep my self-control?" you ask. The answer, they say, is this: if you feel you're about to explode don't be in a hurry to talk. Pretend you're thinking . . . while you take a few deep breaths . . . know how to listen, too, when they (the workers) point out your shortcomings. . . . Criticism must be constructive. The ability to notice a person and simply call him by his first name at the right time, to say hello, remember his birthday, ask how his children are doing, is the most effective way to put

Professor Argyris wrote: "No one tells the boss about the conformity he is creating, because to do so would be to focus on a 'personal' issue which would violate 'rational' values. So the boss is kept ignorant of the true facts. I know of one executive who prides himself on liking 'the wild ducks' in his organization. But when he leaves the room, his subordinates sometimes mumble—'Yes, all flying in the same direction.'

"All new social science is developing what is relevant to modern life, and can help make values such as trust, openness, risk taking, and self responsibility more than glowing generalities. But authentic relationships cannot be cheaply constructed, plugged in, and then discarded because their use creates risk. What we must create is a basic change in the bone and fabric, the guts and heart of our whole mode of life. Our experience leads us to be optimistic about the potential."

While Tom railed against the conformity IBM enforced, it was a clear case of conflict, of an intellectual, or perhaps emotional, disposition to honor what corporate policy stifled. No wonder he sometimes seemed irrational, or lost his temper. Tom's style frequently was petulant and lighthearted by turns, although he had a substantial number of detractors who called him a brutal shadow of the substance that was his father, with an underlying contempt for people masked in contrived affability and personal attractiveness. When the corporate headquarters were moved from midtown Manhattan to Westchester, the character and pettiness of IBM supervision over its people seemed, after some years of quiescence, to reappear.

One of the functions of Dean R. McKay, who entered the ranks of vice-presidents in the mid-sixties, was to control insofar as possible the content of material published about IBM. McKay was a former salesman in charge of sustaining an image made largely by and for a company that was born and reared on sales. Over the years, many well-known and unknown reporters and editors sought to penetrate the corporate redoubts of IBM to write about it and interpret its effect on industrial and social America. McKay would, if such attempts persisted, inevitably call a meeting, not to expedite the requests, but to devise means of fending off any interested journalist or historian.

Articles were published from time to time in *Business Week, Forbes,*

---

people in a good frame of mind and establish rapport in an organization. . . . It produces excellent results.

Thus, not only did Tom Watson think the Soviet organization plan valid for American industry, but Soviet observers seem to think the IBM doctrine, or a variant of it, quite worth importing to that Communist country. (Translation taken from *Atlas Magazine*, April, 1968.)

271

Sales Management, The Saturday Review (which named Watson in 1967 as "The Man in League with the Future"), *Fortune,* and news periodicals. With some notable exceptions, most were as close to the IBM-policy line as if they had been conceived and written on the company's premises. Dean McKay, the salesman, did his information, editorial, and public relations job very well indeed.

McKay was one of twenty-two vice presidents who shared the title in various forms, and he enjoyed considerable authority as long as one of the Group Executives or the Watsons did not intervene. A writer in pursuit of an article or book would be researched and a dossier compiled on him. He would be discussed at McKay's meeting, his characteristics and vulnerability reviewed, and a consensus sought on whether he could be "handled." A writer for *Fortune,* wearying of inconclusive answers to requests for what he felt was legitimate information sought from a public corporation, once made a grandstand play, as McKay interpreted it, and declared he would do a book *without* IBM cooperation. McKay said it could simply not be done. When one of the consultants in the department proposed cooperation with the writer as a technique of influencing his published output, Richard Wight, who was second in command to McKay, announced coldly: "IBM doesn't have to talk to anybody."

The book did not materialize.

After Tom Watson authorized publication of the biography, *The Lengthening Shadow,* there were reports that Watson's widow, Jeannette, was unhappy with the work. It contained a number of between-the-lines inferences that were unflattering, along with some well-reported objective passages and a reasonably complete chronology of the old man's life. An IBM bulletin indicated a certain amount of self-consciousness about the book, and no promotion or exploitation of it followed.

Few critical or questioning paragraphs about the corporation were published over a period of fifteen years, except federal court judgments, until a perceptive and persevering *Fortune* editor, T. A. Wise, wrote two articles about IBM's half-billion dollar gamble to redesign and market a whole new generation of computers (the 360 Series). The articles were published in September and October of 1966 and raised the roof at Armonk, where Tom Watson issued a memorandum suggesting that the appearance of the piece should serve as a lesson to everyone in the company to remain uncommunicative and present a united front to the public, keeping internal differences behind closed doors. After that, no further peeking into IBM closets was permitted, although even prior to that time no IBM spokesman had been allowed to talk with a journalist unless authorized corporate or public relations personnel were present.

Tom Wise was never alone with any of the pepole he talked with in his comprehensive analysis of the IBM computer story of 1966. Sometimes, two or three corporation people stood by to listen in on any dialogue that ensued. But Wise and such men as Theodore Merrill of *Business Week,* among others, are journalists of thorough competence, and Wise's published articles were masterpieces of that particular genre of industrial reporting. They did not, however, lavish any excessive praise on selected leaders. The failure to approach IBM with an appropriate mixture of awe and deference was irritating to the upper echelon of corporation leadership—as was the fact that, on this rare occasion, the articles revealed some of the inner problems of IBM.

But in not allowing an occasional outside objective investigator or historian to look in on their corporate world, IBM did not differ substantially from other self-protective industrial domains. The fact that a corporation like IBM might be making decisions and implementing policies that shape the most profound details of personal and public life at no time has induced industrial leadership to establish mechanisms for providing insight into their operations.

Tom Watson and his brother have indicated on occasion that they personally feel some qualms about the matter, at which point the expression of concern appears to die out. Tom has expressed the fear that the American monopoly, or near-monopoly, on world wide technology in many fields might make lesser nations the hewers of wood and the drawers of water, while the United States continues to drain brains from the rest of the world. As the leaders of a company which more than any other in the world dominates the International Chamber of Commerce, IBM management men have long been in a position to press—as certain economists in the United Nations would recommend—for a form of anti-trust regulation on an international scale. Of course, a shaky monetary system is involved, too, and no corporation can, alone, institute such necessary reforms.

IBM has been welcomed in many countries because it has invested hundreds of millions of dollars in manufacturing, service, and distribution systems, providing jobs for citizens in their home lands. Simultaneously, however, the company by its very presence and its commanding leadership in technological development within those countries has, in enriching itself and in pumping strength into weakened economies, grabbed off the best investment opportunities, captured the best of the brains and talent for itself.

In a report published in Paris in January of 1968, a 701-page document prepared by the Organization for Economic Cooperation and Development, a dismal assessment of the American scientific policy was offered in terms of its effect on much of the world. The report was the work of representatives of twenty-one industrialized, non-Communist nations in the northern hemisphere. It concluded that the directions of American technology, in which IBM plays a role of nearly unregulated importance, were out of control. Concurrently, the report found merit in the American domestic system under which industrial and science specialists move freely back and forth between goverment, industry, and the universities, and urged its adoption among European nations. Yet it is this breakdown of boundaries, the blurring of lines, that puts the American educational system, so admired by Europe, "too strongly in the service of economic goals," in the words of economist John Kenneth Galbraith: "Our present method of underwriting advanced technology is exceedingly dangerous. It could cost us our existence. . . . Our contentions that no economic system in history has provided such a high standard of living, take for granted that the level of consumption is the proper measure of social merit. . . ."[3]

Acknowledgement of a frightening situation does not mitigate it. Neither Watson nor IBM can, or would want to, retreat from practice and policy that has become so profitable, with the certainty of more of the same, regardless of the extent to which industrial leaders fret about the consequences.

One of IBM's international scouts, who frequently has gone abroad to acquire land and property, select sites for plant expansion, and report on regional factors affecting company development, has said that the Watsons, Learson, and the company have to be pragmatic, regardless of feelings they may personally reflect. They try, he said, never to offend, to adapt to the social and cultural establishment of a host country, to avoid at all costs practices associated with American competition, and to utilize native talent and skills as much as possible.

"They are *really* good men," he said, "and they care about the people and their problems. All they want is the money."

[3] *The New Industrial State,* John Kenneth Galbraith; Houghton Mifflin Co., Boston, 1967.

15.
Portrait
of a
Twenty-first
Century
Corporation

WITH THE APPROACH OF the twenty-first century and the mystical year of 2000 that is to greet the third millennium of western civilization, IBM was in the most exalted position of the corporate world. It was by far the most internationally extended of all the companies on earth, had perhaps the closest affinity with the variables of technology in the process of development, and from its lofty protected position in the economic universe exerted a far-flung—sometimes direct and more often subtle—influence over the shape of the future.

The third generation of computers arrived before the new tool had been in existence twenty years, and the fourth generation is embryonic, waiting to be born at the will, convenience, or possibly the defensive reaction of IBM. Because of the enormous investment in programming and software in which both IBM and its competitors and satellite companies have large stakes, the emerging fourth generation of computer technology will doubtless be more evolutionary than revolutionary. Computer users could not possibly afford another revolution of convenience at costs and prices prevailing in 1969, but then, as writer William D. Smith said in *The New York Times*, they couldn't afford the third generation revolution five years earlier, either.

Three years after IBM, responding to fears of being outmaneuvered in scientific advances, introduced the third generation Systems 360 in 1964, the company shipped more than fifteen thousand installations at an average manufacturing cost of $300,000 each, for a total of about $4.5 billion worth of business. Since the company gambled more than five billion on the revolution in the first place, more years of sales and profits must be elicited from the present stage of development; gradual, not comprehensive, changes are in order.

275

Bit by bit, and over the next few years, computer systems will become more readily adaptable for use by people with only marginal training in technical aspects of their functions. Lawyers, architects, run-of-the-mill engineers, middle management men, and in due course, ordinary households will be encompassed by the computer market. There is no escape from convenience, whether it is desired or not. For the very forces which produce and promote the products and gadgets of convenience mandate the withdrawal of alternatives, enforcing changes in a way of life whether or not those whose lives are changed welcome, ignore, or fight it. What was once a luxury, as in the case of electricity, the telephone, and the automobile, becomes essential to daily life and mobility. When suburban sidewalks and bicycle paths were obliterated and public transportation either diminished or did not expand, ownership of an automobile became less a matter of choice than a matter of mobility essential to employment.

Extension of electricity into individual households was perhaps the greatest blessing of the twentieth century. It powered washing machines, heated laundry irons, and illuminated rooms to diminish drudgery and gloom in millions of lives. With time, electricity invaded and intruded upon every aspect of household, office, and commercial life until it became pervasive, ubiquitous, and indispensable. In any modern power failure, people often cannot find their way home after dark, cook a meal, heat a household, write a message, get a garage door open, reach the upper floors of a building, carve a roast, brush their teeth, get a drink of water, dispose of sewage, ring a doorbell, sharpen a pencil, read a newspaper, and so on. Without special preparations they are improbably helpless, wholly and in many instances needlessly dependent on convenience, which is the marketable output of technology.

In a relatively short time, no more than five years in many urban areas, the process is certain to repeat itself in another vast range of individual, household, and commercial services. The telephone hookups to computers that are becoming commonplace in office applications will spread to homes and apartments, first among the curious, the affluent, and the showoffs, the wasteful, the status seekers determined to be among the first to acquire newly promoted products—and in due course to nearly everyone else. Payment of bills, applications for credit, loan and bank balances, the ordering of groceries, the preparation and cooking of meals, inventories of clothing and possessions, family medical, tax, and school records, insurance information, and the like will be accomplished or recorded through data processing, information retrieval, and instructional systems bought or subscribed to as an addition to ordinary telephone service. It will seem needless and fanciful, perhaps an indulgence to the lazy, at first. But only at first. Like the push-buttons that raise and lower windows in automobiles—and eliminate any other means of opening or shutting a window when the automatic system fails —computerized conveniences are on the way to becoming standard and, like electricity, unavoidable. Once they gain a foothold in household life, they are very likely, as in industry, to proliferate wildly. Telephone companies late in 1968 began to send brochures with monthly statements touting the services of "your computer consultant," who was likened to Professor Henry Higgins; the computer, of course, was Eliza Doolittle, an adorable machine which can be taught to communicate with the appropriate accent and princess style. A telephone subscriber may obtain Data Phone Service, a "low cost" system for sending and receiving data for six-level or eight-level punch tape, wide band facilities for transmission speeds at a modest 250,000 bits per second. "In no time at all," a New York Telephone Company brochure pointed out, Professor Higgins "can have your computer chattering away directly to branches, warehouses, distributors, and even customers."

The message was, presumably, addressed to people in households with outside business and commercial interests, but in the language of public relations, the housewife and the home owner were being prepared to "capitalize on the opportunities" offered by the entire Bell Telephone system. One opportunity, said the brochure, would allow "anyone to call you free from the area you choose"—as palpable a falsehood as even a computer could devise, since no one calls anyone free of charge over telephone lines except company officials, employees making installations or credit representatives running down something called unpaid message units.

While the bait of "free" telephone service is part of the corrupt dialect of public relations, the promise of the computer replacing ordinary chores is all but fulfilled, although many of the blessings exist more in the language of allusion and promotion than in the needs of reality. After a while, it will not be possible to sit down with one's bank book, add up the deposits, subtract penalties and fees, and determine how much, if anything, is left in an account. A code query to an information system will flash or print out the data for a fee, like those telephone message units that subscribers just assume are covered by the basic monthly bill. Few people will want to be without such devices providing services declared to be indispensable.

IBM will be a major part of all this. When each of fifty million telephones produces a hundred dollars worth of computer service a year, a development which is being hurried along, another five billion dollars will be injected into the economy, with profits to be split among a few select corporations now prodding progress so assiduously. For this convenience is defined as progress, whether it is demanded by the public or thrust upon it.

Computer systems will become too costly to permit breakdowns, so that backup systems will be standing by with duplicate capability, especially in utility and time-sharing operations. Fail-safe or redundant systems will be as commonplace as auxiliary power generating units as soon as the new convenience becomes so necessary that dependence on it is inescapable. A computer system costing a million dollars to install at the end of the nineteen-sixties will be available by 1973 for perhaps $50,000, according to acknowledged experts. The fourth generation of computers, with services in any household characterized by a steady income and family life, is already a foregone conclusion. Like the automobile which increased in horsepower year after year, increasing in price, too, as the life of an automobile for a first owner was reduced from six to five to four to three and, in millions of cases, to two years or less, the computer and its services is attracting consumers who will become vulnerable to additional marketing and trade-up persuasion. It is a way of life for industrial society and for IBM.

It is a way of life that already has begun to develop lively prospects, reminiscent of both the old cash register market and used car lots, in secondhand computers. The high cost of programming and service stands in the way of the secondhand market, but it is on the way. There are warehouses in Europe and the U.S. bulging with used machines.

However, the horizon is not altogether free of a dark cloud; nothing ominous, to be sure, nothing that cannot be resolved and accommodated. The cloud, no bigger than the hand of mild government intervention, is the threat of anti-trust action. It is scarcely any more threatening than inclement weather but is nevertheless a problem, especially in the burgeoning field of shared-time computers. In this lucrative business, which produced a gross of $50 million for all manufacturers in 1967 and will expand to twenty times that, or a billion dollars, by 1972, IBM has felt it necessary to move carefully, keeping an over-the-shoulder eye on the lightly pursuing Department of Justice.

Time-sharing involves use by many customers of the same computer. As many as 800 customers are able to use, through terminal connections, General Electric's Model 635 installation. Two hundred can make use of the computer at the same time, each paying $10 to $20 an hour, which can easily add up to three thousand dollars an hour. Although under a federal court consent order to stay out of anything resembling the old service bureau operations that IBM was forced to dispose of in 1956, the shared-time business has remained irresistible to the corporation. Consequently, in June of 1968, IBM introduced something it designated as *Call 360 Basic.* It was a time-sharing application of the Model 50 in the System 360 computers and was linked to customer terminals in thirty-four cities. Customers were charged a $100 monthly subscription fee, and by dialing a local number, could gain access to the computer for an additional hourly fee.

According to complaints reaching the Department of Justice, IBM found this promising market so attractive it offered time-sharing at rates below the actual cost of the service, thereby threatening to drive out competitors who were pretty well entrenched.

In Washington an irate lady berated IBM in a trade publication for obtaining computers from itself at "heavily discounted prices" that made it impossible for any independent service company, which did not manufacture the machines, to stay in the business at standard commercial rates. Since the corporation is under a court edict to charge a subsidiary the same price for equipment as it charges others, the complaint of Joan Van Horn, president of her own VIP Systems, Inc., was regarded as serious enough to warrant high level response. IBM vice-president and general counsel Burke Marshall informed a Senate subcommittee that IBM's prices for time-sharing computers were "set at a level intended to be profitable after taking into account the retail price of the equipment . . . and all other properly allocable costs," etc., etc.

Another complaint against IBM also had serious overtones in view of the fact that long before, its service bureau was forbidden to identify itself in any way as an arm of IBM. This sort of thing is an example of how silly anti-trust rulings can get, since it would require a person of extraordinary ignorance in the computer field to be unaware of the relationship between IBM and a service bureau, whether or not it was made clear on a letterhead or in a telephone listing. The mere knowledge on the part of a prospective customer that a time-sharing operation is associated with IBM makes life difficult for competitors. IBM, with an eye on a business headed for a billion dollars in revenue by 1972, is loath to retreat from time-sharing. It is a company that, as was pointed out earlier here, can endure the presence of competing corporations doing business in the millions, but is understandably reluctant to see anything in the range of a billion dollars passing exclusively into hostile hands.

Yet some IBM competitors are anything but hostile. Max B. E. Clarkson, president of Graphic Controls Corporation, a Buffalo firm, was quoted on October 1, 1968, in the *Wall Street Journal* as stating that he preferred to see IBM in the time-sharing field. The company, he said, would be a key factor in expanding sales by dominating the "major educational job to be done." His feeling seemed to be that after IBM had sufficiently educated and sold the market, it would be large enough to support an increased number of lesser competitors. Just gathering crumbs in the computer field can be rewarding.

No matter which way IBM turned or what policies it developed, anti-trust problems were foreseen. If it bought up other corporations, as it bought out in 1968 the firm *Call 360 Datatext Co.*, an improved version of an old text-editing system using IBM equipment, it was subject to charges of crashing into the time-sharing business. If IBM were to reduce computer prices across the board, it would drive out of business those firms which, lacking large capital resources, could not withstand the assault. Anti-trust actions would almost certainly intervene. If, however, the company devoted more resources to sales research and development, it would extend its lead and draw legal fire. Intensified sales and promotion, if blatantly undertaken or if done apparently to smother a specific competitor or carry off all of a given market, would cause IBM more problems than it solved. Such is the woe and anguish of the sovereign.

The IBM of the modern world seems willing to bargain with the Department of Justice through consent decrees as it goes along. Anti-trust procedures are, with rare exceptions, rather a farce anyway, but they are a joke that IBM neither laughs at nor fears. Calmly, if not serenely, secure in its strength, the acknowledged master of the sales and marketing methods with which it has conquered the world, IBM faces a future of perhaps uncertain duration, but confident that it will get not quite all, but nearly all, of the business there is.

The capacity of International Business Machines Corporation and its computer-guided management to sustain efficiency in phenomenal growth and to command leadership in markets it chooses to dominate remains unimpaired. The world-wide empire, built on solid foundations of technology, sales, and service, had no peer and, until now, except in more or less permissible specialties, no threatening competitors.

Yet its capacity to hold its quarter of a million employees in the happy-family image that once characterized the corporation has substantially changed. Considering its multi-billion dollar sales level, and its contributions to causes and institutions in 1967 of $10.5 million—

under .002 per cent of gross income—any assumption of benevolence is pretentious. One million dollars of that trifling amount went to IBM's old friend Columbia University, and the rest was parceled out under a closely held and arbitrary formula that denies even a stockholder knowledge of its disposition. In recent years evidence has been piling up that IBM's corporate philanthropy is largely directed to computer customers in the form of below-cost pricing and services that prevent competitors from encroaching on its vast market. The myth of IBM benevolence cannot be sustained.

The last effort on the part of Tom Watson, Junior, to interpret the "principles and beliefs" of the company in the subjective terms dear to his father came in 1962. The effort was a series of lectures given by Tom at Columbia University, and published—the only work printed as a book over his name—a year later by McGraw-Hill as *The McKinsey Foundation Lecture Series*. They were an exercise in public relations and in futility, a description and analysis of personal attitudes untransferable to a corporate entity.

But to Courtney C. Brown, dean of the Graduate School of Business at Columbia, where old Watson's shadow at times cuts off some of the light, Tom's lectures constituted a significant statement of much that is best in America, "a forthright expression of the enlightened attitudes that serve as our most effective defense of the free way of life." IBM, said Courtney Brown, was "governed in its daily affairs by the verities of human relations," and, "Enduring truths of the personal conduct learned by the company's founder in an uncomplicated rural community setting have successfully served as management guidelines in the development of a highly complex business organization which operates in the most scientific areas of contemporary times."

The company, of course, does operate in scientific areas, but nothing of the influence of an old rural community remains, and the beliefs and principles of the past are unrecognizable to seven or eight out of every ten employees who entered the ranks after old Watson's death. The way it was managed, the products it made, the human verities attributable to the corporate institution, even the promise of happiness through affluence— these are gone with the songbooks, the evangelism, the IBM spirit, the "family," the meat slicers, butcher scales, and coffee grinders. Only the myth has persisted, and few take it seriously.

Tom said he believed a corporation like IBM "owes its resiliency, not to its form of organization or administrative skills, but to the power of what we call beliefs and the appeal these beliefs have for its peo-

281

ple. . . . In other words, the basic philosophy, spirit, and drive of an organization have far more to do with its relative achievements than do technological or economic resources, organizational structure, innovation, and timing. . . . IBM is still very much the same company it has always been and what we intend it shall always be. For while everything else has altered, our beliefs remain unchanged."

When an old colleague of Tom reviewed this comment, he smiled tolerantly, and said: "Well, what the hell could he say? He couldn't very well tell graduate students that IBM had the money, recruited the scientists, or was ready to spend half a billion dollars—which they hadn't done yet—to take over the computer market by making everything in it, including IBM's own machines, obsolete. He couldn't very well say that it didn't make any difference what the company, or the employees, believed if they got eighty per cent of the market. Nobody believes that stuff. Tom doesn't believe it; he probably just wishes it was true. Life might be simpler and better that way. And who wouldn't like that?"

Tom made his own life simpler, or at least that was his official intention, when he moved corporation headquarters in 1964 to Armonk in Westchester County, New York. In answer to a flood of inquiries about why IBM, which Tom's father had said would never leave Manhattan, was relocated in the suburbs, the company's spokesmen were directed to respond with a prescribed catechistic statement that Tom wanted to spend more time with his family in nearby Greenwich, Connecticut. While there were other reasons why corporate executive offices were moving from the inner cities to outlying districts, Tom was said to order the move as a categorical imperative, under which his own motive and conscience were transferable to, and shared by, the displaced families. People of IBM, conditioned by the "family" philosophy, were just naturally expected to find such reasoning unobjectionable. It was in their spirit.

The twelve hundred people whose jobs were involved, most of them in the middle income range, scrambled around in the protected zoning areas of Westchester trying to locate dwellings already in short supply. Uprooted from rent-controlled apartments in Brooklyn and Queens, their pensions, equity in benefits, and promotions at stake, some commuted forty miles a day by automobile, some quit, taking their loss, and some thought the company should pay their moving bills and the cost of interim housing while quarters were being built or sought. It was reasoned that because an executive, when ordered to a new assignment, had his costs covered, hotel bills paid, and the like, the policy should be extended in the case of the relocated families. A good deal of acrimony developed when the company decided against this idea, especially after word spread that Tom's motive for the move had its origins in his fear that New York City would be an early target in nuclear warfare, while the suburb, where he built an elaborate bomb shelter which gossips said was the largest in Connecticut, would be theoretically safer. A company offer of free-interest loans to others who might want to build shelters was not noticeably mollifying.

An executive of twelve years with the corporation who quit to become an aide to a former member of the presidential cabinet in another industry said that IBM loyalty had become no longer reciprocal; "the company no longer gives anything back, its reputation for benevolence and concern is a façade, a fraud." He said further that the character and pettiness of supervision, restricted to working hours in the metropolis, became worse in the suburbs where employees without urban anonymity were more visible at all times.

Watson frequently addressed himself to management level people through a special communication in an easily recognizable format, an Executive Letter containing both explicit and interpretive statements of Tom's personal views. The letters were prepared and written by an unidentified man who thought it odd that he had never been required, or asked, to meet or speak with Tom, whom he had never seen.

Arthur K. Watson made plans to move the World Trade Corporation to the suburbs, too, after acquiring a site of two hundred and fifty acres, but a rebellion developed to frustrate the project. So many complaints were "kicked up" to the Watsons from old hands in the international end of the IBM operation, citing old Thomas J. Watson's pledge not to leave New York, that the pledge was honored. Someone reminded Tom of another promise of his father's, one he had apparently forgotten. Old Watson had offered a vacation in Europe to salesmen exceeding their quotas by some designated amount, but World War II had intervened and the tours abroad had never materialized. Some years later, the successful salesmen and their wives were sent en masse to the south of Europe, where much of their vacation time was spent in company reserved hotels and resorts, free of wine and frolic, until the travelers dispersed to make their way back to the United States individually, enjoying two or three days of unsupervised life among the dissolute, the museums, or fellow tourists, as they chose.

The "half a billion dollars" which an apologist for Tom said IBM was ready to spend to enforce obsolescence on its own and competing computers—and thereby guarantee market dominance—was unquestionably the biggest and boldest gamble in the company's history and one which, apparently successful, gave IBM possession of computer territory. Management men did not have to be reminded, as J. J. Servan-Schreiber told Europeans, that "force today is the capacity to invent, that is—research. It is the capacity for converting inventions into products that is technology." If ever there was a principle or a belief on which a corporation was built, it was this one for IBM.

Nevertheless, the company made incredible and costly mistakes, both of a financial and of a technological variety, mistakes that could cripple a competitor, but it always had the resources to operate around them. By the end of 1963, with a cash balance of nearly a billion dollars on hand, the company actually *prepaid* $160 million in loans to the Prudential Insurance Company, which waived a stipulated premium; probably it was glad enough to get back money it had put out at three and one half per cent interest, in order to pass it around to other borrowers at five per cent. But within three years IBM had to go on the financial market to borrow back the same $160 million, this time paying about an additional two per cent for any funds that were used. Even a naïve household borrower wouldn't turn in cheap money and borrow it back at higher cost.

In the years between the mid-fifties and early sixties, a number of companies, whose assets included highly educated, inventive, and daring men, put capital and brains into developing diversity and specialty in computer technology. IBM, on the other hand, faced with the need to stabilize production, programming, and service in order to supply market demands, had neither the freedom nor the economic need at the time to build into its systems all of the improvements, capacity, and variables of which they were capable. Improvements in computer design and technology were developing at such a rapid rate that they could not be incorporated into stabilized, long-run production. As a sales and service company, IBM consistently sought to meet demands and sustain its grip on most of the market, persuading its large volume of customers that stability, reliability, and guaranteed service were more important than piecemeal technological advancement. Concurrently, companies like Honeywell, Control Data, Remington-Rand, Burroughs, and others were developing computer ideas and specialization that put them, collectively, ahead of IBM in virtually every area except sales and marketing. Because of the enormous capital commitments required for sales and marketing programs capable of competing with IBM, none of the companies except IBM was making much money, even though they were stepping out front with research and design ideas.

In order to guarantee continued command of the market, it became necessary for IBM to take a massive step forward—at a risk which some old company hands feared might, notwithstanding its great resources, break the company. Over a period of four years in the nineteen-sixties, IBM spent nearly as much money to develop, redesign, program, and systematize its full line of computers as its gross sales of $5,345,000,000 in 1967. By dumping in staggering amounts of capital, far more than any combination of competing companies could or would commit, and by striding into the market armed with systems and equipment distinguished by all of the advanced design and compatibility technology the company could develop, imitate, or buy, IBM could keep most of the market to itself. Otherwise, the market might become fragmented, even thoroughly competitive, with quite a few separate companies carving out segments of the burgeoning field, leaving IBM one among many. The vision of rampant free enterprise developing in a market overwhelmingly dominated by IBM was a recurring nightmare to management.

The fact was that IBM had been caught short in research, planning, and—more importantly—in applying what was known to its product lines. By committing five billion dollars to continuing dominance of the market, the corporation was taking a terrible financial risk. While the decision appalled some IBM men, Bob O. Evans, head of the Federal Systems Division, which produced computers for the government market, told writer T. A. Wise that he called the project "you bet your company . . . but it was a damn good risk, and a lot less risk than it would have been to do anything else, or do nothing at all."

Wise compared the operation to one in which General Motors, for example, might decide to scrap every existing make and model of its vehicles, covering the entire spectrum of demand, with a radically redesigned engine and the use of a new exotic fuel.

But having taken the risk, the corporation emerged with what it called the System 360, a compatible multiple model system using hybrid microcircuitry, 30,000 components per cubic foot; it performed at high speed and allowed computer users to move up from one model to another over a vast range of powers. All peripheral equipment had to be redesigned, too, so that auxiliary machines could feed information into, or receive it from, processing units. In the end, the cost of processing 100,000 computations on the old first generation models was reduced, according to IBM, from $1.38 to three and a half cents.

During the anxiety-ridden gestation period of the System 360 line,

IBM held the competition at bay by continuing to promote the future and to out-service customers, inducing them to wait for new models. The object was to operate within the corridor of consent established by the last anti-trust decree which restricted overt methods of intimidating competitors, at the same time fencing in prospects with promises to be honored later. IBM had two generations of experience in the mastery of this industrial art form, and as it turned out, the management's anxiety, while intense, was needless.

By the end of 1966, the talent recruitment program necessitated by the research and development project added sixty thousand employees to the payroll, and from 1964 to 1967, five new plants were added to IBM operations in the U.S. and abroad. It was the most costly privately financed commercial project in history, two and one-half times the cost of the Manhattan (atomic bomb) Project up to the catastrophic day at Hiroshima. But IBM's position in the world seems to have been made secure, leaving other corporations operating in specialty areas and segments of the market where millions of dollars may be made, but closing out for some time the major segments—where the billions are. It softened the fiasco of the STRETCH Computer, on which the company lost $20 million and some of its reputation when Control Data stood up to IBM's guns and moved into the massive computer field.

Many IBM managers and executives disappeared into obscurity—or into other companies, which was considered the same thing—during the portentous System 360 project. But Learson emerged as the strong man, laying low the stragglers and the doubters and getting across to Tom and Dick and everybody else the evidence of his superiority as a man of ability, foresight, and dominance. He was the undisputed hero of the 360 project.

Learson threatened to resign at one point in the System 360 development, but the issue that provoked the threat was resolved in his favor. Then he demonstrated his willingness to risk his IBM career with an exercise of personal competitiveness that symbolized his transference of gladitorial combat to the executive suite. He competed with Tom Watson before the world and won, and in a far more offhand manner usurped a prerogative from Arthur Watson that could scarcely avoid inflicting some form of humiliation. The incidents reveal something about the Watsons and, more significantly, about Learson.

Tom had been a yachtsman for many years, sailing his beautiful *Palowan* in the Newport to Bermuda race, enjoying himself hugely in the social life attendant upon completion of the race. Someone walked into The Reefs, a well-known and beautiful resort on a cliff over the sea

in Bermuda one night and found the place fully and exclusively occupied by Tom, his crew, and a party, having a merry evening of drinking,
dancing, dining, and song, enlivened by the consumption of twenty-six
cases of champagne.

Learson studied the history of the race and recruited the best yacht-
ing talent he could find. One of the experts he engaged was a navigator
who had plotted the course to victory three times. Another was a famous
boat designer, Bill Lapworth, who joined his crew. In California, TV
persuaded a noted spinnaker man to join him, having made the trip to
the West just for that purpose. As Learson's plans progressed, IBM
people responded with apprehension and fascination. Tom Watson, with
either real or feigned lightheartedness, said at a board meeting that
Learson probably couldn't expect to stay at IBM if he should happen to
win the race with his own boat, the *Thunderbird*. But Learson did win.
Watson's *Palowan* finished twenty-fourth on corrected time.

Dick was taken care of in quite another manner, one that involved
one-upmanship within corporate ranks. After the STRETCH failure and
the loss of that part of the scientific market it was presumably intended
to serve, another computer called SCAMP emerged from the company's
internal development operations with high promise and powerful support. SCAMP was a small scientific computer, its design attributed
largely to John Fairclough, a young man then not past thirty, who
worked in the World Trade Corporation's Hursley Laboratory sixty
miles southwest of London. The Hursley group had been trying for
some time to develop a computer specifically suited to European
markets, but failing to do so, had to sell U.S.-made machines on the
continent. Both Fairclough and his boss, Dick Watson, when SCAMP
seemed to measure up to exacting standards specified back in the United
States, were confident and delighted. Dick's men had produced a fine
computer on their own, a compliment to the company's international
operations and a real plum to a sales-oriented, as opposed to a scientific,
research program.

However, Learson was leary of it. He preferred to stretch out the
IBM 7000 line, as it was called, specifically a model known as the 7044,
arguing that IBM should not add to the proliferation of models. Dick
could have set Learson down and gone ahead with Fairclough, producing SCAMP in Europe and winning a good deal of favor there at the
same time. But, responsive to rational argument, he thought Learson's
misgivings about proliferation were valid. Reluctantly, he ordered Fairclough to scrap SCAMP and sell the 7044 in its place. Fairclough was
bitter over the death of the computer he and his associates felt so

strongly about. His people had to be reassigned, the staff at Hursley dispersed.

The old feeling that the U.S. IBM headquarters considered them all stepchildren intensified his disappointment. Dick Watson had nurtured the idea that the divisions in Europe, where brains were being drained off by the United States, might produce the machine and calm the uneasiness of some European governments about computer concentration back in America. Fairclough thought he would resign, but after a night of brooding and drinking Scotch, he reconsidered.

Learson conceded that SCAMP had come close to a life of its own. It had done as well as the 7044. Nevertheless, Learson said, "I had to kill it."

A man who knew of his emotional concern for Fairclough and his staff, asked, disbelieving, whether Learson, then heading the domestic manufacturing division in the United States, had the right to veto an operation in Europe.

"Oh, yes," said Learson.

Dick Watson and his associates abroad believed that *he* had made a reasoned, though tortured, decision against production of SCAMP in Europe. It was not long, however, before they knew that Learson, a man of lesser executive rank, in apparent usurpation of Dick's prestige and authority, had done the actual killing. Dick hadn't counted for much. Nor, for that matter, had Albert Williams, then president of the corporation, whom Tom Watson had often praised warmly and who presumably stood above Learson in the exercise of power. Williams, unaccountably, had begun to say that he was going to retire at the upcoming age of fifty-five. It was curious talk for a healthy IBM man who had been with old Watson. Others began to comment on the impending retirement: "Al is going to quit when he's fifty-five," they would say, unnecessarily. But Williams didn't quit or retire. He dropped down to become chairman of the Executive Committee, and Learson, the IBM man of the future, took over as president.

Promises made by the company, which had scheduled delivery of System 360 models for April of 1965, were not kept. Software problems and programming costs caused an uproar, and Tom himself had to concede that the company's announcements had been "ill advised." A typical IBM euphemism was devised—the word was "decommitted" —to cover broken promises. Competing companies pointedly reminded the market in advertisements that, unlike IBM, they did not promise what could not be produced. It was recalled that the STRETCH computer, the promise of which produced havoc at Control Data by inhibiting sales of that corporation's large scientific model, had not materialized as announced.

As it developed, parts of the 360 line were not fully compatible. Two thousand programming specialists and support personnel labored on the project, as estimated costs for this aspect of the innovative operation alone rose from sixty, to seventy-five, to one hundred, to two hundred million dollars. Delay produced urgency, almost frenzy. In the meantime, Honeywell had figured out a way by which users of IBM's well-known 1401 computer could convert inexpensively to the Honeywell 200 computer, which sold for thirty per cent less than the IBM machine. In fact, customers could use Honeywell's computer with more compatibility than an IBM model intended for just that purpose. More of the gloss was being rubbed off IBM.

In the fall of 1964 M.I.T. announced the purchase of a General Electric 600 Series computer, to the dismay of IBM, which then lagged in time-sharing developments. Eugene Fubini, former Assistant Secretary of Defense at the Pentagon, was brought into one of the highest level jobs ever offered to an outsider. Stephen Dunwell, who had been the upper echelon "goat," above Charles De Carlo, in the STRETCH failure, was brought back to get the System 360 project completed. It was discovered that a good deal of STRETCH research was applicable and valuable. Dunwell was appointed an IBM Fellow, one of many well-paid thinkers, scientists, and scholars privileged to work, or not work, for five years on projects of their own selection.

The company took over its own transatlantic line for communications to and from England and Europe. By 1966 it had two Atlantic channels and was asking for direct access to the Comsat satellite, which the Federal Communications Commission turned down. Nevertheless, plants and laboratories all over IBM's world, linked in an instantaneously responsive communications network, functioned as a multifaceted unit as no corporate operation had ever done before. IBM had become, in fact, a truly international and integrated industrial system. Although it will take a few more years, with unpredictable but unfeared plans of competitors to be unveiled, for IBM's half-billion-dollar gamble to be fully evaluated, the verdict is that it has won. But the mystique of automatic success is, as *Fortune* reported, gone for good at IBM. Even the awesome bonus services offered by the corporation with its products no longer intimidates other companies or customers.

In 1967, after demonstrations and tests among bidders who included Honeywell, Burroughs, and RCA, the U.S. Air Force awarded IBM a contract to provide $114 million worth of computers and services, the largest order ever placed. Cries of outrage greeted announcement of the contract, and pressure was exerted on Congress and the General Services Administration. It was charged that the computer systems intended for 135 Air Force bases could be provided for half of what IBM had bid. The contract was "restudied" for a time, then canceled altogether and given to Burroughs in new bidding for $60 million. An unidentified "spokesman" at IBM said, "Naturally, we're disappointed." He was quoted in the *Wall Street Journal* as saying that his company had offered "an even better system . . . and even greater savings to the government" in the second round of bidding than it had offered the first time, but that apparently Burroughs was able to meet the requirements at a "lower price."

Loss of the Air Force contract to Burroughs provided some small comfort to IBM, which could claim with conviction that the federal systems market had become more competitive. It is a valuable point in anti-trust cases, and there was no doubt that the relatively small Burroughs corporation had walked off with a very large and prized piece of business. By its very act of favoring Burroughs and rejecting the costlier system proposed by IBM, the government had strengthened a competitor and perhaps neutralized a prosecution argument in an anti-trust action.

Although the mystique and myths about IBM are dispelled, no one doubts that it will continue, in one of old Thomas J. Watson's favored phrases, Onward and Upward—perhaps not through eternity, but for a long, long time. But the seriousness with which it took itself—and, in fact, the lugubrious seriousness of the whole computer industry—has changed. One company has even gone so far as to poke fun at it, getting a good deal of public relations attention in the process.

Honeywell hired the late celebrated British cartoonist, Rowland Emett, to create something called the Forget-Me-Not Computer, controlled by FRED, a Frightfully Rapid Evaluator and Dispenser of information. FRED was a whimsical Victorian spoof of the science of automated calculation, a three-dimensional construction of bamboo and metal, incorporating motion, blinking lights, noise-making contraptions, birds, doorknobs, lampshades, playing cards, and measuring tapes. It did not compute, but it made people laugh on an exhibition tour, which gave company spokesmen an opportunity to say that mankind need not fear computers any more than pushbutton telephones or sliced bread.

In Stockholm, a wake was held for BESK, one of the twenty or so oldest computers operating in 1967. It was famous for its ability, originating in an attached device, to sing the Swedish drinking song "First Drink Goes," and for correctly predicting the decline of Communist strength in elections. It had been in operation for eighteen years and was put to death in a simple ceremony involving pulling a plug from an electric socket.

In London, after thirty-three-year-old Walter Davis and his wife, Barbara, had been divorced, Mr. Davis became lonely. He went to a dating bureau, filled out a questionnaire, and was matched by computer punch card with thirty thousand "prospects," one of whom Mr. Davis hoped would be a proper mate for him. The computer's first choice was his former wife, Barbara, who had turned herself in as a prospect.

Cosmopolitan for October, 1967, published an account of the use of computers in matching the lovelorn. The report cited a young lady named Vicki who, a stranger in New York City, invoked the help of a computer dating service in finding a beau. She found him, a fellow named Ben, and they were married. They had very much in common. Among other things, both were employed by IBM.

E. B. White, a serious humorist and essayist, wrote that he did not believe in computers very much, since the convenience they afforded some people was regarded as more important than the inconvenience they caused to all. "In short," he wrote in *The New York Times,* "I don't think computers should wear the pants or make the decisions. They are deficient in humor. . . . The men who feed them seem to believe that everything is made out of ponderables, which isn't the case. I read a poem once that a computer had written, but didn't care much for it. It seemed to me I could write a better one myself, if I put my mind to it."

A computerized St. Louis, Missouri, insurance company sent one of its clients a bill for $0.00, and an automatically produced letter ordering him to pay up. Examining the amount, he ignored the message. A second letter followed, threatening to cancel his automobile insurance policy. He capitulated and mailed off a check for $0.00. According to *The National Underwriter,* he received a most courteous letter, thanking him and advising that the policy would remain in force.

The *Wall Street Journal* reported on March 27, 1968, that Joe Rodman's computer almost put him out of the wholesale grocery business in Boston. He had leased an IBM RAMAC 305, with visions of ending warehouse inventory snarls. When Mr. Rodman began to get shipments of twenty times more merchandise than he ordered, with no place in the warehouse to store it, he summoned a battery of "customer engineers," who said they fixed it. Then he asked the computer how many cases of canned peas, or something, he had in stock, and the computer said none. A nonelectronic warehouseman, however, observed cases of peas stacked to the ceiling. When he paid, through computer error, $200 for a $13 item and $39.00 instead of $3.90, Mr. Rodman filed a lawsuit and quit paying the IBM leasing fee. The company's attorney said they had "made the best possible installation under the circumstances," which Mr. Rodman thought was overstating the case. So did the judge, who ruled in his favor. Just the same, Mr. Rodman had to pay the withheld leasing fee of $26,620. Without anything resembling the ceremony held for old BESK in Stockholm, Mr. Rodman pulled the plug.

At M.I.T. and other locations as well, students have amused and enlightened themselves by programming a computer to play chess, and otherwise rigging the mechanism to serve their sense of competition, play, and humor. Early experiments turned out poorly for the machine, thus supporting the "vitalists"—those who believe that the human mind is a vital force beyond mechanical imitation—in their contention that no computer could be designed to match the imagination and logic of man. The M.I.T. computer, in response to an appropriate signal, printed out the message, "I am ready to play chess. It's your move." After a time, with the machine losing more often than it won—once the students got onto it—the chess program was wiped out and the computer devoted on a time-sharing basis to more scientific and educational matters associated with research contracts. The signal to start the computer off on a game was not, however, removed; one of these days someone is inadvertently going to give the signal, and the computer, apparently on its own initiative, is going to ask someone for a game. At that point, some startled student will doubtless be convinced that the computer has a mind of its own, is weary of turning out tedious work, and simply wants to play. It might alter a scientist's whole outlook.

The most sophisticated, large-scale time-sharing experiment at M.I.T. was Project MAC, meaning Multiple Access Computer. Data representing records and accumulated knowledge of different corporations could be brought forth only to those who, knowing the operational password or code, were capable of extracting it. In what could have been out-and-out criminality, had their intention been other than professional experimentation, graduate students devised means of "bugging" the system. It was an exercise in program raiding, or hijacking of data, by which secrets locked into a memory core were printed out at the will of an unauthorized experimenter. It provokes shivers of horror among scientists and industrialists aware of the probability that if a sufficiently skilled opportunist is determined to do so, he can theoretically not only make data espionage raids but, in the possession of the right identifying codes, charge the time used for making the raid to the corporation already robbed of its secrets.

Some scientists see in this kind of intrusion the likelihood that if highly secret data is computerized by the government, a good spy could pick up twenty years of espionage on a well-planned raid. Looking at the matter broadly, however, they do not necessarily fear the result. The possession of information, even where predictable outcome is measurable, is not felt by many scientists to constitute much danger. Even a spy with a pass allowing him full access to Atomic Energy Commission data does not by itself give tremors to men who know, if the public does not, that any small band of technicians with ten pounds of plutonium in a good laboratory workshop can make a bomb of enough power to obliterate a city. Safeguards could, theoretically, prevent access to nuclear material, but keeping knowledge from scientists is an acknowledged impossibility. Release of the Smythe report, after Hiroshima and Nagasaki, probably had more to do with curtailing otherwise wasteful efforts on the part of the Soviet Government than any information from espionage agents, including Ethel and Julius Rosenberg. All the French, the Russians, and the Chinese did was follow up on the U.S. demonstration that the bomb functioned. The Smythe report proved it could be done. In science, proof of fact reduces espionage in search of proof to redundancy.

The possession of knowledge, whether stolen from a computer in an invasion of privacy or acquired through pure research, is felt to be inevitable in the most pragmatic long range sense. Determination, resources, and policy to apply such knowledge to designated goals are, in the judgment of scientists, questions of value and political judgment. Herbert Grosch, the highest ranking authority on computers in the U.S. Bureau of Standards, has suggested that Gunnar Myrdal's prediction in the nineteen-forties of American racial strife was a compendium of knowledge which, widely published in several countries, produced virtually no action to alleviate human degradation and prevent the destruction of cities by burning and anarchy. He does not fear the computer, IBM, or any technological capability, but sensibly doubts the readiness of men and mankind to apply what they learn to problems at hand.

Nearly everyone in the computer field knows and many have recalled these anecdotes, and dozens more like them. Daniel McCracken, author of ten textbooks on computers and a well-known lecturer on the subject, has said that these stories and jokes, which became painful and boring to old computer hands, were authentic in their original forms but reappear in apocryphal variations. The most chilling and widely known item of black humor relating to the electronic brain appeared in print in a short story by Fred Brown twenty years ago; it has been recounted to scientists, programmers, and salesmen over the years without credit to the writer—an oversight which the novelist and astrophysicist Arthur C. Clarke has pointed out. Mr. Brown's story was about the super-computer which had become so sophisticated that it was independent of human sources for its own power control. The great machine was asked the ultimate question:

"Is there a God?"

In tones of Jovian thunder, the ultimate machine answered:

"There is now."

Arthur Clarke declared that the story was "more than a brilliant myth; it is an echo from the future." Theologians, he wrote in a 1968 magazine article, may have made a "slight but understandable error —which, among other things, makes totally irrelevant the recent debates about the death of God. It may be that our role on this planet is not to worship God—but to create him."

In the Christmas season of 1968, as three American astronauts pro-pelled themselves to the moon and back in a projectile spawned by com-puters, some earthbound people thrilled to the radioed Bible readings of one of the trio and found in them an allegorical relationship to the Three Wise Men of Bethlehem proclaiming the religion of redemption and love. It was history's most exalted day for the computers and for technology, even though the sociological usefulness of the demonstra-tion remained to be perceived. Commercial benefits of space flights, how-ever, had more than computer corporations all but licking their chops at the prospect of long-range benefits. One of the largest beneficiaries of space expenditures, for example, sponsored a television show proclaiming that "North American Rockwell and the future were made for each other" and showed photographs of large sectors of the planet in which coloration and configuration indicated the presence of vast unsuspected oil and mineral resources which had somehow escaped exploitation. The space photos encouraged opportunistic corporate enterprises to set about remedying this apparent oversight.

Tom Watson at IBM, like Howard Aiken, the designer of the original Mark I, has assured the world that the computer is no more than a tool, a view held by most people who profit by, or in, this field of technology. Others are certain that it is already something of a monster, corrupting values and causing distortion of viewpoints. Some fear it is an instru-ment that, by compiling a lifetime accumulation of details about each person's life, will doom human beings to a loss of privacy.

Writer Daniel McCracken who, except as an occasional consultant, has left the computer field to become a Unitarian clergyman, sees the computer as a slave becoming a master, and does not accept the easy argument that it is incapable of thought; man will probably use it as a substitute for thought. McCracken has written that it is possible for society to become financially and physically dependent on the computer, which will change society's evaluation of it. Also, "computers are so much fun . . . that the tool has become dominant through the enjoyability of working with it. It can dominate us in a subtle way because it makes problems solvable. Then we tend to work on these problems because they are solvable, not because they are important." He has called upon computer people to "speak out" for socially useful applications of computer technology and warns that "colossal blunders" are possible. In effect, he seems to be sounding the same warning as Norbert Wiener: the technology may be owned by the wrong people. Mr. McCracken has been joined by other spokesmen in this respect, including some who saw the enormous cost of the race to the moon as an exercise in problem solving and the use of programmed astronauts as an extension of technology for nationalistic purposes rather than the pursuit of science.

In America, committees in Congress and the Federal Communications Commission have under study proposals to regulate computer information transmission, guard individual privacy, and in general keep a legislative eye on the computer invasion. Constitutional lawyers, humanists, and people concerned with the preservation of individual rights stand by warily, knowing from past experience that expediency and commercialism, along with outright avarice, often show small concern for the human scale of things.

One such group of suspicious thinkers in 1968 decided to commemorate the twentieth anniversary of the adoption by the United Nations of the Universal Declaration of Human Rights, a great document significant for the hopefulness of its content and dishonored substantially in its international application. A private research agency, the Commission to Study the Organization of Peace, released a report of a study that raised some alarming questions about computers and their unregulated use.

Drafted by Professor Louis B. Sohn, Beamis Professor of Law at Harvard, the report called on the United States to support the UN in studying "the implications of scientific and technological developments for human rights . . . and recommend procedures for making the experience of each country available to other countries."

Although some countries might prefer not to share certain experiences, the study commission viewed inaction on computer controls as perilous. Most dangerous is the fact that "actual decisions will be no longer in the hands of duly elected representatives of the people but instead in the hands of those who feed the data to the computers on which decisions are based and who are the interpreters and implementers of the answers. . . ." The United States should take the initiative in devising means "to control the precious few who know how to run the machines, and on whose wisdom and impartiality the fate of mankind may depend." Seventy-four men and women, nearly all of them noted in fields of scholarship, law, economics, labor, and publishing, signed the report, which dwelt further on the possibility that "a dangerous combination of government officials and experts" might start prescribing, in the name of the greatest good, "who can marry whom and for how long, who cannot have any children and who should have the maximum possible."

Explicit proposals to guard the interests of mankind, or even to determine what they are, have never been agreed upon to any substantial extent. Any mechanism for regulation and enforcement would require multilateral action that is politically, emotionally, and diplomatically difficult to achieve. Even the issue of whether elected, as differentiated from appointed, officials should exercise regulatory controls is vague. The capacity to win elections confers upon men and women little expertise in so profound a field. The achievement of a consensus in support of a demonstrably destructive policy is to be feared. A good deal more time and dialogue must pass before theories, fears, and uncrystallized expectations can be incorporated into international action. Experience of the past two or three generations contributes little comfort to the idea that global thinking and planning, rather than separatist or nationalist outlooks, can be organized in good time.

Intelligent or effective regulation probably cannot be applied to phenomena whose projections are neither known nor predictable. Not much is expected to happen for some time, except peripherally, in the area of individual privacy. But the truth is that there is virtually no privacy left to anyone, in terms of data and information, against whom official forces—and sometimes unofficial ones, as well—may choose to move. Even before Senator Joseph McCarthy and a vast sector of American officialdom, including much of the press, made an obscene mockery of privacy in the nineteen-fifties, before computers were applied to its invasion, modern man was helpless to prevent the accumulation of fact and conjecture about himself. His best defense against intrusion was apathy and official disinterest. Unclassified F.B.I. data have been leaked when appropriately placed protectors thought it safe to do so. Fingerprints compelled by procedure and law, tax and income data, credit reports covering human lifetimes, hotel registers, medical and telephone records, employment data, the most private associations, voice prints, dental charts—all are obtainable to virtually anyone with the resources to get them. All that remains is to institutionalize and formalize their acquisition.

The real fear of an F.B.I. dossier lies in its truth or falsity, as the real objection to disclosure lies in the shame and outrage of the individual being exposed. The computer makes exposure both practical and inevitable. It is argued that if no one cared, if it was irrelevant and immaterial in general whom an individual had affairs with, or how many, what money he made, what he did with it, whether he was arrested, indicted, or jailed—if all was known about everyone, what importance would private information have? Sexual conduct, as a moral issue, is already a matter of uninterest to oncoming generations. The salaries of corporation executives, school teachers, policemen, everyone on a public payroll, are already virtually public information; so are individual stock holdings of corporation officers. What is left to privacy as far as data are concerned? It would be better, the argument goes, to have data correctly assembled, free of error, with erasure and correction possible, than gossip and unclassified trash about a person in a dossier, the leakage of which can be arranged without knowledge of the victim. In a world where individuals will live in compressed space, in rooms of broom closet size, perhaps, what difference will it all make?

Assurances that locked-in data cannot be disclosed are worthless; any lock can be broken. One that cannot be broken, or that offers nearly perfect protection—as in the case of presumptive fail-safe mechanisms applicable to nuclear weapons—offers too much protection to serve the practical considerations involved. What might be applicable in the case of a bomb that could blow up a world would be out of place in guarding a credit rating or covering up a love affair.

Tom Watson was unsuccessfully approached in 1960 with an idea for creating a good public image against the day when IBM might be accused, with other corporations in a technocracy, of being the master of a brutalizing, dehumanizing machine. The idea involved a giant simulation of transportation problems, urban congestion, city planning, programmed on assumptions that might determine the quality of human life. It was proposed that a variable grain simulation, as it was called, of detail and experiments could suggest—again, with a variety of assumptions—where to place escalators and open space, how to use or not use resources, how and whether to move people to and from jobs—all possible things. The technology necessary to provide a remedy is here.

The two major factors preventing its application are the nature of man, of course, and the exaltation of materialism as an index of accomplishment. The latter is most prevalent in the United States, where old Thomas J. Watson, as much as any man who ever lived, helped make it a characteristic of national life. An increasing quantitative measure of material production and profit became the goal of corporate life. IBM and the computer technology it has led are revealing the depth of the human crisis, but social action, as always, must provide solutions. With the ultimate control of human intelligence conceded as possible; with much of the century's political discussion irrelevant; and with the artificial intelligence of the computer available to reconcile doubts about the quantitative measurement of man's problems, basic dilemmas are unresolved. Mankind's social action lags; objectives go undefined; society is, by and large, irrational if not—as more militant philosophers insist—insane.

In the United States, the principal breeding ground of the computer and the technological revolution it set off, the Congress of a compromise society requires months, even years, to come to grips with a single monumental problem. The increasing technical expertise required in deciding between alternatives under the slow democratic process of consensus, and under a traditional value system, discourage optimism. Dr. Fred Hoyle, of England's Cambridge University, an eminent scientist, has outraged many people with his assertion that western civilization's terminal point may be reached within thirty-five years. The kind of people who can win elections in ordinary times are not likely, he says in his lectures, to be the kind who can cope with the proliferation of emergencies engulfing the world. Dr. Grosch is afraid America cannot afford to take even twenty years to repair the fissures in its society. America, a land which taught its citizens the great moral truths, the difference between right and wrong in government, was even more effective in inducing its citizens to accept, rationalize, and defend its wrongs, as long as industrial growth and affluence was the mark of achievement.

At IBM, the corporation's president, T. V. Learson, believes, "It is not as important to make the right decision, as it is to make the decision right." Although in his personal life he sometimes devotes his enormous skill and energy to public causes—such as raising funds for private charities and the like—Learson says it like it is; he is an unsentimental spokesman of tremendous drive and authority for the new spirit at IBM.

Arthur Watson, as president of the International Chamber of Commerce, a forum that has been the province of the company and the family for two generations, makes periodic speeches in support of free trade. Like the oilman-governor and occasional candidate for President, Nelson A. Rockefeller, he has extensive and profitable interests throughout Latin America, a kinship Mr. Rockefeller acknowledged when he asked Arthur Watson to accompany him on a fact-finding tour for President Nixon in May of 1969. The tour was interrupted by outbreaks of violence in several Latin American republics, not all of whose citizens appreciated or welcomed the visiting millionaires on what was felt to be a gratuitous public relations junket.

Arthur's brother, Tom, also makes important speeches expressing concern about what will happen to countries whose best brains are claimed by American companies, including IBM, and supporting Dow Chemical Company in public protests against the manufacture and use of napalm by U.S. Forces in Vietnam. Tom Watson now and then takes a flirtatious interest in politics, and in 1968 writer Jimmy Breslin published a peculiar column asserting that unidentified powerful interests were seeking to maneuver Tom into the presidential race. No report of the movement appeared in print except the column by Mr. Breslin. Yet, Tom's yearning for public service was not stilled, and he is sometimes talked about as a possible candidate for Governor of Connecticut. Meanwhile, Tom would have one believe that he walks undisturbed in the ways of his father; that the company, as in its earlier era, finds the old principles and beliefs more important than executive talent, research, and technology. It is not believable. Corporate life is not like that.

In the time between 1957, IBM's first billion-dollar year, and 1961, the corporation's sales grew to two billion dollars. In 1964 they exceeded three billion. Two years later the total rose to four and a quarter billion. In 1968 it approached seven billion dollars. Thus in a little more than one decade, IBM growth was eight and one-half times greater than the sales volume it took old Thomas J. Watson forty-two years to achieve.

That's the way things are measured around IBM and, for the most part, around any other corporation. Some forms of liberalism have come into corporate life, and to the men who run it. Non-unionized IBM's record is no sorrier, and indeed more defensible in many respects, than once-militant, humanistic labor unions that have become vested conservative interests, self-serving fixtures of a productive establishment. But the quantitative value system, with its priority on materialism, seems at present immutable. IBM, in fact, plans on that changeless probability. Learson is sure that computer technology is only beginning.

"The computer business is as vast as the mind," he says. "Use hasn't really begun. We're just at the capital accretion stage."

If he is right, where will the computer take the world and the company? Norbert Wiener's apprehensions are thought-provoking, but not deeply troubling, to the community of industrial scientists, who feel that J. Robert Oppenheimer's measure of the computer as primarily an instrument for the accumulation of knowledge was a sketchy vision of what it will, in application, become. It will THINK in a world Watson helped to make. It is certain to become a universal utility, at least in the industrialized world, a tool of utilitarianism beyond present comprehension.

Dr. Irving John Good of Trinity College at Oxford has suggested that the "ultra-intelligent machine is the last invention that man need make." Such a supercomputer, Arthur Clarke wrote, "will force us to think about the purpose and meaning of human existence. It will compel us to make some far-reaching and perhaps painful decisions, just as thermonuclear weapons have made us face the realities of war and aggression after 5,000 years of pious jabber."

While the supercomputer and its capabilities have not yet been put into service, the question of whether or not it will take over much of the human thinking process has been answered. It will. It is already doing so. It remembers and deduces, analyzes and evaluates, free of distractions and deflection produced by compassion and by questions about the usefulness or necessity of outcomes sought. In a technologically ambitious world, distraction and deflection from the process of analysis are held in disfavor, and in this respect computers achieve the perfection of which man is incapable. The ordinary thinking individual has been all but replaced. In tasks where intuition and reflection are neither important nor tolerated, the argument is over. Jokes about the vulnerability of the computer to ludicrous error, illustrating man's apparent transcendence over mechanisms, give comfort to the uninformed and the mystically hopeful. They reflect a wish but not a truth. It is altogether possible that the slogan THINK is becoming less the function of the people directed to do so than it is of the machines they produce. And because of it, human beings perhaps face fewer rather than more choices in a demanding life of diminishing freedom and tranquility.

A compelling illustration of the point emerged from the reflections of the American heavyweight prize fighter Sonny Liston, whose knowledge of a rough and competitive world possibly did not include familiarity with the musings of Norbert Wiener. Sonny Liston was philosophically prepared, he said, to go back to digging ditches—work he was physically endowed to do—if defeats in the ring ended his career as a boxer. His discovery that, his prowess notwithstanding, there was no livelihood to be found in hard physical labor, no ditches to be dug by men, drove him somewhat unwillingly back to fighting.

It is the position of the Watsons, IBM scientists, and technicians that the computer does only what it is told, or programmed, to do. Its role in decision-making is far from limited to the rigidity of any program, however. When the quantitative measuring devices are applied to highway planning, real estate expansion, siting of nuclear power plants, and calculation of tax revenues, for example, it is a relatively simple matter to determine the preferred economics and preferred alternatives, even though subsequent changes in conditions sometimes make it appear that the computer erred. Injustices and disruption follow less because of error, however, than because of factors left out, or considered irrelevant, in the program. There are innumerable examples of inequities in the assessment of taxes, or failure to assess them. Data processing equipment and computers early in 1969 authoritatively informed Governor Nelson Rockefeller of New York and his fiscal experts that an increase in the state sales levy, which would tax New York City residents six per cent of nearly everything they buy, would bring in an additional $200 million or so. They determined further that if such things as milk, bread, butter, baby food and other previously exempted items were included in taxable purchases, the revenue could be increased to $360 million. But what the computers could not determine, since it wasn't programmed or asked to do so, was the despair, pain, and injustice inflicted on families of marginal and low incomes whose tax payments, in relation to income, were many times more than those of people of some affluence. The computers made the decision right, it could be argued, but was it the right decision? Who programmed that computer? Who will program the computers of the future?

16.
The
Future

FEW CORPORATIONS ENDURE FOR the three score and ten years promised to man. Consolidations and mergers, holding companies and conglomerates, acquisitions and failures eat most of them up in the course of growth and change. IBM in 1971 will have endured for sixty years, all but the first thousand days under the management of Thomas J. Watson and his sons. Once more, in its advancing age, it is in the coils of the slow-moving, seldom effective United States anti-trust laws. Once again, IBM and the Watsons believe application of the law is "unwarranted and without foundation," as Tom Watson in January, 1969, wrote his stockholders. But conditions are different in the age of technology. The federal government, in moving against IBM, has the encouragement and help of powerful but lesser computer corporations, managed by angry and ambitious men, which have achieved multimillion dollar growth at the feet of Watson's monument to monopoly and enterprise. It is altogether possible that, in some manner, IBM will be broken up, but like old John D. Rockefeller's oil monopoly, the fragments can be counted on to grow in size and market dominance separately, perhaps to greater range and size than is possible in unity.

With the impending change of administrations in Washington, IBM was fully aware that the law was in motion against it. The company took official cognizance of the fact in newspaper and magazine advertisements that conceded the existence, but not any guilt in, charges being raised against it. IBM began to behave rather like the electric light or the telephone company used to behave, by reminding the public that it was functioning in a world that contained healthy and welcome competitors. IBM made a better case for itself than utility monopolies because, for one thing, risk-free utilities did not truly face the competition said to be vital in the capitalistic system, while IBM had, at some market levels, very real if not especially dangerous competition which it allowed, off and on, to thrive.

With the confirmation of reports of anti-trust action before and after President Richard Nixon was elected, IBM reminded the world of the existence of companies and computers other than its own. It was one of the times when the corporation seemed, if not humbled, almost embarrassed by its staggering growth, as though perhaps it would just as soon not engage in discussion about it which pending threats made necessary. Yet, with a grace induced by its overpowering strength, it acknowledged problems exposed by its own supremacy.

In an advertisement that was one of a series in periodicals and newspapers, the story was told of an Oakland, California, man who inherited a small chain of tool, hardware, and houseware stores, and who let the word out that he was in the market for a small computer. Five good and reputable manufacturers, said IBM, submitted bids to sell the businessman this relatively inconsequential bit of office equipment. The computers were, said the advertisements, all of fine quality, and any one of them would have served equally well. But because of the company's long experience and knowledge of the buyer's own business, combined with assurances of continuing service, the prospect chose an IBM computer.

The image of four other enterprising, voracious computer manufacturers out there in the market snapping at IBM's heels for a miniscule bit of business prevailed in the courteously presented picture. It was faintly reminiscent of old advertising campaigns of A.T. & T. and Mother Bell, praising in photographs and prose the little enterprising independently owned rural telephone companies, in which a lonesome "Central" presided through the night over a switchboard, relaying instructions on the delivery of a baby, while the country doctor fought his way through storms to reach the remote household. Appropriate parallels were drawn between a great system that spanned the nation and a brave company with thirty-two subscribers, each serving a spirited, free, God-fearing country with courage and Yankee ingenuity.

While it is perhaps cynical to suggest that the complete truth is obscured in such a presentation, the suspicion was inescapable that when a very large corporation of near monopoly stature and enormous capital reserves takes to costly advertising media to cite the courage and virtues of its competitors, it must need those competitors very much.

IBM had indeed become just a little nervous about anti-trust interference on the domestic scene, disregarding grumblings concurrently audible in Europe. It was, despite the nervousness, all right with IBM and its World Trade arm if all the governments and competing corporations in the world got together to compete among themselves, scramble for, or amicably share, that lesser portion of the great electronic computer market growing to unpredictable size. For in all probability IBM will continue to possess the four-fifths, or maybe three-quarters, of a world-wide industry on which expansion, even from a base level approaching $8 billion, can only continue year after year, decade after decade, as long as the world of electronic technology lasts. Nothing has occurred to nullify old Thomas J. Watson's promise that IBM would go on forever. It is forever itself that seems to get less measurable. Thus, while IBM may have needed most of the sixty competing manufacturing systems which have grown in its shadow, and four thousand companies dealing in related computer equipment, it did not need the open combat and gang warfare which unexpectedly broke out as the corporation in 1969 entered its fifty-eighth year of life. The warfare emerged in the wake of a year, 1968, when IBM's income rose to $6,888,500,000, with earnings up 43.7 per cent.

Thomas J. Watson, Junior, noted that such earnings were abnormally high, and attributed the $1.5 billion growth during the year to the swing from rental of computer equipment to outright purchase. This trend to final sales instead of leasing would probably curb such high annual gains in the future, Mr. Watson explained. He did not exactly tug his forelock and promise not to let such expansion happen again, but the implication was clear that earnings would not continue at this accelerated rate. Three months later, in April of 1969, Watson had to report that first quarter sales had gone up another $200,000,000 over the same period of the preceding year, but that on a percentage basis, growth had indeed—as he had surmised—declined. Income for the three months was up only 13.8 per cent, compared to 34 per cent a year earlier. Nevertheless, IBM seemed to be moving toward an eight-billion-dollar volume for 1969.

The gang war of litigation, unrelated to damage lawsuits being directed against IBM and other computer systems for other reasons, put the Department of Justice and competitors of IBM into an armed camp of unintended allies. Grounds for the combat on one of the fronts closing in on IBM originated in 1965. In that year Control Data Corporation was the only U.S. computer company besides IBM showing a profit, and William C. Norris, president and board chairman of Control Data, was counting on his big 6600 system to assault the Watson stronghold.

IBM has had long and refined practice trying to live within the consent decree of 1956. Around headquarters offices, a familiar and hefty document has long been in evidence. It is called the Bible, and it is a special edition of the text of the consent decree plus intra-company rules instructing salesmen and managers how to behave to stay out of conflict with the law. The Bible and the comprehensive rule book was Tom Watson's idea after he took command from his father, and every employee above a designated level in the hierarchy is compelled to read it once a year, go to a lecture relating to its application, and attend a showing of an instructive motion picture on anti-trust decrees as they affect the company. This attention to detail and indoctrination of men in the field were expressions of Tom's determination to reduce the likelihood of complaints from competitors and from the U.S. Department of Justice. The employment at high salaries of Burke Marshall and Nicholas deB. Katzenbach, former top ranking officials in the Attorney General's office, was a further reflection of Tom's preparations for combat if caution failed—which it did.

/ Pressure, obedience to rules, and attendance at lectures and motion picture showings were not sufficient to keep the law at bay. Enforcement yielded to laziness, inattention, and opportunism, or so it seemed as marketing men began to tell prospective buyers of large scientific computers that they would be best advised to wait for the arrival of large-scale IBM computers already past the drawing board stage. /

Talked into a state of expectancy, customers who had otherwise planned to buy Control Data's system, waited. While waiting, according to William Norris, they cancelled his orders. As it turned out, IBM delivered very few of the big computers while Control Data's stock slithered to frightening lows, and the company's 1965 profits were wiped out by losses the next year. Complaints began reaching the Department of Justice from more wounded competitors than Norris alone. /

Contrary to Norris's expectations, however, the government took no action against IBM's modern refinement of the old cash register "knock-out" machine brought into the computer age. Norris and his extraordinarily able engineers emerged from the distress of 1966 with a surprising recovery the following year. In 1967 Control Data stock, which had slid to thirty-two and one-quarter as marketing troubles plagued the 6600, made one of the best gains on the New York Stock Exchange by climbing back to one hundred thirty-six and one-half. It was the kind of financial character assessment which money and management men often prefer to more subjective forms of judgment. Norris decided to open the attack.

As the days of Lyndon Johnson's administration dwindled to a few, rumors that the Justice Department might move against IBM remained unconfirmed. In December, Norris introduced the most powerful computer on earth, called the 7600. A week later, on December 11, he stunned the computer community by filing a suit against IBM in Federal Court in St. Paul, Minnesota, supported it with thirteen pages of damning complaints, called for a breakup of the offending corporation, and demanded triple damages for losses inflicted on Control Data by IBM—losses computed by Norris, of course. The suit stipulated thirty-seven charges of monopolizing, or attempting to monopolize, the computer market and estimated IBM's share of the $18 billion market at seventy-seven to ninety per cent.

As the strongest and most ambitious challenger IBM ever had, Norris declared he wanted Control Data to be the "Ford" of the computer business and that IBM could go on being "General Motors," but he was not content with a small percentage of the business divided among those sixty competitors for which IBM had shown such high regard. As far as Norris was concerned, IBM might measure its tribulations against sixty competitors, but he had only one. Tom Watson and T. V. Learson doubtless wished they could have confined their advertising campaign to fifty-nine.

The Control Data suit produced an uproar at the Joint Computer Conference in San Francisco, which was in session when the damage suit was disclosed. Some computer authorities deduced that Norris was making an effective power play in his challenge to IBM, an exercise in tactics that would chase IBM out of the large scientific computer field for good and dissuade the giant from "announcing" any more knockout machines that might inhibit Control Data sales. The request for dissolution of the IBM corporation was an audacious touch of Norris drama. Preparations had been made in deep secrecy, and Norris had withheld instituting the action until it appeared that a new administration would come to power without any anti-trust action against IBM at all.

The lights burned late in the chancellery at Armonk, but the only response came in the form of "IBM statements," attributed to no one at all but channeled through the anonymity of the public relations office. IBM "intends to fight the suit vigorously," it was said in *The New York Times* and *The Wall Street Journal:* "IBM issued a statement denying any violations of the anti-trust laws." No one really spoke for IBM. *It* spoke for *itself*. Ordinarily, identified men do not address themselves to the public or to the press at IBM. A statement appears and the contents are what IBM, thereafter sometimes referred to as *it*, says.

While Nicholas Katzenbach, under-secretary of state and former attorney general, prepared to leave the government and transfer to the chancellery at Armonk, another treble damage suit hit IBM, thus assuring Mr. Katzenbach, the new general counsel, that there would be plenty of work for him to do as soon as he showed up in the troubled suburb following the transfer of power in Washington.

The second damage suit, obviously long under consideration, was filed by a leasing concern, Data Processing Financial & General Corporation, in New York. The company owned $175 million worth of IBM computers which it leased to users at a discount from IBM rates. A young company, Data Processing was trying at the time it brought suit to buy a one-third interest in the Great Atlantic & Pacific Tea Company. One never knows in the era of conglomerates when a computer leasing firm will find itself in the food chain business. The one-third interest was to be a down payment, more or less, a preliminary quest intended to end in full ownership of the A. & P.

Where Control Data was content to let the court decide how much injury IBM had done to it, Data Processing added up the pain IBM was said to have inflicted and found it totaled $351.5 million. Triple damages of this amount was $1,054,500,000, quite enough to soothe the agony, with enough left over to buy A. & P., especially if beleagured old IBM had to pay all the lawyers, too.

Again, anonymous spokesmen at Armonk said the whole case was "without merit," and that, anyway, concessions already had been made to computer lessor companies, such as Data Processing, which had applauded the adjustment of grievances. Data Processing said IBM sold at less than cost, or gave away free, services for which the plaintiff liked to get paid, there being no pretensions on the part of the leasing company of indulging in the kind of customer philanthropy IBM, it was charged, practiced on a carefully discriminating scale. Like Control Data, the leasing company asked the government to break up IBM into separate manufacturing, leasing, and service operations. Harvey Goodman, president of Data Processing, was frank to say that his suit was welcomed by other leasing companies—which it surely was—and which had been "intimidated" or in other ways injured by "IBM's illegal practices."

IBM stock wavered around $312 a share, having dipped from the 1968–69 high of $375, then held firm as a feeling of relief and resignation settled over Armonk. It was felt that the long period of litigation between competitors could begin, now that the action had started without, it seemed, any tactical support from the Attorney General's office. At this point, the inauguration of President-elect Nixon was two weeks away, and things at the Department of Justice seemed more or less calm.

/ On Friday, January 17, the last working day of the departing administration, the United States Department of Justice filed its own anti-trust suit accusing IBM of monopolizing the computer market and indicated, in a lugubrious phrase, that it would seek "relief by way of divorcement, divestiture and reorganization with respect to the business properties of the defendant as the court may consider necessary or appropriate to dissipate the effects of the defendant's unlawful activities."

A statement issued by "the company," as the newspapers put it, called the government action "unwarranted and without foundation." *It* said: "Evidence of the open and strongly competitive nature of the computer business is abundant. Virtually non-existent 20 years ago, it has grown into a multi-billion dollar industry that has attracted more than 60 manufacturers and some 4,000 companies dealing in related equipment support and services."/

IBM, with extraordinary efficiency, put into action a project which in two working days explained its position in well-mannered prose to most of the newspaper readers of the United States. In double page spreads, it asked the eight-column question, "Has IBM spoiled the computer business for others?" and on an adjoining page, it answered, "Let's look at the record." It was a convincing and compelling story— quite accurate, but perhaps not relevant to economic and political issues that would doubtless bear on the ultimate resolution of the legal actions.

In essence, IBM said it had not stifled competition because the computer business was open, in addition to sixty manufacturers who had entered the field, to thousands of other growth companies in related services. It was a record that General Motors, the dominant power in the automobile industry, for example, could not equal, although G.M. remained inviolate to anti-trust action through years of deplorable policy and conduct that escaped government notice until critic Ralph Nader and others acted in the public interest. Anti-trust policy has seldom been fair and is generally something less than rational. When, however, in the spring of 1969 rumors spread that the Justice Department had General Motors in its sights, the bully of the automotive industry addressed itself belligerently to the public through Ross L. Malone, former deputy attorney general of the U.S., an office which trains corporation lawyers to serve industry.

Mr. Malone found, with less provocation than IBM management had, that "any attempt to artificially restructure industry or business enter-prises that have developed over many years in response to competitive pressures, inevitably risks a loss of economic efficiency." Anti-trust action that would break up a monolithic corporation or require divestiture "could defeat the very objectives of the anti-trust laws themselves by reducing the incentives which make the competitive system work." He said further that General Motors, which enjoyed sacrosanct status at government hands for many years, was sick of being kicked around by innuendo and government threat. G.M. knew how to take care of competitive pressures.

IBM, on the other hand, was, with less although no doubt adequate cause, beyond the range of innuendo and threat; it was already cited in the United States, while in Europe authorities of the Common Market Executive Commission were looking into the possibility of prohibiting, under its charter and treaty, IBM and other possible offenders from taking "improper advantage of a dominant position" in Continental markets. In England, efforts were under way to challenge IBM supremacy by coordinating computer technology in the British Isles, West Germany, and the Netherlands. The Common Market was increasingly determined to establish an anti-trust policy to deal with what the Executive Commission described as "thousands of cartels."

Under a barrage of fire, and in spite of its embarrassingly expansive growth, IBM's stock fell to 295 when the market opened on Inauguration Day. Mr. Katzenbach went to work, now to defend what his government oath formerly required him to prosecute, on perhaps the most important anti-trust action—unless General Motors succumbs—of the century.

Regardless of the damage and divestiture actions started by competing computer firms, which would be resolved by jury trials, the federal government would require a year or two to reach the courts, and perhaps several more years before a complex consent decree or juridical decisions could be reached. It would have a decisive bearing on the fastest growing industry in the world—the computer industry in general, and IBM in particular.

In any case, IBM the giant will remain so, even if among competing companies of gigantic size. Broken up, a situation could be created "where instead of having one IBM, you have two or three," said Isaac Auderbach, former president of the International Federation of Information Processing Societies. Stock market analysts saw the possibility that divestiture would make shares in spin-off companies worth more than stock in a single giant concern. The classic Rockefeller-Standard Oil case is remembered for the presumption that punishment and restrictive decree were involved when, in fact, the separated companies went on to great growth and riches, with the same people made increasingly wealthy. The Rockefeller fortunes never faltered, but grew more and more vast with each succeeding generation. Thus, no one need tremble for IBM or the computer industry.

As individuals and as "the company," IBM could find a note of cheer and relief from anti-trust publicity in an unintentionally well-timed full-page advertisement that appeared in *The Wall Street Journal* on Inauguration Day, January 20, 1969. It was an institutional ad over the signature of Scientific Resources Corporation, of Philadelphia, with which Dr. John Mauchly, inventor (with J. Presper Eckert) of the first electronic computer, is associated. Scientific Resources Corporation became the first independent systems and software company listed on the New York Stock Exchange. The advertisement simply commended the computer companies and mentioned Mauchly and ENIAC. But in view of the facts of history, and in view of the tidal wave of charges filed against the company, the large black headline at the top of the page seemed amusingly pointed:

"WE LOVE YOU IBM (anyway)!"

IBM's low spirits were lifted by a report of an important study published on the same day the Justice Department filed its suit. The report covered the first year of a prolonged project for which IBM passed out $5,000,000 in research grants and stipends to fifty scholars in eleven universities, including the usual ones involved in such work—Columbia, M.I.T., Harvard, Yale, etc. While there were certain foreboding aspects of the report—such as the idea that computer-trained analysts might have to govern, and that they might not be accountable to the citizenry—one important commerical fact emerged with clarity. The computers more and more will run the technological world, irrespective of the competitive factor.

For its $5,000,000 in grants to universities and scholars, IBM was advised in the first year report that technology is making more room for individualism at a time when there is no end in view for the proliferated usage of computers. Even the computers have not computed the ultimate dimensions of the market. But then the project under study will not be completed until 1974, and these early findings, which are nonsense as far as offering more individualism is concerned, could conceivably be contradicted.

As all roads once led to Rome, all studies involving the application of computer technology lead in the ultimate to the issue of human values, to the question: Who programmed the computer? Who selected the questions at input and who determined the questions to be unasked?

Tom Watson, his brother Arthur, and T. V. Learson are mortal men—although not everyone readily believes it in the case of Mr. Learson, who sometimes appears as vital and indefatigable as a supercomputer. While they remain among the quick, wielding enormous power in the industrial-governmental technocracy their energy and their company have helped create, than can, if they will, help the monster that is industry chart new paths to the old equivalent of Rome, new roads to a foreshortened future in which the human community is in peril.

By 1974 or thereabouts, when IBM's anti-trust cases will be resolved and its own position in the world more clearly defined, the corporation nourished by a backwoods peddler who was the patriarch of a popular but false American dream will have to decide what it will do about going on forever.

Bibliography

———◆———

ABELS, JULES. *The Rockefeller Billions: The Story of the World's Most Stupendous Fortune.* New York, 1965.

BELDEN, THOMAS and MARVA. *The Lengthening Shadow: The Life of Thomas J. Watson.* Boston, 1962.

BELL, WILLIAM D. *A Management Guide to Electronic Computers.* New York, 1957.

BERKELEY, EDMUND C. *The Computer Revolution.* Garden City, N.Y., 1962.

BERNSTEIN, JEREMY. *The Analytical Engine: Computers—Past, Present and Future.* New York, 1963.

CROWTHER, SAMUEL. *John H. Patterson.* New York, 1923.

DOWNEY, MATTHEW T. *Ben D. Wood, Educational Reformer.* Princeton, N.J., 1965.

ECKERT, WALLACE J. *Punched Card Methods in Scientific Computation.* New York, 1940.

EISENHOWER, DWIGHT D. *The White House Years, 1953–56: Mandate for Change.* Garden City, New York, 1963.

FLINT, CHARLES R. *Memories of an Active Life.* New York and London, 1923.

GALBRAITH, JOHN KENNETH. *The New Industrial State.* Boston, 1967.

INGLIS, WILLIAM. *George F. Johnson and His Industrial Democracy.* Binghamton, N.Y.; first edition, 1935; second edition, 1947.

LEUCHTENBURG, WILLIAM. *Franklin D. Roosevelt and the New Deal.* New York, 1963.

MARCOSSON, ISAAC FREDERICK. *John Henry Patterson.* New York, 1945.

McMILLAN, JAMES and BERNARD HARRIS. *The American Take-Over of Britain.* New York, 1968.

MEAD, MARGARET. *Soviet Attitudes Toward Authority: An Interdisciplinary Approach to Problems of Soviet Character.* Researched and written in collaboration with the RAND staff. New York, 1951.

MILLS, C. WRIGHT. *White Collar: American Middle Classes.* New York, 1951.

312

Bibliography

PFEIFFER, JOHN. *The Thinking Machine: Everyman's Introduction to the World of Electronic Devices.* Philadelphia and New York, 1962.

POOL, ITHIEL DE SOLA (with ROBERT P. ABELSON and SAMUEL POPKIN). *Candidates, Issues & Strategies: A Computer Simulation of the 1960 and 1964 Presidential Elections.* Cambridge, 1964.

RIDGEWAY, GEORGE L. *Merchants of Peace: The History of the International Chamber of Commerce.* Boston, 1938; revised, 1959.

RIDGEWAY, JAMES. *The Closed Corporation: American Universities in Crisis.* New York, 1968.

ROSEN, SAUL. *Electronic Computers: A Historical Survey.* Purdue University Computer Sciences Department, 1968.

SCHLESINGER, ARTHUR, JR. *The Politics of Upheaval.* Boston, 1960.

SERVAN-SCHREIBER, JEAN-JACQUES. *Le Défi Americain.* Published in English as *The American Challenge.* New York, 1968.

WATSON, THOS. J. *Men, Minutes, Money.* A collection of excerpts from talks and messages delivered and written at various times. Published and circulated by International Business Machines Corporation.

WATSON, THOMAS J., JR. *McKinsey Lectures of T. J. Watson, Jr.* New York, 1962.

WILKINSON, J. B. *The annals of Binghamton and the County Connected With It, From the Earliest Settlement.* Published by Cooke & Davis, Printers, 1840. Third printing, with an appraisal by Tom Cawley, published by the Broome County and Old Onaquaga Historical Societies, 1967. Illustrated by John Hart.

WRIGHT, ORVILLE and WILBUR. *The Miracle at Kitty Hawk: The Letters of Wilbur and Orville Wright.* Edited by Fred C. Kelly; New York, 1951.

As a Man Thinks. A collection of editorials and thoughts expressed by THOMAS J. WATSON. Published undated as a tribute to Mr. and Mrs. Thomas J. Watson by the International Business Machines Corporation over the printed signature "The IBM Family."

National Cash Register Co., Suggestions From Employees. Compiled by ALFRED A. THOMAS, secretary of the company; published by the company in 1905.

THINK, A Collection. Edited by ROBERT COUSINS. New York, 1957.

Volume No. 760, transcript record of the Federal Court, Southern District of New York: *National Cash Register Company vs. American Cash Register Company.*

Volumes 549, 550, 551, and 552 of the United States Court of Appeals, Sixth District.

Index

314